BARRON'S

NYSTCE

EAS
ALST
Multi-Subject CST
Overview of the edTPA

4TH EDITION

Dr. Robert D. Postman
Professor
New York

BARRON'S

To my wife Liz, who showed me the way

And my children Chad, Blaire, and Ryan, who lit the way

And to my grandson Quinn, who is the way

This book is dedicated to you.

Acknowledgment

Special acknowledgment is due to Elena Nitecki, a Professor of Education and Department Chair, who conducted the field trial of the practice tests in this book. Her feedback and the feedback of graduate students who had taken the actual tests, as well as those taking the tests for the first time, is found throughout the tests and answer explanations.

All inquiries should be addressed to:
Barron's Educational Series, Inc.
250 Wireless Boulevard
Hauppauge, New York 11788
www.barronseduc.com

Library of Congress Catalog Card No.: 2015934252

ISBN: 978-1-4380-0618-5

PRINTED IN THE UNITED STATES OF AMERICA
9 8 7 6 5 4 3 2

CONTENTS

SECTION III ACADEMIC LITERACY SKILLS TEST (ALST)

Preface

This book is crafted to show you how to achieve passing scores on the New York State Certification tests. We know the tests and we show you a clear path to success. The contents of this book have been field tested by prospective teachers, and reviewed by experienced teachers and by those familiar with the NYSTCE tests.

My wife Liz, a teacher and professor, has been a constant source of support and has made significant contributions to this book. She continues to accept my regrets for the lost months, and pretends to believe my repeated promises that it won't happen again. My children Chad, Blaire, and Ryan, and my grandson Quinn, make it all worthwhile.

Kristen Giardi of Barron's did an absolutely masterful job with this manuscript. Kristen and I have worked harmoniously on a number of books. Many special touches in the book are the result of her caring attention.

Special thanks to the undergraduate and graduate students and those changing careers for their assistance. I am also grateful to those in the New York State Education Department who took the time to talk to me and to those at New York colleges, particularly Elena Nitecki, who talked to me about their experiences with the testing.

I look forward with you to a time when these tests are barely a memory and when you are actively engaged in the most important profession.

Robert D. Postman

SECTION I
Overview and Strategies

New York State Teacher Certification Examinations

1

This Book Is Mobile Device Ready

All of the links in this book are accompanied by a QR code that you can scan directly into your phone, tablet, or computer. That makes things a lot easier.

Try out the two QR codes in the box below.

TEST INFO BOX

The NYSTCE assessments are offered through Evaluation Systems, a subdivision of Pearson Education.

NYSTCE CONTACT INFORMATION:
Evaluation Systems–Pearson
Box 660, Amherst, MA 01004-9008

www.nystce.nesinc.com (most up-to-date information)

1-413-256-2882
Recording (24 hours) 1-800-309-5225
Fax: 1-413-256-7088

Computer-Delivered Test Appointments

www.pearsonvue.com/nystce

1-800-989-8532

All tests covered in this book are computer delivered.

The edTPA Assessment is not computer delivered.

NYSTCE ASSESSMENTS COVERED IN THIS BOOK

Passing the NYSTCE Tests

Each NYSTCE test is based on an enormous number of topics. Each topic could generate an equally enormous number of tests. The NYSTCE tests described below have a scale score range from 400 to 600. The passing score for each test is a scale score of 520. A scale score of 520 may result from a wide range of raw scores (number of points actually earned) and may vary from test to test and year to year.

Students report a wide variation in the similarity of administered tests. One student reported taking the same test twice. Other students reported tests based on the objectives and test format, but with questions that had a very different focus and difficulty level. State testing officials can adjust the scale scores to account for these variations.

This indicates that the tests you take may have a different focus and difficulty level than the practice tests in this book. The practice tests will be very helpful as you prepare for the real test; however, because of this variation, you will not be able to predict the scale score you would receive on a practice test.

All Teaching Certificates

In general, all teacher certification candidates must complete two tests and the edTPA. This book helps you prepare for all three: Academic Literacy Skills Test (ALST), Educating All Students (EAS), and the Education Teacher Performance Assessment (edTPA).

ALST

(computer delivered only, 2 hours 30 minutes)
The ALST consists of two focused constructed-response items and one extended response (essay) based on two passages with opposing positions on a common topic and a supporting graphic. It also includes forty selected-response items: five long passages, each with eight selected response items. Selected-response items often show the portion of the passage you will use to select your answer.

Constructed responses: 60% of the score (focused responses 15%, each extended response 30%). Students say to complete the constructed responses first.

Selected response: 40% of the score

EAS

(computer delivered only, 2 hours 15 minutes)
The EAS consists of forty-two selected-response items (eight teaching scenarios, each with four selected response items; ten selected response items without scenarios) and three embedded constructed-response items, each based on a scenario.

Selected response: 70% of score
Constructed response: 30% of score

edTPA

The edTPA is not a test. It is actually a developmental process in which you work with faculty mentors, cooperating teachers, and college supervisors to develop an electronic portfolio, which includes lesson plans, assessments, and brief unedited video lessons. This developmental process typically stretches over several semesters. You submit the completed portfolio electronically to Pearson through a secure submission link. The scoring is completely different from the other tests and is described in Chapter 7.

Individual Teacher Certificates

Each teaching certificate typically has a required Content Specialty Test (CST). You must pass the CST in each certification area. This book prepares you for the multi-subject CSTs.

MULTI-SUBJECT ELEMENTARY EDUCATION AND EARLY CHILDHOOD CSTS

(computer delivered only)

Each Multi-Subject CST consists of three distinct tests. You must achieve a passing score on each test. The content of the elementary and early childhood CSTs are quite similar.

LITERACY AND ENGLISH LANGUAGE ARTS CST

(2 hours)

Includes both knowledge of Literacy and English Language Arts and Literacy and English Language Arts Instruction. It is comprised of forty selected-response items and one extended constructed-response item based on a teaching-learning situation.

    Selected response: 70% of the score

    Constructed response: 30% of the score

MATHEMATICS CST

(2 hours 15 minutes)

Includes knowledge of numbers and operations, ratios and proportions, algebra, geometry, measurement, data, applications, and teaching these subjects. It includes forty selected-response items and one extended constructed-response item based on a teaching-learning situation.

    Selected response: 70% of the score

    Constructed response: 30% of the score

ARTS AND SCIENCES CST

(1 hour)

Includes science, technology, social studies, arts, health, family, consumer and careers, and teaching those subjects. Forty selected-response items.

Selected response: 100% of the score

WHAT'S GOING ON WITH THE NYSTCE?

The State of New York has just finished implementing a new assessment system for teachers. The new system requires most teacher candidates to take and pass at least four tests and assessments. A candidate seeking certification in Early Childhood and Elementary Education will have to take and pass seven tests and assessments, including two CSTs. The ALST, the EAS, and the CSTs are actual tests, given only in a computer-delivered setting. The edTPA is a digital record of the work in your teacher certification program, including videos of lessons you will usually complete during student teaching.

It's only fair to say that these tests are more comprehensive than the previous tests, and there may have been an increase in the number of "raw score" points you need to reach a scale score of 520, the passing scale score for all the tests. This book will take you through the steps to pass. Most important are the seven full-length model tests with explained answers found in Chapters 4, 6, and 9.

We know it can seem overwhelming to deal with all these tests. However, everyone has to do it. Take things one step at a time, one test at a time, and you will dramatically increase your chances of passing on the first try. However, you may take a test as often as needed, and this is not high stakes testing, so it does not hurt to relax.

This book shows you how to use proven test preparation and test-taking strategies. These are not tricks, but rather effective ways to mark the correct answer or write an acceptable constructed response. Some of the strategies are more general, while others apply specifically to computerized tests. The EAS, ALST, and CSTs covered in this book are computerized tests. The edTPA is not really a test in the traditional sense, so these preparation strategies do not apply.

TAKING THE NYSTCE TESTS

NYSTCE Website

www.nystce. nesinc.com/

Start by visiting the main NYSTCE website: *www.nystce.nesinc.com/*. Just searching for NYSTCE will usually take you right there. This site will have the most up-to-date information. It has registration information, including a link to the preferred online registration site and the optional phone registration. You can also print out and mail the registration form. Many colleges have course progress requirements tied to passing test scores. Always check with a college advisor about the order in which you should take the tests.

NYSTCE Test Centers

The Pearson nationwide network of test centers offers more than 300 computer-based tests in addition to the NYSTCE. These tests include the GMAT, Microsoft tests, and many other tests you've never heard of. The centers we visited were simple but appropriate, and the staff members were usually helpful. The waiting rooms are not unlike a dentist's waiting room.

Remember, though, that the centers are in the test administration business, and schedules are usually tight. Be sure to arrive before the scheduled test time and be sure to cancel well in advance if you can't make a test. If you miss a test and fail to cancel in advance, you will be charged the full test fee.

Security is a big deal, and you will be well aware that you are being monitored during testing. Lockers are provided to store food and other necessary items. You can't bring anything into the testing area without specific permission. You will be carefully screened and digital photos and palm prints are common. You may also find additional screening measures in place.

It is a good idea to check with the test center at which you registered to learn about what you may bring to the center, what you may bring into the testing room, and about the center's rules and identification requirements.

It's also good to visit the center in advance. Our GPS once took us to a location across town, and we had to call the center for directions. Centers can be in storefronts or in office buildings, and you want to be sure you know how to get there.

You must bring one piece of current, government-issued photographic and signed identification in the name in which you registered. You may not use identification such as a credit card, a Social Security card, or a student ID. Check for specific requirements, which may change from time to time.

It can be difficult to arrange an appointment at a site close to you. It makes sense since most people who take the NYSTCE tests are from New York. We often found nearby test sites that had no seats available for as long as two months, so set up your account and register as early as you can.

We often found more "seats" available at sites in states bordering New York State. So when you schedule your test, be sure to examine the full geographic range of test center options. If you are going to be away from the area, check around. We found available appointments for the next day at a center in San Francisco.

Your Scores

You will be able to view scores online. You may also arrange to have the scores sent to you via e-mail. The score report will show your test score and clearly indicate whether you passed or did not pass the test. Your test scores are also reported to the New York State Education Department and the college you listed on your registration form. Be sure to list the college at which you are pursuing certification, or there may be a delay in your ability to take additional coursework.

Alternative Test Arrangements

There are a wide range of test adaptations and alternative testing arrangements available. To view the most current arrangements, visit the Alternative Testing Arrangements link under Registration at the main NYSTCE website (*http://www.nystce.nesinc.com/*).

NYSTCE Statewide Passing Rates and Individual Campus Passing Rates

In late fall, New York State releases NYSTCE statewide passing rates and passing rates for every New York State college campus that offers teacher certification programs. The 2013–2014 scores were released just before this book went to the typesetter. The statewide passing percent for the ALST was 68%, and the statewide rate for the EAS was 77%. It appears that these passing rates include retakes, and that a student who took a test three times, and passed on the final try, would be recorded as passing.

The edTPA results are reported in Chapter 7. The new Multi-Subject CSTs were not offered during the 2013–2014 school year. We will post current passing rate information each fall, as it is made available.

There is a wide variation in passing rates among individual college campuses. Each college campus has its own score reports to share with you.

REVIEW CHECKLIST AND TEST SELECTION IDENTIFIER

Proven Test-Preparation and Test-Taking Strategies

2

These strategies apply to the EAS, ALST, and the CST. The edTPA strategies are reviewed in the section about that test.

QUICK START

It is not the best strategy, but some people get this book just a few days before a test, even the day before or the night before. If that's you, and the pressure is on, follow this strategy: The model tests with explained answers are the most useful preparation. Review this section and go right to the applicable model test(s), take the test(s) and review the answers. Each test takes more than two hours, and you should leave another hour at least to review the answers.

REGULAR REVIEW

If you have left yourself some time, then follow the steps below and read the preparation steps and available review in each chapter.

Follow These General Strategies

SELECTED RESPONSE

Eliminate and then guess. There is no penalty for wrong answers. Never leave any answer blank.

Suppose a selected-response test has 40 items with four answer choices. If you eliminate two incorrect answer choices on all the items and guess every answer, then on average, you would get 20 correct.

CONSTRUCTED RESPONSE

WRITE AN OUTLINE: Then write the constructed response.

TOPIC PARAGRAPH: Begin the written assignment with an introduction to orient the reader to the topic. The first paragraph should clearly state the main idea of your entire written assignment.

TOPIC SENTENCE: Begin each paragraph with a topic sentence that supports the main idea.

DETAILS: Provide details, examples, and arguments to support the topic sentence.

CONCLUSION: End the written assignment with a paragraph that summarizes your main points.

GRAMMAR, PUNCTUATION, SPELLING: Edit sentences to conform to standard usage.

AVOID PASSIVE CONSTRUCTION: Write actively and avoid the passive voice.

BE SURE YOUR RESPONSE IS COMPLETE: Respond to all parts of the response prompt, and be sure your response is of sufficient length.

ALST, EAS, AND CST PROVEN TEST-PREPARATION STRATEGIES

Here are several strategies and steps to follow as you prepare for the test. These strategies take you right up to test day. You will take the ALST, CST, and EAS on a computer at a test center.

Get Yourself Ready for the Test

Most people feel at least a little bit uncomfortable about tests. You are probably one of them. No book is going to make you feel comfortable, but here are some suggestions to help ease your concerns.

Most people are less tense when they exercise. Set up a *reasonable* exercise program for yourself. The program should involve exercising in a way that is appropriate for you. Aim for 30 to 45 minutes of exercise each day. This exercise may be just as important as other preparation.

Prepare with another person. You will feel less isolated if you have a friend or colleague to study with.

Accept this important truth: You are not going to get all the answers correct, and you do not have to. You can take this test again if necessary. There is no penalty for taking the test again. This is not a do-or-die, life-or-death situation. You will survive. You may be able to get an immediate test appointment. It is almost always best to give yourself more time to get ready. Your education course work will be particularly helpful for the EAS and edTPA.

Follow This Study Plan

Begin preparing four to ten weeks before the test. Use the longer time if you are very busy or you don't feel comfortable about the test.

Look in turn at each chapter you have to use and review the description of each test you have to take.

Use the available strategies and review for each test. Complete your review two weeks before the test. Then, complete the model test(s). Have someone proctor the test. Take the test under exact test conditions. No television. No extra time. No breaks that are not normally included in the test. Nothing.

Grade your own test or have someone grade it for you. Either way, review each incorrect answer and read all the explanations.

TWO WEEKS TO GO

During this week look over those areas you answered incorrectly on the practice test(s). Go over the answer explanations. Get help for things you are not sure about.

ONE WEEK TO GO

The hard work is over. You are coasting in for a landing. You know the material on the test. You do not even have to get an A. You just have to pass.

Get up each day at the time you will have to get up on test day. Sit down at the time the test will start and spend about one hour answering questions on the practice test(s). It is okay that you have answered these questions before.

FOUR DAYS TO GO

Make sure you:

- have your admission ticket.
- know where the test is given.
- know how you will get there.

THREE DAYS TO GO

- Write on 3×5 index cards any special terms or formulas you must remember for the test.
- Visit the test site or the test center, if you have not done so already. You do not want any surprises. The worst stories are about people who miss the test appointment.

ONE DAY TO GO

- Review your index cards one last time.
- Complete any forms you have to take to the test.
- Prepare any snacks or food you want to bring with you. You will not be able to take them into the testing area.
- Talk to someone who makes you feel good or do something enjoyable and relaxing.
- Have a good night's sleep.

TEST DAY

- Plan to be at the test site or center for at least four hours.
- Dress comfortably. There are no points for appearance.
- Do not eat too much before the test. You want your blood racing through your brain, not your stomach.
- Get to the test room or the test center, not the parking lot, about 10 to 15 minutes before test time. Remember to leave time for parking and walking to the test site or test center.
- Hand in your forms. You are ready. This is the easy part.
- Follow the test-taking strategies in the next section.
- Pay close attention to the computer delivered tutorial.

PROVEN TEST-TAKING STRATEGIES

Testing companies like to pretend that test-taking strategies do not help that much. They act like that because they want everyone to think that their tests only measure your knowledge of the subject. Of course, they are just pretending; test-taking strategies can make a big difference.

However, there is nothing better than being prepared for the subject matter on the test. These strategies will do you little good if you lack this fundamental knowledge. If you are prepared, then these strategies can make a difference. Not using them may very well lower your score.

You Will Make Mistakes

You are going to make mistakes on this test. The people who wrote the test expect you to make them.

You Are Not Competing with Anyone

Your score does not depend on others. When the score report comes out it does not say, "Nancy got a 500, but Blaire got a 520." You just want to get the required score. If you can do better, that is great. Stay focused. Remember your goal.

Some Multiple-Choice Questions Are Traps

Some questions include the words *not, least,* or *except*. You are being asked for the answer that does not fit with the rest. Be alert for these types of questions.

Save the Hard Questions for Last

You are not supposed to get all the questions correct, and some of them will be too difficult for you. Work through the questions and answer the easy ones and come back to the other ones.

They Show You the Answer

Every multiple-choice test shows you the correct answer for each question. The answer is staring right at you. You just have to figure out which one it is. There is a 25 percent chance you will get it right by just guessing.

Some Answers Are Traps

When a test writer writes a test question, he or she often include distracters. Distracters are traps—incorrect answers that look like correct answers. It might be an answer to an addition problem when you should be multiplying. It might be a correct answer to a different question. It might just be an answer that catches your eye. Watch out for this type of incorrect answer.

Eliminate the Incorrect Answers

If you cannot figure out which answer is correct, then decide which answers can't be correct. Choose the answers you are sure are incorrect. Write them on the scrap paper. Only one left? That is the correct answer.

Guess, Guess, Guess

If there are still two or more answers left, then guess. Guess the answer from those remaining. Never leave any item blank. There is no penalty for guessing.

It Is Not What You Know That Matters, It Is Just Which Circle You Fill In

No one you know or care about will see your test. An impersonal machine scores all selected-response questions. The machine just senses whether the correct circle on the computer screen is selected. That is the way the test makers want it. If that is good enough for them, it should be good enough for you. Concentrate on filling in the correct circle.

You Can Be Right but Be Marked Wrong

If you get the right answer but fill in the wrong circle, the machine will mark it wrong. We told you that filling in the right circle was what mattered.

Pay Attention During the Computerized Tutorial

The tutorial shows you how to use the computer and how to mark your answers. The tutorial also shows you how to use a tool to mark items to which you want to return. You will also learn how to use the review page to see the items you marked. Pay close attention. Point out any issues with the testing equipment to the test monitor. There is no way to get additional help once the test is underway.

You Do Not Have to Answer Every Item When It First Appears

If you come across an item you are not ready to answer, mark it with the special marking tool you learned about during the tutorial. You can also mark an item you have not answered as a reminder to review the item later and/or perhaps change an answer.

All the items you mark are recorded on this review screen.

Use the Review Screen

Leave time at the end of the test to look at the review screen. The screen shows all the items you marked with the marking tool, as well as those items you revisited. Use the information on this screen to be sure you entered an answer for every item. There is no penalty for guessing.

It Is Easy to Change Your Answer

You can change the answer to any multiple-choice item. Just click on the oval for another answer.

Use the Scrap Paper or the White Board

The test center staff should provide you with scrap paper or an erasable white board and marker. Use the scrap paper or the white board to do calculations, draw diagrams, or to make any notes you need to arrive at the correct answer.

Your Constructed Responses Are Graded Holistically

Holistic rating means the readers assign a score based on their informed sense about your writing. Readers look at a lot of responses, and they do not do a detailed analysis.

Pearson typically sends your essay to readers via a computer. Readers can review the responses anywhere there is Internet or cell phone access. Readers typically consist of teachers. At first, representatives of Pearson show the readers the topics for the recent test and review the types of responses that should be rated. The readers are trained to evaluate the responses according to Pearson's guidelines.

Each response is evaluated twice, without the second reader knowing the evaluation given by the first reader. If the two evaluations differ significantly, other readers review the assignment.

Readers have a tedious, tiring assignment, and they work quickly. Think about them as you write. Write a response that makes it easy for the reader to give you a high score.

PASSING THE NYSTCE

This section reviews scoring and gives you some information about what it takes to get a passing score on the ALST, EAS, and CSTs. edTPA scoring is discussed in Chapter 7.

Raw Scores and Scale Scores

Your raw score is the number of items you answer correctly, or the number of points you actually earn. Your scale score converts your raw score to a score that can be compared to those of everyone else who has taken that test.

It works this way. Test items, test sections, and different forms of the test have different difficulty levels. For example, an item on one form might be harder than a comparable item on another form. To make up for this difference in difficulty, the harder item might earn a 0.9 scale points, while the easier item might earn a 0.8 scale points. A scale score can be compared to the scale score on all forms of a test.

This is the fair way to do it. To maintain this fairness, scores are reported to you as scale scores. All the scores discussed here are scale scores.

PASSING RAW SCORES

It is tricky to figure out the raw score you will need to get a passing scale score. That is because passing raw scores can vary from test to test and the state does not release information about passing raw scores. Indications are the state has recently increased passing raw scores.

This means we have to be cautious. However, this is information readers often request, so we will help as best we can. Please remember that these are just estimates. Policy makers may adjust the required raw score, or the test versions it designs may be harder or easier. The test you take may be a harder or easier version. Any of these things could significantly reduce the meaning of the following estimates.

Of course, the idea is to do your best. Remember that you can pick up raw score points by using the fundamental test strategies. Eliminate every answer you know is incorrect. Never leave an answer blank. You may also find that a good constructed response score may reduce the selected response raw score you will need.

So here it is—ESTIMATES. There is absolutely no assurance that they will apply to the test you take. The best approach is to assume you will have to do better than these guidelines indicate.

Generally speaking, a raw score of at or above the 20th to 30th percentile on the test is a good score for most test takers.

SECTION II
Educating All Students (EAS)

Preparing for the Educating All Students Test (EAS)

3

TEST INFO BOX

The Educating All Students (EAS) test is built around six teaching-related areas.

There are forty-two selected-response items and three brief constructed responses. Thirty-two of the selected responses and all three constructed-response answers are built around eight teaching scenarios. Each scenario includes a description of a learning situation, data about the situation, and a draft lesson plan. Each scenario includes four selected-response items. Three of these scenarios also include a constructed-response item.

Selected response: 70% of score   Constructed response: 30% of score

The approximate distribution of selected-response and constructed-response items is shown below.

	Approximate Number	
	Selected Response	Constructed Response
Diverse Student Populations	12	1
English Language Learners	12	1
Students with Disabilities and Other Special Learning Needs	8	1
Teacher Responsibility (What a teacher should do)	5 (no scenario)	
School-Home Relationships (A focus on communication)	5 (no scenario)	

SCORES

In the school year ending June 2014, the state average EAS score was about 530 higher than the average ALST average score. New York State reports EAS scores as Level 1 or Level 2 (Mastery). Passing scale scores below 563 are classified as Level 1, while scale scores 563 and above are classified as Mastery. Less than 10% of the statewide scores were at the Mastery level. It is not clear whether this dual classification will be meaningful.

PREPARATION STRATEGIES

The scenarios can be very detailed and may appear complex. However, the items address only a small portion of the material in the scenario. Reading the scenario in detail will only waste time and likely slow you down. Any test about teaching methods may include a certain amount of subjectivity. We give the most likely correct answers based on our review of test scoring practices.

For the selected-response items, the best strategy is to skim the scenario, and then review each item in turn. Use the information in the item to locate the needed information in the scenario.

Write constructed responses of about 150 to 200 words. Answer all parts of the prompt. A well-written response can help make up for any selected-response items you may have missed.

USING THIS CHAPTER

This chapter contains a summary EAS review built around the five teaching-related areas. Most people find the review helps focus attention on the tests main areas. You can study the review in as much detail as is needed.

You should complete the practice EAS scenario with selected-response and constructed-response items. The explained answers appear immediately after the practice items.

A BRIEF EAS REVIEW

This Brief EAS Review is designed to focus your attention on the five EAS Strands and some of the topics you may encounter. The primary source of EAS information is your extensive college course work in these five areas.

ETHNIC DIVERSITY

The statistics from the U.S. Census Bureau show the ethnic diversity in New York State compared to the ethnic diversity in the United States as a whole. The most striking results show the much higher proportions of New Yorkers who are foreign born and equally higher numbers who do not speak English at home. In many areas of the state, these differences are even more striking. With a population of about 20,000,000, a few percentage points represents a lot of people.

U.S. Census Bureau 2013

	New York State	United States
Black or African American alone	17.5%	13.2%
Asian alone	8.2%	5.3%
Two or more races	2.3%	2.4%
Hispanic or Latino	18.4%	17.1%
White alone, not Hispanic or Latino	57.2%	62.6%
Foreign born persons	22.0%	12.9%
Language other than English spoken at home	29.8%	20.5%

This diversity is compounded by the persistent level of poverty in New York State. Recent reports indicate New York ranks fourth in the United States for the number of people living in poverty. Those same reports indicate that nearly 40 percent of female-led households with children live in poverty. About 27 percent of Latinos and 25 percent of African Americans live in poverty compared to less than half that number for other ethnicities. In some areas, nearly 50 percent of children live in poverty. The number of known homeless children in New York State exceeds 100,000 at any one time.

Income inequality is a striking feature of New York State. In the United States, the level of income inequality is at the highest level since this index was first measured about twenty-five years ago. New York is second only to Washington, DC in income disparities between wage earners in all income categories.

Being an educator in New York State means being prepared to respond to an ethnically and economically diverse population, as well as to childhood poverty and childhood homelessness.

STUDENT MOTIVATION

Motivation

Most good lessons begin with motivation. Motivation keeps learners interested and focused on the lesson. It is important to maintain students' motivation for the duration of the lesson.

The motivation for a lesson may be intrinsic or extrinsic. Intrinsic motivation refers to topics that students like or enjoy. Effective intrinsic motivations are based on a knowledge of what is popular or interesting to students of a particular age.

For example, you might introduce a lesson about the French and Indian War to older students by discussing the book and movie *Last of the Mohicans.* You might introduce a lesson on patterns to young children by picking out patterns in children's clothes. You might introduce a lesson on fractions to middle school students with a discussion about the stock market.

Extrinsic motivation focuses on external rewards for good work or goal attainment. Extrinsic rewards are most successful when used in conjunction with more routine work. Extrinsic motivations may offer an appropriate reward for completing an assignment or for other acceptable performance. Establish rewards for activities that most students can achieve and take care to eliminate unnecessary competition.

For example, you might grant a period of free time to students who successfully complete a routine but necessary assignment. You might offer the whole class a trip or a party when a class project is successfully completed. Special education programs feature token reinforcement in which students receive or lose points or small plastic tokens for appropriate or inappropriate activity.

Motivation needs to be maintained during the lesson itself. Follow these guidelines for teaching lessons in which the students remain motivated. Lessons will be more motivating if you have clear and unambiguous objectives, give the students stimulating tasks at an appropriate level, get and hold the students' attention, and allow students some choices. Students will be most motivated if they like the topic or activity, believe that the lesson has to do with them, believe that they will succeed, and have a positive reaction to your efforts to motivate them.

Individual work gives a further opportunity to use intrinsic motivation. Use the interests and likes of individual students to spark and maintain their motivation.

The extrinsic motivation of praise can be used effectively during a lesson. For praise to be successful, it must be given for a specific accomplishment (including effort) and it must focus on the student's own behavior. It does not compare behavior with other students or establish competitive situations.

SUCCESSFUL LEARNING

Research indicates that the following factors are likely to lead to successful learning.

- Students who are engaged in the learning process tend to be more successful learners, particularly when they are engaged in activities at the appropriate level of difficulty.
- Students learn most successfully when they are being taught or supervised as opposed to working independently.
- Students who are exposed to material at the appropriate level of difficulty are more successful learners.
- Students are successful learners when their teachers expect them to master the curriculum and use available instructional time for learning activities.
- Students who are in a positive, uncritical classroom environment are more successful learners than students who are in a negative, critical classroom environment. This does not mean that students cannot be corrected or criticized, but that students learn best when the corrections are done positively and when the criticisms are constructive.
- Students generally develop positive attitudes to teachers who appear warm, have a student orientation, praise students, listen to students, accept student ideas, and interact with them.

CLASSROOM APPROACHES

Effective classrooms are characterized by a variety of teaching approaches. The approaches should be tailored to the ability of the learner and the lesson objectives. When utilizing these approaches, the teacher should also keep in mind the varied ways children develop cognitively. Some of the methods used follow here.

Zone of Proximal Development

Lev Vygotsky developed the concept of the zone of proximal development (ZPD). The ZPD consists of those tasks the student cannot do without help but can do with help. Vygotsky held that teachers should present activities that are in a student's ZPD to encourage a realistic opportunity for advancement of student learning.

SCAFFOLDING

Scaffolding applies Vygotsky's ZPD to the classroom, although scaffolding was not developed by Vygotsky. In scaffolding, a student receives help to learn something in his or her ZPD. The help is withdrawn in a measured way until the help becomes unnecessary. The term *scaffolding* was chosen because of its conceptual resemblance to the way a scaffold is removed, say, from a building as it is no longer needed for construction.

Gardner's Multiple Intelligences

Howard Gardner presented a theory of multiple intelligences. He proposed a list of nine because he felt that the traditional view of intelligence did not reflect the wide range of ability demonstrated by students. His theory has received a cool reception from many psychologists because of a lack of empirical evidence. However, it has received a much better reception from those involved in education because of the theory's practical usefulness. Many educators believe that attention to the theory may encourage teachers to try alternate approaches when students are having difficulty learning. A list of Gardner's intelligences with brief explanations follows.

1. Spatial thinkers learn best by visualizing problems and solutions.
2. Linguistic thinkers may learn best through words and language.
3. Logical-mathematical thinkers may learn best through abstract and scientific thinking, and through solving numerical problems. It is said that this type of thinking is strongly related to traditional measures of intelligence.
4. Students with bodily-kinesthetic intelligence may learn best through physical activity and are generally good at sports and dance.
5. Musical students may learn best by listening and tend to excel at singing and playing instruments.
6. Interpersonal thinkers may learn best by working with others and tend to be sensitive to the needs of others.
7. Intrapersonal thinkers may learn best by working alone and tend to be intuitive and introverted.
8. Naturalistic thinkers may learn best by relating subject matter to nature and to the world around them.
9. Existential thinkers may comprehend concepts beyond the actual information given.

Maslow's Hierarchy of Needs and Human Motivation

Maslow's hierarchy of needs is a linear description of levels leading to the top level of self-transcendence. There are basic (deficiency) needs, which Maslow holds must be met for a person to be motivated to achieve the higher-level (being) needs. It is the achievement of one level of needs that "motivates" someone to pursue the next level of needs. Maslow holds that without motivation, it is unlikely that the higher level of needs will be achieved.

DEFICIENCY NEEDS

1. Biological and physiological: hunger, thirst, bodily comforts
2. Safety: feel safe, personally secure, free from danger; and for adults, a secure employment
3. Belongingness and love: be affiliated with others; and with a family, feel accepted and loved
4. Esteem: to gain approval, be seen as capable and have self-respect

BEING NEEDS

5. Cognitive: to know, to understand, and explore
6. Aesthetic: the appreciation of and search for beauty, order, and form
7. Self-actualization: to find self-fulfillment and realize one's potential
8. Self-transcendence: to help others find self-fulfillment and self-realization

LEARNING STYLES IN THE CLASSROOM

There is an incredible variety of learning styles. A student's learning style may change as he or she matures, and the style may be different for different types of learning and different subjects. There are some fundamental learning styles for a teacher to consider as he or she teaches. The three most frequently discussed styles are given below.

Auditory

The student learns best through listening to spoken information.

Try books on CD or books that can be "read" aloud by an e-reader. Encourage students to make oral reports and repeat aloud difficult words or ideas. In general, allow for periods in which oral expression is as important as written expression.

Visual-Spatial

The student learns best through reading and viewing tables, charts, and maps.

Try writing words on the board as you speak, make provisions for a rich selection of books and other written learning materials, and encouraging students to write reports or create PowerPoint presentations. Try handing out typed versions of complex instructions that you are giving orally.

Kinesthetic

The student learns best through physical activity and hands-on activities.

The ideal is for a teacher to structure classroom learning to incorporate opportunities for all these learning styles. Naturally, there are physical and emotional needs to be met as well, and these needs may well be a determining factor in student success. Teaching is a complex business. Here is a brief summary of some ways that teachers can account for each of the listed learning styles.

Particularly in mathematics and science, give students opportunities to learn through hands-on experiences and experiments. Incorporate projects that students can work on in small groups at their own pace. Some educators recommend giving kinesthetic learners an opportunity to take breaks and to participate in field trips and role-playing.

Metacognition

Metacognition is "knowing about knowing." In the classroom, metacognition includes what a student knows about him- or herself, what a student knows about strategies, or what a student knows about the topic to be learned or the problem to be solved. The term *metacognition* sounds exceptionally complex, but it can be as simple as noticing that one concept or skill is more difficult to learn than another.

Metacognition can help students perform cognitive tasks more effectively. Teachers can encourage metacognition in a number of ways. One metacognitive strategy is self-questioning (Have I solved a similar problem? What do I already know about this topic?). Other suggested strategies include using graphic representations such as flowcharts or concept maps. Still other educators recommend writing out thoughts or "thinking aloud" as effective metacognitive strategies.

Teacher-Centered Approaches

Teacher-centered approaches are characterized by teacher presentation, a factual question, and a knowledge-based response from the student.

Lecture or Explanation

You can present material through a lecture or an explanation. A lecture is a fairly long verbal presentation of material. Explanation refers to a shorter presentation. Lecture and explanation are efficient ways to present information that must be arranged and structured in a particular way. However, lecture and explanation may place learners in too passive a role.

Lecture and explanation work best under the following circumstances: (1) the lesson begins with a motivation, (2) the teacher maintains eye contact, (3) the teacher supplies accentuating gestures but without extraneous movements, (4) the presentation is limited to about 5–40 minutes depending on the age of the student, and (5) the objective is clear and the presentation is easy to follow and at an appropriate level.

Demonstrations

Demonstrations are lectures or explanations in which you model what you want students to learn. That is, you exhibit a behavior, show a technique, or demonstrate a skill to help students reach the objective. Demonstrations should follow the same general rules as lectures, and the actual demonstration should be clear and easy to follow.

Teacher Questions

Teachers frequently ask questions during class. The following guidelines describe successful questions.

- Formulate questions so that they are clear, purposeful, brief, and at an appropriate level for the class.
- Address the vast majority of questions to the entire class. Individually addressed questions are appropriate to prepare "shy" students to answer the question.
- Avoid rhetorical questions.
- Use both higher and lower level questions on Bloom's Revised Taxonomy. All types of questions have their place.
- Avoid question-and-answer drills. A consistent pattern of teacher questions that call for responses at the first level of Bloom's Taxonomy is too limiting for most classrooms.
- Pause before you call on a student to answer the question, giving students an opportunity to formulate their responses.
- Call on a wide range of students to answer. Do not pick students just because they are either likely or unlikely to respond correctly.
- Wait 4 or 5 seconds for an answer. Do not cut off students who are struggling with an answer.
- Rephrase a question if it seems unclear or vague.
- Set a target for about 70 percent or so of questions to be answered correctly.

Student-Centered Approaches—Active Learning

In a student-centered or active learning environment, the teacher ceases to be the prime presenter of information. The teacher's questions are more open-ended and indirect. Students will be encouraged to be more active participants in the class. This type of instruction is characterized by student-initiated comments, praise from the teacher, and the teacher's use of students' ideas.

Just because there is student involvement does not mean that the teacher is using a student-centered or active approach. For example, the pattern of questions and answers referred to as drill is not a student-centered approach.

Cooperative Learning

Students involved in cooperative learning work together in groups to learn a concept or skill or to complete a project. Students, in groups of two to six, are assigned or choose a specific learning task or project presented by the teacher. The group consults with the teacher and devises a plan for working together.

Students use many resources, including the teacher, to help and teach one another and to accept responsibilities for tasks as they complete their work. The students summarize their efforts and, typically, make a presentation to the entire class or the teacher.

Cooperative learning is characterized by active learning, full participation, and democracy within a clearly established structure. Cooperative learning also engages students in discovering how to establish personal relationships and a cooperative working style.

Inquiry Learning

Inquiry learning uses students' own thought processes to help them learn a concept, solve a problem, or discover a relationship. This kind of instruction has also been referred to as Socratic. Inquiry learning often requires the most structure and preparation by the teacher. The teacher must know that the situation under study will yield useful results.

The teacher begins by explaining inquiry procedures to students, usually through examples. Next, the teacher presents the problem to be solved or the situation that will lead to the concept or relationship. Students gather information and ask questions of the teacher to gain additional information. The teacher supports students as they make predictions and provide tentative solutions or results. Once the process is complete, the teacher asks students to think over and describe the process they used to arrive at the solution. This last step is referred to as a metacognition.

Resources for Instruction

You may have to assemble a number of resources for instruction. It often helps to jot down the resources you will need to teach a lesson or a unit. The materials you select should help the students meet the lesson objectives and match the teaching-learning approach you will use. The resources may include textual, manipulative, technological, and human resources.

Be sure to assemble in advance the materials you need to teach a lesson. The materials may include texts, workbooks, teacher-made handouts, or other printed materials. Check the materials to ensure that they are intact and in appropriate condition.

You may use manipulative materials to teach a lesson. Be sure that the materials are assembled and complete. Any laboratory materials should be tested and safe. Be sure that the materials are at an appropriate level for the students.

You may use technological resources, such as a computer, during your lesson. Be sure that the computer will be available during your lesson. Try the computer out and be sure that it is working. Be sure that any software you will use is at an appropriate grade and interest level and matches the objectives of the lesson.

You will frequently use human resources in your lesson. You may decide to cooperatively teach a lesson or unit with another teacher. This approach requires advanced planning and regular communication. You may need to arrange for a guest speaker to speak to the class about a particular topic.

Special education teachers frequently teach in consultive or collaborative roles. That is, they work in classrooms with regular education teachers. In this arrangement, teachers must coordinate their activities and agree on how they will interact during the lesson.

CHARACTERISTICS OF SUCCESSFUL TEACHERS

In general effective teachers have these general characteristics.

- Accept children within a teacher–student relationship.
- Set firm and clear but flexible limits.
- Enforce rules clearly and consistently.
- Have positive, realistic expectations about students' achievements and adaptations.
- Have clear reasons for expectations about students.
- Practice what they preach (model acceptable behavior).
- Don't take students' actions personally. Students usually misbehave or act out because of who they are, not because of who the teacher is.

CRITICAL THINKING

Critical thinking involves logical thinking and reasoning, including skills such as comparison, classification, sequencing, cause/effect, patterning, webbing, analogies, deductive and inductive reasoning, forecasting, planning, hypothesizing, and critiquing.

CREATIVE THINKING

Creative thinking involves creating something new or original. It involves the skills of flexibility, originality, fluency, elaboration, brainstorming, modification, imagery, associative thinking, attribute listing, and metaphorical thinking. The aim of creative thinking is to stimulate curiosity.

HIGHER-ORDER THINKING

This type of thinking is based on the higher levels of Bloom's revised taxonomy of educational objectives: cognitive domain, discussed on page 387. For example, skills and concepts that involve analysis, evaluation, and the creation of new knowledge are classified as higher-level thinking. Encouraging higher-order thinking is worth the extra effort because this type of thinking is more likely to be applied to new or unique situations.

INDUCTIVE AND DEDUCTIVE REASONING

Inductive reasoning leads the learner from the specific to the general. Deductive reasoning takes the learner from the general to the specific. A student who bases a conclusion on an observation is thinking inductively. In general, a student drawing a conclusion based on an established scientific fact is thinking deductively. Discovery and inquiry learning in science and mathematics are examples of inductive thinking.

PROBLEM SOLVING

In this approach students apply critical and creative thinking with established steps to solve a problem. This term is used most frequently in mathematics education in which students may use specific strategies such as clue words, working backward, and interpreting the remainder to solve a problem.

INVENTION

This approach asks students to create something new or better. As simple examples, a student might be challenged to invent a better approach to checking out at a food store or a better way to store books in a classroom.

MEMORIZATION AND RECALL

Memorizing and recalling information is at the lowest rungs on Bloom's taxonomy. Still, it is often important to remember and recall details and there are mnemonic devices available to improve recall. Examples of these devices are "Roy G. Biv" to remember the colors of the rainbow or "Please Excuse My Dear Aunt Sally" to recall the order in which arithmetic operations should be performed.

CONCEPT MAP

A concept map is a graphical tool for representing and organizing concepts. These concepts are usually shown as squares or circles and are connected with labeled arrows to show the downward flow of concept development. This technique is often referred to as concept mapping.

PROJECT APPROACH

This approach builds learning around the study of a particular topic rather than a particular skill or concept. In this way students learn a wide range of subject skills and concepts in the context of the topic.

LOCAL EXPERTS

This approach uses local experts from the community to help students learn. The experts may be parents or guardians of students in the class.

PRIMARY DOCUMENTS

This approach relies on original documents rather than a description of the document. For example, students would learn about the Revolutionary War by studying the Declaration of Independence rather than reading about the Declaration.

SERVICE LEARNING

This integrates service to the community and learning. This experiential approach to instruction seeks to teach students about civic responsibility while encouraging a lifetime of engagement with the community.

COMPUTERS AND THE INTERNET IN EDUCATION INCLUDING E-MAIL, WEB PAGES, CDS, DVDS, AND SMART BOARDS

Computers and computer-related technology are widely used in schools for tasks ranging from word processing to the presentation of graphics and sound. There are many computer-based effective instructional programs available. The Internet and SMART Boards are among the many technological applications being fully integrated into the schools. The Internet makes a wide array of information and media available to teachers and students. Hyperlinks to Internet websites can be integrated with text as students prepare papers and reports. Electronic e-mail gives those in the schools the ability to communicate electronically throughout the world. Services such as Skype permit students to videoconference using only a computer, a portable camera, and a microphone.

Teachers should be aware that the Internet also presents a number of dangers, from inappropriate content to an adult's ability to make inappropriate contact with students. Social networking sites are also very popular among students. These sites carry their own problems, as it is possible for someone to misrepresent someone else's picture and personal information, and because a person may be able to learn his or her personal information. Schools and teachers typically take steps to reduce the likelihood that these dangers will be present on a school's computers, but these efforts may not be universally successful.

Students may create copies of documents, images, and video on CDs and DVDs. Most modern computers are equipped with players for recording or playing these flat round disks. School are increasingly using e-book readers.

Interactive white boards, typically the trademarked SMART Boards, give teachers an interactive "chalk board" that can integrate text, images, and sound. Teachers frequently use SMART Boards to display PowerPoint presentations. The Board enables the teacher to write directly on the presentation images and to save the presentation along with the handwritten text. The graphic capabilities of the SMART Board increase each month and the use of these boards is becoming widespread.

In addition to the technology available for use in any learning setting, there is a wide array of adaptive devices to support learning and living for students who are disabled.

PLANNING INSTRUCTION

Common Core State Standards Initiative

The Common Core State Standards Initiative is a state-led effort coordinated by the National Governors Association Center for Best Practices (NGA Center) and the Council of Chief State School Officers (CCSSO). These standards define the knowledge and skills students should have within their K–12 education careers so that they will graduate high school able to succeed in entry-level, credit-bearing academic college courses and in workforce training programs. The standards:

- are aligned with college and work expectations;
- are clear, understandable, and consistent;
- include rigorous content and application of knowledge through high-order skills;
- build upon strengths and lessons of current state standards;
- are informed by other top performing countries, so that all students are prepared to succeed in our global economy and society; and
- are evidence based.

Objectives

All useful instruction has some purpose. Planning for instruction begins with choosing an objective that expresses this purpose. Objectives usually refer to outcomes, while goals usually refer to more general purposes of instruction. The terms *aim, competency, outcome,* and *behavioral objective* are also used to refer to an objective.

Objectives are often established by national or state organizations. The national or state English, mathematics, and science professional organizations may recommend objectives for their subject. The national or state organizations for speech, primary education, elementary education, preschool education, and special education may recommend objectives for specific grades or specialties.

Most school texts contain objectives, usually given for each text unit or lesson. These objectives are also reflected in national, state, and local achievement tests.

School districts usually have their own written objectives. There may be a scope and sequence chart that outlines the objectives for each subject and grade. The district may also have a comprehensive set of objectives for each subject and grade level.

Taxonomy of Objectives

Benjamin Bloom and others described three domains of learning: cognitive, affective, and psychomotor. The cognitive domain refers to knowledge, intellectual ability, and the other things we associate with school learning. The affective domain refers to values, interests, attitudes, and the other things we associate with feelings. The psychomotor domain refers to motor skills and other things we associate with movement.

Each domain describes various levels of objectives. The six levels on the revised cognitive domain, noted below, are most useful in classifying objectives. Students should be exposed to objectives at all levels of the taxonomy.

1. **REMEMBERING**—Remembering specifics, recalling terms and theories.
2. **UNDERSTANDING**—Understanding or using an idea but not relating it to other ideas.
3. **APPLYING**—Using concepts or abstractions in actual situations.
4. **ANALYZING**—Breaking down a statement to relate ideas in the statement.
5. **EVALUATING**—Judging a decision or critiquing according to a particular criteria.
6. **CREATING**—Creating new ideas or a new product or perspective.

Choosing and Modifying Objectives

Initially, you will identify an objective from one of the sources noted previously. Consider these criteria when choosing and sequencing objectives.

- The objective should meet the overall goals of the school district.
- The objective should be appropriate for the achievement and maturation level of students in the class.
- The objective should be generally accepted by appropriate national, regional, or state professional organizations.

The objective you select may not exactly describe the lesson or unit you are going to teach. Modify the objective to meet your needs. You also may need to select or modify objectives and other plans to meet the needs of diverse student populations.

Your class may be academically diverse. You may teach special-needs students or you may have special-needs students in your class under the inclusion model. When you select and modify objectives for academically diverse students, consider the different achievement levels or learning styles of these students.

Your class may be culturally diverse. When you select and modify objectives for a culturally diverse class, consider the range of experiences and backgrounds found among the class. Do not reduce the difficulty of the objective.

Your class may be linguistically diverse. You may have limited English proficiency (LEP) students in your class. For a linguistically diverse class, take into account the limits that language places on learning. You may have to select or modify objectives to help these students learn English.

Writing Objectives

An objective should answer the question: "What are students expected to do once instruction is complete?" Objectives should not describe what the teacher does during the lesson. Objectives should not be overly specific, involved, or complicated.

Whenever possible, objectives should begin with a verb. Here are some examples.

Not an objective:	I will teach students how to pronounce words with a silent *e*. [This is a statement of what the teacher will do.]
Not an objective:	While in the reading group, looking at the reading book, students will pronounce words with a silent *e*. [This statement is overly specific.]
Objective:	Sounds out words with a silent *e*. [This is an objective. It tells what the student is expected to do.]
Objective:	States what he or she liked about the trip to the zoo.
Objective:	Reads a book from the story shelf.
Objective:	Serves a tennis ball successfully twice in a row.

Do not limit objectives to skills or tiny bits of strictly observable behavior. Specific objectives are not limited objectives. Objectives can include statements that students will appreciate or participate in some activity. Objectives should include integrating subject matter, applying concepts, problem solving, decision making, writing essays, researching projects, preparing reports, exploring, observing, appreciating, experimenting, and constructing and making art work and other projects.

Planning to Teach the Lesson

Once you have decided what to teach, you must plan how to teach it. Consider these factors as you plan the lesson or unit.

- Determine the prerequisite competencies. This is the knowledge and skills students must possess before they can learn the objective. Draw up a plan that ensures students will demonstrate prerequisite competencies before you teach the lesson.
- Determine the resources you need to help students reach the objective. The resources could include books, manipulatives, overhead transparencies, and other materials for you or the students to use. The resources could also include technological resources including computers or computer software and human resources including teacher aides, students, or outside presenters.
- Devise a plan to help students reach the objective. In addition to the factors discussed previously, the plan will usually include motivation and procedures.

Madeline Hunter posited the following important stages for effective lessons.

- Anticipatory set—Something that is said or done to prepare students and focus the students on the lesson.
- Objective and purpose—The teacher should state the objective of the lesson, and the students should be aware of the objective.
- Input—New information is presented during this stage.
- Modeling—The skills or procedures being taught or demonstrated.
- Checking for understanding—Following the instructional components in the previous two stages, the teacher should ensure that students understand the concept before moving to the next phases of the lesson.

- Guided practice—Students are given the opportunity to practice or use the concept or skill with the teacher's guidance.
- Independent practice—Students practice or use the concept on their own.

Classrooms are filled with the teacher's verbal and nonverbal communication. While most verbal communication is deliberate, much of nonverbal communication is expressed in ways that the teacher did not intend. A teacher can overtly develop a set of meanings for particular nonverbal communication that furthers the goal of a smoothly functioning classroom. These gestures should be carefully explained to students so that the students know the appropriate response. There are gestures that communicate approval, whereas others signal it is time to get back to work. Teachers can use gestures to tell students to take their seats, to get out their books, and for a whole host of routine classroom activities. Teachers should be sensitive to the cultural norms among their students. Moving into a student's personal space can be seen as approval by some students whereas others will see it as an unwanted intrusion. Even simple gestures like a "thumbs-up," universally seen as a sign of approval in this country, may be offensive to some learners.

A main focus of a teacher's communication is always to foster interactions and to stimulate discussions. The teacher pursues a wide range of strategies that embrace the full range of Bloom's Taxonomy and an energized approach to teaching.

The teacher will be there to help students formulate and flush out their ideas while continuing to probe learners for a deeper understanding of the subject matter. The teacher will create a safe environment where students feel comfortable taking risks and he or she will help students question facts and opinions to stimulate their curiosity in a way that furthers learning. The teacher will help students recall factual information needed for learning and then build on the recall to help students explore concepts. The teacher will help students learn how to engage in both convergent and divergent thinking.

TEACHING FOR STUDENT LEARNING

Planning instruction and implementing instruction are intertwined. Many of the points discussed here will have been considered during the planning process.

Classrooms are dynamic places. Students and teachers interact to further a student's learning and development. Follow these guidelines to establish a successful classroom and teach successful lessons.

MANAGING THE INSTRUCTIONAL ENVIRONMENT

Classroom management is a more encompassing idea than discipline or classroom control. Classroom management deals with all the things a classroom teacher can do to help students become productive learners. The best management system for any classroom will establish an effective learning environment with the least restrictions.

Teachers who are proactive and take charge stand the best chance of establishing an effective learning environment. Classroom management is designed to prevent problems, not react to them.

Classroom management begins with understanding the characteristics of students in your class.

Characteristics of Students

Some general statements about the students in a class can be made. For example, 3–7 percent of girls and 12–18 percent of boys will have some substantial adjustment problems. Prepare yourself for these predictable sex differences.

Boys are more physically active and younger children have shorter attention spans. Respond to this situation by scheduling activities when students are most likely to be able to complete them.

A teacher's management role is different at different grade levels. Prepare for these predictable differences in student reaction to teacher authority.

In the primary grades, students see teachers as authority figures and respond well to instruction and directions about how they should act in school. In the middle grades, students have learned how to act in school and still react well to the teacher's instruction.

In seventh through tenth grade, students turn to their peer group for leadership and resist the teacher's authority. The teacher must spend more time fostering appropriate behavior among students. By the last two years of high school, students are somewhat less resistant and the teacher's role is more academic.

Adolescents resent being touched and that teachers may anger adolescents by taking something from them. Avoid this problem by not confronting adolescent students.

There will be cultural differences among students. Many minority students, and other students, may be accustomed to harsh, authoritarian treatment. Respond to these students with warmth and acceptance. Many minority students will feel completely out of place in school. These students also need to be treated warmly and with the positive expectation that they will succeed in school.

Many other students may be too distracted to study effectively in school. These students may need quiet places to work and the opportunity to schedule some of their own work time.

Other factors, such as low self-esteem, anxiety, and tension, can also cause students to have difficulty in school.

Classroom Management Techniques

The following guidelines for effective classroom management include techniques for dealing with student misbehavior.

Teacher's Role

Teachers who are good classroom managers understand their dual role as an authority figure and as someone who helps children adapt to school and to life. Teachers are authority figures. Students expect the teacher to be an authority figure and expect teachers to establish a clear and consistent classroom structure.

Teachers must also help students learn how to fit into the classroom and how to get along with others. Teachers fare better in their role as authority figures than they do in this latter role. But teachers who have realistic expectations and know how to respond to problems can have some success.

Establishing an Effective Climate for Management

CLASSROOM PHYSICAL LAYOUT

There are several general rules to follow for a successful classroom layout. Set up the initial layout of the room so that you can see the faces of all the students. Rearrange the desks for individual and group work. Ensure that heavily used areas are free of all obstacles. Arrange the room so students do not have to stand in line, by having books and supplies available at several locations.

CLASSROOM LEADERSHIP

Research indicates that the following factors are most important in establishing effective classroom leadership. Develop a cohesive class by promoting cooperative experiences and minimizing competition among class members. Identify and gain the confidence of peer leaders, particularly in Grades 7–10. Establish an authoritative, but not authoritarian, leadership style.

Depending on the grade level, set three to six reasonable, adaptable rules that describe the overall nature of acceptable and unacceptable behavior. The expectations that accompany these rules should be stated clearly. The rules should be posted for students to see.

Much of the first two weeks of school should be spent establishing these rules, which may be stated by the teacher and/or developed through class discussion. Once the rules are established and the expectations are understood, the teacher should follow through. Student misbehavior should be handled immediately and appropriately but without causing a confrontation or alienating the student from the class.

Effective classroom managers take steps to ensure that the majority of class time is spent on instruction. They also take steps to ensure that students use their seat work and other inclass study time to complete assignments.

Specific Management Techniques

There are some specific management techniques that a teacher can apply to all classes. These techniques are summarized here.

KOUNIN

Kounin is a well-known expert on classroom management. Research results show that a number of Kounin's management techniques are effective. The following techniques have the most research support.

Kounin noted that teacher with-it-ness is an important aspect of classroom management. In other words, teachers who are constantly monitoring and are aware of what is happening in the classroom are better managers.

Kounin also showed that effective managers' lessons have smoothness and momentum. By this he meant that these lessons are free of teacher behavior that interrupts the flow of activities or slows down lesson pacing.

Finally, Kounin showed that group alerting was an effective technique. In group alerting, the teacher keeps bringing uninvolved students back into the lesson by calling their attention to what is happening and forewarning them of future events.

CANTER AND CANTER

Canter and Canter developed an approach called assertive discipline. Their approach is popular but lacks the research support of the approach recommended by Kounin.

The Canters recommend a direct and assertive approach to problem children. They point out that passive and hostile reactions to student misbehavior are not effective. Among other approaches, they recommend that the teacher and students establish rules and post those rules in the classroom. During each class session, the teacher writes and then marks the names of students who have violated rules. One rule violation in a session requires no action. Two rule violations, and the student meets with the teacher after school. Three violations require a parental visit to the school.

CUEING

Cues are words, gestures, or other signals that alert students to a coming transition or that gain their attention. A cue may be spoken, such as "We'll be leaving for art in about 5 minutes. Take this time to get ready." Another cue might be, "Your group has about 15 minutes to complete your project."

Other cues are nonverbal. You may glance at a student or make eye contact to re-engage the student in the lesson. You may raise your arm or hold your hand in a particular way to gain attention. You may flick the classroom lights quickly to indicate that groups should stop working and return to whole-class instruction.

OTHER EFFECTIVE TECHNIQUES FOR
MAINTAINING ATTENTION DURING A LESSON

The techniques listed below have proven effective in classrooms.

- Stand where you can scan and see the entire class.
- Ask questions of the whole class and then call on individuals for a response.
- Involve all students in the question-and-answer sessions and do not call on students just to catch them in a wrong answer or because they will give the correct answer.
- Gain attention through eye contact or a gesture.
- If a comment is required, make it very brief.
- Ensure that the material being taught is at an appropriate level.
- Base seat work or group work on an established system that is monitored closely and positively.

ASSESSMENT PROGRAMS

Every teacher evaluates instruction. The assessment program and the assessment instruments should measure mastery and understanding of important topics. The assessment program should also be used as a teaching tool. That is, the program should be used to help students learn and to improve instruction. The program should include authentic assessment of students' work as well as teacher-made and standardized tests.

Formative assessment information is usually gathered before or during teaching. Formative information is used to help you prepare appropriate lessons and assist students. Formative evaluations help teachers decide which objectives to teach, which instructional techniques to use, and which special help or services to provide to individual students.

Summative assessment information is usually gathered once instruction is complete. Summative evaluation is used to make judgments about student achievement and the effectiveness of the instructional programs. Summative evaluations lead to grades, to reports about a student's relative level of accomplishment, and to alterations of instructional programs.

Assessment information may be used for both purposes. For example, you may give a test to determine grades for a marking period or unit. You may then use the information from this test to plan further instruction and arrange individual help for students.

You may informally gather formative and summative information. Just walking around the room observing students' work can yield a lot of useful information. You can frequently discern the additional work that students need and identify different levels of student achievement.

Assessment Instruments

Tests have long been used to determine what students have learned and to compare students. Every test is imperfect. Many tests are so imperfect that they are useless. It is important to realize how this imperfection affects test results.

Some students are poor test takers. Every test assumes that the test takers have the opportunity to demonstrate what they know. A student may know something but be unable to demonstrate it on a particular test. Teachers must also consider alternative assessment strategies for these students.

Familiarize yourself with these basic assessment concepts.

- **ERRORS OF MEASUREMENT**—Every test contains errors of measurement. In other words, no one test accurately measures a student's achievement or ability. Carefully designed standardized tests may have measurement errors of 5 percent or 10 percent. Teacher-designed tests typically have large errors of measurement.

  A test result shows that a student falls into a range of scores and not just the single reported score. Focusing on a single score and ignoring the score range is among the most serious of score-reporting errors.

- **RELIABILITY**—A reliable test is consistent. That is, a reliable test will give similar results when given to the same person in a short time span. You cannot count on unreliable tests to give you useful scores. Use only very reliable standardized tests and be very aware of how important reliability is when you make up your own tests.

- **VALIDITY**—Valid tests measure what they are supposed to measure. There are two important types of validity: content validity and criterion validity.

  A test with high content validity measures the material covered in the curriculum or unit being tested. Tests that lack high content validity are unfair. When you make up a test it should have complete content validity. This does not mean that the test has to be unchallenging. It does mean that the questions should refer to the subject matter covered.

  A test with high criterion validity successfully predicts the ability to do other work. For example a test to be an automobile mechanic with high criterion validity will successfully predict who will be a good mechanic.

NORM-REFERENCED AND CRITERION-REFERENCED TESTS

Norm-referenced tests are designed to compare students. Intelligence tests are probably the best-known norm-referenced tests. These tests yield a number that purports to show how one person's intelligence compares to everyone else's. The average IQ score is 100.

Standardized achievement tests yield grade-level equivalent scores. These tests purport to show how student achievement compares to the achievement of all other students of the same grade level.

A fifth grader who earns a grade level equivalent of 5.5 might be thought of as average. A second-grade student with the same grade equivalent score would be thought of as above average. About half of all the students taking these tests will be below average.

Standardized tests also yield percentile scores. Percentile scores are reported as a number from 0 through 100. A percentile of 50 indicates that the student did as well as or better than 50 percent of the students at that grade level who took the test. The higher the percentile, the better the relative performance.

Criterion-referenced tests are designed to determine the degree to which an objective has been reached. Teacher-made tests and tests found in teachers' editions of texts are usually criterion-referenced tests. Criterion-referenced tests have very high content validity.

AUTHENTIC ASSESSMENT

Standardized and teacher-made tests have significant drawbacks. These types of tests do not evaluate a student's ability to perform a task or demonstrate a skill in a real-life situation. These tests do not evaluate a student's ability to work cooperatively or consistently.

In authentic assessment, students are asked to demonstrate the skill or knowledge in a real-life setting. The teacher and students collaborate in the learning assessment process and discuss how learning is progressing and how to facilitate that learning. The idea is to get an authentic picture of the student's work and progress.

Students have an opportunity to demonstrate what they know or can do in a variety of settings. Students can also demonstrate their ability to work independently or as part of a group.

Portfolio assessment is another name for authentic assessment. Students evaluated through a system of authentic assessment frequently keep a portfolio of their work.

EFFECTIVE BRIDGES

Creating Bridges Among Curriculum Goals and Students' Prior Experiences

One effective approach to instruction is to connect the curriculum goals with a student's prior experiences and knowledge. Consider these four ways to build a bridge between the curriculum and a student's prior knowledge.

Modeling

The term *modeling* means demonstrating a desired behavior or presenting a representation of an important theory, idea, or object. Each of these meanings can link curriculum goals with students' prior knowledge and experience.

Activating Prior Knowledge

Activating prior knowledge helps students recall what they already know about the material being studied. The teacher may encourage students to discuss what they already know, or the teacher may take the lead and directly discuss their prior knowledge. In either case, the activated prior knowledge is incorporated in instruction.

CULTURAL AND LINGUISTIC DIVERSITY AND ELL STUDENTS

SES (socioeconomic status)—Socioeconomic status and school achievement are highly correlated. Overall, students with higher SES will have higher achievement scores. In America, SES differences are typically associated with differences in race and ethnicity. However, the achievement differences are not caused by and are not a function of these differences in race or ethnicity. Rather, achievement differences are typically caused by differences in home environment, opportunity for enriched experiences, and parental expectations.

Teachers frequently have a higher SES than their students. These students often behave differently than teachers expect. The crushing problems of poor and homeless children may produce an overlay of acting out and attention problems. All this frequently leads the teacher to erroneously conclude that these students are less capable of learning. In turn, the teacher may erroneously lower learning expectations. This leads to lower school performance and a compounding of students' difficulty.

A teacher must consciously and forcibly remind herself or himself that lower SES students are capable learners. These teachers must also actively guard against reducing learning expectations for lower SES students.

There are appropriate ways of adapting instruction for students with different SES levels. For high SES students, minimize competitiveness, provide less structure, and present more material. For low SES students, be more encouraging, guard against feelings of failure or low self-esteem, and provide more structure. Do not lower learning expectations, but do present less material and emphasize mastery of the material.

CULTURALLY DIVERSE—Almost every class will have students from diverse cultural backgrounds. Use the values embedded in these cultures to motivate individual learners.

LINGUISTICALLY DIVERSE—The first language for many students is not English. In addition, a number of American students speak local variants of the English language. Teachers frequently, and erroneously, lower their learning expectations for these students. There are a number of useful strategies for adapting instruction for these students.

A number of students are referred to as Limited English Proficiency (LEP) who need English as a second language (ESL) instruction. Teaching English as a second language to ELL students can be accomplished in the classroom, but often requires a specialist who works with students in "pull-out programs."

ELL STUDENTS

We often think of ELL students as those children who enter the classrooms without a word of English. These ELL students are frequently recent newcomers to the country and frequently do not communicate effectively for some time.

This so-called "silent period" may last anywhere from just a few days to several months or in extreme cases even close to a year. This is a time of uncertainty for the ELL student and the teacher. The student is trying to understand written and spoken communication and to fit into the cultural framework of the school. The teacher may be concerned about the student's progress and in search of promising approaches.

How a second language is acquired is still not fully understood. Students show varying patterns, rates, and styles of acquisition. One student may seem to "take off" and become quickly conversant in English, while others continue to struggle even after lengthy periods of exposure. At other times, self-confident children will attempt verbal interactions in the second language more quickly, which helps with social adjustment.

Prior language development and competence are also a key in determining how well a student acquires English as a second language. Adequate development in the primary language at home helps students learn English. Students frequently come without the necessary competence in their native language to allow an easy bridge into second language learning. Difficulties in vocabulary development and syntax, poor writing skills, and difficulty keeping up and participating in class may all be symptoms of an earlier lack of competence in a first language.

CORRECTED MISUNDERSTANDINGS ABOUT ELL STUDENTS

There are several key misunderstandings about ELL students and second language acquisition.

MISUNDERSTANDING: Students can learn English quickly by being exposed to and surrounded by native language speakers.

CORRECTED: Mere exposure to English does not itself ensure English proficiency. Reports also indicate that while grammatical proficiency may be established in a few years, academic competence comparable to that of native language peers takes much longer, perhaps even between five and as much as 10 years.

MISUNDERSTANDING: The ability to converse comfortably in English signals proficiency and means the child should be achieving academically.

CORRECTED: It is easy to confuse conversational competence with academic competence in a language. Proficiency in social language interaction in English is not the most important indicator of school success. Spoken practice in English may not be necessary for development of English proficiency and may retard it in some instances. Emphasis on interpersonal communication may even inhibit academic achievement

MISUNDERSTANDING: Students should learn English before attempting to study an academic subject in that language.

CORRECTED: While pull-out ELL classes may make ELL students more comfortable, much of the English taught in these classes focuses on social interaction. This does little to assist the student in learning an academic discipline. Academic disciplines have their own vocabularies and performance expectations. These are rarely taught outside the subject area classroom, except perhaps in sheltered content courses.

MISUNDERSTANDING: ELL students should stop speaking their native language and concentrate on speaking English.

CORRECTED: Full proficiency in the native language facilitates second language development, and academic achievement is significantly enhanced when ELL students are able to use their native languages to learn in school. Some studies have found that second language students who achieved the greatest academic success were enrolled in bilingual programs that provided solid cognitive academic instruction in both the first and second language.

SECOND-LANGUAGE ACQUISITION AND STRATEGIES FOR LEARNING ENGLISH AS A SECOND LANGUAGE

Second-language acquisition refers to learning a second language once a first language has already been learned. This typically happens in the United States when a student has learned the second language before the child comes to school.

The field of second-language acquisition often includes a number of terms such as English language learners (ELLs), English as a second language (ESL), English for speakers of other languages (ESOL), and English as a foreign language (EFL).

The ability of a student to learn a second language depends in large part on whether the second language is spoken at home. That makes it important to involve parents and guardians in an effective second-language acquisition program.

Sheltered Instruction

The term *sheltered instruction* describes one approach teachers use to help ELLs. Sheltered instruction provides meaningful instruction in the content areas while students move toward English proficiency. The approach is notable since it frequently integrates Vygotsky's ZPD and Gardner's multiple intelligences. The approach is contrasted with other approaches for ELLs that offer content instruction below grade level while focusing primarily on a student's development of English skills.

One approach to sheltered instruction is the sheltered instruction observation protocol (SIOP). The SIOP model includes activities associated with the following interrelated activities.

- Lesson Preparation
- Building Background
- Comprehensible Input
- Strategies
- Interaction
- Practice/Application
- Lesson Delivery
- Review/Assessment

Each of the strategies is accompanied by a series of specific activities.

ADDITIONAL ELL RECOMMENDATIONS

RECOMMENDATION 1

Teach a set of academic vocabulary words intensively across several days using a variety of instructional activities.

- Choose a brief, engaging piece of informational text that includes academic vocabulary as a platform for intensive academic vocabulary instruction.
- Choose a small set of academic vocabulary for in-depth instruction.
- Teach academic vocabulary in depth using multiple modalities (writing, speaking, listening).
- Teach word-learning strategies to help students independently figure out the meaning of words.

RECOMMENDATION 2

Integrate oral and written English language instruction into content-area teaching.

- Strategically use instructional tools—such as short videos, visuals, and graphic organizers—to anchor instruction and help students make sense of content.
- Explicitly teach the content-specific academic vocabulary, as well as the general academic vocabulary that supports it, during content-area instruction.
- Provide daily opportunities for students to talk about content in pairs or small groups.
- Provide writing opportunities to extend student learning and understanding of the content material.

RECOMMENDATION 3

Provide regular, structured opportunities to develop written language skills.

- Provide writing assignments that are anchored in content and focused on developing academic language and writing skills.
- For all writing assignments, provide language-based supports to facilitate students' entry into, and continued development of, writing.
- Use small groups or pairs to provide opportunities for students to work and talk together on varied aspects of writing.
- Assess students' writing periodically to identify instructional needs and provide positive, constructive feedback in response.

RECOMMENDATION 4

Provide small-group instructional intervention to students struggling in areas of literacy and English language development.

- Use available assessment information to identify students who demonstrate persistent struggles with aspects of language and literacy development.
- Design the content of small-group instruction to target students' identified needs.
- Provide additional instruction in small groups consisting of three to five students to students struggling with language and literacy.
- For students who struggle with basic foundational reading skills, spend time not only on these skills but also on vocabulary development and listening and reading comprehension strategies.

VISUAL-PROCESSING PROBLEMS

Visual-processing problems arise when students have difficulty processing visual input. Visual-processing problems are particularly important in the elementary grades. Students can have perfect vision and still have visual-processing problems.

The most appropriate action for a teacher who suspects that a student may have difficulty processing visual information is to refer the child for a special test that can identify students with this problem. A regular vision test will not identify this problem and eyeglasses will not correct it.

Visual-processing problems usually create reading problems, but visual processing problems can create learning problems in other school subjects. Experts believe that as many as 80 percent of students may have visual-processing problems not severe enough to interfere with learning.

LEARNING DISABILITIES

The formal definition of learning disability comes from the Individuals with Disabilities Education Act (IDEA).

A learning disability is . . . a disorder in one or more of the basic psychological processes involved in understanding or in using language, spoken or written, that may manifest itself in an imperfect ability to listen, think, speak, read, write, spell, or do mathematical calculations, including conditions such as perceptual disabilities, brain injury, minimal brain dysfunction, dyslexia, and developmental aphasia.

Learning disabilities do not include, . . . learning problems that are primarily the result of visual, hearing, or motor disabilities, of mental retardation, of emotional disturbance, or of environmental, cultural, or economic disadvantage.

There are many different types of learning disabilities. A partial list is given below.

Dyslexia	Difficulty processing language	Problems reading, writing, spelling, speaking
Dyscalculia	Difficulty with math	Problems doing math problems, understanding time, using money
Dysgraphia	Difficulty with writing	Problems with handwriting, spelling, organizing ideas
Dyspraxia (Sensory Integration Disorder)	Difficulty with fine motor skills	Problems with hand-eye coordination, balance, manual dexterity
Auditory Processing Disorder	Difficulty hearing differences between sounds	Problems with reading, comprehension, language
Visual Processing Disorder	Difficulty interpreting visual information	Problems with reading, math, maps, charts, symbols, pictures

ATTENTION-DEFICIT DISORDER AND ATTENTION-DEFICIT HYPERACTIVITY DISORDER

The three main symptoms of a child with attention-deficit disorder (ADD) or attention-deficit hyperactivity disorder (ADHD) are inattention, hyperactivity, and impulsivity. Usually one of these symptoms is predominant. Not everything about students with ADD/ADHD has a negative impact on learning, and there are many successful people with ADD/ADHD. However, students who fit these classifications usually present a problem in a typical school setting.

INATTENTIVE: Inattentive students may be harder to identify because these students may not be disruptive. However, these students may not follow rules and directions, whether it is in interactions with teachers or with other students. These students may be unorganized.

HYPERACTIVE: Students are normally active, but students with hyperactive symptoms seem to be constantly on the move. They move suddenly from one activity to the next. Attempts to be still may be accompanied by what seems an involuntary movement such as tapping fingers or feet.

IMPULSIVE: Impulsive students lack self-control. They may make off-the-topic comments or ask irrelevant questions. They may break into other people's conversations or inappropriately move into another student's personal space.

There are many intervention programs for learning disabled students. However, the teacher should see the symptoms of these problems as behavior the student can likely not control. This step will help the teacher work with special educators and parents to develop effective classroom strategies.

MENTAL RETARDATION

A child under the age of 18 must meet two specific criteria to be classified as mentally retarded: (1) The child must have an IQ below 70; and (2) There must be meaningful limitations in at least two of three areas of adaptive behavior: social skills, daily living skills, and communication skills. Mental retardation is a disability and not a disease. There is no known cure for mental retardation. However, students with mental retardation can learn to function effectively within the limits of their disability.

An IQ score is determined by an IQ test. These tests have a mean score of 100 with a standard deviation of 15. That means a student classified as mentally retarded on the basis of these tests is at least two standard deviations below the mean. There are many causes of a low IQ score other than low intelligence, and it is very important to eliminate these causes before accepting the validity of the score.

Here are the categories of mental retardation based solely on IQ scores.

Degree of Mental Retardation	IQ Score
Profound	less than 20
Severe	20–34
Moderate	35–49
Mild	50–69

The other limitation required for a diagnosis of mental retardation is based on scores from an adaptive rating scale, which is based on the abilities a person is known to possess at a particular age. The evaluation and scale are administered and scored by a professional evaluator, and are typically beyond the responsibilities of a classroom teacher.

There are many such scales and each focuses on these three important areas of adaptive behavior.

Social skills as demonstrated by interactions with family members, teachers, and peers.

Daily living skills such as self-feeding, personal toilet habits, and dressing oneself.

Communication skills such as understanding what someone is saying and the ability to respond orally to comments and questions.

BEHAVIOR DISORDERS IN CHILDREN

Students classified with behavior disorders exhibit aberrant behavior that goes well beyond the problems normally demonstrated by children. These behavior disorders are particularly noticeable in the preschool years and in adolescence. The following biological and family factors make children most at risk for behavioral disorders: (1) low birth weight, (2) neurological damage, (3) early rejection, (4) separation from their parents, (5) physical and sexual abuse, or (6) being raised by mothers who have suffered physical or sexual abuse or who are living in poverty.

TYPES OF BEHAVIOR DISORDERS

Oppositional Defiant Disorder

Students exhibiting this disorder disobey rules formulated at home or in school. These students frequently argue and have temper tantrums, refuse to obey rules, defy authority, reject responsibility for their behavior, and show evidence of resentment and revenge seeking.

Conduct Disorder Behavior

Students exhibiting this disorder are usually older children or teens who disobey rules and laws formulated by the larger society, including laws that may lead to arrest and incarceration. These students may run away from home, not attend school, destroy property, or set fires. They may bully other students or steal, they may threaten to injure people or animals, and they may find themselves in youth detention facilities or in special programs.

DEVELOPMENTAL DELAYS

The IDEA is the source of the definition of developmental delay. These are students who [are] experiencing developmental delays as defined by the State and as measured by appropriate diagnostic instruments and procedures in one or more of the following areas: physical development, cognitive development, communication development, social or emotional development, or adaptive development; and who, by reason thereof, need special education and related services.

A teacher must be familiar with his or her state's definition of *developmental delay*, and, indeed, whether the state uses this term. A student may qualify for services as a developmentally delayed student in one state but not in another.

Developmental delays are determined by comparing what a child can do compared to the normal range of performance for children the same age. Developmental evaluations must be conducted by a trained professional. The evaluation typically focuses on five developmental areas.

Physical development
Cognitive development
Speech and language development
Social skills and emotional development
Child's ability to care for him- or herself

As long as a state defines the term and requires local school districts to use the term, a finding of developmental disabilities means special education services are available free of charge through the school system for children over the age of three.

AMERICANS WITH DISABILITIES ACT AND AMERICANS WITH DISABILITIES ACT AMENDED

The Americans with Disabilities Act (ADA) includes five main titles, but most important for education are the life activities defined more clearly in the Americans with Disabilities Act Amended (ADAA).

The ADA defines a covered disability as "a physical or mental impairment that substantially limits a major life activity."

Recently, the ADAA broadened the interpretations and added to the ADA examples of "major life activities" including, but not limited to, "caring for oneself, performing manual tasks, seeing, hearing, eating, sleeping, walking, standing, lifting, bending, speaking, breathing, learning, reading, concentrating, thinking, communicating, and working," as well as the operation of several specified "major bodily functions."

INCLUSION, MAINSTREAMING, AND LEAST RESTRICTIVE ENVIRONMENT

Inclusion, mainstreaming, and least restrictive environment (LRE) have different meanings.

LRE comes from the IDEA mandate that disabled students should be placed in learning settings whenever possible with students without disabilities. The term *LRE* does not refer to any particular setting, but emphasizes that the less a learning setting is like a traditional setting the more restrictive it is.

Inclusion has a more specific meaning. It means deliberately placing disabled students in regular classrooms with students who have no disabilities, when the disabled student can receive an appropriate education in the class. Inclusion reflects a more comprehensive plan than the less-used term *mainstreaming*, although the two terms still tend to be used interchangeably.

INDIVIDUALIZED EDUCATION PLAN

An individualized education plan (IEP) is required by the IDEA for a child who is classified as disabled by federal or state regulations. To qualify, the child's disability must have an adverse effect on the child's educational progress.

Once a child is found eligible for services, the school sets up an IEP team to develop the IEP. Specific IEP requirements may vary from state to state. An IEP team established by the school typically includes the student's teacher, the student's parents or guardian, a special education teacher, and someone to evaluate the child's evaluation reports, such as a school psychologist. The school may invite other experts to the meeting, and it is not unusual for the parents or guardian to arrange for an advocate or an attorney to join the team. It is also not unheard of for students beyond the primary grades to participate in the meeting.

The whole purpose of this effort is to bring everyone together to consider a child's strengths and deficits and to develop a plan that will best meet the child's educational needs. The IEP may include a wide variety of educational adaptations as well as work in a regular class.

The initial IEP must be accepted by the parents or guardian, or appealed within a set time, typically 10 days. Any member of the team may call a meeting to request an alteration to the IEP. An extensive system of conflict resolution procedures are set out in the statutory provisions.

SECTION 504 OF THE REHABILITATION SERVICES ACT

The best way to understand Section 504 of the Rehabilitation Services Act is to understand how it differs from the IDEA.

Section 504 has more lax requirements than the IDEA. That is, students may receive less assistance from schools with less overview and regulations under Section 504 than under IDEA. Section 504 covers a person's entire life span and safeguards the rights of persons with disabilities beyond education.

Schools are not required to identify students who qualify for services under Section 504, and parental permission is not required for students receiving 504 services. However, parents may raise concerns about the services and petition for a 504 hearing. Section 504 students have a plan but not an IEP. A Section 504 student is typically not placed in a special education setting.

ADAPTING INSTRUCTION

Adapt instruction for the following factors, types of learners, and students.

AGE—Primary students should have more structure, shorter lessons, less explanation, more public praise, more small group and individual instruction, and more experiences with manipulatives and pictures. Older students should have less structure, increasingly longer lessons, more explanation, less public praise, more whole-class instruction, more independent work, and less work with manipulatives.

ACADEMICALLY DIVERSE

APTITUDE—Students exhibit different abilities to learn. You can provide differentiated assignments to enable students at different aptitude levels to maximize their potential.

READING LEVEL—Ensure that a student is capable of understanding the reading material. Do not ask students to learn from material that is too difficult. Identify materials at an appropriate reading level or with an alternative learning mode (tapes, material read to student). Remember that a low reading level does not mean that a student cannot learn a difficult concept.

LEARNING DISABLED—Learning-disabled students evidence at least a 2-year discrepancy between measures of ability and performance. Learning-disabled students should be given structured, brief assignments, manipulative experiences, and many opportunities for auditory learning.

VISUALLY IMPAIRED—Place the visually impaired student where he or she can most easily see the instruction. Use large learning aids and large print books. Use a multisensory approach.

HEARING IMPAIRED—Ensure that students are wearing an appropriate hearing aid. Students with less than 50 percent hearing loss will probably be able to hear you if you stand about 3 to 5 feet away.

MILDLY HANDICAPPED—Focus on a few, highly relevant skills, more learning time, and lots of practice. Provide students with concrete experiences. Do not do for students what they can do for themselves, even if it takes these students an extended time.

GIFTED—Gifted students have above average ability, creativity, and a high degree of task commitment. Provide these students with enriched or differentiated units. Permit them to test out of required units. Do not isolate these students from the rest of the class.

Changing Behavior

Students may act so unacceptably that their behavior must be changed. Here are some suggestions for changing behavior.

REINFORCEMENT

All teachers use positive reinforcement, whether through grades, praise, tokens, or other means. Teachers also use negative reinforcement by showing students how to avoid an undesirable consequence (poor grade) by doing acceptable work. Negative reinforcement is not punishment.

CONTRACTS AND LOGS

You may be able to help children change behavior by using contracts or by asking students to maintain logs. These approaches cause students to think about their behavior and both have been proven effective.

When writing a contract, work with a student to establish desired learning goals or classroom behavior. The contract, signed by the teacher and the student, sets short-term goals for classroom conduct and academic achievement. A teacher may also ask students to maintain a log of their classroom behavior. A brief daily review of the log may improve behavior.

PUNISHMENT

Punishment is a temporary measure. It should be administered to improve student performance, not to make the teacher feel better. Limited punishment given for a specific reason when students are emotionally stable can be effective. Other punishments, such as extra work, punishment of the entire class, and corporal punishment, are usually not effective.

Effective punishment should be reasonable, deliberate, and unemotional. The punishment should also be short and somewhat unpleasant. The reason for the punishment should be clear, and the punishment should be accompanied by examples of appropriate behavior.

NEW YORK STATE TEACHER RESPONSIBILITY AND EDUCATION LAW

These links take you to specific information about New York State Education Laws and Regulations and New York State Teaching Standards.

New York State Education Laws and Regulations

www.p12.nysed.gov/sss/lawsregs

Search for "New York State Education Law"

New York State Teaching Standards Page

www.highered.nysed.gov/tcert/pdf/teachingstandards9122011.pdf

Search for "New York State Teacher Responsibility

LEGAL, LEGISLATIVE, AND POLITICAL INFLUENCES

WHO'S IN CHARGE OF EDUCATION

The Constitution of the United States does not assign the responsibility for education to the federal government, leaving this responsibility to each state. The state government, including the governor, the legislature, and the courts have the ultimate responsibility for public education. A state board or commission is usually responsible for the operation of the schools. A state commissioner of education reports to the state board.

The commissioner, in turn, oversees a state education department. The state education department is responsible for the state's daily responsibility for the schools. Other organizations in a state, including regional and county authorities, may have education responsibilities.

Local or regional boards of education are directly responsible for operating schools in their district or town. In more than 80 percent of the cases, these boards are elected. A local or regional superintendent of schools reports to the board and, along with other administrators and support staff, has the daily responsibility for operating the schools.

Building principals report to the superintendent and are responsible for the daily operations of their school building. Teachers have the responsibility for teaching their students and carrying out district and state education policies.

IT'S THE LAW

A complex set of federal, state, and local laws govern education. Court cases are changing the interpretation of these laws each day. Here is a brief summary of legal rights as they may apply to schools, teachers, and students. This summary should not be used to make any decisions related to school laws. Any specific interest in legal issues should be referred to a competent attorney.

Schools

- Schools may not discriminate against students, teachers, or others because of their race, sex, ethnicity, or religion. "Reverse discrimination" *may* be legal when hiring teachers, but it is not legal when dismissing teachers.
- Schools must make children's school records available to parents and legal guardians.
- Schools may remove books from the school library. However, a book may not be removed from the library just because a school board member or other school official does not agree with its content.

Teachers

- Nontenured teachers usually have very limited rights to reappointment. Generally speaking, schools may not rehire a nontenured teacher for any reason. For example, the schools may simply say that they want to find someone better, that the teacher doesn't fit in, or that they just do not want to renew the contract.
- Teachers cannot be fired for behavior that does not disrupt or interfere with their effectiveness as teachers. However, even personal behavior away from school, which significantly reduces teaching effectiveness, might be grounds for dismissal.
- Teachers may be dismissed or suspended for not doing their job. Any such action must follow a due process procedure.
- Teachers may be sued and be liable for negligence. Successful suits and actions against teachers have occurred when the evidence showed that the teacher could have reasonably foreseen what was going to happen or that the teacher acted differently than a reasonable teacher would have acted in that same situation.
- Teachers have freedom of speech. Teachers have the same free speech rights as other citizens. They may comment publicly on all issues, including decisions of the school administrators or the school board. However, a teacher may not disclose confidential information or be malicious, and the statements cannot interfere with teaching performance. Teachers do not have unlimited academic freedom or freedom of speech in the classroom or elsewhere in the school. Teachers are not permitted to disrupt the school or the school curriculum.

Students

- Handicapped students from ages 3 to 21 are entitled to a free and appropriate public education as a matter of federal law. This education should take place in the least restrictive environment available.
- Students have limited freedom of the press. Student newspapers supported by school funds may be reviewed and edited by school officials. However, papers paid for and produced by students off school property may not be censored by school officials.
- Students are entitled to due process. In particular, students have a right to a hearing and an opportunity to present a defense before being suspended. Students who pose a threat to others in the school are not entitled to this due process.

TEACHER–PARENT COMMUNICATION

Communication between parents and teachers is an essential part of effective instruction. The approaches listed below are proven strategies for effectively involving parents in a child's education.

Parent Surveys	Parent Classroom Visit
Positive Phone Calls	Weekly Folders
Class Newsletters	Flexible Scheduling for Conferences
Class Website and E-mail Updates	

DIVERSITY IN SOCIETY AND CULTURE

America is a multiethnic and multicultural society. Consequently, the culture of the community and the culture of the school varies widely depending on the school's geographic location, socioeconomic setting, and local norms. To understand schools, we must understand society and culture.

Anthropology and sociology provide a scientific basis for studying society and culture. Anthropology is the formal study of culture and the development of society. Much of the early anthropological work dealt with primitive cultures. However, in recent years anthropologists have turned their attention to communities and schools. Sociology is the study of how people behave in a group. Sociology can help us understand how students behave in school, how teachers function on a faculty, and how citizens interact in the community.

Culture is directly affected by the ethnicity of the community. Each ethnic group brings its own culture, its own language, and its own customs to this country.

Until recently, most immigrant groups have been acculturated. That is, they have largely adopted the dominant language and culture of the United States. Lately there has been a shift toward cultural pluralism in which immigrants maintain their cultural, and occasionally linguistic, identity.

Under cultural pluralism, the challenge is to provide equal educational opportunity while also providing for these cultural differences among students. There is little prospect, however, that non-English speakers will realize their full potential in the United States.

Socioeconomic status has a direct effect on culture and on the schools. As noted earlier, there is a strong correlation between SES and academic achievement. In the United States, groups, communities, and schools are stratified by social class. Social stratification often occurs within schools. Unlike many other countries, individuals are able to move among social classes, usually in an upward direction.

THE SCHOOL AND SOCIETY

The School in Society

The school is a part of society. It reflects the society and socializes students. To that end, the schools prepare students to function in society. Students are taught, directly and indirectly, acceptable social values and behavior.

The academic curriculum reflects society's expectations. Students are taught a generally accepted body of knowledge. Students are also prepared for society by being exposed to potential careers as a part of the school curriculum.

Every society has a culture. The culture combines the history of the society and the society's current norms. The culture includes customs, values, ethical and moral structures, religions and beliefs, laws, and a hierarchy of most valued contributions by members of society.

The School as a Society

The school is a society in itself. The school society consists of a complex interrelationship of teachers, students, administrators, parents, and others. Each school has its own character, practices, and informal hierarchy. Generally speaking, new teachers must find a niche in the school's society to be successful. The school has a formal decision-making hierarchy of teachers, supervisors, principals, superintendents, and school boards. The new teacher must usually gain acceptance at each level of this hierarchy to experience success.

Each state in the United States has its own system of education. States are legally responsible for education. Locally elected or appointed school boards usually have the most direct legal impact on the schools. Within state and federal laws, school boards pay for the schools from tax receipts and other funds, hire teachers and administrators, approve curricula, and set school policy.

Many of the decisions made by school boards are affected by the amount of money available to the schools. Generally speaking, wealthier districts have more money to spend on schools. The difference in the funds available may create a difference in the quality of schooling.

THE FAMILY

The family remains the predominant influence in the early lives of children. However, the nature of the American family has changed.

Divorce rates are very high, and some say that a majority of Americans under the age of forty will be divorced. American families are fragmented, with about 30 percent of children living with a step-parent. About one-third of children are raised in single-parent families, and about two-thirds of these children live below the poverty level.

An increasing number of children, called latchkey children, return from school with no parents at home. School programs developed for these students cannot replace effective parenting.

In many respects, the school, social or religious institutions, peer groups, and even gangs have replaced parents. This means that parents and families have less influence on children's values and beliefs.

The pressures of economic needs have drastically changed the American family. Less than 10 percent of American families have children, a mother at home, and a father at work. More than 30 percent of married couples have no children, and more than 70 percent of mothers with children are working mothers.

SOCIETAL PROBLEMS

This decade finds our society beset with unprecedented problems of crime and violence, alcohol and drug abuse, sex, AIDS, high dropout rates, and child abuse. Many of these problems can be traced directly to poverty. Schools are a part of society, so they too are affected by these problems.

Crime and Violence

Students bring guns to school. More than 70 percent of those who commit serious crimes are never caught. We live in a society where crime is rampant.

Crime in school presents a particular problem for teachers. Some estimate that 3 to 7 percent of all students bring a gun with them to school. Students attack teachers every day in the United States. While this behavior is not defensible, attention to the principles of classroom management mentioned earlier can help in averting some of these incidents.

Alcohol and Drug Abuse

Alcohol is the most used and abused drug. Even though it is legal, there are serious short- and long-term consequences of alcohol use. Alcoholism is the most widespread drug addiction and untreated alcoholism can lead to death.

Tobacco is the next most widely used and abused substance. Some efforts are being made to declare tobacco a drug. Irrefutable evidence shows that tobacco use is a causative factor in hundreds of thousands of deaths each year.

Other drugs including marijuana, cocaine, heroin, and various drugs in pill form carry with them serious health, addiction, and emotional problems. The widespread illicit availability of these drugs creates additional problems. Many students engage in crimes to get money to pay for drugs. Others may commit crimes while under the influence of drugs. Still others may commit crimes by selling drugs to make money.

More than 90 percent of students have used alcohol by the time they leave high school. About 70 percent of high school graduates have used other illegal drugs. Awareness programs that focus on drug use can have some positive effects. However, most drug and alcohol abuse and addiction has other underlying causes. These causes must be addressed for any program to be effective.

Sex

Many teens and preteens are sexually active, and many of these children know little about sexual education. It is in this environment that we find increases in teenage pregnancies, abortions, dropouts, and ruined lives. Sex spreads disease. So we also note increases in syphilis, gonorrhea, and other sexually transmitted diseases.

About 10 percent of teenage girls will become pregnant. Teenage pregnancy is the primary reason why girls drop out of high school. These girls seldom receive appropriate help from the child's father and are often destined for a life of poverty and dependence.

AIDS

Acquired immune deficiency syndrome (AIDS) is a breakdown in the body's immune system caused by the human immunodeficiency virus (HIV). This virus can be detected with blood tests. People with the HIV may take ten years or longer to develop AIDS.

HIV is transmitted by infected blood and other bodily fluids. Sexual relations and contact with infected blood, including blood injected with shared hypodermic needles, are all examples of ways that HIV can be transmitted. Some 2 to 5 percent of the teens in some urban areas may be HIV-positive.

Students can try to avoid becoming HIV-positive by reducing their risk factors. Abstinence from sex and never injecting drugs will virtually eliminate the likelihood that a teenager will become HIV-positive. Less effective measures, such as using condoms, can be taken to help sexually active students reduce the likelihood of becoming HIV-positive. Girls run a higher risk than boys of becoming HIV-positive through sexual activity.

Acquiring HIV is associated with drug and alcohol use. Even when students know the risks and how to avoid them, alcohol and drug use can lower inhibitions and lead to unsafe practices.

Dropouts

Dropout rates are worst in urban areas, with over half the students dropping out of some schools. High school dropouts are usually headed for a life of lower wages and poorer living conditions.

Many of these students feel alienated from society or school and need support or alternative learning environments. Intervention, counseling, and alternative programs such as therapeutic high schools, vocational high schools, and other special learning arrangements can help prevent a student from dropping out.

Child Abuse

Child abuse is the secret destroyer of children's lives. Some estimate that between two and three million children are abused each year. Child abuse is a primary cause of violent youth, runaways, and drug abusers.

Physical and sexual abuse are the most destructive of the abuses heaped upon children. Contrary to popular belief, most child abuse is perpetrated by family members, relatives, and friends. Younger children are often incapable of talking about their abuse and may not reveal it even when asked.

In many states, teachers are required to report suspected child abuse. When child abuse is suspected, a teacher should follow the guidelines given by the school, the district, or the state.

DESCRIPTION

This is Ms. Daley's first year as a fifth-grade teacher. She was previously a third-grade teacher, and the difference between the grades is noticeable. Her class of 24 students is culturally and linguistically diverse, although most of the students are high performing. In recent years, another ethnic group has moved into this town and quickly became 20 percent of the school population. Performance among this new population has eclipsed that of the longer-term residents and these newer students tend to win most of the academic awards. Last year, the top 10 percent of ACT and SAT scores in the high school were from this new group.

Ms. Daley is just learning about this particular mix of students at this grade, and she is maintaining a daily log. She watches students' interactions in class and during lunch, and she reviews last year's assessment data. It is quite daunting because she finds that all the students in the class perform above grade level and most of the students from the newer group receive the highest scores. She also notes that there is friction between a few members of each of the distinct class groups.

DATA

Ms. Daley's Notes

I can see immediately what my biggest challenge will be. The students in this class are smart and accomplished. Even at this early stage they do more than asked and there is a competitive atmosphere among students in the classroom. I hear only one foreign language being spoken, but even those students seem to have a fairly good command of English. It's going to be a lot of late nights for me to keep up with these students.

I was an English major in college and the school administration asked me to teach fifth grade to strengthen the literature part of the curriculum. I previously taught third grade. But moving from that grade to fifth grade seems like moving to the high school with these students. In one recent lesson, I introduced the idea of an unstated topic or main idea. I expected this lesson to be difficult because the topic and main idea have to be assembled from among the details in the passage. There are a few students who have difficulty, and I noticed those students often spoke the foreign language, but overall the students mastered the lesson objective quickly.

There is a real tendency among students in the second language group to be very quiet in class. They seem to follow a "don't speak unless spoken to" approach to class participation. At first I thought that the issue was primarily language, and that is true for some students. However I am becoming aware that this behavior is more cultural than linguistic. I am learning that in the second language culture it is considered rude to speak out, and it is never acceptable to criticize or even question the teacher's authority. I am going to have to find some way to loosen up the class discussion to have the kind of interchanges and discussion that will deepen and expand learning.

LESSON PLAN
New York Standard Determine the meaning of words and phrases as they are used in a text, including figurative language such as metaphors and similes.
Objective Write a brief poem using both metaphors and similes.
Preview Figurative language is not meant to be taken literally; it does not mean exactly what the words say. Today we are going to begin learning about metaphors and similes, two different types of figurative language.
Teach Explain: A metaphor is a comparison between two things. A simile is a comparison of two things using the words "like" or "as." Say: Here are a few examples of metaphors. I'm jumping for joy. It is raining cats and dogs. Ask students to give their own examples of metaphors. Help students who make mistakes. Continue until it is clear students understand. Say: Here are a few examples of similes. The coins were as bright as sunlight. The raindrops looked like little pearls. Ask students to give their own examples of similes. Help students who make errors. Continue until it is clear students understand.
Activity Ask students to write a brief four-line poem that includes two metaphors and two similes. Explain that the poem need not rhyme.

BASE YOUR RESPONSES ON THE INFORMATION IN THE SCENARIO.

1. What is the most likely cause for the biggest challenge Ms. Daley will face?

   Ⓐ Her move from a third-grade teacher to a fifth-grade teacher
   Ⓑ Having to deal with second language students in her class
   Ⓒ Emphasis of education at home for the second language group
   Ⓓ The lack of classroom engagement among the second language students compared to other students in the class

2. Which of the following would be the best assessment of the lesson on similes and metaphors?

   Ⓐ The end of chapter test in the textbook about similes and metaphors
   Ⓑ An informal review of the poems written during the activity stage
   Ⓒ An informal review of the simile and metaphor examples given during each portion of the lesson
   Ⓓ An informal assessment of students' knowledge of similes and metaphors during the Preview stage of the lesson.

3. The overview of Ms. Daley's class reveals that students would benefit most from which of the following types of activities?

   Ⓐ Carefully structured lessons built around central curricular themes
   Ⓑ Activities that show a cultural sensitivity to both the native speakers and the second language students
   Ⓒ Small group work intended to provide help for students who are having difficulty keeping up with the rest of the class
   Ⓓ Open-ended lessons that enable students to pursue concepts and ideas beyond the lesson's objectives

4. Which of the following actions by Ms. Daley is most likely to address the participation of second language students?

   Ⓐ Enable these students to work in pairs to share ideas in a more private setting
   Ⓑ Encourage students to just speak up when they have something to offer
   Ⓒ Wait until after the discussion is over and then ask these students to share ideas
   Ⓓ Ask very challenging questions that these students are likely to have an answer to

Constructed-Response

5. Review the exhibits, and then write a brief response in which you
   - describe a unique learning issue that Ms. Daley has in this class;
   - present a strategy that would address this unique learning issue; and
   - support your decision to use the strategy and explain why it would be successful.

Answer Explanations

1. **(C)** Ms. Daley identifies the high functioning of students as her biggest challenge, and the second language group as the highest functioning. So her challenge is most likely dealing with the high achievement resulting from an emphasis on education at home among the second language students.

2. **(B)** The poems come at the end of the lesson and are thus the best way to assess the lesson's effectiveness. An informal review by Ms. Daley is sufficient to reveal the general grasp of these concepts by students in the class.

3. **(D)** The students in this class are capable and would benefit most from lessons that enable them to pursue and explore the full range of their capabilities.

4. **(A)** Of all the strategies listed, this choice has been shown to have the most success in eliciting comments and participation from students.

EAS Constructed-Response Scoring Guide

SCORING EXPECTATIONS

The response should meet the stated specific requirements.
The response should demonstrate an understanding of the applicable exhibits.
The response should provide e-mails to support the main themes.

SCORING

4 The response demonstrates a STRONG grasp of the applicable content and skills and always includes all required response elements.

3 The response demonstrates an ACCEPTABLE grasp of the applicable content and skills and always includes all required response elements.

2 The response demonstrates a LESS THAN ACCEPTABLE grasp of the applicable content and skills and may not include all required response elements.

1 The response is INCOMPLETE AND/OR OFF TRACK and usually does not include required response elements.

U The response can't be scored because it is off topic, written in a language other than English, or contains too little information to score. Note, a well-written but off-topic response will be scored U.

B You did not write anything.

CONSTRUCTED-RESPONSE EXAMPLE

5. This response would be graded a 4 or perhaps a 3.

The unique learning issue I see is the competition in the class, and that 80 percent of longer-term resident students in the class seem to be at a competitive disadvantage to the newer group of advanced second language students. This kind of competition can cause significant conflicts as the school year progresses. There is nothing to be done about gaps in ability. However, there is something to be done to have an effective classroom environment.

As a whole, the students are self-motivated. Ms. Daley should take advantage of that ability to act independently and make more use of cooperative learning groups. Each group could be crafted to represent the full range of students in the class. The cooperative groups would have specific directions with specific desired outcomes, and groups should benefit as a whole from the results of the groups' work.

I choose this strategy because it emphasizes group and not individual responsibility. The emphasis on cooperation removes some, but not all, of the competition noted in the class. The approach emphasizes the contribution of each individual to the larger whole and gives an opportunity for students to learn from each other. I believe the strategy will be successful because of the ability of the students in this class to work without a lot of close scrutiny, and because, as a whole, they may be able to learn more from each other than from Ms. Daley.

Discussion

It is important to note immediately that there are many possible responses to this assignment. This assignment responds specifically to each of the three elements of the response prompt. The unique learning issue is creatively devised and clearly explained. The approach of using cooperative learning is supported by details and explains the benefits to be gained by students. The reasons for selecting this approach are clearly stated and detailed, while the expectation of success is directly tied to the information in the exhibits. Overall, the response could be very useful to a teacher in the same situation as Ms. Daley.

Two Model EAS Tests with Answer Explanations

4

EDUCATING ALL STUDENTS TEST ONE

45 items

32 selected-response items based on a scenario

3 constructed-response items based on a scenario

10 selected-response items not based on a scenario

Darken the lettered oval to show your choice for the selected-response items.

Use a word processor, without the spell or grammar checker, and type your constructed-response answers.

SCENARIO 1

Renea Jacson is a primary teacher with a class consisting mainly of ELL students. These students often have as much difficulty with their native language as with English. Fortunately for Ms. Jacson, the parents of the students in her class are generally well motivated to help their children acquire English language skills and to achieve in school subjects. The parents are generally not proficient in English.

After language and reading, mathematics is the main focus of instruction in Ms. Jacson's class. To prepare for instruction Ms. Jacson gave students an individual assessment to determine each student's knowledge of place value. In preparation for instruction, students were given access to a number of physical models that represented place value.

Ms. Jacson plans to use the experiences with physical models and the individualized pretest results for planning lessons on place value.

DATA

Individualized Assessment of Place Value Skills

	No Mastery	Partial Mastery	Mastery
Name numerals in the one place.	25%	15%	60%
Name numerals in the tens place.	35%	20%	45%
Name a numeral with digits in the tens and ones places.	55%	20%	25%
Demonstrate that 10 ones makes one 10.	45%	25%	30%

DRAFT LESSON PLAN

New York State Standard
Understand that the two digits of a two-digit number represent amounts of tens and ones.

Objective
Students will identify numerals in the ones place and tens place and name a numeral with digits in the tens and ones places.

Resources for Instruction
Tens and ones charts, SMART Board tens and one animations, worksheets

Teach
Begin the lesson with a discussion of how a digit can mean different things depending on the place it occupies. Show students the SMART Board animation depicting tens and one place values. Complete the lesson by asking students to write numbers on the tens and one chart.

Practice
Distribute worksheets, in English, that ask students to write and recognize numerals in the tens and ones places.

Accommodation(s)
Circulate among ELL students. Encourage students to explain answers in English with appropriate support.

BASE YOUR RESPONSES ON THE INFORMATION IN THE SCENARIO.

1. What appropriate support during the Accommodation is most likely to help English Language Learners use English words for 1 and for 10?

   Ⓐ Use manipulatives to represent ones and tens.
   Ⓑ Encourage English Language Learners to work with other ELL students in the class.
   Ⓒ Help ELL students master the number words in their native language and English.
   Ⓓ Allow the students to answer using their native Language and then translate into English.

2. According to the Individualized Assessment results, which of the following skills requires the most attention before Ms. Jacson teaches the lesson?

   Ⓐ Name numerals in the ones place.
   Ⓑ Name numerals in the tens place.
   Ⓒ Name a numeral with digits in the tens and ones places.
   Ⓓ Demonstrate that 10 ones makes one 10.

3. What is the best way for Ms. Jacson to incorporate a high level of motivation among parents to further students' acquisition of English skills?

   Ⓐ Encourage parents to help their children learn English skills.
   Ⓑ Involve parents in students homework assignments.
   Ⓒ Involve available parents as aids in the classroom.
   Ⓓ Work with parents to encourage their children to bring completed homework to school each day.

4. Ms. Jacson wants to develop some real world activities to help students understand the different meaning of a numeral in the ones place and that same numeral in the tens place. Which of the following would likely be the most appropriate activity?

   Ⓐ Give students objects and ask them to group the objects into tens and ones.
   Ⓑ Ask students to write amounts with the same number of dimes and cents and discuss different meanings of the digits in each amount.
   Ⓒ Ask students to cut out pictures from newspapers and magazines showing ones and tens.
   Ⓓ Partition the class into collaborative learning groups and ask each group to discuss the difference between one ten and ten ones.

SCENARIO 2

Ms. Del Corso teaches six fifth-grade science classes. She is working on her Personal Improvement Plan (PIP), which every teacher in the district completes each spring. Her PIP will be about science, and she is very interested in a continuing question about science learning. This question stems from two issues about experiments.

1. Students learn more if they observe an experiment, record the results, and then "discover" the cause of the results.
2. Students learn more if the science behind an experiment is explained, and then students observe the experiment itself.

She realizes that her examination of this issue will have too small a sample to draw any general conclusions, but she hopes her own experiment will give her insight into how her students learn—Insight she can put to work in the classroom.

Ms. Del Corso uses the "egg in the bottle" experiment. In the experiment, a lighted piece of paper is put in a bottle, and then a hardboiled egg is put in the opening to the bottle. After a little time, the egg is "sucked into the bottle."

In half the classes, she performs the experiment first, and then leads students in a discussion of the results. She uses the last fifteen minutes of the class to give a test on the concept. In the other half of the classes, she explains about air pressure, completes the experiment as an example of air pressure, and then gives the test.

The results of the test are shown below.

DATA

Classes: Experiment First (A, C, F)
Explanation First (B, D, E)

Test results	Less than 60% correct	60% to 80% correct	More than 80% correct
A	20%	65%	15%
B	35%	50%	15%
C	25%	55%	20%
D	45%	30%	25%
E	35%	40%	25%
F	25%	65%	10%

LESSON PLAN
New York State Standard Observe and discuss objects and events and record observations.
Objective Students will identify the cause and effect of lowered air pressure.
Resources for Instruction Appropriately shaped bottle, shredded newspaper, hardboiled egg, recording forms
Teach Begin the lesson with a discussion of safety. Set up the bottle for the experiment. Explain to students the steps you are going to take and ask students to predict what will happen by the conclusion of the experiment. Instruct students to write predictions on their recording forms.
Experiment Conduct the experiment (as in the Class Description).
Discussion Ask students to discuss their predictions as compared to the actual results. Promote a discussion among students of what caused the egg to be drawn into the bottle, and lead students to the conclusion that it was lowered air pressure in the bottle that caused the egg to be pushed in by higher air pressure outside the bottle.
Extension Involve students in a discussion of other natural phenomena involving lowered air pressure, such as tornadoes and hurricanes.

5. The "do the experiment first and observe" approach is best described as

    Ⓐ inquiry learning.
    Ⓑ deductive learning.
    Ⓒ learning by trial and error.
    Ⓓ inferential learning.

6. The test results give most support for Ms. Del Corso to use the Experiment First approaches because the approach is

    Ⓐ most likely to result in students earning more than 80% correct.
    Ⓑ most likely to result in students earning less than 60%.
    Ⓒ most likely to result in students earning between 60% and 80% correct.
    Ⓓ least likely to result in students earning between 60% and 80% correct.

7. Which explanation could students give that would best explain why the egg ended up in the bottle?

    Ⓐ The air pressure in the bottle is raised causing the egg to be sucked into the bottle.
    Ⓑ The air pressure in the bottle is lowered causing the egg to be pulled into the bottle.
    Ⓒ The air pressure outside the bottle is increased causing the egg to be pushed into the bottle.
    Ⓓ The air pressure in the bottle is lowered causing the egg to be pushed into the bottle.

8. The most beneficial outcome of the Extension activity in the lesson plan is that it encourages students to

    Ⓐ do higher order thinking.
    Ⓑ identify other events related to a single scientific concept.
    Ⓒ identify phenomena that occur naturally.
    Ⓓ help extend the lesson into a discussion of weather.

28

SCENARIO 3

Alex Whitby is an eighth-grade teacher with twenty-eight students in a school well known for its multicultural student body, which reflects the population of the town as a whole. The students in his class generally read below grade level, and some students' reading levels are even three, four, or more years below grade level. A special education teacher works in the classroom with Mr. Whitby.

The class is studying Native Americans in New York. Mr. Whitby wants students to read *The Iroquois Trail: Dickon among the Onondagas and Senecas*, by Mark Harrington, as part of a research project. The book is at about a seventh-grade reading level.

The book describes the Iroquois "Long House." In the book this term has two meanings. The first meaning is a type of long hut with several rooms in which the Native Americans lived. The second meaning refers to the arrangement of the five Iroquois tribes arranged across New York in a geographically large Long House. Mr. Whitby wants students to complete a research project about the Long House of the Iroquois.

Mr. Whitby wants to devise an effective instructional strategy before his students read the book. To help prepare, he is reviewing some reading test results and consulting with a special education teacher.

DATA

Grade Reading Level for Mr. Whitby's Eighth-Grade Class (28 Students)

Eighth Grade or Above	4
Seventh to Eighth Grade	14
Sixth to Seventh Grade	6
Fifth to Sixth Grade	2
Below Fifth Grade	2

DRAFT LESSON PLAN
New York Standards Identify, describe, and evaluate evidence about events from diverse sources (including written documents, works of art, photographs, charts and graphs, artifacts, oral histories, and other primary and secondary sources). Identify a region by describing multiple characteristics common to places within it, and then identify other similar regions. Write informative/explanatory texts, including the narration of historical events or technical processes.
Objective Prepare a collaborative report on the dual meanings of the term "Long House."
Vocabulary Identify all vocabulary words unfamiliar to any student in the class.
Resources for Instruction *The Iroquois Trail: Dickon among the Onondagas and Senecas*, by Mark Harrington Map of the Long House of the Iroquois tribes Internet access
Teach Begin the lesson with a discussion of all the appropriate vocabulary words, using images to support word understanding. Ask students to read selected passages of *The Iroquois Trail*, which set the stage for the story and focus on passages related to the Long House of the Iroquois. Introduce students to appropriate Internet resources for the Iroquois.
Research Partition students into collaborative groups to prepare a brief research report on the Long House of the Iroquois using the book, Internet resources, and other available resources identified by students. Ensure that each group has the full range of reading ability represented in the class.
Discussion Arrange for each group to present the group's research report and encourage a discussion of each report.
Extension Encourage students to read the entire book, *The Iroquois Trail*.

BASE YOUR RESPONSES ON THE INFORMATION IN THE SCENARIO.

9. The description of the students in the class and the reading grade level assessments indicate which of the following is the most important step for Mr. Whitby to take in this class?

   Ⓐ Partition the class during instruction to account for the range of reading levels.
   Ⓑ Provide students in the class with a vocabulary list based on the reading.
   Ⓒ Arrange for additional support in the class from an ESOL teacher.
   Ⓓ Assign the co-teacher to help the poorest readers learn English as a second language.

10. Which of the following would most likely help the students benefit from reading *The Iroquois Trail*?

   Ⓐ Discuss a biography of the author, who has written other books about Native Americans.
   Ⓑ Activate prior knowledge about Native Americans before reading.
   Ⓒ Provide a list of questions for students to answer as they read the story.
   Ⓓ Establish the students' zone of proximal development about Native Americans.

11. Which of the following is the primary way of creating a character trait diagram after reading the book?

   Ⓐ Students list all the characters in the book along the top of a page, and list under each character his or her main traits.
   Ⓑ Students identify desirable traits and then identify the character that possesses most of those traits.
   Ⓒ A branching diagram begins with the primary trait of the main character and then shows how the other traits are related to the main trait.
   Ⓓ A Venn diagram that compares the traits of two main characters.

12. Mr. Whitby included a collaborative learning activity in his lesson plan. Which of the following is the most appropriate cultural responsive outcome to that activity?

   Ⓐ A collaborative group reports on cultural aspects of the Iroquois culture.
   Ⓑ A collaborative group relates the cultural aspects of the Iroquois culture to cultural aspects of their own culture.
   Ⓒ A collaborative group describes what lives of members of the group might have been like if they lived in the Iroquois culture.
   Ⓓ A collaborative group describes the aspects of the Iroquois culture that should be reflected in the town's culture.

Constructed Response

13. Based on your review of the exhibits, write a brief response in which you

   ▪ discuss a way to address the diverse student population needs during the use of Internet activities in the lesson; and
   ▪ describe a strategy Mr. Whitby could employ to address the wide range of reading levels in the class.

SCENARIO 4

Ms. Kelly is a third-grade teacher in a K–5 school. This is her fourth year teaching. "I'm going to get this teaching down—definitely in the next 20 years" is her favorite thing to say to the more experienced teachers in the school.

The students in Ms. Kelly's class come from diverse cultural backgrounds, but only three of the students are ELL students: Janice, James, and Elizabeth. These students converse very well in English but need help with reading comprehension. Ms. Kelly has been working with these students to help them improve reading skills, particularly reading in the content area of science.

Ms. Kelly plans to teach a lesson about living things that will involve students germinating beans in the classroom. As a part of the lesson, students will read *From Bean to Bean Plant*, by Anita Ganeri. Ms. Kelly plans to use her contemporaneous notes about students' reading performance as she prepares for the lesson. Ms. Kelly has often found these "pretest" observations to help her to truly personalize instruction.

DATA

Ms. Kelly's Observations about Three Students' Reading Process and Performance

Janice: Janice has the most trouble when she tries to sound out new words while reading. However, Janice easily remembers new sight words when I present them before she reads the story.

James: James knows the sound of every phoneme and can frequently "sound out" new words while reading. However, James has trouble with new sight words when I present them. James, quick at computation, has great difficulty when he has to solve word problems in mathematics.

Elizabeth: Elizabeth has trouble when she reads stories from a basal text. But give her a book with many pictures at the same reading level as the basal text, and she will be able to get as much information from the book as any student in the class. Still, I am concerned about Elizabeth's ability to read individual words, and she may get most of her information from the pictures.

DRAFT LESSON PLAN
New York Standards
Ask "why" questions in attempts to seek greater understanding concerning objects and events they have observed and heard about.
Observe and discuss objects and events and record observations.
Articulate appropriate questions based on observations.
Each plant has different structures that serve different functions in growth, survival, and reproduction.
Roots help support the plant and take in water and nutrients.
Objective
Plan, conduct, and evaluate an experiment with the germination of a bean sprout.
Vocabulary
Identify all vocabulary words in the book noted below that are unfamiliar to any student in the class.
Resources for Instruction
From Bean to Bean Plant, by Anita Ganeri
Lima beans
Clear plastic cups
Metric ruler
Teach
Begin the lesson with a discussion of all the appropriate vocabulary words, using images to support word understanding.
Ask students to read *From Bean to Bean Plant,* which fully discusses the germination of a lima bean.
Experiment
Ask each student to place masking tape with her or his name on the bottom of a plastic cup, fill the cup 3/4 full with water, and place four lima beans in the water.
Direct students to place the cup near the window or other consistent light source.
Observation
Each day for two weeks students keep a log describing their bean plants' growth including the approximate height of the stalk and the depth of the roots.
At the completion of two weeks, students prepare a line graph showing the plant's development.
Discussion
Each student describes the growth of her or his bean plant and shows the final graph. Students discuss the variations that appear among the plant's growth and present possible reasons for these variations.

14. In conjunction with the vocabulary portion of the Teach section of the lesson, Ms. Kelly could most help Janice by

    Ⓐ helping her rely on the pictures that Ms. Kelly presents along with vocabulary words to understand these words.
    Ⓑ helping her recognize the meaning of science words from the context of the word.
    Ⓒ presenting her with a list of vocabulary words before the lesson and helping her learn the meaning of each word on the list.
    Ⓓ helping her complete a phonemic analysis of each word presented during the vocabulary section and "sound out" each word to develop word meaning.

15. The lag in reading comprehension in the three ELL students when compared to verbal communication is most likely because

    Ⓐ these ELL students watch too much television and rely on what they hear and see on television and not on written materials.
    Ⓑ these students are more likely to speak English at home than to read English at home.
    Ⓒ learning to read a language takes longer than learning to speak a language.
    Ⓓ these students are more likely to converse in English with their peers outside school.

16. Ms. Kelly's plan to use images to support vocabulary development is effective primarily because the images

    Ⓐ motivate students and maintain their interest in learning the vocabulary.
    Ⓑ reflect the multicultural makeup of the classroom and help solidify cultural identity.
    Ⓒ provide a visual reference for the word and further comprehension.
    Ⓓ appeal to the visual nature of the culture from which these students come.

17. Planning this lesson built around an "experiment" helps address the ELL students' learning needs by

    Ⓐ enabling the ELL students to learn through observation without relying on English language skills.
    Ⓑ encouraging the ELL students to use ELA skills to record the results of the experiment in English.
    Ⓒ helping the ELL students prepare for careers in STEM-oriented jobs.
    Ⓓ helping the teacher prepare for the language needs required to understand directions and complete the experiment.

SCENARIO 5

Mr. Zoll is a high school teacher who teaches classes and supervises students in a work study program. Students spend each morning taking classes, and each afternoon they serve as interns in a business setting. Almost all of the students are ELL students. The two primary issues Mr. Zoll faces are the poor health habits and certain diseases found among these students in addition to extreme difficulty with English.

Mr. Zoll often mentions two specific examples. Roberto is in eleventh grade. Roberto comes from a remote part of a Central American country and speaks a language unfamiliar to anyone in the school. It appears that he never attended school until he came to this country at 14 years old. He had a number of health problems as a youth, including excessive tobacco use.

Darlene is a native Spanish speaker and her language needs are easier to address. However, Darlene has the same previous and continuing tobacco use issues found in Roberto.

Tobacco use is generally forbidden in most workplaces, and to help these two students avoid additional health problems and to help them learn how to gain employment, Mr. Zoll is designing a program to help students deal with tobacco use, while at the same time accounting for their language issues.

To help plan the project, Mr. Zoll is reviewing classifications based on the New York State English as a Second Language Achievement Test (NYSESLAT), which measures reading, speaking, listening, and writing. A student may receive Proficient, Advanced, Intermediate, or Beginning for each area.

DATA

Roberto's and Darlene's Classifications on the New York State English as a Second Language Achievement Test (NYSESLAT)

Roberto	Beginning
Darlene	Intermediate

Proficient: Students function fluently in listening, reading, writing, and speaking; their skills are equal to those of native English speakers at their appropriate grade level. These students have attained the skills necessary to participate in an English-speaking classroom.

Advanced: Students are able to use skills at a higher level than intermediate students. Although their knowledge and use of English is at a more advanced level, mistakes are made, usually involving more subtle use of language and more difficult levels of vocabulary and grammar.

Intermediate: Students have better English skills than students at the basic level; however, their skills are often not well developed, and they make significant errors in the four skill areas.

Beginning: Students are simply at the beginning level in the four skill areas. These students' English skills are minimal.

DRAFT LESSON PLAN
New York Standards
Demonstrate a variety of problem-solving, communication, and stress management skills to address health-compromising behaviors such as fad dieting; alcohol, tobacco, and other drug use; early sexual involvement; and violent behavior.
Predict how decisions regarding health behaviors have consequences for self and others.
Objective
Prepare a report that explains the negative health and job-related aspects of smoking.
Vocabulary
addiction, tobacco, smoking, cancer
Resources for Instruction
Centers for Disease Control and Prevention's Smoking and Tobacco Use website with resources http://www.cdc.gov/TOBACCO/youth/index.htm
Images of lungs of smokers
New York State laws about smoking at work and in public places
Teach
Begin the lesson with a discussion of tobacco use and share the images of lungs of smokers.
Point out how New York State law prevents smoking in most workplaces.
Ask students to review the CDC website and to use the electronic text resources to prepare a two-page report.
Discussion
Each student gives an overview of her or his report and demonstrates an understanding that tobacco use has a serious impact on health and on job opportunities.

BASE YOUR RESPONSES ON THE INFORMATION IN THE SCENARIO.

18. In reviewing how to respond to Roberto's youthful exposure to excessive tobacco use and his unawareness of when tobacco use is unacceptable, Mr. Zoll should be aware that

- Ⓐ his first responsibility is to help these students get jobs and that reasonable but firm action is required to deal with Roberto's tobacco use.
- Ⓑ because of his language problems and his health problems, Roberto is likely to be limited to very low-paying jobs, where tobacco use may be an unimportant factor.
- Ⓒ the combination of the youthful link to tobacco use and Roberto's lack of schooling will make the issue of his tobacco use a particularly difficult one to solve.
- Ⓓ for someone like Roberto, who is so far behind educationally and linguistically and so unaccustomed to the culture in this country, the best approach is to do nothing.

19. Based on what we know about Roberto's and Darlene's ELL categories, Mr. Zoll can best help develop their English language skills by

   Ⓐ ensuring that each student receives the maximum exposure to English language experiences.

   Ⓑ planning completely different programs for each student.

   Ⓒ ensuring that these students are assigned to a workplace where others speak their native language.

   Ⓓ helping students learn how helpful it is to speak English if you want a good job.

20. Compared to Roberto, Darlene's proficiency with English indicates that Mr. Zoll could do which of the following to enhance her learning during the lesson?

   Ⓐ Permit Darlene to identify the language skills she wants to pursue.

   Ⓑ Rely more on Darlene's English language skills during the lesson.

   Ⓒ Rely more on Darlene's native language during the lesson.

   Ⓓ Expect Darlene to respond to a greater degree toward the goal of smoking cessation.

21. How can Mr. Zoll most effectively enhance the learning of the ELL students in the class during the Discussion section of the lesson?

   Ⓐ Ensure that the students demonstrate a full understanding of the dangers of tobacco use.

   Ⓑ Arrange for students to review their partners reports before making the presentation.

   Ⓒ Encourage students in the class to present a brief critique of each presentation.

   Ⓓ Require students to present evidence from the workplace that they had abstained from smoking on the job.

Constructed Response

22. Fully review all the information available about Roberto. Then, present this three-step plan.

- Describe a unique learning issue.
- Enumerate a specific adaptation for the lesson that addresses the learning issue described above.
- Support your decision to use that strategy and an explanation of why it would be effective.

SCENARIO 6

Ms. Almon is a fifth-grade teacher with a class of twenty-five students, including two ELL students, Lung Se and Wee Hong, who receive additional instruction that includes the help of a reading specialist and an ESOL teacher. The two ELL students seem quite similar to the other students in the class, until the time comes for reading and writing in English. Each of the ELL students performs well below grade level in reading comprehension and writing.

The problems each student has with English are compounded by the harsh conditions in their native country, North Korea, including the torture, imprisonment, and killing of family members. Although they arrived in this country three years ago, these students still demonstrate a fear of authority and a withdrawal from the society in school and out of school. Each student was adopted, and their foster parents are not Asian.

Ms. Almon tries to use the Zone of Proximal Development (ZPD) technique as she works with these students. The difficulty is that their social withdrawal and stressful circumstances often prevent them from demonstrating their true ability, and it is usually hard to identify the appropriate ZPD.

Ms. Almon is planning a lesson on the Koreas, which aligns with the grade-level standard and is directly related to the cultural experiences of Lung See and Wee Hong. Ms. Almon is reviewing some reading and summary data related to speaking English.

DATA

	Lung See	Wee Hong
Reading Grade Level	3.4	3.4
English as a Second Language Achievement Test (NYSESLAT)	Beginning	Beginning
Time spent each week reading English books outside class	None	About 1 hour
Approximate time spent each week interacting with other students in the class	1 to 2 hours	3 to 5 hours

DRAFT LESSON PLAN
New York Standards Determine the central ideas or information of a primary or secondary source; provide an accurate summary of the source distinct from prior knowledge or opinions. Study the Eastern Hemisphere, particularly East Asia and most particularly North Korea and South Korea.
Objective Compare and contrast the cultures of North Korea and South Korea with a particular focus on the 38th Parallel border.
Resources for Instruction Map of North and South Korea Newspaper articles about the "Peace Village" (secondary source) Presentations by Lung See and Wee Hong about their lives in North Korea (primary source)
Teach Begin the lesson with a map of North and South Korea, which may be presented on a SMART Board or as a projection of maps from the Internet. Discuss the relative size and proximity of the two Koreas. Distribute and discuss newspaper articles about the Korean War, the partial truce, and how each Korea has developed economically. Offer Lung See and Wee Hong an opportunity to talk about their experiences in North Korea. Emphasize that the free expression of experiences and views are always acceptable.
Prepare Report Ask each student in the class to prepare a brief 150-word report comparing the two Koreas. The report will include citations from the newspapers and the oral presentations, distinguishing between primary and secondary sources.
Discussion Each student gives an overview of her or his report and discusses how primary and secondary sources were used as citations.

23. Which of the following would negatively impact Lung See's and Wee Hong's learning during the Report phase of the lesson plan?

    Ⓐ Reduce the length of the report for Lung See and Wee Hong to 50 words.
    Ⓑ Present a graphic organizer that lists South Korea in one column and North Korea in another column.
    Ⓒ Arrange for Lung See and Wee Hong to work with a class partner when preparing the report.
    Ⓓ Involve the ESOL teacher as a support agent for the two students as they prepare their reports.

24. When it comes to these ELL students' performance in reading and writing English, Ms. Almon might also expect

    Ⓐ similarly low levels of conversation in their native language.
    Ⓑ somewhat higher levels in conversational English.
    Ⓒ low reading comprehension skills in their native language that matches their English reading skill levels.
    Ⓓ high writing scores in their native language because they have had more time to practice.

25. Which of the following approaches would best promote success for the two ELL students as newspaper articles and Internet resources are shared with the class?

    Ⓐ Provide translations of the articles for the ELL students to use.
    Ⓑ Provide the ELL students with graphic organizers that lists important words from the articles and online resources.
    Ⓒ Give the ELL students the articles in advance so they can read them and be prepared for class.
    Ⓓ Read the articles aloud so that the ELL students can rely more on their listening comprehension skills.

26. Which of the following is the first step Ms. Almon should take while designing and implementing the instructional plan for ELL students in the class?

    Ⓐ Complete a full assessment of the ELL students' language skills.
    Ⓑ Actively work with the ESOL teacher to plan appropriate support steps and instructional strategies for the ELL students.
    Ⓒ Actively involve the students' parents in planning the instructional strategies for their ELL child.
    Ⓓ Establish a postinstructional assessment plan to accurately determine what the ELL students have learned and what they still need to learn.

SCENARIO 7

Ms. Alberto is a teacher in a fourth-grade self-contained classroom. As is often the case, Ms. Alberto has several "classified" students in her classroom. Lena and Rory are two of these students and each one of them has an IEP. These students have IEPs for very different reasons. Lena has a classification of Learning Disabled, which means she has a disorder in one or more of the basic psychological processes involved in understanding or using language, spoken or written, which manifests itself in an imperfect ability to listen, think, speak, read, write, spell, or to do mathematical calculations with a discrepancy of 50 percent or more between actual achievement and expected achievement. Lena exhibits no behavior problems. She spends an hour each day working with a special education teacher in a resource room.

Rory has a classification of Emotional Disturbance. Specifically, his performance is adversely affected to a marked degree because he has an inability to build or maintain satisfactory interpersonal relationships with peers and teachers and exhibits inappropriate types of behavior or feeling under normal circumstances. Rory does not act out physically. He meets for 45 minutes with a school psychologist twice a week and with a guidance counselor the other three days. Ms. Alberto is planning a lesson about using prefixes in context to determine word meaning and is reviewing the available notes to help her prepare for the lesson.

DATA

IEP Goals and Progress

Lena	
Goal and Criteria	**Progress To Date**
1. Lena will earn a score of 75% correct on her in-class tests in Reading and Mathematics	Lena has made progress, but her score on in-class tests is steady at 60%.
2. Lena will demonstrate that she can decode a generated list of vocabulary words to 100% accuracy.	Again, Lena has made progress, but she is still unable to decode more that 50% of the words on the list.
3. Lena will complete all homework and submit it in a timely manner 100% of the time.	Lena has made significant progress and now completes over 90% of her homework on time.

Summary
Goals 1 and 2 are considered not met, while goal 3 is considered met.

Rory	
Goal and Criteria	**Progress To Date**
1. Rory will reduce his inappropriate interactions with the teacher to no more than once a day.	Rory has made no progress. He still has inappropriate interactions with the teacher at least once every hour.
2. Rory will demonstrate positive verbal interactions with students at least twice a day.	Rory has made progress and one or two days out of the week he demonstrated two or more personal interactions with other students.

3. Rory will demonstrate an ability to accept constructive guidance from the teacher.	Rory's difficulty accepting constructive guidance has not gotten worse. However, he still demonstrates a marked tendency to resist this guidance.

Summary

Goal 1 is considered a significant continuing problem and will be given more focus for Rory's work with the school psychologist and the social worker. Goal 2 is considered partially met, and goal 3 is considered not met.

DRAFT LESSON PLAN

New York Standard

Use combined knowledge of all letter-sound correspondences, syllabication patterns, and morphology (e.g., roots and affixes) to read accurately unfamiliar multisyllabic words in context and out of context.

Objective

Use prefixes to determine the meaning of words in context.

Resources for Instruction

SMART Board if available

Teach

Begin by writing these words on the SMART Board and reviewing the meaning of the prefix "re" and the meaning of these words:

Reread, Redo, Rewrite and similar words

Point out for "re-write" that "re" is the prefix and "write" is the base word.

Explain that "rewrite" means to write again.

Ask students to write their own "re" words on the SMART Board while describing the prefix and the base word.

Write this sentence followed by other examples.

I have to rewash my hands.

Point out that the context tells "you" that "rewash" is about hands.

So in the sentence, rewash means washing your hands again.

Application

Write a few examples of "re" words in a sentence and discuss how to determine the meaning of the word.

Ask students to come to the SMART Board and write their own "re" sentences and describe how to decode the meaning of the word.

Extension

Ask students to find examples of "re" words in sentences and to bring the examples to class. Ask students to further explain how they determined each word's meaning.

27. Which of the following could Ms. Alberto do to best help Lena succeed in this lesson?

    Ⓐ Teach the words in a direct explicit fashion.
    Ⓑ Give Lena a list of the base words to learn.
    Ⓒ Give Lena a series of different prefixes to learn.
    Ⓓ Ask Lena to read the word out loud during the lesson.

28. Which of the following is the most appropriate step to help Rory maintain his interest in the lesson?

    Ⓐ Establish a reward system, such as token reinforcement, that rewards continued attention.
    Ⓑ Allow Rory to absent himself from the lesson if it becomes too overwhelming.
    Ⓒ Allow Rory to lead the class discussion during the lesson.
    Ⓓ Arrange for Rory to complete the lesson using an individualized lesson on a computer.

29. As the weeks progress, Lena has been having more and more difficulty with lessons and often appears to be under stress. Ms. Alberto is unsure about how to facilitate Lena's participation in the lesson, but the best steps would be to

    Ⓐ consult with Lena's special education teacher to devise a plan to help reestablish participation.
    Ⓑ engage Lena in a discussion of what is bothering her to find an approach based on her needs that would work with this lesson.
    Ⓒ reassure her that she is making adequate progress and that sometimes learning seems hard but the effort she makes will pay off in the long run.
    Ⓓ do everything necessary to help Lena avoid failure in the lesson.

30. In order to address the social isolation, partly because of Rory's tendency to display inappropriate behavior, which of the following is the best approach for Ms. Alberto and the special education teacher to employ?

    Ⓐ Role-play appropriate behavioral strategies in the resource room to model those appropriate strategies in the classroom.
    Ⓑ Identify a small group of willing students and engage them in a project designed to help Rory feel more accepted and to receive more positive comments.
    Ⓒ In a very clear and direct way, explain to Rory some of the behaviors he exhibits that isolate him and make specific suggestion for specific actions on his part to change those behaviors.
    Ⓓ Spend time after school listening to Rory's recounting of his problems, further analyze those problems, and identify specific steps for Rory to follow,

SCENARIO 8

Ms. Levine teaches required tenth-grade mathematics courses. Ms. Levine has several "classified" students in her classroom. Gulaka and Morgan are two of these students, and each one of them has an IEP. In addition, both students come from homes in which English is a second language.

Gulaka has a classification of Learning Disabled, which means that she functions at least two years below her expected achievement level and has great difficulty learning mathematics. She spends an hour in a learning center with a small supplemental mathematics group.

Morgan has a classification of Emotional Disturbance. This generalized emotional disturbance makes it difficult for Morgan to maintain a calm composure. He has trouble controlling his handwriting, often making it difficult for him to accurately place mathematical symbols on a page. Morgan meets with a school psychologist for 45 minutes three times a week.

Each student has an IEP, and Ms. Levine maintains daily notes on the progress of the IEP objectives.

Ms. Levine is planning a lesson on rational exponents and is reviewing her notes in advance of planning the lesson.

DATA

Summary of Ms. Levine's Notes

Gulaka

There is no doubt that Gulaka's difficulty with English interferes with her ability to learn mathematics. In addition I have seen a number of examples that indicate there are still some problems learning mathematics. I will continue to try to interpret mathematics word problems to make them accessible to Gulaka.

I have also noted that Gulaka's learning disability is the most significant issue when it comes to learning mathematics. These difficulties are quite pronounced, and Gulaka seems to be falling even further behind the class.

Morgan

One can only feel for Morgan as he struggles to write the simplest mathematics numerals and symbols. I am as reassuring as I can be, but to no avail. His difficulty also makes the calculator a poor aide because he cannot even press the keys. I will seek approval for Morgan to use a large-key calculator in class and on the tests, but this approach will only partially address his problems.

The emotional problems that interfere so dramatically with his work in mathematics make it hard for me to be sure exactly what role his non-English–speaking background has on mathematics learning. He is so tense and unreceptive throughout the class that it is clear the emotional issues must be solved before we can turn our attention to a language learning problems that might exist.

DRAFT LESSON PLAN
New York Standard
Extend the properties of exponents to rational exponents.
Objective
Write a whole number with a rational exponent of ½ as a square root.
Resources for Instruction
SMART Board if available   Rational exponent worksheets
Teach
Begin by writing on a SMART Board (if available) this whole number with an exponent 3^2.   Explain that this means 3×3.   Give a few more similar examples.   Ask a few students to come to the SMART Board and write his or her own "square examples."   Then, show students the example $3^{½}$.   Give this example $3^{½} \times 3^{½} = 3^{(½ + ½)} = 3^1 = 3$.   Say, "we multiplied $3^{½}$ by itself (or squared $3^{½}$) and we got 3. We know from whole numbers that $3^{½}$ must be the square root of 3.   So $3^{½}$ means the same as $\sqrt{3}$."   [Students may have difficulty with this explanation but press ahead.]
Participation
Ask students to come to the SMART Board and write their own examples of a number written to the ½ power as a square root.
Practice
Ask students to complete work sheets, which ask them to write whole numbers raised to the ½ power as a square root and to write square roots as a whole number raised to the ½ power.
Extension
Ask students to predict the value of a whole number raised to the $\frac{1}{3}$ power.

BASE YOUR RESPONSES ON THE INFORMATION IN THE SCENARIO.

31. As a high school mathematics teacher, Ms. Levine has little exposure to Morgan's emotional problems and the symptoms of those problems. Which of the following issues is the special education teacher most likely to alert Ms. Levine to expect from Morgan?

Ⓐ Morgan may have difficulty with the elementary concept of place value.
Ⓑ You won't encounter many issues with Morgan in your math class. Things would be different in an English class.
Ⓒ You must keep the windows closed at the bottom as Morgan may be suicidal.
Ⓓ Sometimes he may look bothered, but that's not the way he really feels.

32. A student in Ms. Levine's class acted out to the extent that it was a violation of a school rule and that student is subject to discipline. The student is not classified as a disabled student. Under these circumstances, the student shall be presumed to have a disability for discipline purposes under New York State regulations when

Ⓐ the student applies to the school administration for such a classification.
Ⓑ a literate nondisabled parent of the student had expressed concern verbally to a teacher or supervisor.
Ⓒ the student requests his or her own evaluation pursuant to section 200.4.
Ⓓ any school personnel specifically expressed concerns about the student to supervisory personnel.

33. Ms. Levine believes that Gulaka may have dyscalculia as well as being learning disabled. Which of the following would NOT indicate that Gulaka has dyscalculia?

Ⓐ Difficulty with abstract concepts of time and direction
Ⓑ Inability to recall schedules and sequences of past or future events
Ⓒ May be chronically early or late
Ⓓ Consistent calculation results in addition, subtraction, multiplication, and division

34. Ms. Levine has a plan to use raised expectations with the classified students in her class. The most likely reason that Ms. Levine devised this plan was to

Ⓐ meet parents' expectations.
Ⓑ increase student participation.
Ⓒ treat all students alike.
Ⓓ have these students appropriately placed in remedial classes.

Constructed Response

35. ▪ Identify one part of the lesson plan with which Gulaka will likely have the most difficulty.
    ▪ Describe an adaptation you would make to help Gulaka overcome that difficulty.
    ▪ Explain why the adaptation you suggested would help Gulaka.

There are no scenarios for items 36–45.

36. When it comes to the language of instruction, it is the responsibility of a teacher to provide instruction

    Ⓐ in English even for ELL students.
    Ⓑ to ELL students in the students' native language.
    Ⓒ in English unless waived by the commissioner because an ELL student has a foreign ancestry.
    Ⓓ in English with augmented instruction in the foreign language for students in New York identified as ELL students.

37. Economically disadvantaged students as a whole tend to have lower achievement scores than other students. The teacher's most important responsibility in this situation is to realize that

    Ⓐ economically disadvantaged students are less capable learners than other students.
    Ⓑ minority teachers are more effective teachers of minority students.
    Ⓒ learning expectations should be lowered for economically disadvantaged students.
    Ⓓ economically disadvantaged students typically have fewer enriched learning opportunities at home.

38. A principal distributes guidelines that describes appropriate classroom questioning techniques. Which of the following most likely describes the teacher's responsibility in this situation?

    Ⓐ Ensure that students know who will answer a question before it is asked.
    Ⓑ Ask questions of the entire class, and then call on a student.
    Ⓒ Ask questions of students who are not paying attention.
    Ⓓ Ask questions of students who usually have the correct answer.

39. A teacher wants to use effective modeling techniques. The teacher's most important responsibility in this situation is to

    Ⓐ show students how to construct replicas of historic buildings.
    Ⓑ respond courteously to students' questions.
    Ⓒ correct mispronounced words.
    Ⓓ recreate students' inappropriate behavior.

40. A teacher has a class that is culturally and linguistically diverse. Which of the following best describes the teacher's responsibility in this situation?

    Ⓐ Modify the lesson objectives to focus more on basic skills.
    Ⓑ Modify the lesson objectives to reduce the objective's difficulty level.
    Ⓒ Modify the teaching method and teach the class in the predominant foreign language.
    Ⓓ Modify the plans to focus on the cultural heritage of students in the class.

41. A parent's child will be the subject of a Committee on Special Education meeting. When it comes to the parent's attendance at the meeting

Ⓐ both parents are required to be at the meeting.
Ⓑ only one parent has a right to attend the meeting.
Ⓒ a second parent can be required to attend the meeting only by written request.
Ⓓ neither parent has a right to attend the meeting, but parents may be invited at the discretion of the CSE Chair.

42. Mr. Bataswani meets with the principal to discuss ways of communicating effectively with parents. Which of the following is LEAST likely to promote good communication with parents or guardians?

Ⓐ Make phone calls to parents.
Ⓑ Write personal notes on report cards.
Ⓒ Initiate a series of home/school letters.
Ⓓ Meet with groups of parents to discuss individual student achievement.

43. Teachers who support the public school budget vote but do not live in the town are at a school board meeting along with a large group of parents. Which of the following is the most appropriate communication a teacher can make to the parents or guardians?

Ⓐ Tell parents that the school needs their support and ask them to get out and vote.
Ⓑ Tell parents to vote "yes" on the school budget.
Ⓒ Tell the parents that the voting records of board candidates are clear and to vote for the pro-school candidate.
Ⓓ Tell parents that a vote for antibudget candidates is a vote against school programs.

44. The appropriate way for a teacher to effectively communicate with parents or guardians about the problems with a tracking system is by saying:

Ⓐ "The standardized tests used to place students in the tracking program are deliberately designed to trick minority students."
Ⓑ "Tracking programs have been shown to consistently discriminate against minority students."
Ⓒ "The best teachers are always assigned to the highest and lowest tracks."
Ⓓ "The schools cannot be counted on to accurately report test scores."

45. Ms. Lenoir, a teacher in a public school, inadvertently views the health records of Student "X" and correctly concludes that this student has AIDS. The parents or guardians of Student X should know that the teacher

Ⓐ has the right to refuse to have Student X in her class because of concerns for her safety.
Ⓑ must keep this information to herself even though it may be a concern to other school personnel.
Ⓒ has a responsibility to inform parents of other students in the class so that these parents may safeguard their children's safety.
Ⓓ has a legal responsibility under New York law to confidentially inform other teachers so that they may protect students in their classes.

ANSWER EXPLANATIONS

EAS Constructed-Response Scoring Guide

SCORING EXPECTATIONS

The response should meet the stated specific requirements.
The response should demonstrate an understanding of the applicable exhibits.
The response should provide details to support the main themes.

SCORING

4 The response demonstrates a STRONG grasp of the applicable content and skills and always includes all required response elements.

3 The response demonstrates an ACCEPABLE grasp of the applicable content and skills and always includes all required response elements.

2 The response demonstrates a LESS THAN ACCEPTABLE grasp of the applicable content and skills and may not include all required response elements.

1 The response is INCOMPLETE AND/OR OFF TRACK and usually does not include required response elements.

U The response can't be scored because it is off topic, written in a language other than English, or contains too little information to score. Note, a well written but off-topic response will be scored U.

B You did not write anything

1. **(C)** We can tell from the description that these students have difficulty in their native language and in English. This is not an uncommon problem, and the best approach among those given is to help students learn the words from both languages.

2. **(B)** The question asks what Ms. Jackson should review before the lesson. The pretest indicates that naming numerals in the tens place requires the most pre-lesson help. That is choice (B). Students demonstrate a higher level of mastery of choice (A) than choice (B). Eliminate choice (C) because that is the lesson objective, and eliminate (D) because that choice is more difficult than the objective.

3. **(D)** Parents who don't know English cannot help their children learn the language or check homework, which will be in English. The parents can be most helpful by ensuring that the students bring completed homework to school, even though parents may not know if it is correct or complete.

4. **(B)** This is the only activity that matches Ms. Jacson's specific intent to help students understand the difference between the same digit in the ones place and the tens place. There is absolutely no connection between the other activities and that specific objective.

5. **(A)** This approach to learning science is called inquiry learning because students learn as the result of the inquiry and their own explorations, and not through an explanation by the teacher.

6. **(C)** The question asks which answer has the most support for the Experiment First Group. We are not comparing the Experiment First Group with the Explanation First Group. Most of the students in the Experiment First groups (A, C, F) receive scores between 60% and 80% correct, which gives the most support to use that approach.

7. **(D)** The air pressure inside the bottle is lowered to the point where the outside pressure is more than the lowered inside pressure. The outside air pressure actually pushes the egg into the bottle.

8. **(B)** Among the choices given, identifying other events that represent the same scientific concept is the most beneficial outcome of the Extension. This answer is directly related to the lesson, unlike choice (C) which makes a more general reference to natural phenomena, but does not incorporate the objective of the lesson. There is neither evidence (A) of higher order thinking related to the lesson objective or (D) any relationship between the lesson and weather.

9. **(A)** The class description and the assessment data reveal a class with an exceptionally wide range of reading levels. Mr. Whitby should work with the special education teacher, partition the class, and assign a group of the poorest readers to that teacher. (B) The vocabulary list alone will not help if students cannot read the definitions. (C) There is nothing in the description or the assessment data that reveals particular problems with English as a second language. (D) There is no reason to believe, based on the information we have, that the poorer readers have difficulty because they are ESL students.

10. **(B)** Among all the choices given, unlocking what students already know about Native Americans, and even the Iroquois, is the best help to give students. It prepares them for the reading experience and involves them in the process.

11. **(D)** A character trait diagram displays the relationship among the traits of two characters, or the traits of a character and a real person such as the student. A Venn diagram with overlapping rings is the best way to diagram that relationship.

12. **(B)** Cultural responsiveness refers to giving students an opportunity to discuss their own culture in the context of another culture.

13. **Example of a response that would likely receive a rating of 3 or 4:**

One way that Mr. Whitby could address the needs of the diverse student population while using the Internet is to help students find sites that reflect their own culture as well as the Iroquois culture. Students could use these sites to find similarities and differences between their culture and the Iroquois culture, which would strengthen their own cultural identity.

Mr. Whitby must exercise care when using the Internet since students may encounter sites which are both inappropriate and culturally insensitive. Careful monitoring of student Internet usage is strongly indicated.

Mr. Whitby has an opportunity with this lesson to recognize that students at every level can help each other in a culturally diverse classroom. He could establish collaborative groups so that each group has a wide range of reading levels. By mixing reading levels in each group, all students will gain. Some students will explain while other students will listen, and these roles will evolve as the group works. Beyond the obvious learning benefits of this peer-mediated instruction, students will have an opportunity to share and understand the various cultures represented in the group.

14. **(C)** The data section reveals that Janice has the most trouble when sounding out new words, but does well with "sight" words presented before the lesson. This choice comes closest to the approach we know works with Janice. Nothing in the data suggests that (A) pictures, (B) meaning from context, nor (D) a phonemic analysis are successful approaches for Janice.

15. **(C)** ELL students first want to learn to speak a language to carry on daily affairs in the second-language country. That means learning to speak typically comes before learning to read. Learning the new sounds for letters is much more difficult when students are beyond the primary grades and is one reason why many people who are illiterate cannot read nor write a language, but can speak it.

16. **(C)** Seeing the words and images together establishes a visual basis for the word's meaning and helps ELL students overcome their difficulty developing word meaning. (A) may be true; however, it is not the primary reason why this approach is effective.

17. **(D)** The question asks about planning, and the only benefit among the four choices related to planning the lesson is that it will help the teacher prepare for the language needs of the ELL students.

18. **(C)** It is impossible for us to understand what Roberto has been through, or to gauge the tremendous difficulty he has in school. But we can understand that things will not happen quickly and, although helping him deal with his tobacco addiction will take time and patience, it is the only way through for him. Pressing too hard or ignoring his problem will not help.

19. **(B)** The ESL results show that Roberto and Darlene are at two different levels, and that there are significant differences between those levels. Based on this information, Mr. Zoll should plan different programs because each student needs a different type of help.

20. **(B)** The question asks us to compare Darlene's and Roberto's proficiency with English and base our answer on that comparison. Darlene is more proficient with English than Roberto, so it makes the most sense that Mr. Zoll could rely more on her English language skills.

21. **(B)** This question asks about *enhancing* learning *during* the discussion. This type of interaction is well recognized as an effective technique to enhance his or her English vocabulary and to practice English language skills in a nonthreatening atmosphere. Choice (A) and choice (D) are incorrect because these are already part of the discussion. Choice (C) is incorrect because a critique during discussion does not enhance learning.

22. **Example of a response that would likely receive a rating of 3 or 4:**

Roberto's unique learning issue as the description indicates is that no one is familiar with the language he speaks. This can be the case in isolated areas of Central America in which only tribal languages are spoken.

The adaptation is amazingly simple, if hard to implement. In any lesson, Roberto's work would improve if he had someone to talk to. Even if no one in the school is familiar with Roberto's language, there are adults outside the school who speak the language and could serve as resource aides. The adaptation is for Roberto to have a teacher aide who can speak his language and interact with him during lessons.

Roberto's learning issue makes it impossible to build on his native language to learn about English. The meanings of words are not known and cannot be related to English words. Finding someone who speaks Roberto's language is the most effective way to address this issue.

23. **(A)** It may seem like a good idea to just make things easier for these students. However, this approach sends the wrong message to these two students: that we think less of them as learners and have lower expectations. It also makes the work easier than it is for their fellow classmates. It is better to use some or all of the remaining three choices to support students as they work on the report.

24. **(B)** ELL students generally develop second-language speaking skills before they develop comparable second-language reading skills, and of all the choices given, this is the most likely result for Ms. Almon to encounter.

25. **(B)** The newspaper articles and Internet resources are a step toward preparing the written report. Of all the choices given, this choice gives ELL students the best opportunity to organize their thinking before reading in preparation for writing.

26. **(B)** The very first step before designing and implementing the instructional plan should be a close collaboration with the ESOL teacher. Pre- and post-assessment are not a part of the instructional plan.

27. **(A)** The National Reading Study established that Learning Disabled students learn words best when the words are taught directly, in a clear and explicit fashion.

28. **(A)** The best way among those listed to keep Rory involved is to establish a reward system for continued attention. Choices (B) and (D) actually remove Rory from the lesson, and his difficulty with interpersonal relationships makes choice (C) a poor option at this stage of his development.

29. **(A)** Ms. Alberto is not a special education teacher, and he should consult with an expert so that the combination of her daily experiences with Lena and the special education teacher's expertise can create a collaborative approach to the problem. There are no guarantees for success, but this approach is far superior to all the others.

30. **(A)** Rory does not know how to act, and of all the choices given, this one exposes Rory to a range of situations in which he observes appropriate behaviors. This is the best these two teachers can do to help Rory. The other approaches are likely to make things worse.

31. **(A)** We can tell from the description that Morgan has trouble controlling his handwriting and placing mathematical symbols on a page. That combination of problems will most likely make it difficult for him to align numerals in place value, and that is the issue from among those listed that will most likely be evident in Ms. Levine's class.

32. **(D)** This choice is the correct interpretation of the New York State regulation regarding the classification of a student as disabled for disciplinary purposes. Choice (B) is incorrect because a literate nondisabled parent must have made a prior request in writing;

however, an illiterate disabled parent may just make prior verbal statements. Student requests are not a factor.

33. **(D)** A student with consistent calculation results, as described, does NOT have dyscalculia. The other choices describe traits of students with dyscalculia, including having inconsistent results in addition, subtraction, multiplication, and division.

34. **(B)** The results of many studies make it clear that increased expectations are likely to lead to more student participation. An increased expectation for a classified student may or may not place them at the same level as unclassified students; however, these increased expectations are likely to increase participation, and will likely be viewed as affirmation that the teacher sees the potential in these students to do more. Note the term "likely," which means increased expectations do not always lead to increased participation.

35. **Example of a response that would likely receive a rating of 3 or 4:**

   The mathematical explanation in the lesson plan is correct, but it may be too difficult for Gulaka to understand. Gulaka will almost certainly have trouble understanding how fractional exponents are represented with the radical sign. The obvious first step understands that $3^{\frac{1}{2}}$ means the same as $\sqrt{3}$. This relationship is not intuitive, and it is difficult for even more advanced students. We may have to settle for a more rote grasp of this relationship with a student like Gulaka.

   The first step is to help Gulaka see the pattern of relationships between fractional exponents of ½ and square roots. I would give Gulaka a sheet showing several examples of this pattern. The sheet would look something like this.

   $3^{\frac{1}{2}}$ $\sqrt{3}$
   $4^{\frac{1}{2}}$ $\sqrt{4}$
   $5^{\frac{1}{2}}$ $\sqrt{5}$
   $6^{\frac{1}{2}}$ $\sqrt{6}$

   I would point out the pattern that shows a number raised to the ½ power is the square root of that number. Then I would ask Gulaka to continue the pattern for the next five numerals. Finally, I would give examples such as $26^{\frac{1}{2}}$ and ask her to write that number in radical form, followed by a similar example of square roots in radical form and ask her to represent the radical with a fractional exponent of ½. At this time I would not work with fractional exponents other than ½.

36. **(C)** This choice best summarizes the New York State Education law that requires instruction in English unless waived by the commissioner if an ELL student is of foreign birth or ancestry. The regulation limits this extension period to six years.

37. **(D)** Economically disadvantaged students are not less capable, but, as a group, economically disadvantaged students do have fewer home learning opportunities, which leads to lower achievement scores. Choices (A), (B), and (C) are false.

38. **(B)** It is generally most appropriate to address questions to the entire class. This maximizes the number of students who are thinking about the answer. Choices (A), (C), and (D) are incorrect and represent incorrect questioning techniques.

39. **(B)** Modeling means demonstrating the behavior students should replicate. Choices (A), (C), and (D) are not examples of appropriate modeling behavior.

40. **(D)** It is appropriate to alter the objectives or plans to focus on the cultural heritage of those in the class. Choices (A), (B), and (C) are not appropriate practices to adopt in a culturally and linguistically diverse class.

41. **(C)** According to the law, the additional parent member may only be required to attend any CSE meeting if requested in writing by the first parent or others at least 72 hours prior to each meeting.

42. **(D)** Note, the question asks for the choice LEAST likely to help Mr. Batsawani promote communication. The communication described to this choice is likely to lead parents to talk among themselves or with school administrators. The teacher should never discuss individual test scores with groups of parents. The remaining choices are examples of effective techniques for promoting good communication with parents.

43. **(A)** This action furthers the teacher's aims and does not run the risk of alienating parents. (B) is too self-serving; it does not give parents a reason to vote "yes," and may not further the teacher's goal. (C) and (D) are incorrect because they inject the teachers into town politics, in which they have an interest but no standing, and would likely not further the teachers' goal.

44. **(B)** Minority students' standardized test scores tend to fall below their actual ability and that is one of the reasons minority students are disproportionately represented in the lower tracks of a tracking system. (A) is incorrect because the flaws in standardized tests are not deliberately designed for that purpose, but that is often the outcome. (C) is incorrect because this statement is not necessarily true and is more properly a suggestion for how teachers are assigned to classes. (D) is incorrect because as a general rule, administrators do accurately report scores.

45. **(B)** Health information about students, and particularly about students with AIDS, is confidential and should not be shared. (A) is incorrect because a teacher has no right to have a child with AIDS removed from his or her class. (C) is incorrect because teachers are not permitted to inform anyone that a student has AIDS. (D) is incorrect because a teacher should not inform other teachers that a student has AIDS.

> 45 items
>
> 32 selected-response items based on a scenario
>
> 3 constructed-response items based on a scenario
>
> 10 selected-response items not based on a scenario
>
> Darken the lettered oval to show your choice for the selected-response items.
>
> Use a word processor, without the spell or grammar checker, and type your constructed-response answers.

SCENARIO 1

Ms. Erino is a fourth-grade teacher with a class of 27 students from diverse populations. In this class, all of the students were born outside the United States and come from Central and South America. Most students came to the United States with their families, but some are living in foster homes. Some of the intact families are living in homeless shelters. Academic achievement levels are as diverse as the cultures. Ms. Erino reports very few incidents of acting out in class.

Ms. Erino has worked closely with her students to develop an informal reading inventory that reflects some of the most important fourth-grade reading standards. The results of that inventory are found in the next section.

Ms. Erino will plan and teach a reading lesson based on these inventory results. To help ensure some success, Ms. Erino will choose the standard for which students show the most progress.

DATA

Individual Assessment of Fourth-Grade Reading Skills

	No Mastery	Partial Mastery	Mastery
Details and examples	30%	30%	40%
Theme	45%	50%	5%
Describe character and setting	40%	40%	20%
Word meaning in context	35%	35%	30%

DRAFT LESSON PLAN
New York Standard
Refer to details and examples in a text when explaining what the text says explicitly and when drawing inferences from the text.
Objective
Identify a detail in a text that answers a specific question.
Resources for Instruction
SMART Board
Example passages
Worksheets
Vocabulary
Review the meanings of words as students encounter difficulty.
Teach
Present students with this passage about Native Americans on the SMART Board:
Native Americans first came here about 60,000 years ago. They first traveled through Alaska. They first lived in Alaska about 7,000 years ago. They first lived in New York about 5,000 years ago. Eskimos first lived in northern Alaska about 4,000 years ago.
Point out that the passage contains many details. Our job as readers is to know what these details say and mean.
Explore
We can find details that answer these questions.
When did the Native Americans first live in New York?
When did Native Americans first come here?
Where in Alaska did Eskimos first live?
Ask students to answer these questions and come to the SMART Board to point to the sentence that supplies the details.
Ask students to provide their own detailed questions and engage the class in answering them.
Inference
Ask this inference question: Why did Native Americans first settle in Alaska?
Point out that no detail in the passage directly answers this question.
Ask students to answer the question and show that the second sentence provides the basis for this inference.
Ask students to provide their own inference questions and engage the class in answering them.
Practice
Ask students to complete a worksheet with passages followed by detail and inference questions based on each passage.
Extension
Distribute index cards. For homework, students should choose a passage from an available source and write one detail and one inference question based on the source.

BASE YOUR RESPONSES ON THE INFORMATION IN THE SCENARIO.

1. Which of the following additional strategies would Ms. Erino most successfully employ to help ELL students identify details from the passage in the lesson plan?

    Ⓐ Tell students not to look for details in the first or last sentence in a paragraph.
    Ⓑ Ask students to point to the sentences that contain the details.
    Ⓒ Present students with a graphic organizer that contains a main point in the passage with room for the students to write details next to the main point.
    Ⓓ Pair students to take advantage of their shared language as the students identify the details.

2. Considering that Ms. Erino's goal is for students to move beyond "No Mastery," which of the following skills from the Individual Assessment requires the most attention in her class?

    Ⓐ Details and examples
    Ⓑ Theme
    Ⓒ Describe character and setting
    Ⓓ Word meaning in context

3. Which issue is most important for Ms. Erino to consider when planning a lesson for students who are living in foster homes and in homeless shelters?

    Ⓐ Arrange for these students to receive adequate nutrition in school to maximize learning.
    Ⓑ Work on a plan to help students in homeless shelters move into real home settings.
    Ⓒ Ensure that students living in these circumstances are not being abused.
    Ⓓ Adapt instruction for students living in these circumstances.

4. Ms. Erino wants to establish a voluntary after-school learning community that will involve the students in reading books. Which of the following is the most effective step Ms. Erino could take to establish an effective learning community?

    Ⓐ Ensure that topical, relevant books at appropriate reading levels are available for students.
    Ⓑ Incorporate participation in the learning community into the students' grades.
    Ⓒ Invite community leaders to participate in learning community activities.
    Ⓓ Arrange for transportation to take the students home after the activities.

SCENARIO 2

This is Ms. Anderson's second year as an eighth-grade social studies teacher. She teaches six periods a day, and the fourth period class with thirty students is the most culturally and linguistically diverse. Still, performance in the class is quite good, with about half the students performing at or above grade level. There is a group of students who are a year or two below grade level and five students who are more than two years below grade level.

Ms. Anderson has arranged for some extra classroom support two days a week so that she may work with the group of five very low-performing students.

Ms. Anderson's school incorporates Gardner's Theory of Multiple Intelligences into instruction. Ms. Anderson has gone to great lengths to identify the primary Intelligence of each of the five very low-performing students. Her classification of the students follows.

Ms. Anderson wants to incorporate each Intelligence as a lesson adaptation in an upcoming social studies lesson.

DATA

Classification of low-performing students using four of Gardner's Intelligences

Visual-spatial   Cora, Jonah
Students with high spatial judgment possess the ability to visualize with the mind's eye.

Verbal-linguistic   Frances
People with high verbal-linguistic intelligence display a facility with words and languages.

Logical-mathematical   No students
Students with high logical-mathematical intelligence have the capacity to understand the underlying principles of a logical system.

Bodily-kinesthetic   Jacob, Liam
Students who have high bodily-kinesthetic intelligence should be generally good at physical activities such as sports, dance, acting, and making things.

DRAFT LESSON PLAN
New York Standards
Recognize, analyze, and evaluate dynamics of historical continuity and change over periods of time. Students will evaluate the United States' actions taken under the Roosevelt Corollary and their effects on relationships between the United States and Latin American nations, including the building of the Panama Canal.
Objective
Explain how the Roosevelt Corollary and the Monroe Doctrine are related and how they developed successfully
Resources for Instruction
Copies of the Roosevelt Corollary and the Monroe Doctrine
Vocabulary
doctrine, corollary
Teach
Briefly discuss President Monroe and President Roosevelt. Present students with the brief summaries of the Monroe Doctrine and the Roosevelt Corollary. The Monroe Doctrine issued in 1823 indicates that further efforts by European nations to colonize land or interfere with states in North or South America would be viewed as acts of aggression requiring U.S. intervention. The Roosevelt Corollary issued in 1904 indicates that the United States would intervene in conflicts between European countries and Latin American countries to enforce legitimate claims of the European powers. Point out the time relationship between these two statements of foreign policy. The Roosevelt Corollary came after the Monroe Doctrine and built on the doctrine.
Research
Use the Intelligences identified in the data to engage students in research activities. Cora and Jonah: Ask Cora and Jonah to meet and discuss the two summaries. Ask them to visualize the relationship between these two documents and prepare a brief summary of their conclusions. Ask Frances to conduct Internet research about the two documents and prepare a brief written summary of her findings. Jacob and Liam: Ask Jacob and Liam to prepare and rehearse a brief skit involving Roosevelt and Madison.
Presentation
Ask each group to present its report or skit.

BASE YOUR RESPONSES ON THE INFORMATION IN THE SCENARIO.

5. Ms. Anderson meets with her supervisor to discuss the integration of Multiple Intelligences in a lesson. The supervisor is most likely to think the most important issue is

  Ⓐ the validity of the Theory of Multiple Intelligences.
  Ⓑ the appropriateness of the Multiple Intelligences approach for this school district.
  Ⓒ the accuracy of Ms. Anderson's classification of the students.
  Ⓓ how Multiple Intelligences are integrated into the lesson plan.

6. What is the best explanation of the learning tasks assigned to Jacob and Liam in the lesson plan?

  Ⓐ Ms. Anderson wants to involve a full range of learning activities in the lesson.
  Ⓑ Jacob and Liam are classified primarily as bodily-kinesthetic learners.
  Ⓒ Jacob and Liam are classified as visual-spatial learners and this activity involves both visualization and space.
  Ⓓ The other learners were assigned to the tasks based on their primary learning styles, and this remaining activity was assigned to Jacob and Liam because their evaluation showed only a weak Multiple Intelligence association.

7. Which of the following activities would be the best way for Ms. Anderson to differentiate instruction for the students who perform above average?

  Ⓐ Ask students to explore why Roosevelt's document is referred to as a Corollary.
  Ⓑ Ask students to explore the biography of President Theodore Roosevelt.
  Ⓒ Ask students to explore the biography of President James Monroe.
  Ⓓ Ask students to distinguish between President Theodore Roosevelt and President Franklin Roosevelt.

8. What is the main advantage to choosing this lesson objective to represent the lesson's learning standard?

  Ⓐ The lesson shows development of government over a prolonged period of time.
  Ⓑ The lesson shows the relationship between two related historic events.
  Ⓒ The lesson involves students in events in the history of the United States.
  Ⓓ The lesson gives the teacher an opportunity to present the topic dynamically.

Constructed Response

9. Review the information in the scenario.

  ▪ Identify an additional approach related to the diverse students described in this scenario that Ms. Anderson should incorporate in the lesson.
  ▪ Describe the approach you recommend.
  ▪ Detail why the approach you suggest is likely to be effective.

SCENARIO 3

Mr. Lee is a fifth-grade teacher with thirty students in his crowded class. The class is culturally diverse, with students whose families come from around the world. The school district budget is very tight and all the teachers have limited access to materials. The students themselves also have limited access to computers and other reading material at home. Mr. Lee's class does not have a computer.

In addition to the cultural diversity, Mr. Lee's class has several students with learning disabilities who have accompanying reading problems. There is no access to additional instruction for these students. However, Mr. Lee works with the school's Child Study Team support staff to augment instruction.

The class is studying the portion of the fifth-grade standards devoted to the U.S. Constitution and the separation of powers. Mr. Lee has been reading aloud to the class from *Our Constitution Rocks*, by Juliette Turner, which he purchased himself.

Mr. Lee knows someone who is an expert on the Constitution and separation of powers and who visits local schools to show students a replica of the document and answer questions about how the Constitution was written and how it is interpreted. This person will visit Mr. Lee's class next week, and Mr. Lee wants to be prepared to arrange a discussion that will meet the students' needs. He has been gathering student reading data from the most recent state reading test. He also consults with his supervisor prior to the visit.

DATA

New York State Reading Test

Reading Decile Data for the School (Higher numbers are better scores)	
Economically disadvantaged	3
Not economically disadvantaged	8
Students with disabilities	2
English language learners	1
Proficient in English	9
Non-migrant	7
All students	7

DRAFT LESSON PLAN
New York Standard Students will examine the basic structure of the United States federal government, including the president, Congress, and the courts.
Objective Students examine the basic structure of the federal government as outlined by the Constitution. Students identify the various functions of the three branches of government.
Resources for Instruction
Our Constitution Rocks, by Juliette Turner Visiting expert
Teach *Before the Visit* Review the portions of *Our Constitution Rocks* that address separation of powers. Explain that in a few days we will have a visitor who knows how to explain the Constitution to fifth graders and that this expert will bring a replica of the Constitution. Ask each student to write one question to ask the expert. Review the questions with individual students and help them rephrase or restate the questions. *During the Visit* Introduce the visitor and help the students maintain attention during the presentation. As was prearranged, enable each student to read his or her question and to note the expert's response. *After the Visit* Engage the students in a discussion of the visit. Ask them to talk about what they learned about the Constitution. Ask each student to share his or her question and to discuss the helpfulness of the expert's response. Encourage students to discuss each question and the response.

10. Mr. Lee wants to make the best use of his meeting with the supervisor to discuss the lesson. Which of the following questions would best meet his needs?

    Ⓐ How can I best maintain discipline during the visitor's class discussion?
    Ⓑ How much time should I allocate to the visitor's presentation to the class?
    Ⓒ What is the best way for me to use the visitor's expertise during the visit?
    Ⓓ How much information should I share with the visitor about students' reading levels?

11. Based on the test results, which of the following conclusions can Mr. Lee draw about the reading performance of students in his class?

    Ⓐ Students with disabilities are more likely than migrants to have reading difficulties.
    Ⓑ ELL students and students with disabilities are likely to have comparable problems with reading.
    Ⓒ Students who are economically disadvantaged can be proficient readers.
    Ⓓ Students who are proficient in English do not do better than students as a whole.

12. How could Mr. Lee and the class visitor work together most effectively to improve the overall effectiveness of the lesson?

    Ⓐ Mr. Lee could prepare the class in advance for the visit.
    Ⓑ Mr. Lee and the visitor could discuss the makeup of the class and strategies that could be most effective.
    Ⓒ The visitor could take steps to relate the discussion to the cultural backgrounds of students in the class.
    Ⓓ The visitor and Mr. Lee could meet with a delegation of students from the class to discuss the visit.

13. What is the main advantage in the Before the Visit section of the lesson to asking students to prepare written questions?

    Ⓐ It ensures that the students will be prepared with questions during the visit.
    Ⓑ It helps students distinguish between "off the cuff" questions and prepared questions.
    Ⓒ It gives students an opportunity to incorporate his or her own cultural experience in preparation for the visit.
    Ⓓ It involves students in a further study of the lesson topic.

SCENARIO 4

Mr. Elojas is a second-grade teacher. His class includes several ELL students who were born outside the United States. These students receive individual help each day from Ms. Fabrione, an ESOL specialist. Each teacher works to ensure that the students in the ESOL group receive the same content instruction as other students in the class.

Mikail is the student who requires the most help. His family escaped from a country in which the entire family had been facing imprisonment. Their escape across many countries took years and was a dangerous and frightening time for young Mikail. During that time, Mikail received no schooling. Even so, Mikail is resilient and intelligent, but very shy and withdrawn in the classroom. He is making good progress. It's just that there is a lot to make up.

During one of their regular meetings, Mr. Elojas and Ms. Fabrione are planning a science lesson based on the second-grade standard about the similarities between adult and baby animals. They are reviewing some of their anecdotal notes to prepare.

DATA

Relevant notes from the second-grade teacher Mr. Elojas

I noticed that Mikail is starting to work more closely with some of the other students in the class. I also see that a few students seem to object to the attention he is getting, and I will have to be careful to ensure that these students feel equally important.

I don't need a reading test to tell that Mikail is reading at the pre-K level. This very low reading level interferes with everything he does in class and significantly inhibits his ability to learn, despite the fact that he is quite intelligent.

I received a call from a friend of Mikail's parents to pass on in English some of their concerns. It seems that Mikail can be up half the night after awaking from a terrible nightmare. He does not share what the nightmare is about, but his mother feels it is related to some frightening events from their past.

Relevant notes from Ms. Fabrione, the ESOL specialist

I can't remember the last time I worked with a student as determined as Mikail. He wants very much to learn English and to read just like the other students. His progress is steady, but he is unfamiliar with many vocabulary words and is still at the lowest level on the ESL test scale.

I must admit that sometimes I feel inadequate. I know how to help students develop English language skills, but I am completely unfamiliar with Mikail's language. Things would be different if it was Spanish or Italian, but it is not. I try to learn as much about the language as I can, and at least I know exactly how Mikail feels. Sometimes I think he's learning faster than I am, and I love to tell him that. It makes him happy. "OK" he says, "we do gether."

DRAFT LESSON PLAN
New York Standard Plants and animals closely resemble their parents and other individuals in their species.
Objective Identify adult animals and the offspring and note the similarities between them.
Resources for Instruction Pictures of rabbits, cats, dogs, horses, cows, and their offspring *Born in the Wild: Baby Mammals and Their Parents*, by Lita Judge
Teach Talk about animals' offspring and how they are usually very similar to the adults, except for size. "Stick" the adult pictures on one side of the board and the baby pictures on the other. Ask students to come up and move the baby animal's picture next to the adult picture. Each time, engage students in a conversation about the similarities between the adult and the "child." Use the pictures from *Born in the Wild* to give more examples of how adult and baby animals look very similar.
Adaptation Ms. Fabrione will work with Mikail during the lesson.
Integration Ask Mikail to tell the class the names of some of the animals in his language. Discuss that although the names for the animals are different, each name refers to the same animal.

BASE YOUR RESPONSES ON THE INFORMATION IN THE SCENARIO.

14. What is the most important learning advantage in the Integration portion of the lesson when Mikail tells the class the names of the animals in his native language?

  Ⓐ It provides additional information about animal names to students in the class.
  Ⓑ It gives Mikail an opportunity to demonstrate that his unfamiliarity with the English language does not mean that he is unintelligent.
  Ⓒ It reinforces the important concept that one object may have many different names.
  Ⓓ It gives Mikail an opportunity to relate his native language to English.

15. From what we know of Mikail, it is most likely that

  Ⓐ his fears and nightmares will significantly inhibit his learning growth.
  Ⓑ he is likely to develop English skills at a faster pace than other similar students.
  Ⓒ Ms. Fabrione's unfamiliarity with his language will delay Mikail's language development.
  Ⓓ having parents who do not speak English means that he will have more learning problems than other ELL students.

16. Mr. Elojas uses the effective approach of scaffolding to help Mikail learn English, most likely meaning that

  Ⓐ he provides temporary support to help students achieve higher levels of learning that they would not be able to achieve without that support.
  Ⓑ he uses a detailed diagram, a framework, of learning activities that Mikail will "climb" to achieve higher levels of language learning.
  Ⓒ he provides additional details to the school district's framework for ELL learning to personalize Mikail's learning experience.
  Ⓓ the room contains a series of multilevel bookshelves with motivational reading books that increase in difficulty as Mikail reads books on ever higher shelves.

17. Which of the following is the best approach for Mr. Elojas to take that will address Mikail's vocabulary deficiency noted by Ms. Fabrione?

  Ⓐ Give Mikail carefully chosen words on individual index cards with the definition on the reverse side of the card and ask Mikail to review the words on the way to mastery.
  Ⓑ Instruct Mikail how to use the translation capability on the typical computer browser to translate unfamiliar English words.
  Ⓒ Give Mikail carefully chosen words on individual index cards that Mikail can arrange on a graphic organizer.
  Ⓓ Instruct Mikail how to use a computer connected to the Internet to look up the definitions of unfamiliar English words.

SCENARIO 5

Mr. Longin is a performing arts teacher who has two ELL students, Ernesto and Maria, in his eighth-grade class. Both of the students are able to converse fluently with other English speakers in the class, even though there is a tendency for them to speak privately in the language of their country of origin. The two students are below grade level in reading and language.

Ernesto had almost no schooling until coming to this country when he was in elementary school. He still has relatives in his home country, where living conditions are very poor. His family sends money to relatives in their home country, and Ernesto works after school every day to help support his family.

After leaving her home country, Maria at first lived near the U.S.-Mexico border, but about two years ago her family moved to New York. Maria frequently complains about the cold and that there is often not enough heat in their small apartment. Her family does not speak English at home.

Recently, each family received a report about their child's English language proficiency from New York State. Mr. Longin has been spending time with an interpreter explaining the report to the parents, and he plans to use the test results from the New York State ELA test to help him prepare students to perform brief skits.

DATA

ELA Test Percentile Scores

Ernesto	Percentile Score	22nd (Level 1)
Maria	Percentile Score	19th (Level 1)

Eighth-Grade Level Explanation

NYS Level 4

Students performing at this level excel in standards for their grade. They demonstrate knowledge, skills, and practices embodied by the New York State P-12 Common Core Learning Standards for English Language Arts/Literacy that are considered more than sufficient for the expectations at this grade.

NYS Level 3

Students performing at this level are proficient in standards for their grade. They demonstrate knowledge, skills, and practices embodied by the New York State P-12 Common Core Learning Standards for English Language Arts/Literacy that are considered sufficient for the expectations at this grade.

NYS Level 2

Students performing at this level are below proficient in standards for their grade. They demonstrate knowledge, skills, and practices embodied by the New York State P-12 Common Core Learning Standards for English Language Arts/Literacy that are considered partial but insufficient for the expectations at this grade.

NYS Level 1

Students performing at this level are well below proficient in standards for their grade. They demonstrate limited knowledge, skills, and practices embodied by the New York State P-12 Common Core Learning Standards for English Language Arts/Literacy that are considered insufficient for the expectations at this grade.

Summary

Both Ernesto and Maria scored at eighth-grade level 1, although their percentile scores put them within striking distance of level 2. It was extremely difficult to explain the test report and the test scores to the parents, even with the help of an interpreter. It was hard for them to understand the scores or the 1–4 ranking and to understand that the scores did not represent their child's ability. So we have two issues, students who desperately need reading support and parents who are upset with the school, New York State, and their children.

DRAFT LESSON PLAN
New York Standard Students will actively engage in the processes that constitute creation and performance in the arts (dance, music, theatre, and visual arts) and participate in various roles in the arts.
Objective Students will practice and perform a brief, one-minute skit written by the students.
Teach Preparing the skits On Day 1 students talk about the themes for the one-minute skits they will each write. Students should be given wide latitude to select appropriate topics. On Day 2 students will write and edit the scripts. [Adaptation for this activity: Mr. Longin has arranged for Ernesto to work with an ESOL teacher who is familiar with his native language. The final skits will be in English, but it may go through a stage where it is written in the foreign language.]
Performing the Skits On Day 3, students perform the skits [Adaptation: Mr. Longin has arranged for an ESOL teacher to be present to help Ernesto and Maria understand the spoken words and to speak aloud the words they have each written.] Students are encouraged to give attention and respect to the student presenting the skit.

BASE YOUR RESPONSES ON THE INFORMATION IN THE SCENARIO.

18. Based on Mr. Longin's observation of Ernesto and Maria, the most effective approach to promote reading skills from among those described below is to

Ⓐ explore cultural linkages between the language of their home country and English.

Ⓑ help the students develop a spoken vocabulary of English words.

Ⓒ draw on their spoken English skills.

Ⓓ use literature that addresses the success of immigrants in the United States.

19. Mr. Longin is concerned when Ernesto and Maria speak privately in their native language. His concerns are reduced when an ESOL teacher explains that

Ⓐ it's actually better for students to speak in their native language.

Ⓑ this will actually help the students complete class assignments.

Ⓒ this will help build a bond of friendship between these two students.

Ⓓ there is nothing he can do about it, so just relax and let nature take its course.

20. Based on the New York ELA test percentile scores for these two students, Mr. Longin can conclude that

Ⓐ there is very little chance that Maria and Ernesto will move to Level 3 on the scale.

Ⓑ Ernesto and Maria performed at about the same level on the assessment.

Ⓒ Maria and Ernesto cannot read or write in English.

Ⓓ Ernesto reads English more fluently than Maria.

21. Which of the following changes would best improve the adaptation on the second day of the lesson?

Ⓐ Eliminate the transition from the native language to English.

Ⓑ Include Maria along with Ernesto for this adaptation.

Ⓒ Have higher expectations for Ernesto's ability to write in English.

Ⓓ Permit Ernesto to write the entire skit in his native language.

Constructed Response

22. In the data section, Mr. Longin describes the challenges of interpreting the report for parents.

■ Outline a plan for him to follow that describes approaches for explaining the assessment report for parents.

■ Explain why the approaches you describe would be effective.

SCENARIO 6

Ms. Bora is a fifth-grade teacher with a class of 28 students, including a number of ELL students. Several of the students, with very limited English proficiency, spend time outside class with an ESOL teacher. Ms. Bora is glad these students receive extra language learning help, but she is concerned that the students are missing out on regular class work. We will focus on two of the ELL students in the class who do not share a common second language.

Mei Sing came to this country with school records from her native country. These records show superior performance. However, there are questions about the educational achievement overall in that country and about the meaning of these records. Mei Sing can converse easily with other students in the class, although her ELL tests do not indicate the higher level of performance observed in class.

Lerone just arrived in the United States at the beginning of last year and lives with his mother and sister. There are serious economic and political problems in his country, and his father and brother are trying to escape through a roundabout route. He and his mother have not heard from them since they arrived in this country, but relatives overseas report recent contact. Lerone can communicate effectively with the other students and his gregarious personality has earned him a measure of acceptance among other students.

Ms. Bora is planning a fifth-grade social studies lesson about Christopher Columbus not reaching the mainland of North America, and she is reviewing the results of Mei Sing's and Lerone's ELL achievement tests in preparation of the lesson.

DATA

English as a Second Language Achievement Test

Mei Sing   Beginning
Lerone   Beginning

Ms. Bora's Comments

Based on my classroom observations these test results do not accurately capture Mei Sing's or Lerone's progress learning English. Their class interactions are more like a student in the middle of the Intermediate Level. I believe their scores appear lower because of their difficulty with taking tests and not their difficulty with English. I will interact with each of them according to my observations.

Four Levels of NYSESLAT Scores

Proficient: Students function fluently in listening, reading, writing, and speaking; their skills are equal to those of native English speakers at their appropriate grade level. These students have attained the skills necessary to participate in an English-speaking classroom.

Advanced: Students are able to use skills at a higher level than intermediate students. Although their knowledge and use of English is at a more advanced level, mistakes are made, usually involving more subtle use of language and more difficult levels of vocabulary and grammar.

Intermediate: Students have better English skills than students at the basic level; however, their skills are often not well developed and they make significant errors in the four skill areas.

Beginning: Students are simply at the beginning level in the four skill areas. These students' English skills are minimal.

DRAFT LESSON PLAN
New York Standard Students will investigate explorers from different European countries and map the areas of the Western Hemisphere where they explored, including Christopher Columbus, John Cabot, Jacques Cartier, Pedro Cabral, and Vasco Nunez de Balboa
Objective Students will explore and understand that Christopher Columbus never reached the mainland of the United States.
Resources for Instruction *Pedro's Journal: A Voyage with Christopher Columbus, August 3, 1492–February 14, 1493*, written by Pam Conrad and illustrated by Peter Koeppen SMART Board maps of the four voyages Columbus made from 1492 to 1500 Internet access
Teach Read excerpts from the book, *Pedro's Journal*. Have students discuss what they think it might have been like to be on a voyage with Columbus. Reveal one by one the voyages of Columbus. Show that on the first voyages Columbus reached Cuba and Hispaniola. Show that it was only on a later voyage that he landed in South America. Elicit from students that Columbus never reached the mainland of North America or the current United States.
Participation Involve students in a discussion of why the popular myth exists that Columbus "discovered" North America and what is now the United States.
Extension Partition students into groups of three or four. Ask them to conduct Internet research to try to determine when humans first reached the United States and when Europeans first reached the United States. The first humans were most likely Native Americans, although there may have been an earlier Nordic colony. Ask students to "present" their findings and discuss that there can be uncertainty about some historic events.

23. How appropriate is it for Ms. Bora to base her work with the ELL students on her own observations and not on the test results?

    (A) It is inappropriate because Ms. Bora is not an ELL expert, and she would be better off using the test results.
    (B) It is appropriate because Ms. Bora has the most up-to-date information about the students.
    (C) It is inappropriate because Ms. Bora is unlikely to detect the subtle differences in English proficiency measured by the test.
    (D) It is appropriate because we should not rely on this kind of high-stakes testing when working with ELL students.

24. During the teaching phase of the lesson, which of the following is the most effective approach to help the ELL students distinguish among the voyages of Columbus?

    (A) The individual voyages do not really matter for this lesson, what is important is that Columbus never reached North America.
    (B) Number the voyages on the maps presented in class.
    (C) Present students with a graphic organizer that permits them to record and organize the voyages.
    (D) Encourage the ELL students to use the number words from their native language to label the voyages.

25. As the school year progresses, Ms. Bora notes that Mei Sing demonstrates an advanced ability to learn science and can achieve well beyond the fifth-grade curriculum with language support. The most appropriate step for Ms. Bora to take is to

    (A) stay focused on English Language learning because Mei Sing's proficiency scores are so low.
    (B) seek support from a science specialist or science teacher to develop a curriculum for Mei Sing.
    (C) wait until Mei Sing can achieve at or above grade level in science without language support before raising curricular standards.
    (D) secure a sixth-grade science book for Mei Sing to use.

26. The Extension activity involves students in Internet research, which is the most common way for students to access information. The most important actions for Ms. Bora to take during this Internet research time is to

    (A) provide websites related to the subject for students to access.
    (B) account for the different levels of Internet access that students have at home.
    (C) carefully monitor the sites that students visit.
    (D) allow students to visit sites that display his or her native language.

SCENARIO 7

Mr. Bateman teaches mathematics in fifth grade. The class includes two "classified students" who have IEPs.

One student, Maureen, is a child with Attention Deficit Disorder (ADD). She spends 45 minutes three times a week out of class receiving services from a special education teacher. It is very difficult for Maureen to stay on task and to follow the teacher's directions or respond to requests. Her desk is a mess, filled with partially completed work, and her homework is never completed. She constantly seeks attention by talking out in class or by bothering other students. While not a social outcast in class, Maureen lacks the awareness to know when to interact with other students.

The other student, Jacob, is classified with Traumatic Brain Injury (TBI) caused by a fall from a window when he was just six years old. It was a life-threatening injury, and doctors believe the brain was deprived of oxygen for a period of time. By all reports, Jacob was reading above grade level, seemed better at learning than most students in his first-grade class, and was a happy child. Today Jacob is very unhappy and has difficulty with learning and memory, perceptual-motor activities, and speech. Jacob spends half the school day working with a collection of specially trained professionals, including a special education teacher, a speech pathologist, and a physical therapist.

Mr. Bateman is working with the support teachers and specialists to prepare a lesson on multiplying by powers of 10. He is reviewing the notes and some pretest information about the two classified students in his class in preparation for the lesson.

DATA

Pretest Results

Mr. Bateman wanted to rely on specific student data, so he gave students an "open-ended" pretest for which the students would not rely on the selected-response answers and guessing. Here are the responses for two questions related to the lesson topic from Maureen and Jacob:

Pretest

Question A	$10^6 =$		Question B	$10^3 \times 27 =$
Maureen	$10 \times 6 = 60$		Maureen	30×27
Jacob	$10^6 = 1{,}000{,}000$		Jacob	$10 \times 10 \times 10 \times 27$

Related IEP Objective

Maureen

Maureen will attend to a task for at least 15 minutes.

Maureen will not call out in class more than once every 30 minutes.

Maureen will not engage with other students while those students are completing schoolwork.

Jacob

Jacob will increase his reading and mathematics proficiency by at least one grade level.

Jacob will have a teacher available for social support in testing situations.

DRAFT LESSON PLAN

New York Standard

Explain patterns in the number of zeros of the product when multiplying a number by powers of 10, and explain patterns in the placement of the decimal point when a decimal is multiplied or divided by a power of 10. Use whole number exponents to denote powers of 10.

Objective

Multiply whole numbers by a positive whole number power of 10.

Resources for Instruction

Practice worksheet

Review

Review the symbols for powers of 10.

Remind students that 10^0 is always equal to 1.

10 to any other whole number power shows how many zero digits follow the 1.

$10^1 = 10$ [one zero]

$10^2 = 100$ [two zeros]

and so on.

Teach

Explain that multiplying a number by a power of ten adds that many zeros to the number.

$10^1 \times 27 = 270$ [one zero]

$10^2 \times 27 = 2700$ [two zeros]

$10^3 \times 17 = 27000$ [three zeros]

Participation

Ask students to provide their own examples of multiplying 27 by a power of 10.

Ask questions such as, "If we multiplied a number by 10 to the 50th power, how many zeros would that add to the number?"

Practice

Give students the "Multiplying by Powers of Ten" practice sheet and monitor them as they complete the worksheets.

Extension

Ask students to name the numbers they create when they multiply by powers of 10.

For example, ask students, "What would we call 70 multiplied by 10 to the third power?"

[$70 \times 10^3 = 70{,}000$ is 70 thousand]

27. Which of the following would be the LEAST appropriate school-related response for Jacob when he is ready to return to school?

    Ⓐ The use of assistive devices including augmentative communication devices
    Ⓑ The use of external cues such as timers and alarms
    Ⓒ A flexible daily routine featuring student choice of activities
    Ⓓ A gradual return to school slowly increasing over time

28. Based on the pretest conducted by Mr. Bateman, the most accurate statement of Maureen's understanding of exponents is that Maureen

    Ⓐ has some trouble with exponents but knows the meaning of "power."
    Ⓑ confuses an exponent with a factor.
    Ⓒ understands exponents but has trouble using exponents to multiply.
    Ⓓ confuses exponents and raising a number to a power.

29. Which of the following is the best approach for Mr. Bateman to take when teaching about powers of 10 to Maureen?

    Ⓐ Reduce stress by providing a flexible learning experience with exponents that enables her to make choices and opt out of the lesson.
    Ⓑ Help her see the pattern of raising 10 to a power. That is, the exponent shows how many zeroes follow the digit 1.
    Ⓒ In order to hold Maureen's attention, avoid being predictable in your discussion of exponents and call on her when she least expects it.
    Ⓓ Avoid overtly stating what Maureen is expected to learn about exponents during the lesson.

30. Mr. Bateman has students in his class who participate in school sports, meaning he should be aware of the New York State law that

    Ⓐ forbids students from participating in "contact sports" who are in the same class as a student with TBI.
    Ⓑ requires teachers to conduct seminars about TBI for parents when students in their class plan to participate in sports.
    Ⓒ requires an information pamphlet on mild traumatic brain injuries to be distributed to parents of pupils who have suffered a mild traumatic brain injury.
    Ⓓ requires a full-time teacher certified to work with students with TBI to be assigned to work one on one with the student for the first 180 days in school.

SCENARIO 8

Mr. Rasish teaches earth science in high school. All of his students are English language learners. There is also a wide range of ability and learning issues among students in his class. However, two students in the class have official classifications and IEPs.

Lena is classified as Learning Disabled, which includes a wide range of learning issues marked by performance two years below the expected performance level. Lena's issues are primarily with reading. She has a below grade level vocabulary and is not able to sound out new words or identify the meaning of the words from their context. Lena often shows an interest in science, but difficulty identifying words in context will significantly inhibit her progress in class.

Rodney is classified as Emotionally Disturbed. He is usually distracted, often responds inappropriately in social situations, and has demonstrated an inability to learn that has no obvious explanation. Rodney is the biggest challenge for Mr. Rasish because just when Rodney starts to make progress, something will happen, and Rodney will be right back where he started. Other times, Rodney will just not pay attention at all, turning his attention to some unrelated task.

Both of these students receive "pull-out" services from a special education teacher in a resource room, and Rodney receives additional services from a psychologist and a behavior therapist specially employed by the district to help Rodney and to avoid the expense of sending Rodney to a specialized school.

However, Mr. Rasish prefers to rely on his notes on each student's classroom behavior, which he finds most useful and most up to date. He is reviewing those notes now in preparation for a lesson on the Coriolis effect.

DATA

Mr. Rasish's Notes

I have to keep reminding myself that this is a "special" earth science class and overall most students in this class are not performing at the higher level found in other earth science classes in the school.

Lena

Lena has been working hard in class. However, her difficulty with reading has been quite noticeable in the last few weeks. Lena is somewhat unfamiliar with English, but her parents speak English at home, so that is not the problem. Early last week I met with the parents, which gave me a little more insight about Lena. It seems that Lena had some of the same reading problems in her native language in the early grades just before the family moved to the United Sates. So it seems the problems with words are long-standing, and it is difficult to address the problem directly at this stage in her life.

I think I may have come upon an effective strategy for Lena. The Earth Science book series comes with a separate glossary and dictionary that show meanings of English science terms in her foreign language. I've given this supplementary book to her along with a list of science terms I have compiled for this course. Just reminding Lena to check these sources when she comes across an unfamiliar word has met with initial success. I am hoping that once she has looked up a word a few times and learned its meaning in context, then the words will eventually become a part of her regular vocabulary.

Rodney

Rodney is a real challenge and the past two weeks have pretty much been a disaster. He's refusing more and more to do any work. He bothers everyone. I notice that things get worse as he senses that he is falling behind, and I can understand his frustration since he seems not to be in control of any of the difficulties he is having. I am concerned that things will get worse, and a decision will be made to send him to a special school, where I do not expect things to be any better for him.

I have been trying to give Rodney very small tasks and to work with the specialists to help him complete some of the small tasks with them and some with me. I hope this approach helps account for Rodney's easily distracted nature and gives him small morsels of success that may help his confidence. I am getting great cooperation from the specialists, but it is hard to tell about the long-term success of this approach.

DRAFT LESSON PLAN
New York Standard The Foucault pendulum and the Coriolis effect provide evidence of Earth's rotation.
Objective Observe the effect of the Coriolis effect and explain what causes it.
Resources for Instruction "Lazy Susans" or some other device that can spin Paper Markers
Preview Air travels clockwise around high pressure in the Northern Hemisphere and counter-clockwise in the Southern Hemisphere. Why?
Teach Ask the students to record their prediction of how a drawn straight line will turn on a page spinning clockwise (to the right). Ask students to record a prediction for a page spinning counterclockwise. After the students have recorded their predictions, partition them into working groups of four students each. Be prepared to help students with the experiments that follow.
Experiment Mention that in the experiment, turning the paper clockwise represents the Northern Hemisphere and turning counterclockwise represents the Southern Hemisphere. One student holds the paper in the center. The second slowly spins the paper clockwise. The third student draws a straight line from the top of the paper to the bottom. The fourth student keeps notes. Students repeat the experiment with a counterclockwise spin.

Discussion

Students share and discuss the results. Lead the discussion to the conclusion that the Coriolis effect causes an object to be deflected to the east (right) in the Northern Hemisphere and to the west (left) in the Southern Hemisphere.

Extension

Ask students to find other examples of the Coriolis effect and describe the effects during class.

Example: A swirl of water filtering down will turn to the right in the Northern Hemisphere and will turn to the left in the Southern Hemisphere.

BASE YOUR RESPONSES ON THE INFORMATION IN THE SCENARIO.

31. Mr. Rasish has written extensive notes, including a strategy for using a bilingual glossary he prepared to help Lena learn science terms. Which of the following would be the best further adaptation for his approach?

    Ⓐ Limit Lena's use of the glossary by keeping it at his desk.
    Ⓑ Have Lena use the glossary in a small group.
    Ⓒ Switch to a glossary that uses only the English language.
    Ⓓ Rely on the glossary he developed and avoid a commercial product.

32. Which of the following would be the most effective choice to use in the classroom to help reduce Rodney's disruptive behavior?

    Ⓐ Make arrangements to remove him from the class and send him to a time-out area with an aide when the disruptions become too pronounced.
    Ⓑ Give Rodney a set number of "passes" on pieces of paper. He gives Mr. Rasish one pass each time he acts out. When the "passes" are all gone, his acting out will be expected to stop.
    Ⓒ Arrange a meeting with the school psychologist to gain a comprehensive view of the reasons for the cause of Rodney's problems in the classroom, and develop a plan of action for dealing with these problems.
    Ⓓ Separate Rodney from the rest of the class by placing him at a desk in the back of the classroom so that he will be away from other students.

33. Mr. Rasish knows that Lena will have problems with the concepts of clockwise and counterclockwise. The approach by Mr. Rashish most likely to help Lena is to arrange for her to

    Ⓐ meet in a small group to discuss clockwise and counterclockwise.
    Ⓑ physically turn her body to simulate clockwise and counterclockwise.
    Ⓒ draw clockwise and counterclockwise ovals on paper.
    Ⓓ discuss the difference in hemispheres between the clockwise and counterclockwise movements of the swirl of water.

34. Rodney is administered a Functional Behavioral Assessment. A primary outcome of this assessment is always

    (A) strategies that include positive behavioral supports and services to address the behavior.
    (B) a disciplinary plan including suspension that is administered by the building principal.
    (C) the assignment of a one-on-one aide to work with Rodney throughout the day.
    (D) a referral for placement in an alternate school environment that is not a part of the high school.

Constructed Response

35. After reviewing the information in the scenario, write a response to the following:

    ■ Identify one element of the lesson plan that would be difficult for Rodney.
    ■ Describe an accommodation to the lesson plan that will help Rodney with this difficulty.
    ■ Explain why the adaptation you describe is likely to be effective.

There are no scenarios for these items.

36. When monitoring student attendance in school,

    (A) it is the teacher's responsibility to maintain attendance records.
    (B) it is the school's responsibility to maintain attendance records.
    (C) the teacher's responsibility is limited to reporting when students are absent.
    (D) the school will appoint an attendance officer who is responsible for maintaining attendance records.

37. The teacher's primary responsibility as a classroom manager is to ensure that the majority of class time is spent on

    (A) individual work.
    (B) on-task activities.
    (C) cooperative learning.
    (D) activities that embrace all the cultural identities in the classroom.

38. When using authentic assessment, the teacher's primary responsibility is to

    (A) collect and evaluate student work.
    (B) use standardized tests.
    (C) use only tests that have been authenticated.
    (D) collect evaluative information from other teachers.

39. When using a cooperative learning approach in the classroom, it is NOT an appropriate teacher responsibility to

    Ⓐ arrange for students to get help from other students.
    Ⓑ arrange for groups of two to six students to work together.
    Ⓒ arrange for group members to consult with the teacher.
    Ⓓ summarize students' work.

40. The teacher's responsibility when using a constructivist approach is to encourage students to

    Ⓐ respond quickly and alertly to questions.
    Ⓑ construct diagrams of their thought processes.
    Ⓒ elaborate on their initial responses.
    Ⓓ avoid using metaphors.

41. Parents or guardians wish to instruct their children at home. They should understand

    Ⓐ any tutors hired to conduct home schooling must have the appropriate New York teacher certification.
    Ⓑ everyone conducting home schooling must have a bachelor's degree.
    Ⓒ there are no education requirements for those providing home schooling.
    Ⓓ a person must be designated as the Home Schooling Director, and that person must be certified as a teacher in New York State or in a state that has reciprocal certification agreements with New York.

42. A parent or guardian expresses extreme concern to the teacher about her eighth-grade child's school performance. The parent is concerned that continued academic problems will make it impossible for her child to be successful in college or in life. Which of the following is the most appropriate way for the teacher to communicate with the parent/guardian?

    Ⓐ "Don't be concerned. We are convinced that your child will be fine and be successful."
    Ⓑ "We enjoy working with your child, and we have the highest hopes for him."
    Ⓒ "Your child is in a special education setting, and, at this age, there are likely some real problems that may or may not be resolved over time."
    Ⓓ "We are concerned too, but we are not allowed to discuss these issues with parents."

43. A teacher sends home a detailed newsletter every month. The newsletter is distributed via e-mail to those parents who have shared an e-mail address, and each student in the class receives a hard copy to take home. The newsletter is most likely to improve communication with parents and guardians by

Ⓐ increasing the teacher's visibility.

Ⓑ keeping parents abreast of classroom activities.

Ⓒ emphasizing the use of e-mail as a communication tool.

Ⓓ demonstrating the teacher's familiarity with technology.

44. Which of the following is most likely to involve parents or guardians in a school?

Ⓐ Establish a Home School Association with regular meetings and ensure that all parents and guardians are members of the association.

Ⓑ Establish an active Board of Advisors consisting of parents, which meets regularly with school administrators to discuss school issues and school policy.

Ⓒ Arrange for teachers to engage parents and guardians in conversation as they encounter these people in the school.

Ⓓ Appoint two parent/guardian leaders for each class and arrange for these class leaders to meet regularly with the teacher.

45. A secondary school offers a wide range of courses at many different levels of ability and difficulty. Which of the following is most likely to include parents or guardians in their children's educational choices?

Ⓐ Disseminate widely the full course schedule before course assignments for the coming school year along with the prerequisites for each course.

Ⓑ Appoint parents or guardians to the school's scheduling committee and carefully consider the view of parents and guardians in any scheduling decision.

Ⓒ Arrange for direct participation of a parent or guardian in any class scheduling or assignment decisions involving their child.

Ⓓ Allow parents or guardians to review the class schedule before it is finally published and solicit the parents' or guardians' opinions about recommendations for changes.

ANSWER EXPLANATIONS

EAS Constructed-Response Scoring Guide

SCORING EXPECTATIONS

The response should meet the stated specific requirements.

The response should demonstrate an understanding of the applicable exhibits.

The response should provide details to support the main themes.

SCORING

4 The response demonstrates a STRONG grasp of the applicable content and skills and always includes all required response elements.

3 The response demonstrates an ACCEPABLE grasp of the applicable content and skills and always includes all required response elements.

2 The response demonstrates a LESS THAN ACCEPTABLE grasp of the applicable content and skills and may not include all required response elements.

1 The response is INCOMPLETE AND/OR OFF TRACK and usually does not include required response elements.

U The response can't be scored because it is off topic, written in a language other than English, or contains too little information to score. Note, a well written but off-topic response will be scored U.

B You did not write anything

1. **(C)** Of all the choices given, this graphic organizer offers the best chance for students to identify the details. The organizer provides a visual way of engaging the students and associating the details with the main point the details support. Note that choice (D) is an excellent approach if the students share a common language, but these students come from Central and South America where there are innumerable tribal languages beyond the predominant languages of Spanish, Portuguese, and Italian.

2. **(B)** This question is straightforward. Look in the "no mastery" column in the Data section and find the skill with the highest percent. The highest percent represents the students who have the furthest to go to move beyond "no mastery." That's choice (B), Theme, with 45% No Mastery.

3. **(D)** The focus of this question is on the lesson, and the most important consideration among those listed is the lesson adaptations Ms. Erino will make.

4. **(A)** The books available to students are the essence of the learning community. Without a range of books at the appropriate reading level that interest students, the learning community will not be effective. Inviting local leaders might or might not increase interest in the learning community, but not in its effectiveness.

5. **(C)** The effectiveness of the approach depends on the accuracy of Ms. Anderson's classification of the students. If the students are not properly "diagnosed," then the wrong approaches for them will be used during the lesson.

6. **(B)** Jacob and Liam were assigned to this bodily-kinesthetic activity because Ms. Anderson classified them as bodily-kinesthetic learners. The idea of Multiple Intelligence theory is to match students learning activities to the students' predominate intelligence.

7. **(A)** This choice is most appropriate because it is directly related to the lesson and gives students an opportunity to learn about the word "corollary" and to identify what about Roosevelt's pronouncement made it a corollary.

8. **(A)** The lesson shows continuity and change of U.S. government policy over a prolonged period of time mentioned in the learning standard. The other choices do not fully integrate all of these factors. The remaining choices are cognitively less challenging.

9. **Example of a response that would likely receive a rating of 3 or 4.**

   Ms. Anderson identified the primary "intelligence" for the five identified students in the class. It is unlikely that these are the sole "intelligences" present in these students. Ms. Anderson should identify other "intelligences" present in these students.

   Ms. Anderson should include appropriate adaptations for these other intelligences in the lesson. For example, if she recognized that Frances also possessed visual-spatial intelligence, she should incorporate Frances's facility with words and languages with visual-spatial approaches.

   There are many benefits to this adaptation, but let me discuss the students identified as bodily-kinesthetic learners. It is fine for them to put on a skit or play, but this does not match well with what might be expected of them in the workplace. There is certainly one other intelligence that applies to these two students, and Ms. Anderson could bring the activities more into the mainstream and strengthen the students' preparedness for the world of work.

   There are many reasons why this approach would be effective. It broadens the range of learning activities available to students based on a more inclusive and comprehensive assessment of students' intelligences. It helps Ms. Anderson account for any errors she may have made in her initial assessment and avoids tying students to a single range of learning.

10. **(C)** The visitor is to be the centerpiece of the lesson, and the best advice for Mr. Lee is to determine how to make best use of the visitor's expertise. That advice is most likely to lay a firm foundation for an effective lesson. The allocation of time in choice (B) is essentially predetermined.

11. **(B)** The aggregate scores of ELL students and students with disabilities differ by a single decile, indicating that, based on this data, these two groups of students are likely to have similar difficulties.

12. **(B)** Note, for the answer to be correct, it must involve both Mr. Lee and the visitor. Discussing effective strategies for the class will help the visitor understand the class dynamics and allow him to adapt his presentation and discussion to meet students' needs.

13. **(A)** There are few better ways to learn about something than to write questions that address the topic. In addition, work with the teacher on question structure helps students develop written English skills.

14. **(D)** The emphasis in the question is on learning, and one of the best ways to learn English is to build on the ELL students' native language. Mikail did not have that learning opportunity until this stage of the lesson. Choices (A) and (C) do present learning opportunities, but they are not as significant an opportunity as choice (D).

15. **(B)** Mikail is likely to develop more quickly than other similar students because we can tell from the reports that he is intelligent and determined, and most particularly from Ms. Fabrione's report, that he is cooperative and focused. These personal traits speak well for Mikail's development. It would be nice if he was free from fear and his parents spoke English, but these factors will not stop Mikail from learning.

16. **(A)** This is a working definition of scaffolding, to provide temporary support when students need that support to learn, and then to withdraw that support when the learning objective has been reached.

17. **(C)** Using a graphic organizer will help Mikail arrange the words on the organizer. The description is deliberately vague in the answer, but an organizer may contain examples and definitions of the words. It is the process of organization that leads to learning. Choice (A) can be effective, but it is not as powerful as choice (C).

18. **(C)** These students already have strong spoken English skills as evidenced by their ability to speak fluently in English with other members of the class. The best approach is to build on these oral English skills to develop reading skills.

19. **(A)** While it may be ideal to use English, ELL students can use their native language to understand assignments and ask clarifying questions of each other that will ultimately lead to more learning. In this way, the second language is a strength that can be an appropriate part of classroom instruction.

20. **(B)** The percent differences are so small that the only reasonable conclusion is that they performed at about the same level on the assessment. That does not mean that performance on individual tasks is the same for each student. The assessment just gives us an average of the various components that make up the assessment.

21. **(B)** Working with a partner who speaks the same foreign language is one of the most powerful approaches to working with ELL students. Students can help each other clarify the meaning of words, while having a common language to fall back on to discuss ideas not available to them in English.

22. **Example of a response that would likely receive a rating of 3 or 4.**

Mr. Longin must overcome the main issue: the parents do not speak English, and he does not speak their language. Under those circumstances no discussion is possible, and Mr. Longin will never be successful. The first obvious step is to have an interpreter present, preferably a teacher from the school who is familiar with the assessment. The interpreter should give a verbatim interpretation of the conversation and not add any of the interpreter's own thoughts and ideas.

Once the interpreter is available, Mr. Longin can explain to the parents that the performance level is just a reflection of how long the students have been speaking English and not their performance in class or their ability. He can explain that as the students are in the country longer, their level will naturally improve.

This is a very difficult situation, and these two students have quite a long way to go. There are no great answers for the parents, who have many things to worry about other than their children's performance in school. However, the approach does address the issues that Mr. Longin has control over. It removes the language communication barrier, gives an honest explanation of the scores, provides a little reassurance to the parents, and may reduce some of the parents' concerns. Mr. Longin should also emphasize the progress the students are making.

23. **(B)** Ms. Bora is with these students every day and is in the best position to observe their English language proficiency. Students do not always reveal their actual ability on a test, which is why further corroboration of test results is appropriate.

24. **(C)** The choice does not specify the form of the graphic organizer. However, presenting a graphic organizer in the form of a table on which students can enter the number of the voyage in one column and some details of the voyage in another column is the most effective choice among those given.

25. **(B)** We should not wait for Mei Ling's English to improve before exposing her to a more rigorous science curriculum. Among all subjects, students with science and math backgrounds frequently have the best employment opportunities, and advancement in this area should not be denied to her because of her limited English proficiency.

26. **(C)** The dangers of the Internet cannot be overstated, and Internet safety is the most important concern for every teacher who uses the Internet in the classroom. Most school districts block sites; however, it is still possible for these usually knowledgeable students to access sites with inappropriate images or messages, or even worse, sites that enable students to communicate with others on the Internet.

27. **(C)** TBI students need a regular and consistent schedule when in school—not the undefined schedule described in this choice. All of the other choices describe appropriate responses to TBI students.

28. **(B)** In both examples, Maureen multiplies the power of a number (exponent) by the number itself (base), showing that she does not know the meaning of exponents. By contrast, Jacob's answers are both correct, showing that he understands the meaning of exponents.

29. **(B)** This is the only answer choice that addresses teaching powers of 10 to Maureen. ADD students learn from observing patterns. The other choices do not address teaching powers of 10.

30. **(C)** New York Education Law 305.42 enacted the "concussion management and awareness act," which, among other things, requires an information pamphlet on mild traumatic brain injuries to be distributed to parents of pupils participating in interscholastic sports, or students who have suffered a mild TBI.

31. **(B)** A student's native language is a powerful route to mastering English, and the glossary is an effective tool. Using the glossary in a small group would foster discussion and the interchange of ideas and lead to further language development.

32. **(B)** There are no guarantees. However, this technique, proposed by Dreikurs and others, has the best chance of addressing Rodney's problems in the classroom. It will make Rodney more aware of his behavior and place a fixed limit on those behaviors.

Choices (A) and (C) do not address his behavior in the classroom, and putting Rodney in the back of the room will just make him feel more isolated and likely make things worse.

33. **(B)** Lena's learning disability likely includes difficulty telling left from right, and she may have problems with spatial awareness. LD students typically master concepts related to spatial orientation through activities that involve bodily movement.

34. **(A)** This choice accurately describes the legal intent of a Functional Behavioral Assessment (FBA). The outcomes in other choices may occur; however, the FBA always results in the outcomes described in choice (A).

35. **Example of a response that would likely receive a rating of 3.**

Rodney has difficulty focusing, and the active and involved nature of this plan will cause him difficulty. The notes indicate that he has the most trouble when he feels he is falling behind, and the rather complex ideas of clockwise and counterclockwise, particularly drawing lines that represent these movements, will be particularly challenging for Rodney. It is unlikely that Rodney will successfully complete the drawing activities.

The adaptation should enable Rodney to experience the activities, but relieve him of the direct responsibility for drawing the lines. He should be paired with a more able student in the class and observe that student completing the line-drawing activities. Care should be taken to pair him with a student who is most likely to tolerate his bothersome behavior. He can participate as much as he can, but full participation should not be expected.

This is the most practical way to adapt the lesson for Rodney, while still trying to maintain his involvement in the class. Rodney is likely to experience working with another student as a way to gain attention. That sense, combined with his ability to participate in the lesson with a minimum of frustration, should give Rodney the best opportunity to learn.

36. **(A)** The law clearly states that generally each minor child must attend school, and it is the teacher's responsibility to maintain attendance records.

37. **(B)** Research shows that, more than any other factor, student success increases when they spend more time on task. Choices (A), (C), and (D) are incorrect. These choices can be effective techniques, but are not as important as time spent on task.

38. **(A)** Authentic assessment means a teacher observes students as they work and reviews their work product. Portfolio assessment is a form of authentic assessment. Choices (B), (C), and (D) are incorrect. These choices do not describe authentic assessment.

39. **(D)** Note the word NOT in the item. In cooperative learning, students summarize the results of their cooperative work. Choices (A), (B), and (C) are incorrect. All of these choices are characteristics of cooperative learning groups.

40. **(C)** A constructivist approach encourages students to construct their own understanding of concepts. One way students do this is to build on their initial responses. Choice (A) is not correct. A more reflective approach to questions is in keeping with the constructivist approach. Choice (B) is not correct. This is not the kind of construction that constructivists have in mind. Choice (D) is not correct. The constructivist approach encourages students to create metaphors.

41. **(C)** New York State law does not require any specific credentials for those who provide home instruction.

42. **(B)** This is the best response. It is positive and truthful, but it neither holds out too much hope nor is too negative. (A) is incorrect because this choice is too positive and unrealistically raises a parent's expectations. (C) is incorrect because, while this response is likely the most candid, it is too stark and not the kind of response that should be given at a parent-teacher conference. (D) is incorrect because this response unnecessarily puts the parents off.

43. **(B)** The newsletter helps the parents and guardians feel more connected to the classroom and makes the teacher more available to parents. This combination improves home-school communication. None of the other choices addresses improving communication.

44. **(A)** This choice is the best among those offered because it gives every parent or guardian an opportunity to become involved in the school. The other choices offer promise, but none is as comprehensive as choice (A). Note that there may be better strategies; however, we are limited to the best answer among the given choices.

45. **(A)** This choice alone directly involves the parents/guardians in their children's educational choices and helps ensure full parental awareness. The remaining choices may be helpful; however, none of them includes the wide dissemination of educational choice information found in (A).

SECTION III
Academic Literacy Skills Test (ALST)

Preparing for the Academic Literacy Skills Test (ALST)   5

The ALST is really two separate tests, reading and constructed response (writing), in which most points are assigned to the second constructed-response test. Most students say to complete the constructed response first.

Selected Response Reading Comprehension
The first part is a reading comprehension test consisting of five passages of about 900 to 1,000 words each. Each passage is followed by eight selected-response items for a total of forty items. These forty selected-response items contribute 40% to your score.

Selected-response items often show the portion of the passage you will use to select your answer.

The best strategy is to NOT read the passages. Skim the passage to get an idea of the content, and then go to the items and find the answers to the items in the passage.

Writing from Sources
The second part of the test consists of three exhibits: two fairly complex passages that present contrasting views of a common topic and a graphic related to the topic. The difficulty of the passages and the type of graphic varies.

Focused Constructed Response
The two focused constructed-response items ask you to write about specific questions, first relying on the two passages, and then relying on the two passages and the graphic. The emphasis is on drawing information from these three sources as you write your response. Each focused-response item contributes 15% to your score.

Extended Constructed Response
The extended response (essay) asks you to write a 400- to 600-word persuasive response in favor of or in opposition to a position related to the topic. The assignment gives specific guidance about what the extended response should include. The important features of this response are to stake out a clear point of view, defend it using information from each of the three exhibits, and present and refute a position contrary to the position you take. The extended response contributes 30% to your score.

SCORES

In the school year ending June 2014, the state average ALST score was 526, lower than the statewide average EAS score. ALST passing scores below 563 are classified Level 1, while scores 563 and above are classified as Mastery. Less than 10% of the statewide scores were at the Mastery level. It is not clear whether this dual classification will be meaningful.

USING THIS CHAPTER

The ALST is a writing and reading test, with emphasis on writing. This chapter contains a writing review with sample ALST constructed-response prompts and sample responses, and a reading test-taking practice section with a sample ALST passage, items, and explained answers.

We recommend that you complete the Reading Test-Taking Review until you get the rhythm of answering selected-response reading comprehension items. You should complete the practice ALST reading passage test items and review the answers.

ALST selected-response items very often show the portion of the passage you will use to select your answer. That means your answers will most often be based on a shorter passage.

WRITING REVIEW

USING THIS SECTION

This chapter prepares you to take the multiple-choice writing section and the essay sections of the computer-delivered test. You may want to find an English professor, teacher, or tutor to mark the written portion of the tests.

- **I WANT WRITING HELP.** Complete the Writing review.
- **I WANT TO PRACTICE A FEW CONSTRUCTIVE RESPONSE ITEMS (PAGE 141).** Complete the Writing to Sources Practice at the end of the section.

RATING RESPONSES

Each response is graded holistically by two raters, using two different 4-point scales described on pages 141 and 142. Holistic rating means that the raters base the scores on their informed sense of your response and the elements it contains, not on a detailed analysis of the essay.

In practice, a rater often assigns an essay to top or bottom. Then the rater decides which of the two scores in each half to assign to that essay. If the scores assigned to a response differ by one point or more, the response is resubmitted for further review.

Rating is not an exact science, and it is not unusual for raters to differ by 1 point. That is a bigger difference than you might think because a rating of 3 with a 1-point difference could be a rating of a 2 or 4. That range represents 75 percent of the available scores. This just emphasizes how important it is to focus your efforts on making it easy for a rater to give you a high score.

The rating scales for each essay type are given on pages 141 and 142.

This review section targets the skills and concepts you need to know in order to write effective ALST responses.

HOW TO USE NOUNS AND VERBS

Every sentence has a subject and a predicate. Most sentences are statements. The sentence usually names something (subject). Then the sentence describes the subject or tells what that subject is doing (predicate). Sentences that ask questions also have a subject and a predicate. Here are some examples.

Subject	Predicate
The car	moved.
The tree	grew.
The street	was dark.
The forest	teemed with plants of every type and size.

Many subjects are nouns. Every predicate has a verb. A list of the nouns and verbs from the preceding sentences follows.

Noun	Verb
car	moved
tree	grew
street	was
forest, plants	teemed

Nouns

Nouns name a person, place, thing, characteristic, or concept. Nouns give a name to everything that is, has been, or will be. Here are some simple examples.

Person	Place	Thing	Characteristic	Concept (Idea)
Abe Lincoln	Lincoln Memorial	beard	mystery	freedom
judge	courthouse	gavel	fairness	justice
professor	college	chalkboard	intelligence	number

SINGULAR AND PLURAL NOUNS

Singular nouns refer to only one thing. Plural nouns refer to more than one thing. Plurals are usually formed by adding an *s* or dropping a *y* and adding *ies*. Here are some examples.

Singular	Plural
college	colleges
professor	professors
Lincoln Memorial	Lincoln Memorials
mystery	mysteries

POSSESSIVE NOUNS

Possessive nouns show that the noun possesses a thing or a characteristic. Make a singular noun possessive by adding *'s*. Here are some examples.

> The *child's* sled was in the garage ready for use.
> The *school's* mascot was loose again.
>
> The rain interfered with *Jane's* vacation.
>
> *Ron's* and *Doug's* fathers were born in the same year.
> Ron and *Doug's* teacher kept them after school.

Make a singular noun ending in *s* possessive by adding *'s* unless the pronunciation is too difficult.

> The teacher read *James's* paper several times.
> The angler grabbed the *bass'* fin.

Make a plural noun possessive by adding an apostrophe (') only.

> The *principals'* meeting was delayed.
> The report indicated that *students'* scores had declined.

Verbs

Some verbs are action verbs. Other verbs are linking verbs that link the subject to words that describe it. Here are some examples.

Action Verbs	Linking Verbs
Blaire *runs* down the street.	Blaire *is* tired.
Blaire *told* her story.	The class *was* bored.
The crowd *roared*.	The players *were* inspired.
The old ship *rusted*.	It *had been* a proud ship.

TENSE

A verb has three principal tenses: present tense, past tense, and future tense. The present tense shows that the action is happening now. The past tense shows that the action happened in the past. The future tense shows that something will happen. Here are some examples.

Present:	I *enjoy* my time off.
Past:	I *enjoyed* my time off.
Future:	I *will enjoy* my time off.
Present:	I *hate* working late.
Past:	I *hated* working late.
Future:	I *will hate* working late.

REGULAR AND IRREGULAR VERBS

Regular verbs follow the consistent pattern noted previously. However, a number of verbs are irregular. Irregular verbs have their own unique forms for each tense. A partial list of irregular verbs follows. The past participle is usually preceded by *had, has,* or *have.*

Some Irregular Verbs

Present Tense	Past Tense	Past Participle
am, is, are	was, were	been
begin	began	begun
break	broke	broken
bring	brought	brought
catch	caught	caught
choose	chose	chosen
come	came	come
do	did	done
eat	ate	eaten
give	gave	given
go	went	gone
grow	grew	grown
know	knew	known
lie	lay	lain
lay	laid	laid
raise	raised	raised
ride	rode	ridden
see	saw	seen
set	set	set
sit	sat	sat
speak	spoke	spoken
take	took	taken
tear	tore	torn
throw	threw	thrown
write	wrote	written

TENSE SHIFT

Verbs in a sentence should reflect time sequence. If the actions represented by the verbs happened at the same time, the verbs should have the same tense.

Incorrect:	Beth sits in the boat while she wore a life jacket.
Correct:	Beth sits in the boat while she wears a life jacket. [Both verbs are present tense.]
Correct:	Beth sat in the boat while she wore a life jacket. [Both verbs are past tense.]
Correct:	Beth wears the life jacket she wore last week. [The verbs show time order.]

HOW TO USE PRONOUNS

Pronouns take the place of nouns or noun phrases and help avoid constant repetition of the noun or phrase. Here is an example.

Blaire is in law school. *She* studies in *her* room every day.
[The pronouns *she* and *her* refer to the noun *Blaire*.]

Pronoun Cases

Pronouns take three case forms: subjective, objective, and possessive. The personal pronouns *I, he, she, it, we, they, you* refer to an individual or individuals. The relative pronoun *who* refers to these personal pronouns as well as to an individual or individuals. These pronouns change their case form depending on their use in the sentence.

SUBJECTIVE PRONOUNS: I, WE, HE, IT, SHE, THEY, WHO, YOU

Use the subjective form if the pronoun is, or refers to, the subject of a clause or sentence.

> *He* and *I* studied for the Core.
>
> The proctors for the test were *she* and *I.*
> [*She* and *I* refer to the subject *proctors*.]
>
> She is the woman *who* answered every question correctly.
>
> I do not expect to do as well as *she.*
> [*She* is the subject for the understood verb *does*.]

OBJECTIVE PRONOUNS: ME, US, HIM, IT, HER, THEM, WHOM, YOU

Use the objective form if the pronoun is the object of a verb or preposition.

> Cathy helps both *him* and *me.*
>
> She wanted *them* to pass.
>
> I do not know *whom* she helped most.

POSSESSIVE PRONOUNS: MY, OUR, HIS, ITS, HER, THEIR, WHOSE, YOUR

Use the objective form if the pronoun shows possession.

> I recommended they reduce the time they study with *their* friends.
>
> He was the person *whose* help they relied on.

Clear Reference

The pronoun must clearly refer to a particular noun or noun phrase. Here are some examples.

Unclear

> Quinn and Blaire took turns feeding *her* cat.
> [We can't tell which person *her* refers to. Blaire is involved but we do not know it is her cat.]
>
> Quinn gave *it* to Blaire.
> [The pronoun *it* refers to a noun that is not stated.]

Clear

> Quinn and Blaire took turns feeding Blaire's cat.
> [A pronoun doesn't work here. Use a noun.]
>
> Quinn got the book and gave it to Blaire.
> [The pronoun works once the noun is stated.]

Agreement

Each pronoun must agree in number (singular or plural) and gender (male or female) with the noun it refers to. Here are some examples.

Nonagreement in Number

The children played all day, and *she* came in exhausted.
[*Children* is plural, but *she* is singular.]

The child picked up the hat and brought *them* into the house.
[*Hat* is singular, but *them* is plural.]

Agreement

The children played all day, and *they* came in exhausted.

The child picked up the hat and brought *it* into the house.

Nonagreement in Gender

The lioness picked up *his* cub.
[*Lioness* is female, and *his* is male.]

A child must bring in a doctor's note before *she* comes to school.
[The child may be a male or female but *she* is female.]

Agreement

The lioness picked up *her* cub.

A child must bring in a doctor's note before *he* or *she* comes to school.

FOCUS ON SUBJECT-VERB AGREEMENT

Singular and Plural

Singular nouns take singular verbs. Plural nouns take plural verbs. Singular verbs usually end in *s*, and plural verbs usually do not. Here are some examples.

Singular: My father wants me home early.
Plural: My parents want me home early.

Singular: Ryan runs a mile each day.
Plural: Ryan and Chad run a mile each day.

Singular: She tries her best to do a good job.
Plural: Liz and Ann try their best to do a good job.

Correctly Use Subject and Verb

The subject may not be in front of the verb. In fact, the subject may not be anywhere near the verb. Say the subject and the verb to yourself. If it makes sense, you probably have it right.

Words may come between the subject and the verb.

Chad's final exam score, which he showed to his mother, improved his final grade.

The verb is *improved*. The word *mother* appears just before *improved*.

Is this the subject? Say it to yourself. [Mother improved the grade.]

That cannot be right. *Score* must be the subject. Say it to yourself. **[Score improved the grade.]** That is right. *Score* is the subject, and *improved* is the verb.

The racer running with a sore arm finished first.

Say it to yourself. **[Racer finished first.]** *Racer* is the noun, and *finished* is the verb.

It would not make any sense to say the arm finished first.

The verb may come before the subject.

Over the river and through the woods romps the merry leprechaun.

Leprechaun is the subject, and *romps* is the verb. **[Think: Leprechaun romps.]**

Where are the car keys?

Keys is the subject, and *are* is the verb. **[Think: The car keys are where?]**

Examples of Subject-Verb Agreement

Words such as *each, neither, everyone, nobody, someone,* and *anyone* are singular pronouns. They always take a singular verb.

Everyone needs a good laugh now and then.
Nobody knows more about computers than Bob.

Words that refer to number such as *one-half, any, most,* and *some* can be singular or plural.

One-fifth of the students were absent. [*Students* is plural.]
One-fifth of the cake was eaten. [There is only one cake.]

HOW TO USE ADJECTIVES AND ADVERBS

Adjectives

Adjectives modify nouns and pronouns. Adjectives add detail and clarify nouns and pronouns. Frequently, adjectives come immediately before the nouns or pronouns they are modifying. At other times, the nouns or pronouns come first and are connected directly to the adjectives by linking verbs. Here are some examples.

Direct	**With a Linking Verb**
That is a *large* dog.	That dog is *large*.
He's an *angry* man.	The man seems *angry*.

Adverbs

Adverbs are often formed by adding *ly* to an adjective. However, many adverbs do not end in *ly* (e.g., *always*). Adverbs modify verbs, adjectives, and adverbs. Adverbs can also modify phrases, clauses, and sentences. Here are some examples.

Modify verb:	Ryan *quickly* sought a solution.
Modify adjective:	That is an *exceedingly* large dog.
Modify adverb:	Lisa told her story *quite* truthfully.
Modify sentence:	*Unfortunately*, all good things must end.
Modify phrase:	The instructor arrived *just* in time to start the class.

AVOIDING ADJECTIVE AND ADVERB ERRORS

- Do not use adjectives in place of adverbs.

Correct	**Incorrect**
Lynne read the book quickly.	Lynne read the book quick.
Stan finished his work easily.	Stan finished his work easy.

- Do not confuse the adjectives *good* and *bad* with the adverbs *well* and *badly.*

Correct	**Incorrect**
Adverbs	
She wanted to play the piano well.	She wanted to play the piano good.
Bob sang badly.	Bob sang bad.
Adjectives	
The food tastes good.	The food tastes well.
The food tastes bad.	The food tastes badly.

- Do not confuse the adjectives *real* and *sure* with the adverbs *really* and *surely.*

Correct	**Incorrect**
Chuck played really well.	Chuck played real well.
He was surely correct.	He was sure correct.

Comparison

Adjectives and adverbs can show comparisons. Avoid clumsy modifiers.

Correct	**Incorrect**
Jim is more clingy than Ray.	Jim is clingier than Ray.
Ray is much taller than Jim.	Ray is more taller than Jim.
Jim is more interesting than Ray.	Jim is interesting than Ray.
Ray is happier than Jim.	Ray is more happy than Jim.

Use word comparisons carefully to be sure that the comparison is clear.

Unclear:	Chad lives closer to Ryan than Blaire.
Clear:	Chad lives closer to Ryan than Blaire does.
Clear:	Chad lives closer to Ryan than he does to Blaire.
Unclear:	The bus engines are bigger than cars.
Clear:	The bus engines are bigger than cars' engines.

AVOID MISPLACED AND DANGLING MODIFIERS

Modifiers may be words or groups of words. Modifiers change or qualify the meaning of another word or group of words. Modifiers belong near the words they modify.

Misplaced modifiers appear to modify words in a way that does not make sense.

The modifier in the following sentence is *in a large box*. It does not make sense for *in a large box* to modify *house*. Move the modifier near *pizza* where it belongs.

Misplaced:	Les delivered pizza to the house in a large box.
Revised:	Les delivered pizza in a large box to the house.

The modifier in the next sentence is *paid well*. *Paid well* can't modify *city*. Move it next to *the job* where it belongs.

Misplaced:	Gail wanted the job in the city that paid well.
Revised:	Gail wanted the well-paying job in the city.

Dangling modifiers modify words not present in the sentence. The modifier in the following sentence is *waiting for the concert to begin*.

This modifier describes the audience, but audience is not mentioned in the sentence. The modifier is left dangling with nothing to describe.

Dangling:	Waiting for the concert to begin, the chanting started.
Revised:	Waiting for the concert to begin, the audience began chanting.
Revised:	The audience began chanting while waiting for the concert to begin.

The modifier in the next sentence is *after three weeks in the country*. The modifier describes the person, not the license. But the person is not mentioned in the sentence. The modifier is dangling.

Dangling:	After three weeks in the country, the license was revoked.
Revised:	After he was in the country for three weeks, his license was revoked.
Revised:	His license was revoked after he was in the country three weeks.

AVOID COMMA SPLICES AND RUN-ON SENTENCES

An *independent clause* is a clause that could be a sentence.

Independent clauses should be joined by a semicolon, or by a comma and a conjunction.

A *comma splice* consists of two independent clauses joined by just a comma.

A *run-on* sentence consists of two independent clauses incorrectly joined.

Correct:	The whole family went on vacation; the parents took turns driving. [Two independent clauses are joined by a semicolon.]
	The whole family went on vacation, and the parents took turns driving. [Two independent clauses are joined by a comma and a conjunction.]
Incorrect:	The whole family went on vacation, the parents took turns driving. [Comma splice. Two independent clauses are joined by just a comma.]
	The whole family went on vacation the parents took turns driving. [Run-on sentence. Two independent clauses are incorrectly joined.]

AVOID SENTENCE FRAGMENTS

English sentences require a subject and a predicate (see page 129). Fragments are parts of sentences written as though they were sentences. Fragments are writing mistakes that lack a subject, a predicate, or both subject and predicate. Here are some examples.

> Since when.
> To enjoy the summer months.
> Because he isn't working hard.
> If you can fix old cars.
> What the principal wanted to hear.

Include a subject and/or a verb to rewrite a fragment as a sentence.

Fragment	Sentence
Should be coming up the driveway now.	The *car* should be coming up the driveway now.
Both the lawyer and her client.	Both the lawyer and her client *waited* in court.
Which is my favorite subject.	*I took math*, which is my favorite subject.
If you can play.	If you can play, *you'll improve with* practice.

Verbs such as *to be, to go, winning, starring,* etc., need a main verb.

Fragment	Sentence
The new rules to go into effect in April.	The new rules *will* go into effect in April.
The team winning every game.	The team *was* winning every game.

Often, a fragment is related to a complete sentence. Combine the two to make a single sentence.

Fragment:	Reni loved vegetables. *Particularly corn, celery, lettuce, squash, and eggplant.*
Revised:	Reni loved vegetables, particularly corn, celery, lettuce, squash, and eggplant.
Fragment:	*To see people standing on Mars.* This could happen in the twenty-first century.
Revised:	To see people standing on Mars is one of the things that could happen in the twenty-first century.

Sometimes short fragments can be used for emphasis. However, you should not use fragments in your essay. Here are some examples.

> *Stop!* Do not take one more step toward that apple pie.
> I need some time to myself. *That's why.*

USE PARALLEL FORM

When two or more ideas are connected, use a parallel structure. Parallelism helps the reader follow the passage more clearly. Here are some examples.

Not Parallel: Toni stayed in shape by eating right and exercising daily.

Parallel: Toni stayed in shape by eating right and *by* exercising daily.

Not Parallel: Lisa is a student who works hard and has genuine insight.

Parallel: Lisa is a student who works hard and *who* has genuine insight.

Not Parallel: Art had a choice either to clean his room or take out the garbage.

Parallel: Art had a choice either to clean his room or *to* take out the garbage.

Not Parallel: Derek wanted a success rather than failing.

Parallel: Derek wanted a success rather than a failure.

Parallel: Derek wanted success rather than failure.

WATCH YOUR DICTION

Diction is choosing and using appropriate words. Good diction conveys a thought clearly without unnecessary words. Good diction develops fully over a number of years; however, there are some rules and tips you can follow.

Do not use slang, colloquialisms, or other non-standard English.
One person's slang is another person's confusion. Slang is often regional, and slang meanings change rapidly. We do not give examples of slang here for that very reason. Do not use slang words in your formal writing.

Colloquialisms are words used frequently in spoken language. This informal use of terms such as *dog tired*, *kids*, and *hanging around* is not generally accepted in formal writing. Save these informal terms for daily speech and omit or remove them from your writing except as quotations.

Omit any other non-standard English. Always choose standard English terms that accurately reflect the thought to be conveyed.

AVOID WORDY, REDUNDANT, OR PRETENTIOUS WRITING

Good writing is clear and economical.

Wordy: I chose my career as a teacher because of its high ideals, the truly self-sacrificing idealism of a career in teaching, and for the purpose of receiving the myriad and cascading recognition that one can receive from the community as a whole and from its constituents.

Revised: I chose a career in teaching for its high ideals and for community recognition.

Given below is a partial list of wordy phrases and the replacement word.

Wordy Phrases and Replacements

at the present time	now	because of the fact that	because
for the purpose of	for	in the final analysis	finally
in the event that	if	until such time as	until

HOW TO USE PUNCTUATION

The Comma (,)

The comma may be the most used punctuation mark. This section details a few of these uses.

A clause is part of a sentence that could be a sentence itself. If a clause begins with a conjunction, use a comma before the conjunction.

Incorrect:	I was satisfied with the food but John was grumbling.
Correct:	I was satisfied with the food, but John was grumbling.

Incorrect:	Larry was going fishing or he was going to paint his house.
Correct:	Larry was going fishing, or he was going to paint his house.

A clause or a phrase often introduces a sentence. Introductory phrases or clauses should be set off by a comma. If the introductory element is very short, the comma is optional. Here are some examples.

However, there are other options you may want to consider.

When the deicer hit the plane's wing, the ice began to melt.

To get a driver's license, go to the motor vehicle bureau.

It doesn't matter what you want, you have to take what you get.

Parenthetical expressions interrupt the flow of a sentence. Set off the parenthetical expression with commas. Do not set off expressions that are essential to understanding the sentence. Here are some examples.

Tom, an old friend, showed up at my house the other day.

I was traveling on a train, in car 8200, on my way to Florida.

John and Ron, who are seniors, went on break to Florida.
[Use a comma. The phrase "who are seniors" is extra information.]

All the students who are seniors take an additional course.
[Do not use a comma. The phrase "who are seniors" is essential information.]

Commas are used to set off items in a list or series. Here are some examples.

Jed is interested in computers, surfing, and fishing.
[Notice the comma before the conjunction *and*.]

Mario drives a fast, red car.
[The sentence would make sense with *and* in place of the comma.]

Andy hoped for a bright, sunny, balmy day.
[The sentence would make sense with *and* in place of the commas.]

Lucy had a pale green dress.
[The sentence would not make sense with *and*. The word *pale* modifies *green*. Do not use a comma.]

Randy will go to the movies, pick up some groceries, and then go home.

Semicolon and Colon

THE SEMICOLON (;)

Use the semicolon to connect main clauses not connected by a conjunction. Include a semi-colon with very long clauses connected by a conjunction. Here are some examples.

> The puck was dropped; the hockey game began.
>
> The puck was dropped, and the hockey game began.
>
> The general manager of the hockey team was not sure what should be done about the player who was injured during the game; but he did know that the player's contract stipulated that his pay would continue whether he was able to play or not.

THE COLON (:)

Use the colon after a main clause to introduce a list. Here are some examples.

> Liz kept these items in her car: spare tire, jack, flares, and a blanket.
>
> Liz kept a spare tire, jack, flares, and a blanket in her car.

Period, Question Mark, Exclamation Point

THE PERIOD (.)

Use a period to end every sentence, unless the sentence is a direct question, a strong command, or an interjection.

> You will do well on the ALST.

THE QUESTION MARK (?)

Use a question mark to end every sentence that is a direct question.

> What is the passing score for the ALST?

THE EXCLAMATION POINT (!)

Use an exclamation point to end every sentence that is a strong command or interjection. Do not overuse exclamation points.

> Interjection: Pass that test!
>
> Command: Avalanche, head for cover!

Focused Response and Extended Response

This practice includes one focused response and one extended response.

You will see three exhibits. Two of the exhibits are original passages (shortened here) with differing views on a common topic. Note, the passages are shown exactly as they appear in the original.

The third exhibit is a graphic with information related to the topic.

Focused responses are 100 to 200 words each.

The extended response is 400 to 600 words and fully addresses a question or proposal related to the topic.

Use a word processor with the spell check and grammar check disabled to write your responses.

Plan before you write and do not rely on any outside sources.

Focused-Response Rating Scale

FOCUSED-RESPONSE CHARACTERISTICS

Focused responses are usually 100 to 200 words, but a minimum of 150 words should be your goal.

The content of your response meets the requirements found in the prompt.

Show evidence of engagement with the prompt's exhibits.

Present a clear and coherent response.

4 Your focused response demonstrates a STRONG grasp of the writing skills and meets all the stated requirements of the focused-response prompt, including a reference to the graphic.

3 Your focused response demonstrates a SATISFACTORY grasp of the writing skills and completely meets most of the stated requirements of the focused-response prompt.

2 Your focused response demonstrates a LIMITED grasp of the writing skills and completely meets few of the stated requirements of the focused-response prompt.

1 Your focused response demonstrates NO grasp of the writing skills and generally does not meet the stated requirements of the focused-response prompt.

U Your focused response cannot be scored because it is off topic, too short to score, or written in a language other than English. Even a well-written response that is off topic will be scored "U."

B You did not write a focused response

Extended-Response Rating Scale

EXTENDED-RESPONSE EXPECTATIONS

Extended responses must be 400 to 600 words; however, a minimum of 525 words should be your goal.

Clearly communicate complex concepts and ideas in the context of the exhibits.

Demonstrate that you have command of the evidence in the passages and the graphic.

Organize complex ideas and write in a formal style with excellent word choice.

Employ the standards of written English grammar, usage, and punctuation.

4 Your extended response demonstrates a STRONG grasp of the writing skills and meets all the stated requirements of the extended-response prompt, including a reference to the graphic.

3 Your extended response demonstrates a SATISFACTORY grasp of the writing skills and completely meets most of the stated requirements of the extended-response prompt.

2 Your extended response demonstrates a LIMITED grasp of the writing skills and completely meets few of the stated requirements of the extended-response prompt.

1 Your extended response demonstrates NO grasp of the writing skills and generally does not meet the stated requirements of the extended-response prompt.

U Your extended response cannot be scored because it is off topic, too short to score, or written in a language other than English. Even a well-written response that is off topic will be scored "U."

B You did not write an extended response.

Topic: Nuclear Energy

PASSAGE A

Nuclear Energy . . . The Best Road to Energy Independence Quinson web access 10/12/2014
You have heard about problems with nuclear energy from older reactors. What you may not have heard is that it is the most efficient way of using renewable energy to create electricity. It is better than coal, which is still the main way electricity is produced, and it is better than oil or gas or any other non-renewable energy source. You have heard a lot about solar power but the truth is solar power will not be a commercially viable energy source in this century.

Nuclear power has caused fewer fatalities per unit of energy generated. Nuclear energy produces no greenhouse gases and does not pollute the environment. The new reactors put into service are much safer than the reactors built 50 years ago, and many of those older reactors have already been retired. I am very comfortable living just miles from a reactor that has been safely providing energy to this community for decades with no problems. Most of the world's power is generated by coal. With nuclear power there are no smokestacks, no trains hauling in coal, and no huge pipeline delivering gas or oil. In truth, the air here is cleaner than most of the United States because coal used to create electricity in most places is simply not used. Beyond that there are over 150 naval vessels propelled by nuclear power, vessels which never have to be refueled at sea and never have to come into port for fuel. That's the benefit of an energy source that does not have to constantly be renewed.

I want to close this brief paper by mentioning the Fukushima Daiichi nuclear reactor accident in 2011, associated with a tsunami. The universal assessment of this tragedy is that it was essentially man made. That is, all investigations agree that the reactor should never have been built where it was, and that a reactor like that one over 50 years old should already have been retired. About 20,000 people were killed by the tsunami and its aftermath. There will undoubtedly be some after effects, but not at the level of the number of people killed in the tsunami. Using this accident to argue against nuclear power production is a failed argument.

PASSAGE B

Nuclear Energy: A Ticking Atom Bomb Patrick Web Access 9/28/2014

Nuclear energy is not all bad, and only 6% of the world's power and 15% of the electricity is generated by nuclear reactors. I can think of some specific situations when it might be appropriate. A ship at sea might be one of them, or perhaps a tiny reactor at some remote location away from a populated area, and where the earthquake and tornado risks were close to zero. But that's about it.

A large reactor built anywhere else is nothing more than a ticking bomb—a nuclear bomb. There have been three major accidents in the last 25 years and the number of nuclear reactors is steadily increasing. No one really knows the death toll from these accidents, and the long term impact of radiation exposure, but the toll will be in the many tens of thousands, with many more impairments and diseases. And that's the problem with radiation—you often don't see most of the impact for decades. Just to understand the real safety issue consider if someone blew up a coal generating power plant or a nuclear generating plant. Neither is good, but the impact of a destroyed nuclear plant would be devastation. Millions might be killed and thousands of square miles of land made barren for a century. And all that danger for a power system that serves a tiny portion of electric users.

We don't even have to look at the serious safety issues to question nuclear power. Recently former members of the agency that regulates the nuclear industry has said that nuclear energy is simply not economically viable. They point out that solar energy could fill the void that would be left by the absence of nuclear power. It's just a fact that solar energy could never fill a void left if coal and gas were not available to produce energy. So I guess there is a choice, but I'll take the choice that will not lead to the death of millions.

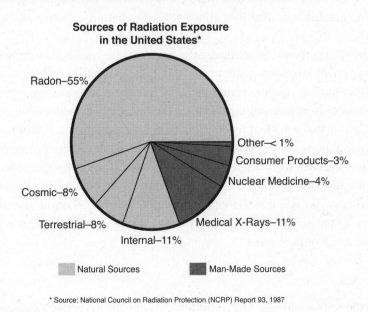

Sources of Radiation Exposure in the United States*

Radon—55%
Other—< 1%
Consumer Products—3%
Nuclear Medicine—4%
Cosmic—8%
Medical X-Rays—11%
Terrestrial—8%
Internal—11%

Natural Sources   Man-Made Sources

* Source: National Council on Radiation Protection (NCRP) Report 93, 1987

Assignment 1: Focused-Response Example

Use passages A and B as you write your response to this assignment.

In about 100 to 200 words, review each passage and compare and contrast the views each takes about nuclear energy. To receive a high score, your response should

- review the claims found in each position paper and explain the contrasting views of nuclear energy;
- contribute to the presentation and make use of evidence;
- include examples from each passage to support your response; and
- represent a first draft for a group of educated adults.

Extended-Response Example

Write in support of or in opposition to this question:

Should steps be taken to make unlawful the construction of additional nuclear power plants in the United States?

Demonstrate that you understand the topic.

Use logical reasoning to expand and extend the points made in the passages.

Provide evidence from both sources to support your claim.

Present and refute a counterclaim. You will certainly want to write 500 to 600 words. Longer responses tend to receive higher scores.

Sample Responses

FOCUSED RESPONSE

This 212-word sample focused response would receive a 4, or possibly a 3.
The authors agree that a strength of nuclear energy is that it is a renewable energy source with low greenhouse gas emissions and that there are health risks associated with nuclear power generation. The graphic indicates that about 18% of radiation exposure comes from "man made" sources.

However, the Quinson seeks to minimize the risks, noting that, "Nuclear power has caused fewer fatalities per unit of energy generated." I don't find that particularly reassuring because Patrick notes that nuclear reactors generates just 6% of the world's energy. Patrick goes on to take a more ominous tone pointing out the three major nuclear accidents that occurred in the last 25 years, writing that a nuclear reactor "is a ticking time bomb—a nuclear bomb."

Each author mentions using coal for power generation. Quinson does point out that coal is far and away the fuel used most often to produce power. Patrick notes that solar power could fill the void left by the absence of nuclear energy but never the void left by the absence of coal.

Quinson brings in an additional point that there are "over 150 naval vessels powered by nuclear energy." Quite unusually, it seems to me, Patrick also believes a "ship at sea" might be an appropriate use of nuclear power.

Discussion

This constructed response meets both requirements needed to receive a high score. It is also of sufficient length to receive a high score. This response summarizes each position paper's point of view and compares and contrasts information from both passages. The source of the information is cited. The response summarizes the writer's opinion of the strength of the argument in each exhibit. The response's structure, use of words, and grammar are generally fine.

EXTENDED RESPONSE

This 559-word sample extended response would receive a 4, or possibly a 3.
Nuclear power uses nuclear processes to generate heat and electricity. The nuclear fission of elements produces the vast majority of nuclear energy. As Patrick points out, nuclear fission power stations produce about 6% of the world's energy and 15% of the world's electricity. Nuclear fission is efficient, but fission and nuclear waste are radioactive, and there is danger, with short term and long term health risks.

Quinson, who favors nuclear power generation, mentions the recent Fukushima nuclear accident at a 50-year-old reactor, has slowed but not stopped the construction of newer and safer reactors worldwide. He points out that using this accident to argue against nuclear power production is a failed argument.

I agree with Quinson's point of view. It would be a serious mistake to halt the development of nuclear power stations in the United States.

The main premise for my position is the dominant role that coal plays in power generation in the United States. While neither position provides details, there are likely more deaths that can be attributed to the environmental effects of coal than the effects of nuclear power. Quinson makes this point directly by noting that with nuclear power there are no smokestacks and so no harmful greenhouse emissions.

The real effort should be to reduce the amount of electricity generated by coal, and one way to do that is through the newer safer nuclear generating facilities. Almost accidentally Patrick actually supports this view by agreeing that alternate choices such as solar power could never reduce dependence on energy produced by coal and oil. He doesn't mention that coal could.

The graph from the Nuclear Regulatory Commission permits us to look at this issue from another perspective. It shows the sources of Radiation exposure in the United States. With all the criticism of nuclear energy one would expect nuclear energy to be a prominent feature of this graph. However, we see that about 80% of the exposure is from natural sources—that does not include nuclear power plants. Medical x-rays are the largest Man Made Source and the exposure from nuclear power can only be one of many things in the Other category that consist of less than 1% of man-made exposure.

The main argument against my position is the acknowledged safety issues of nuclear power. The weakness in that opposing position is there is no discussion of alternatives, and from my perspective the options of air choking coal power generation is much worse. Those opposed to nuclear power would have to provide another viable alternative to coal for their position to have merit. Others engaged in this debate might also point to the report in Patrick's paper that some unnamed group of former officials claimed that nuclear energy was not economically viable. While one cannot just dismiss these concerns, the argument is too vague to stand on its own.

Permit me to summarize my position. While acknowledging the dangers of nuclear power, I see worse dangers in other types of power generation. These dangers are not to be taken lightly, nor are the dangers of other power generation techniques.

The new reactors currently being developed will reduce the danger and until someone has a solution to this country's dependence on coal generated power, I am staunchly opposed to any outright ban on the development of nuclear power facilities in this country.

Discussion

This extended response meets both requirements needed to receive a high score. It is also of sufficient length to receive a high score. This response stakes out a clear position on the proposal to "Make Unlawful the Construction of Additional Nuclear Power Plants in the United States." The extended response incorporates information from all the exhibits, and uses that information to support the position against the ban. The response also mentions a specific counterclaim and provides information from all the exhibits to refute that counterclaim. The response's structure, word use, and grammar are generally fine, although there are some minor issues, including capitalization.

READING REVIEW

USING THIS SECTION

This section prepares you to take the computer-delivered reading tests. Choose one of these approaches.

- **I WANT VOCABULARY AND READING HELP.** Review the entire section and take the practice reading items at the end.
- **I WANT TO PRACTICE READING A PASSAGE (PAGE 169).** Complete the Practice Reading Passage with Items and Answers at the end of this section.

VOCABULARY REVIEW

You cannot read if you do not know the vocabulary. You do not have to know every word in the dictionary. Follow this reasonable approach to developing a good vocabulary for these tests.

CONTEXT CLUES

Many times you can figure out a word from its context. Look at these examples. Synonyms, antonyms, examples, or descriptions may help you figure out the word.

1. The woman's mind wandered as her two friends **prated** on. It really did not bother her though. In all the years she had known them, they had always <u>babbled</u> about their lives. It was almost comforting.
2. The wind **abated** in the late afternoon. Things were different yesterday when the wind had <u>picked up</u> toward the end of the day.
3. The argument with her boss had been her **Waterloo**. She wondered if the defeat suffered by Napoleon <u>at this famous place</u> had felt the same.

4. The events swept the politician into a **vortex** of controversy. The politician knew what it meant to be spun around like a toy boat in the <u>swirl of water</u> that swept down the bathtub drain.

Passage 1 gives a synonym for the unknown word. We can tell that *prated* means babbled. *Babbled* is used as a synonym of *prated* in the passage.

Passage 2 gives an antonym for the unknown word. We can tell that *abated* means slowed down or diminished because *picked up* is used as an antonym of *abated*.

Passage 3 gives a description of the unknown word. The description of Waterloo tells us that the word means defeat.

Passage 4 gives an example of the unknown word. The example of a *swirl of water* going down the bathtub drain gives us a good idea of what a *vortex* is.

ROOTS

A root is the basic element of a word. The root is usually related to the word's origin. Roots can often help you figure out the word's meaning. Here are some roots that may help you.

Root	Meaning	Examples
bio	life	biography, biology
circu	around	circumference, circulate
frac	break	fraction, refract
geo	earth	geology, geography
mal	bad	malicious, malcontent
matr, mater	mother	maternal, matron
neo	new	neonate, neoclassic
patr, pater	father	paternal, patron
spec	look	spectacles, specimen
tele	distant	telephone, television

PREFIXES

Prefixes are syllables that come at the beginning of a word. Prefixes usually have a standard meaning. They can often help you figure out the word's meaning. Here is a list of prefixes that may help you figure out a word.

Prefix	Meaning	Examples
a-	not	amoral, apolitical
il-, im-, ir-	not	illegitimate, immoral, irreversible
un-	not	unbearable, unknown
non-	not	nonbeliever, nonsense
ant-, anti-	against	antiwar, antidote
de-	opposite	defoliate, declaw
mis-	wrong	misstep, misdeed
ante-	before	antedate, antecedent
fore-	before	foretell, forecast
post-	after	postfight, postoperative
re-	again	refurbish, redo
super-	above	superior, superstar
sub-	below	subsonic, subpar

STRATEGIES FOR PASSING THE READING TEST

This section gives an integrated approach to answering the literal and figurative reading items on the computer-delivered ALST.

You do not have to understand the entire passage. In fact, the most common error is to read the entire passage before reading the questions. Do not do that. It just wastes time. You only have to know enough to get the correct answer. Less than half, often less than 25 percent, of the details in a passage are needed to answer a question.

> A great way to develop a vocabulary is to read a paper every day and a news magazine every week, in addition to the other reading you are doing. There are also several inexpensive books, including *1,100 Words You Need to Know* and *Pocket Guide to Vocabulary* from Barron's, which may help you develop your vocabulary further.

THE READING COMPREHENSION STUDY PLAN

All reading questions call for either literal or figurative responses. There are examples and tips for answering each type. Then you will learn about the five steps for taking the Core reading test.

Next come passages and questions to try out. All the questions have explained answers. Do not skip anything. Do not look at the answers until you have answered all of the questions. The important thing is to get the rhythm of answering reading comprehension questions.

ALST READING QUESTION TYPES

This is how ETS classifies the three categories of reading items:

Key Ideas and Details

These questions usually ask for the stated main idea of a passage or about details in the passage.

Craft, Structure, and Language Skills

These questions are usually related to word or phrase meaning, the unstated purpose of a passage, the author's reason or purpose for writing the passage, or the general organization of the passage.

Integration of Knowledge and Ideas

These questions may ask you to draw an inference or implication or to identify the author's point of view, attitude, or reason for mentioning something. In addition, you will be asked about the meaning of a word in quotation, and to compare or contrast two paragraphs. The more difficult questions will ask about which listed statement would support or diminish the author's argument or would provide an alternate explanation.

It is not always easy to categorize questions. That is OK because there are really two categories of reading questions—literal comprehension and figurative comprehension. Literal questions typically ask directly about the passage. Figurative questions typically ask you to interpret, extend, and apply ideas in the passage. The test does not identify these categories.

> Let me repeat, do not begin by reading the passage in detail. In fact, that kind of careful reading will almost certainly get you into trouble. Only read in detail after you have read a question and you are looking for the answer. This section shows you how to do that.

Correct Answers

It all comes down to finding the correct answer. The correct answer will be the best choice available among the choices listed, even if there is a better answer. The correct answer will be based on the passage, not on something not in the passage that you may know is true or think is true.

Literal Comprehension

MAIN IDEA (MAIN PURPOSE)

These questions are the main focus of reading comprehension. Main idea and main purpose questions ask you to identify the topic of the passage or part of the passage, or the main reason the author wrote the passage or part of that passage.

Main idea questions often include the words "main idea":

Which of the following describes the main idea of the passage?

Main purpose questions also often include the words "primary purpose":

The primary purpose of this passage is . . .

Find the central idea of the passage to answer these questions. What was the author really trying to get at? Why did the author write the passage?

Some main ideas may not be directly stated in the passage. However, the main idea or purpose must be from the passage. It cannot be what you think the author might have in mind.

SUPPORTING DETAILS

Authors give details to support the main idea. These details may be facts, opinions, experiences, or discussions.

Here are some examples of supporting details questions:

Which of the following does the author use to support the main idea in the passage?

Which of the following details is not found in this passage?

To explain [a statement] in the passage the author writes. . .

When the passage describes the outcomes of [an event] it mentions. . .

The answer choices will usually include statements or summaries of statements found in the passage. Read the question carefully to be sure what details are asked for.

Answer choices frequently include details you know to be true but that are not found in the passage. Eliminate those. The correct answer will be found in the passage.

VOCABULARY QUESTIONS

A passage has lots of words and phrases. Vocabulary questions typically ask you to show that you know the meaning of one of those words or phrases.

Here are some examples of vocabulary questions:

Which of the following words is a synonym for (the word) in line 99 of the passage?

Which of the following gives the best definition of (word) in line 99 of the passage?

All of the following gives the best meaning for the (phrase/word) in line 99 EXCEPT. . .

The vocabulary review (beginning on page 146) gives a vocabulary review. It also includes ways to identify words from their context. A word in context is not always a strict dictionary definition. Word meaning can be literal or figurative.

Here is an easy example. The author writes, "Stand up for what you believe in." The question asks about the meaning of "stand up." One of the answer choices is (A) "stand up straight." Another choice is (B) "take a position." The main dictionary definition is "stand up straight." However, that is not what these words mean in context. The words mean "take a position." That is the correct answer.

That is not to say that a literal definition will always be wrong, or often wrong. It does mean that you should think about the word's meaning in context.

ORGANIZATION

These questions ask you about the way a passage or part of a passage is organized. It sounds hard, but the answer choices are just plain language descriptions. It is usually more a matter of common sense than any specialized knowledge.

Organization questions are just what you would think they would be:

Which of the following choices best describes the way the passage is organized?

There may be some moderately difficult words in the choices for these types of questions. Use the vocabulary skills you will learn in this chapter to tackle those words if they occur.

Figurative Comprehension

INFERENCE

An inference question asks you to identify something that can be reasonably implied or inferred from a passage. The answers to inference questions will not be directly stated in the passage.

Inference questions look like this:

Which choice below can be inferred from this passage?

What can be inferred about [name or event] from lines ___-___ in the passage?

Test writers try to write five choices for which only one is clearly the "most correct" inference. They usually do a good job. However, sometimes other apparently reasonable inferences appear.

> Choose an inference based on the passage. Do not make a choice just because it is true—you will find choices like that. Do not make a choice because it has some other emotional appeal. The inference has to be based on information in the passage.

CHOOSING AN EXCERPT FROM THE PASSAGE

Some of these questions may ask you to determine if they would strengthen or weaken the author's argument.

Choose which excerpt from the pasage the author uses for a particular purpose.

Which of the following excerpts from the passage best supports an idea or concept from the passage?

Which of the following excerpts from the passage most effectively develops a particular character or theme from the passage?

Focus on the author's intent when writing the excerpt and the relationship to the excerpt to ideas in the pasage and the passage as a whole.

ATTITUDE QUESTIONS

By attitude, these questions mean a position or point of view the author holds that is revealed in a passage. Author's tone may also be used to describe these questions. These questions typically have one-word answers. The idea is to figure out how someone feels about something and then find the vocabulary word that matches the feeling.

Attitude questions are what you would expect.

What is the author's attitude about [some idea or fact]?

Look for a statement in the passage that includes judgment terms such as "bad," "good," "well-thought-out," "I guess," or "questionable," and the like.

DRAWING CONCLUSIONS

These questions ask you to assume that everything in the passage is correct and then to draw a conclusion from that information. Drawing a conclusion usually means drawing a logical conclusion based on two pieces of information. These two pieces of information may not appear near one another in the passage.

Here is a simple example that could lead to a conclusion:

Whenever Liz meets someone she knows she always talks to him or her. (The first bit of information means talking.) Later we could read that when Liz talks to someone she knows she always shakes his or her hand.

We can conclude that if Liz met someone she knows she would shake his or her hand. We can't conclude that if she shakes hands with someone, then she knows him or her. That conclusion is not supported by the passage.

Drawing conclusions questions look like this:

Based on the information in the passage, which of the following is the most reasonable conclusion?

Do not choose an answer just because it is correct or because you agree with it. The answer must flow logically from the information in the passage.

STEPS FOR ANSWERING READING QUESTIONS

This section describes five steps for answering any ALST reading question. You will learn how to apply the steps, and then you will see the steps applied to sample passages.

Reading About Reading

Reading seems to be a natural process. Reading about reading and about steps to taking reading tests can seem contrived and confusing. However, we know that these steps and techniques work. Once you apply the steps to the practice exercises, your reading ability and scores will improve.

FIVE STEPS TO TAKING A READING TEST

During a reading test follow these steps:

STEP 1 Skim to find the topic of each paragraph.

STEP 2 Read the questions and the answers.

STEP 3 Identify the question type, when possible.

STEP 4 Eliminate incorrect answers.

STEP 5 Scan the details to find the answer.

STEP 1 **Skim to Find the Topic of Each Paragraph**

Your first job is to find the topic of each paragraph. The topic is what a paragraph or passage is about.

The topic of a paragraph is usually found in the first and last sentences. Read the first and last sentences just enough to find the topic. Use scrap paper.

READING SENTENCES

Every sentence has a subject that tells what the sentence is about. The sentence also has a verb that tells what the subject is doing or links the subject to the complement. The sentence may also contain a complement that receives the action or describes what is being said about the subject. The words underlined in the following examples are the ones you would focus on as you preview.

1. The famous educator John Dewey founded an educational movement called progressive education.

2. Sad to say, we have learned American school children of all ages are poorly nourished.

You may occasionally encounter a paragraph or passage in which the topic can't be summarized from the first and last sentences. This type of paragraph usually contains factual information. If this happens, you will have to skim the entire paragraph.

STEP 2   **Read the Questions and the Answers**

Now read the questions—one at a time. Read the answers for the question you are working on. Be sure that you understand what each question and its answers mean.

Before you answer a question, be sure you know whether it is asking for a fact, an inference, or a connection to excerpts listed as answer choices. If the question asks for a fact, the correct answer will identify a main idea or supporting detail. The correct answer may also identify a cause and effect relationship among ideas or be a paraphrase or summary of parts of the passage. Look for these.

If the question asks for an inference, the correct answer will identify the author's purpose, assumptions, or attitude. If the question asks for a connection to an excerpt, it will list excerpts as answer choices. The question will ask you to choose the excerpt used for a particular purpose in the passage, or best meets the author's goal. Look for these elements.

STEP 3   **Identify the Question Type, When Possible**

Do your best to identify the question type when possible. It can help focus your thinking.

STEP 4   **Eliminate Incorrect Answers**

Read the answers and eliminate the ones that you absolutely know are incorrect. Read the answers literally. Look for words such as *always, never, must, all.* If you can find a single exception to this type of sweeping statement, then the answer cannot be correct. Eliminate it.

STEP 5   **Scan the Details to Find the Answer**

Once you have eliminated answers, compare the other answers to the passage. When you find the answer that is confirmed by the passage—stop. That is your answer choice. Follow these other suggestions for finding the correct answer.

Who Wrote This Answer?

People who write tests go to great lengths to choose a correct answer that cannot be questioned. That is what they get paid for. They are not paid to write answers that have a higher meaning or include great truths.

Test writers want to be asked to write questions and answers again. They want to avoid valid complaints from test takers like you who raise legitimate concerns about their answers.

Try to think like the person who wrote the test.

A Vague Answer Can Be Correct

How can a person write a vague answer that is correct? Think of it this way. If I wrote that a person is 6 feet 5 inches tall, you could get out a tape measure to check my facts. Since I was very specific, you are more likely to be able to prove me wrong.

On the other hand, if I write that the same person is over 6 feet tall you would be hard pressed to find fault with my statement. So my vague statement was hard to argue with. If the person in question is near 6 feet 5 inches tall, then my vague answer is most likely to be the correct one.

Do not choose an answer just because it seems more detailed or specific. A vague answer may just as likely be correct.

Applying the Steps

Let's apply the five steps to this passage and items 1 and 2.

> Many vocational high schools in the United States give off-site work experience to their students. Students usually work in local businesses part of the school day and attend high school the other part. These programs have made American vocational schools world leaders in making job experience available to teenage students.

1. According to this paragraph, American vocational high schools are world leaders in making job experience available to teenage students because they

   Ⓐ have students attend school only part of the day.
   Ⓑ were quick to move their students to schools off-site.
   Ⓒ require students to work before they can attend the school.
   Ⓓ involve their students in cooperative education programs.

STEP 1 Skim to find the topic of each paragraph. Both the first and last sentences tell us that the topic is vocational schools and work experience.

STEP 2 Read the questions and the answers. Why are American vocational education high schools the world leaders in offering job experience?

STEP 3 Identify the question type. This is a details question.

STEP 4 Eliminate incorrect answers. Answer (C) is obviously wrong. It has to do with work before high school. Answer (B) is also incorrect. This has to do with attending school off-site. This leaves answers (A) and (D).

STEP 5 Scan the details to find the answer. Scan the details and find that parts of answer (A) are found in the passage. In answer (D) you have to know that cooperative education is another name for off-site work during school.

It is down to answer (A) or answer (D). But answer (A) contains only part of the reason that vocational education high schools have gained such acclaim. Answer (D) is the correct answer.

Here's how to apply the steps to the following passage.

Problem Solving

Problem solving has become the main focus of mathematics learning. Students learn problem-solving strategies and then apply them to problems. Many tests now focus on problem solving and limit the number of computational problems. The problem-solving movement is traced to George Polya who wrote several problem-solving books for high school teachers.

Problem Solving Strategies

Problem-solving strategies include guess and check, draw a diagram, and make a list. Many of the strategies are taught as skills, which inhibits flexible and creative thinking. Problems in textbooks can also limit the power of the strategies. However, the problem-solving movement will be with us for some time, and a number of the strategies are useful.

2. According to this passage, a difficulty with teaching problem-solving strategies is:

   Ⓐ The strategies are too difficult for children.
   Ⓑ The strategies are taught as skills.
   Ⓒ The strategies are in textbooks.
   Ⓓ The strategies are part of a movement.

STEP 1 Skim to find the topic of each paragraph. The topic of the first paragraph is problem solving. You find the topic in both the first and last sentences. Write the topic next to the paragraph. The topic for the second paragraph is problem-solving strategies. Write the topic next to the paragraph if you are taking the paper-delivered test.

Now look at the questions. If the question is about problem solving "in general" start looking in the first paragraph for the answer. If the question is about strategies, start looking in the second paragraph for the answer.

STEP 2 Read the questions and the answers. The answer will be a difficulty with teaching problem solving.

STEP 3 Identifying the question type. This is a details question.

STEP 4 Eliminate incorrect answers. Answer (A) cannot be right because difficulty is not mentioned in the passage. That leaves (B), (C), and (D) to consider.

STEP 5 Scan the details to find the answer. The question asks about strategies so look immediately to the second paragraph for the answer. The correct answer is (B). Choice (C) is not correct because the passage does not mention strategies in textbooks. There is no indication that (D) is correct.

The correct choice is (B).

Try Them Out

The ALST often shows the part of the passage that contains the answer. There are many examples of each question type, and you may see completely different examples on the ALST you take.

Remember that you are looking for the best answer from among the ones listed, even if you can think of a better answer. Remember that the answer must be supported by the passage and that you should not pick an answer choice just because it is true or because you agree with it.

Apply the five steps. You should not look ahead at the answers. Looking ahead at the answers will deny you important experiences, and it may well hurt your performance on the ALST.

Mark your choice of the correct answer.

Apply the five steps to these practice passages. Mark the letter of the correct answer. Follow the directions given below. The answers to these questions are found on pages 163–168. Do not look at the answers until you complete your work.

Read the following passage. After reading the passage, choose the best answer to each question from among the four choices. Answer all the questions following the passage on the basis of what is stated or implied in the passage.

Today's students have hand-held calculators that can graph one or even many equations. Students can even type in several equations and the calculator will "solve" them. This is the best way just to see a plotted graph quickly.

Line
(5) This is the worst way to learn about graphing and equations. The calculator can't tell the students anything about the process of graphing and does not teach them how to plot a graph.

Left to this electronic graphing process, students will not have the hands-on experience needed to see the patterns and symmetry that characterize graphing and equations. They may become too dependent on the calculator and be unable to reason
(10) effectively about equations and the process of graphing.

It may be true that graphing and solving equations is taught mechanically in some classrooms. There is also something to be said for these electronic devices, which give students the opportunity to try out several graphs and solutions quickly before deciding on a final solution.

(15) For all their electronic accuracy and patience, these graphing calculators cannot replace the process of graphing and solving equations on your own. For mastery of equations and graphing comes not just from seeing the graph automatically displayed on a screen, but also comes from a hands-on involvement with graphing.

3. The main idea of the passage is that:

   Ⓐ a child can be good at graphing equations only through hands-on experience.
   Ⓑ teaching approaches for graphing equations should be improved.
   Ⓒ accuracy and patience are the keys to effective graphing instruction.
   Ⓓ the new graphing calculators have limited ability to teach students about graphing.

4. According to this passage, what negative impact will graphing calculators have on students who use them?

Ⓐ They will not have experience with four-function calculators.
Ⓑ They will become too dependent on the calculator.
Ⓒ They can quickly try out several graphs before coming up with a final answer.
Ⓓ They will get too much hands-on experience with calculators.

5. According to the passage, which of the following is a major drawback of the graphing calculator?

Ⓐ It graphs many equations with their solutions.
Ⓑ It does not give students hands-on experience with graphing.
Ⓒ It does not give students hands-on experience with calculators.
Ⓓ This electronic method interferes with the mechanical method.

6. Which of the following passages best shows an opposing view to a prior statement?

Ⓐ It may be true that graphing and solving equations is taught mechanically in some classrooms.
Ⓑ This is the worst way to teach about graphing.
Ⓒ These graphing calculators cannot replace the process of graphing.
Ⓓ They may become too dependent on the calculator.

7. The description of a graphing calculator found in this passage tells about which of the following?
Select all that apply.

Ⓐ The equations that can be graphed
Ⓑ The approximate size of the calculator
Ⓒ The advantages of the graphing calculator
Ⓓ Why a computer is better than a calculator

On July 2, 1937, during her famed journey across
the Pacific Ocean to complete flying around the
world, noted aviator Amelia Earhart disappeared.
Line   Speculation remains about the cause and validity of
(5)   her elusive disappearance, and Earhart's whereabouts
remain a mystery. As one of the first female aviators
to attempt an around-the-world flight, Earhart
solidified her reputation as one of the most daring
women of her day. Having achieved a series of
(10)   record-breaking flights—such as surpassing the
women's altitude record of 14,000 feet in 1922
and venturing solo across the Atlantic Ocean
in 1932—this trailblazer not only paved the way
for women aviators but advocated independence,
(15)   self-reliance, and equal rights for all women.

Billed as the "First Lady of the Air" or "Lady Lindy"
(Charles A. Lindbergh's female counterpart),
Earhart challenged gender barriers and influenced
women's position in the nascent aviation industry.
(20)   She was a founding member and president of the
Ninety-Nines, an international organization of
women pilots. In 1932, after completing her solo
flight across the Atlantic Ocean, President Herbert
Hoover presented Earhart with the National
(25)   Geographic Society's gold medal, an honor never
before bestowed to a woman. She was also the
first woman to receive the National Aeronautical
Association's honorary membership.

8. Which of the following is most likely an assumption made by the author of this
    passage?

    Ⓐ Amelia Earhart was an American spy captured by Japanese forces.
    Ⓑ Charles Lindbergh would not have disappeared had he been the pilot on this
       mission.
    Ⓒ Amelia Earhart's daring nature caused her to crash on her flight.
    Ⓓ Amelia Earhart may not have died when she disappeared.

9. Which of the following statements, if added to the passage, would weaken the author's statement that Amelia Earhart's whereabouts are unknown?

   Ⓐ A strong storm was reported by a ship along the flight route that Amelia Earhart was following.

   Ⓑ The last person to see Amelia Earhart's plane, a Lockheed Vega, reported that the plane seemed very heavy as it lifted off.

   Ⓒ A search pilot reported signs of recent human habitation on a deserted island along the flight route that Amelia Earhart took.

   Ⓓ Further research on the radio in Amelia Earhart's plane revealed that all the radios in that version of the Lockheed Vega often failed.

10. The author's attitude toward Amelia Earhart can best be described as

    Ⓐ condescending.
    Ⓑ reverential.
    Ⓒ unsettled.
    Ⓓ abhorrent.

11. In which of the following excerpts does the author most clearly express disbelief?

    Ⓐ Billed as the "First Lady of the Air" or "Lady Lindy."
    Ⓑ Earhart solidifed her reputation as one of the most daring women of her day.
    Ⓒ Speculation remains about the cause and validity of her elusive disappearance.
    Ⓓ Earhart challenged gender barriers.

USE THIS PASSAGE TO ANSWER ITEMS 12–18.

Thousands of different types of rocks and minerals
have been found on Earth. Most rocks at the Earth's
surface are formed from only eight elements (oxygen,
Line silicon, aluminum, iron, magnesium, calcium, potassium,
(5) and sodium), but these elements are combined in a number
of ways to make rocks that are very different.

Rocks are continually changing. Wind and water wear
them down and carry bits of rock away; the tiny particles
accumulate in a lake or ocean and harden into rock again.
(10) Scientists say the oldest rock ever found is more than
3.9 billion years old. The Earth itself is at least 4.5 billion
years old, but rocks from the beginning of Earth's history
have changed so much from their original form that they
have become new kinds of rock.

(15) Rock-forming and rock-destroying processes have been active for billions of years. Today, in the Guadalupe Mountains of western Texas, you find limestone, a sedimentary rock, that was a coral reef in a tropical sea about 250 million years ago. Half Dome in Yosemite

(20) Valley, California, about 8,800 feet above sea level, is composed of quartz monzonite, an igneous rock that solidified several thousand feet within the Earth. A simple rock collection captures the enormous sweep of the history of our planet.

12. What is the main purpose of this passage?

   Ⓐ To provide information that rocks are continually changing

   Ⓑ To emphasize that the Earth is made of rock from the tallest mountains to the floor of the deepest ocean

   Ⓒ To examine that there are thousands of different types of rocks and minerals that have been found on Earth

   Ⓓ To prove that in a simple rock collection of a few dozen samples, one can capture an enormous sweep of the history of our planet and the process that formed it

13. Which of the following words or phrases is the best substitute for the word *accumulate* in line 9?

   Ⓐ Disperse

   Ⓑ Renew

   Ⓒ Break down

   Ⓓ Gather

14. According to the passage, most rocks at the Earth's surface are formed from

   Ⓐ oxygen, silicon, calcium, and potassium.

   Ⓑ aluminum, iron, and magnesium.

   Ⓒ one of eight elements.

   Ⓓ elements combined in a number of ways.

15. What is the author's reason for mentioning that rocks are continually changing?

   Ⓐ To make the reading more technical
   Ⓑ To provide a visual description
   Ⓒ To provide the reader with a physical description of rocks
   Ⓓ To provide information to the reader as to why all rocks look different

16. Which of the following is the best description of the organization of this passage?

   Ⓐ An overall description is followed by some specific examples.
   Ⓑ A discussion of one topic ends up with a discussion of an entirely different topic.
   Ⓒ Specific examples are given followed by an explanation of those examples.
   Ⓓ A significant question is raised followed by possible answers to that question.

17. It can be reasonably inferred from the passage that the author

   Ⓐ believes only what the author can personally observe.
   Ⓑ is open to accepting theories presented by others.
   Ⓒ believes science is a mixture of fact and fiction.
   Ⓓ knows how the Earth itself was created.

18. Which of the following statements from the paragraph is most convincingly an opinion as opposed to a fact?

   Ⓐ Thousands of different types of rocks and minerals have been found on Earth.
   Ⓑ Today, in the Guadalupe Mountains of western Texas you find limestone, a sedimentary rock, that was a coral reef in a tropical sea about 250 million years ago.
   Ⓒ Wind and water wear them down and carry bits of rock away; the tiny particles accumulate in a lake or ocean and again harden into rock.
   Ⓓ A simple rock collection captures the enormous sweep of the history of our planet.

Line

(5)

(10)

(15)

(20)

The potential for instruction provided by cable television in the classroom is eclipsed by the number of educational practitioners who remain uninformed about the concept or who lack proficiency in the use of protocols and strategies necessary to optimize its benefits. Teachers, trainers, and educational administrators nationwide would benefit from structured opportunities, rather than trial and error, to learn how to maximize the potential of the medium. Cable television in the classroom can introduce real events into instruction by reporting the news from a perspective with which young people are familiar. Broadcasts received by television satellite can present issues as opportunities in which young people can play an active role, rather than as overwhelming problems no one can solve. By incorporating current events and televised symposia learners are exposed to perspectives beyond their teacher's own view and can explore truth without sensationalism or condescension. Thus cable television access in the classroom allows learners to make informed judgments about the content under study.

19. Which of the following conclusions can reasonably be drawn from this passage?

Ⓐ The potential for television in the classroom is more prominent than the opposition against it.

Ⓑ A lack of understanding of appropriate strategies is the reason cable television in the classroom has not been fully implemented.

Ⓒ The reason cable television in the classroom has not been accepted goes beyond being informed about this instructional tool.

Ⓓ Cable television in the classroom ensures that the teacher's views will receive appropriate attention.

20. If the analysis of this passage were applied to introducing a completely different type of vacuum cleaner, one might say that success would most likely be a function of

Ⓐ effectiveness.

Ⓑ cost.

Ⓒ name.

Ⓓ advertising.

Answers to Reading Questions Explained

Do not read this section until you have completed the practice passage. Here's how to apply the steps. Use this Step 1 for items 3–7. Complete your own Step 1 for the remaining passages.

STEP 1 Skim to find the topic of each paragraph. You may have written a topic next to each paragraph. Suggested topics are shown next to the following selection. Your topics do not have to be identical, but they should accurately reflect the paragraph's content.

Graphing Calculators

Today's students have hand-held calculators that can graph one or even many equations. Students can even type in several equations and the calculator will "solve" them. This is the best way to just see a plotted graph quickly.

Problem with Graphing Calculators

This is the worst way to learn about graphing and equations. The calculator can't tell the students anything about the process of graphing and does not teach them how to plot a graph.

Why it's a Problem

Left to this electronic graphing process, students will not have the hands-on experience needed to see the patterns and symmetry that characterize graphing and equations. They may become too dependent on the calculator and be unable to reason effectively about equations and the process of graphing.

Good Points

It may be true that graphing and solving equations is taught mechanically in some classrooms. There is also something to be said for these electronic devices, which give students the opportunity to try out several graphs and solutions quickly before deciding on a final solution.

For all their electronic accuracy and patience, these graphing calculators cannot replace the process of graphing and solving equations on your own. Mastery of equations and graphing comes not just from seeing the graph automatically displayed on a screen, but also from a hands-on involvement with graphing.

Apply Steps 2 through 5 to each of the questions.

3. **STEP 2** Read the question and the answers. You have to identify the main idea of the passage. This is a very common question on reading tests. Remember that the main idea is what the writer is trying to say or communicate in the passage.

   STEP 3 Identify the question type. This is a main idea question.

   STEP 4 Eliminate incorrect answers. Answers (B) and (C) are not correct. Answer (C) is not at all correct based on the passage. Even though (B) may be true, it does not reflect what the writer is trying to say in this passage.

STEP 5 Scan the details to find the answer. As we review the details we see that both answer (A) and answer (D) are stated or implied in the passage. A scan of the details alone does not reveal which is the main idea. You must determine that on your own.

The correct answer is (D). The author certainly believes that (A) is true, but uses this point to support the main idea.

4. **STEP 2** Read the question and the answers. This is a straightforward comprehension question. What negative impact will calculators have on students who use them? The second and third paragraphs have topics related to problems with calculators. You will probably find the answer there.

   STEP 3 Identify the question type. This is a main idea question.

   STEP 4 Eliminate incorrect answers. Answer (C) is not a negative impact of graphing calculators. Scan the details to find the correct answer from (A), (B), and (D).

   STEP 5 Scan the details to find the answer. The only detail that matches the question is in paragraph 3. The author says that students may become too dependent on the calculators. That is the answer.

   Answer (B) is the only correct choice.

5. **STEP 2** Read the question and the answers. This is another straightforward comprehension question. This question is somewhat different from Question 2. Notice that the question asks for a drawback of the calculator. It does not ask for something that is wrong with the calculator itself. The topics indicate that we will probably find the answer in paragraph 1 or paragraph 2.

   STEP 3 Identify the question type. This is a details question.

   STEP 4 Eliminate incorrect answers. Answer (C) is obviously wrong. Graphing calculators do give students hands-on experience with calculators. Be careful! It is easy to mix up (C) with (B). Answer (A) is a strength of the calculator and is also incorrect. Now move on to the details.

   STEP 5 Scan the details to find the answer. Choices (B) and (D) remain. The details in paragraph 2 reveal that the correct answer is (B).

   Answer (B) is the only absolutely correct answer.

6. **STEP 2** Read the question and the answers. This is yet another type of reading comprehension question. You are asked to identify the questions that could be answered from the passage.

   STEP 3 Identify the question type. This is a choosing the excerpt question.

   STEP 4 Eliminate incorrect answers. Eliminate choice (D). We are looking for an opposing view and the term "may" in this choice does not reveal an opposing view.

   STEP 5 Look for a word that signals opposition. Choice (C) includes the word "worse," and we can see that this choice shows a directly opposing view to the previous sentence, which includes the word "best." We are done. Choice (C) is the correct answer.

7. **(STEP 2)** Read the question and the answers. This is another classic type of reading comprehension question. You are given several choices. You must decide which combination of these choices is the absolutely correct answer.

   (STEP 3) Identify the question type. This is a details question.

   (STEP 4) Eliminate incorrect answers. If you can determine that A, for example, is not addressed in the passage, you can eliminate it.

   (STEP 5) Scan the details to find which of the original three statements is (are) true.

   Ⓐ No, there is no description of which equations can be graphed.

   Ⓑ Yes, paragraph 1 mentions that the calculators are hand-held, not the exact size.

   Ⓒ Yes, paragraph 4 mentions the advantages.

   Ⓓ No, the passage does not mention computers.

   Choices (B) and (C) are correct.

8. **(STEP 2)** Read the question and the answers. You have to identify an assumption.

   (STEP 3) Identify the question type. This is an assumption question.

   (STEP 4) Eliminate incorrect answers. Always try to eliminate at least one answer. Eliminate (A). There is nothing here at all about this assumption.

   (STEP 5) Scan the details to find the answer. (D) is the correct answer. The author assumes that Amelia Earhart may not have died when she disappeared. The author never states it, but the author questions the validity of her disappearance and calls her whereabouts a mystery. (A) This choice was eliminated even though this is a popular theory among some people. But there is no mention of this assumption in this passage. (B) There is nothing to indicate anything about Lindbergh, except for a nickname for Earhart. (C) is incorrect because there is nothing in the passage to indicate any reason for her disappearance.

9. **(STEP 2)** Read the question and the answers. You have to find the statement that would weaken the author's argument that Earhart's whereabouts are unknown. Remember weaken does not mean disprove.

   (STEP 3) Identify the question type. This is a choosing an excerpt question.

   (STEP 4) Eliminate incorrect answers. Eliminate (B) and (D) because each contains information about why Earhart's plane may have encountered trouble but not about her whereabouts.

   (STEP 5) Scan the details to find the correct answer. (C) The reports of human habitation on a deserted island is the only statement that would weaken that argument, although it would not by itself disprove the statement. The other statements are incorrect: (A) A strong storm, (B) a heavy plane, (D) a malfunctioning radio. Do not be tempted by the specific information about Earhart's plane found in choices (B) and (D).

10. **(STEP 2)** Read the question and the answers. You have to understand how the author feels about Earhart.

    (STEP 3) Identify the question type. This is an attitude question—it says it is.

    (STEP 4) Eliminate incorrect answers. Eliminate (D) abhorrent. It is a negative word and the author thinks the world of Earhart.

(STEP 5) Scan the details to find the answer. Choice (B) is correct. Reverential means to honor and respect. That is obviously how the author feels toward her. Choice (A) is incorrect because condescending means to look down on, someone or something. Choice (C) is incorrect because the author was settled in his opinion of Earhart. Choice (D) was eliminated. Abhorrent means to have strong negative feelings.

11. (STEP 2) Read the question and the answers. You have to identify what Earhart would say about something.

(STEP 3) Identify the question type. This is a choosing an excerpt question.

(STEP 4) Eliminate incorrect answers. Eliminate (B) and (D). Each is a fact based opinion of the author.

(STEP 5) Scan the details to find the answer. Choice (C) is correct. The author reflects disbelief about the circumstances surrounding Earhart's disappearance. Choice (A) is incorrect because the author is reporting a fact, even though the fact may, appear exaggerated.

12. (STEP 2) Read the question and the answers. You have to identify which answer best summarizes the main purpose of the passage. Why was it written? Save lots of time by reading the question and answers before looking at the details in the passage.

(STEP 3) Identify the question type. This is a main purpose question.

(STEP 4) Eliminate incorrect answers. Answer (D) is clearly wrong. The main purpose is not about rock collections. You might be able to eliminate more, but you can be sure of this one. If you had to guess, eliminating just this one answer would increase the odds that you will guess correctly.

(STEP 5) Scan the details to find the answer. The answer to this question is (C) because most of the passage examines that there are thousands of different types of rocks and minerals that have been found on Earth. (A) is incorrect because the passage was not written primarily to discuss that rocks continually change. (B) is incorrect because it states facts found in the passage that are too detailed to be the main purpose.

13. (STEP 2) Read the question and the answers. You have to determine the meaning of a word, perhaps from the context.

(STEP 3) Identify the question type. This is a vocabulary question.

(STEP 4) Eliminate incorrect answers. Eliminate (C) because "accumulate" does not mean "break down."

(STEP 5) Scan the details to find the answer. (D) is the correct answer. If you accumulate something, you gather it. You can actually tell from the context that (A) is incorrect because disperse means the opposite of accumulate. It is an antonym. (B) is incorrect because bits of rock do not renew themselves; rather they combine with other bits of rock. (C) was eliminated because break down also means the opposite of accumulate. The rocks broke down before they accumulated.

14. (STEP 2) Read the question and the answers. You have to find information in the passage.

(STEP 3) Identify the question type. This is a question about details.

STEP 4 Eliminate incorrect answers. Eliminate (A) and (B) because each of them is just a partial list of the elements from which most rocks are formed. Correctly eliminating two choices means you would have a one-half chance of guessing correctly instead of a one-fourth chance. That is a big difference if you had to guess.

STEP 5 Scan the details to find the answer. The correct answer is (D), because the passage states that elements are combined in a number of ways to form rocks. (A) and (B) were eliminated because they do not list all of the eight elements from the passage. (C) is incorrect because the passage says that rocks are a combination of elements, not just one element.

15. **STEP 2** Read the question and the answers. You have to find the author's purpose for writing something in the passage.

STEP 3 Identify the question type. This is a purpose question.

STEP 4 Eliminate incorrect answers. Eliminate all the choices except for (D). If you know that all the other choices are incorrect, then you can be sure (D) is correct. Eliminate (A) because the author does not mention that all rocks are continually changing, primarily to make the reading more technical. Eliminate (B) and (C) because telling the reader that rocks are continually changing does not give him/her a visual or a physical description of rocks.

STEP 5 Scan the details to find the answer. (D) is the correct answer. All the other answer choices were eliminated, and the author mentions that rocks are continually changing to explain why rocks look different.

16. **STEP 2** Read the question and the answers. You have to look at the overall structure of the passage to see how it is organized.

STEP 3 Identify the question type. This is a choosing an excerpt question.

STEP 4 Eliminate incorrect answers. Eliminate choice (D) because no significant question is raised in the passage.

STEP 5 Scan the details to find the answer. Choice (A) is correct. The author writes about how rocks are formed and then discusses rocks formed deep in the Earth or from a coral reef. (B) is incorrect because the last sentence mentions Earth's history, but there is no discussion of Earth's history. (C) is incorrect because this is more or less the opposite of the actual structure of the passage. (D) was eliminated because the author never raises a significant question, although some scientists may have questions about the exact dates in the second paragraph.

17. **STEP 2** Read the question and the answers. You have to draw an inference from the passage.

STEP 3 Identify the question type. This is an inference question.

STEP 4 Eliminate incorrect answers. Eliminate (C) because there is nothing here to suggest that science is a mixture of fact and fiction.

STEP 5 Scan the details to find the answer. (B) is correct. In the second paragraph the author presents a theory from other scientists about the age of rocks found on Earth. (A) is incorrect because most of what the author presents can't be personally observed. (C) was eliminated because there is nothing to indicate that the author has presented or believes that science includes both fact and fiction. (D) is incorrect because the author presents information about the age of rocks and the age of the Earth but nothing about how the Earth was formed.

18. **STEP 2** Read the question and the answers. You have to identify the statement that is most likely an opinion.

    STEP 3 Identify the question type. This is a fact or opinion question.

    STEP 4 Eliminate incorrect answers. Eliminate the choices that are facts. There are many facts in this passage so you should be able to eliminate many of the choices. The first three choices, (A), (B), and (C), are facts. That leaves choice (D).

    STEP 5 Scan the details to find the answer. (D) is the correct answer. It is clearly the author's opinion about a simple rock collection. It could never be proven true or false.

19. **STEP 2** Read the question and the answers. You have to look for several elements in the passage that will lead to a conclusion.

    STEP 4 Identify the question type. This is a conclusion question.

    STEP 4 Eliminate incorrect answers. Eliminate (D) because the passage says learners will be exposed to "perspectives beyond their teacher's own view."

    STEP 5 Scan the details to find the answer. (C) is the correct answer. The first five lines of the passage mention both technical ability and familiarity as the reasons cable television in the classroom has not been accepted. We use those two bits of information to draw the conclusion. (A) is incorrect because the beginning of the passage says the opposite—that acceptance of cable television in the classroom is eclipsed by the number of educational practitioners who do not use it. (B) is incorrect because the passage mentions other reasons beyond strategies as why cable television in the classroom has not been accepted. (D) was eliminated because the passage mentions that cable television in the classroom will be exposed to views other than the teacher's view.

20. **STEP 2** Read the question and the answers. You have to decide how to use the information from the passage in a different setting.

    STEP 3 Identify the question type. This is an application question.

    STEP 4 Eliminate incorrect answers. Eliminate everything but choice (D). The main point of the passage is that teachers do not use cable television in the classroom because they do not know about it and do not know how to use it. One part of that message, applied to introducing a new vacuum cleaner, is that you have to get the word out. One way to do that is through advertising. You can eliminate all the other choices, which will probably be important when the new vacuum cleaner is introduced. Some of them may turn out to be more important than advertising. But none of those other choices are related to knowing about the vacuum or knowing how to use the new vacuum.

    STEP 5 Scan the details to find the answer. (D) is the best answer. Advertising is the only choice from among those given that is supported by this passage.

Adapted from *Pride and Prejudice*, by Jane Austen

1   It is a truth universally acknowledged, that a single man in possession of a good fortune, must *be in want of a wife.*

2   However little known the feelings or views of such a man may be on his first entering a neighbourhood, this truth is so well fixed in the minds of the surrounding families, that he is considered the rightful property of someone or other of their daughters.

3   "My dear Mr. Bennett," said his lady to him one day, "have you heard that Netherfield Park is let at last?"

4   Mr. Bennett replied that he had not.

5   "But it is," returned she; "for Mrs. Long has just been here, and she told me all about it."

6   Mr. Bennett made no answer.

7   "Do you not want to know who has taken it?" cried his wife impatiently.

8   "*You* want to tell me, and I have no objection to hearing it."

9   This was invitation enough.

10   "Why, my dear, you must know, Mrs. Long says that Netherfield is taken by a young man of large fortune from the north of England; that he came down on Monday in a chaise and four to see the place, and was so much delighted with it, that he agreed with Mr. Morris immediately; that he is to take possession before Michaelmas, and some of his servants are to be in the house by the end of next week."

11   "What is his name?"

12   "Bingley."

13   "Is he married or single?"

14   "Oh! Single, my dear, to be sure! A single man of large fortune; four or five thousand a year. What a fine thing for our girls!"

15   "How so? How can it affect them?"

16   "My dear Mr. Bennett," replied his wife, "how can you be so tiresome! You must know that I am thinking of his marrying one of them."

17   "Is that his design in settling here?"

18   "Design! Nonsense, how can you talk so! But it is very likely that he *may* fall in love with one of them, and therefore you must visit him as soon as he comes."

19   "I see no occasion for that. You and the girls may go, or you may send them by them-selves, which perhaps will be still better, for as you are as handsome as any of them, Mr. Bingley may like you the best of the party."

20   "My dear, you flatter me. I certainly *have* had my share of beauty, but I do not pretend to be anything extraordinary now. When a woman has five grown-up daughters, she ought to give over thinking of her own beauty."

21 "In such cases, a woman has not often much beauty to think of."

22 "But, my dear, you must indeed go and see Mr. Bingley when he comes into the neighbourhood."

23 "It is more than I engage for, I assure you."

24 "But consider your daughters. Only think what an establishment it would be for one of them. Sir William and Lady Lucas are determined to go, merely on that account, for in general, you know, they visit no newcomers. Indeed you must go, for it will be impossible for *us* to visit him if you do not."

25 "You are over-scrupulous, surely. I dare say Mr. Bingley will be very glad to see you; and I will send a few lines by you to assure him of my hearty consent to his marrying whichever he chooses of the girls; though I must throw in a good word for my little Lizzy."

26 "I desire you will do no such thing. Lizzy is not a bit better than the others; and I am sure she is not half so handsome as Jane, nor half so good-humoured as Lydia. But you are always giving *her* the preference."

27 "They have none of them much to recommend them," replied he; "they are all silly and ignorant like other girls; but Lizzy has something more of quickness than her sisters."

28 "Mr. Bennett, how *can* you abuse your own children in such a way? You take delight in vexing me. You have no compassion for my poor nerves."

29 "You mistake me, my dear. I have a high respect for your nerves. They are my old friends. I have heard you mention them with consideration these last twenty years at least."

30 "Ah, you do not know what I suffer."

31 "But I hope you will get over it, and live to see many young men of four thousand a year come into the neighbourhood."

32 "It will be no use to us, if twenty such should come, since you will not visit them."

33 "Depend upon it, my dear, that when there are twenty, I will visit them all."

34 Mr. Bennett was so odd a mixture of quick parts, sarcastic humour, reserve, and caprice, that the experience of three-and-twenty years had been insufficient to make his wife understand his character. *Her* mind was less difficult to develop. She was a woman of mean understanding, little information, and uncertain temper. When she was discontented, she fancied herself nervous. The business of her life was to get her daughters married; its solace was visiting and news.

Questions

1. The best analysis of paragraph 10 in the passage is that Mrs. Bennett

Ⓐ sees the young man mentioned in the paragraph as a suitor for one of her daughters.

Ⓑ is letting Mr. Bennett know that "Netherfield" was a piece of property that she wanted Mr. Bennett to purchase.

Ⓒ wants to share the information that the young man who took the property has a large fortune.

Ⓓ is very impressed with all the trappings of wealth, including the expensive "chaise and four," a carriage with four horses, that the young man arrived in.

2. Which of the following comes closest in meaning to the term *over-scrupulous* in paragraph 25?
   Ⓐ Extremely courteous
   Ⓑ Very rigid
   Ⓒ Unusually fastidious
   Ⓓ Notably unconcerned

3. These sentences are in paragraph 29 of the passage:

   "You mistake me, my dear. I have a high respect for your nerves. They are my old friends. I have heard you mention them with consideration these last twenty years at least."

   These sentences help develop the character of Mrs. Bennett by

   Ⓐ setting the stage for further examination of Mrs. Bennett's character.
   Ⓑ establishing that Mr. Bennett has a fixed opinion about Mrs. Bennett.
   Ⓒ revealing that Mr. Bennett has great concern and regard for Mrs. Bennett.
   Ⓓ extending the impression that Mr. Bennett is very concerned about Mrs. Bennett's health.

4. In paragraph 27, which of the following best describes how the author portrays Mr. Bennett?

   Ⓐ He has a prejudice against young women.
   Ⓑ He has an abusive personality where young woman are concerned.
   Ⓒ He is hesitant to recommend women, particularly for well-paying jobs.
   Ⓓ He is partial to those who can rapidly process information.

5. In paragraph 34, the author writes "the experience of three-and-twenty years had been insufficient to make his wife understand his character."

   How does this excerpt relate to the passage as a whole?

   Ⓐ It points out a not uncommon feature of married life.
   Ⓑ It demonstrates that Mr. Bennett did not care enough about family and friends.
   Ⓒ It contrasts Mrs. Bennett's focus on more menial things with Mr. Bennett's more global view.
   Ⓓ It emphasizes that Mrs. Bennett's concern in this marriage was unappreciated by her husband.

6. In the author's view, which of the following passages is best characterized as an aphorism.

   Ⓐ a single man in possession of a good fortune, must *be in want of a wife.*
   Ⓑ "But it is," returned she; "for Mrs. Long has just been here, and she told me all about it."
   Ⓒ "Indeed you must go, for it will be impossible for *us* to visit him if you do not."
   Ⓓ "Ah, you do not know what I suffer."

7. Which of the following sentences from the passage is the best example of self-effacing?
   - Ⓐ "Ah, you do not know what I suffer."
   - Ⓑ "You take delight in vexing me. You have no compassion for my poor nerves."
   - Ⓒ "It is more than I engage for, I assure you."
   - Ⓓ "A woman . . . ought to give over thinking of her own beauty."

8. You will find this sentence in paragraph 3:

   "My dear Mr. Bennett," said his lady to him one day . . .

   In this instance, the lady is

   - Ⓐ the person who found out about the sale of the Netherfield.
   - Ⓑ a woman of means who was related to the young man who bought the Netherfield.
   - Ⓒ a woman he was related to.
   - Ⓓ a woman who worked as a housekeeper for the Bennetts.

Reading Practice Answers

1. **(A)** The thread that runs through the passage is Mrs. Bennett's interest in securing husbands for her daughters. That makes Choice (A) the most obvious reason why Mrs. Bennett would mention this event to Mr. Bennett in paragraph 10.

2. **(C)** "Scrupulous" means someone is diligent, thorough, and extremely attentive to details. "Fastidious" means very attentive to and concerned about accuracy and detail. These two words are the closet in meaning among the answers given.

3. **(B)** Mr. Bennett obviously has a fixed opinion that Mrs. Bennett complains a lot.

4. **(D)** The real focus of this sentence is to single out Lizzy as someone who is quick witted. It is true that he shows some prejudice against this particular group of young women, his daughters. However, that is not the main point of the sentence, and we do not know if this prejudice applies to all young women, or just these young women, or if he literally means what he says. He certainly seems to like his daughter Lizzy well enough.

5. **(C)** Mrs. Bennett has trouble understanding her husband because they are so different. Mr. Bennett has a more global view of the world, while, as this passage points out, Mrs. Bennett is concerned mainly with arranging marriages for her daughters, visiting, and gossip.

6. **(A)** An aphorism is a universal truth, and in paragraph 1 the author clearly states Choice (A) is a "truth universally acknowledged."

7. **(D)** "Self-effacing" means not drawing attention to oneself. In the passage, Mrs. Bennett turns attention away from herself when she refers to her own beauty, but notes that when one has grown daughters, she should put the thought of her own beauty aside.

8. **(C)** The context of the passage shows that Mr. Bennett's wife was the lady who addressed him.

Two Model ALST Tests with Answer Explanations

6

ACADEMIC LITERACY SKILLS TEST ONE

40 Selected-Choice items

3 Constructed-Response Writing to Sources Items

Darken the lettered oval to show your choice for the multiple-choice items.

Use a word processor, without the spell or grammar checker, and type your constructed-response answers.

USE THIS PASSAGE TO ANSWER THE QUESTIONS THAT FOLLOW.

Lincoln's Second Inaugural Address

This address is frequently ranked by historians as the best of all presidential inaugural addresses. As with his Gettysburg address, it is marked by its relative brevity.

Fellow-Countrymen:

1   At this second appearing to take the oath of the Presidential office there is less occasion for an extended address than there was at the first. Then a statement somewhat in detail of a course to be pursued seemed fitting and proper. Now, at the expiration of four years, during which public declarations have been constantly called forth on every point and phase of the great contest which still absorbs the attention and engrosses the energies of the nation, little that is new could be presented. The progress of our arms, upon which all else chiefly depends, is as well known to the public as to myself, and it is, I trust, reasonably satisfactory and encouraging to all. With high hope for the future, no prediction in regard to it is ventured.

2   On the occasion corresponding to this four years ago all thoughts were anxiously directed to an impending civil war. All dreaded it, all sought to avert it. While the inaugural address

was being delivered from this place, devoted altogether to saving the Union without war, insurgent agents were in the city seeking to destroy it without war—seeking to dissolve the Union and divide effects by negotiation.

3   Both parties deprecated war, but one of them would make war rather than let the nation survive, and the other would accept war rather than let it perish, and the war came.

4   One-eighth of the whole population were colored slaves, not distributed generally over the Union, but localized in the southern part of it. These slaves constituted a peculiar and powerful interest. All knew that this interest was somehow the cause of the war. To strengthen, perpetuate, and extend this interest was the object for which the insurgents would rend the Union even by war, while the Government claimed no right to do more than to restrict the territorial enlargement of it.

5   Neither party expected for the war the magnitude or the duration which it has already attained. Neither anticipated that the cause of the conflict might cease with or even before the conflict itself should cease. Each looked for an easier triumph, and a result less fundamental and astounding. Both read the same Bible and pray to the same God, and each invokes His aid against the other. It may seem strange that any men should dare to ask a just God's assistance in wringing their bread from the sweat of other men's faces, but let us judge not, that we be not judged. The prayers of both could not be answered. That of neither has been answered fully.

6   The Almighty has His own purposes. "Woe unto the world because of offenses; for it must needs be that offenses come, but woe to that man by whom the offense cometh." If we shall suppose that American slavery is one of those offenses which, in the providence of God, must needs come, but which, having continued through His appointed time, He now wills to remove, and that He gives to both North and South this terrible war as the woe due to those by whom the offense came, shall we discern therein any departure from those divine attributes which the believers in a living God always ascribe to Him?

7   Fondly do we hope, fervently do we pray, that this mighty scourge of war may speedily pass away. Yet, if God wills that it continue until all the wealth piled by the bondsman's two hundred and fifty years of unrequited toil shall be sunk, and until every drop of blood drawn with the lash shall be paid by another drawn with the sword, as was said three thousand years ago, so still it must be said "the judgments of the Lord are true and righteous altogether."

8   With malice toward none, with charity for all, with firmness in the right as God gives us to see the right, let us strive on to finish the work we are in, to bind up the nation's wounds, to care for him who shall have borne the battle and for his widow and his orphan, to do all which may achieve and cherish a just and lasting peace among ourselves and with all nations.

Questions

1. Which of the following excerpts from the passage best supports Lincoln's primary point in paragraph 1?

   Ⓐ "On the occasion corresponding to this four years ago, all thoughts were anxiously directed to an impending civil war."

   Ⓑ "Neither party expected for the war the magnitude or the duration which it has already attained."

   Ⓒ "Fondly do we hope, fervently do we pray, that this mighty scourge of war may speedily pass away."

   Ⓓ "These slaves constituted a peculiar and powerful interest."

2. In which of the following excerpts does Lincoln most demonstrate reconciliation?

   Ⓐ "Neither party expected for the war the magnitude or the duration which it has already attained."

   Ⓑ "These slaves constituted a peculiar and powerful interest. All knew that this interest was somehow the cause of the war."

   Ⓒ "With malice toward none, with charity for all . . ."

   Ⓓ "With high hope for the future, no prediction in regard to it is ventured."

3. This excerpt is from paragraph 7.

   "Fondly do we hope, fervently do we pray, that this mighty scourge of war may speedily pass away. Yet, if God wills that it continue until all the wealth piled by the bondsman's two hundred and fifty years of unrequited toil shall be sunk, and until every drop of blood drawn with the lash shall be paid by another drawn with the sword . . . "

   Lincoln's reference in this excerpt to "every drop of blood drawn with the lash" is part of a warning that

   Ⓐ the North remains a stronger force than the South.

   Ⓑ if the war continues, the South will pay for its treatment of slaves.

   Ⓒ the South will pay a higher price than defeat in war for its treatment of slaves.

   Ⓓ the lash used to punish slaves will just empower the slaves to be stronger as they resist slavery.

4. In which of the following excerpts does Lincoln describe a moderate reaction to slavery?

   Ⓐ "... but let us judge not, that we be not judged."

   Ⓑ "These slaves constituted a peculiar and powerful interest."

   Ⓒ "Fondly do we hope, fervently do we pray, that this mighty scourge of war may speedily pass away."

   Ⓓ "... while the Government claimed no right to do more than to restrict the territorial enlargement of it."

5. This excerpt appears in paragraph 3.

"Both parties deprecated war, but one of them would make war rather than let the nation survive, and the other would accept war rather than let it perish, and the war came."

In the context of the passage as a whole, this excerpt

Ⓐ places the blame for the war on the South.
Ⓑ places the blame for the war on the North.
Ⓒ suggests a shared responsibility for the war.
Ⓓ suggests that slavery was the cause of the war.

6. This sentence comes from paragraph 1.

"The progress of our arms, upon which all else chiefly depends, is as well known to the public as to myself, and it is, I trust, reasonably satisfactory and encouraging to all."

The sentence conveys Lincoln's notion that

Ⓐ soldiers in the North and South alike are being well treated on the battlefield.
Ⓑ the North is winning the war.
Ⓒ the North has an arms manufacturing advantage.
Ⓓ the North and the South are nearing a negotiated truce.

7. In paragraphs 2 and 3, Lincoln's use of the words "all" and "both" most likely intend to

Ⓐ include both the North and the South.
Ⓑ include both men and women.
Ⓒ emphasize the equality of slaves and non-slaves.
Ⓓ emphasize the strong bond between members of the army and civilians.

8. Which of the following best describes the main tone of this inaugural address?

Ⓐ Lincoln made clear throughout that the North was in the superior moral position.
Ⓑ The main theme was to avoid antagonizing the South.
Ⓒ Lincoln often turned to moral and religious descriptions.
Ⓓ The main theme was to emphasize the horror of slavery.

Edgar Allan Poe's Biography, by Killis Campbell, from *The Cambridge History of American Literature*, Book II, Chapter XIV: "Poe"

1   The saddest and the strangest figure in American literary history is that of Edgar Allan Poe. Few writers have lived a life so full of struggle and disappointment, and none have lived and died more completely out of sympathy with their times. His life has been made the subject of minute and prolonged investigation, yet there are still periods in his history that have not been satisfactorily cleared up. And the widest differences of opinion have existed as to his place and his achievements. But there are few today who will not readily concede to him a place among the foremost writers of America, whether in prose or in verse, and there are not wanting those who account him one of the two or three writers of indisputable genius that America has produced.

2   Poe was born at Boston, 19 January, 1809, the son of actor parents of small means and of romantic proclivities. Before the end of his third year he was left an orphan, his mother dying in wretched poverty at Richmond, Virginia, 8 December, 1811, and his father a few weeks later, if we may believe the poet's own statement.

3   He was promptly taken under the protection of a prosperous tobacco exporter of Richmond, John Allan, in whose family he lived, ostensibly as an adopted child, until 1827. In his sixth year he attended for a short time the school of William Ewing in Richmond. In the summer of 1815 he went with his foster-father to England, and for the next five years, with the exception of a few months spent in Scotland shortly after reaching England, he lived in London, attending first a boarding school kept by the Misses Dubourg in Sloane Street, and later the academy of the Rev. John Bransby in Stoke Newington. He impressed Bransby as a "quick and clever boy," though embarrassed by "an extravagant amount of pocket-money"; and John Allan wrote of him in 1818 that he was "a fine boy" and read "Latin pretty sharply." In 1816 Allan described him as "thin as a razor," but in 1819 he wrote that he was "growing wonderfully."

4   On his return to Richmond in the summer of 1820, Poe entered an academy kept, first, by Joseph H. Clarke and, later, by William Burke, under whom he continued his work in the languages, earning the admiration of his fellows by his readiness at "capping verses" from the Latin and by his skill in declamation. He also wrote verses of his own, and it is said that a sheaf of his juvenilia was collected in 1822 or 1823 in the hope that they might be published in volume form. But before the end of 1824 he had somehow broken with his foster-father, and the breach between the two was never to be entirely healed.

5   "The boy possesses not a spark of affection for us," wrote John Allan in November, 1824, "not a particle of gratitude for all my care and kindness towards him. . . . I fear his associates have led him to adopt a line of thinking and acting very contrary to what he possessed when in England." The immediate cause of the breach we do not know; but a parting of the ways between the two, who were radically dissimilar in tastes and ideals, was inevitable sooner or later.

6   The year 1826 Poe spent as a student at the University of Virginia. Here he made a creditable record in his classes, winning honourable mention in Latin and French; and he at no time fell under the censure of his instructors. At the end of the year, however, because of his having accumulated gambling debts of some twenty-five hundred dollars, he was

withdrawn from college; and with the beginning of the next year he was placed by his adoptive father in his counting-house in Richmond, in the hope that he might develop a taste for a business career. But he had small leaning that way; besides, he had been disappointed in a love-affair, having become engaged before going to college to Miss Sarah Elmira Royster, of Richmond, who, in consequence of a misunderstanding, had jilted him in his absence and had betrothed herself to another.

7   Smarting under this disappointment and completely out of sympathy with the life marked out for him by his foster-father, Poe now determined to run away; and at some time in March, 1827, he left Richmond for parts unknown. In May he appeared at Boston, and there, 26 May, he was mustered into the army of the United States. The next two years he served as a soldier in barracks, being stationed first at Boston, then at Charleston, South Carolina, and finally at Fortress Monroe. In the spring or summer of 1827 he brought out at Boston his first volume of poems, Tamerlane and other poems (1827), a collection of ten fugitive pieces, all brief save one, and all plainly imitative either of Byron or of Moore.

8   In February, 1829, Mrs. Allan died, and in April Poe was discharged from the army, a substitute having been provided, and efforts were made to obtain for him an appointment to West Point. Some time intervened, however, before an appointment could be procured, and it was not until July, 1830, that he was admitted to the Academy. In the preceding December he had published at Baltimore a second volume of poems, made up largely of his earlier pieces revised, but containing his long poem Al Aaraaf, the most ambitious and the most promising of his earlier productions.

9   At West Point he took high rank in his classes; but in October, 1830, John Allan had married a second time, and Poe, concluding that there was no longer any prospect of succeeding to a fortune, determined to bring about his dismissal from the Academy. He adopted the very effective means of absenting himself from roll calls and from classes, was court-martialed was formally expelled.

Questions

9. Which of the following excerpts from the passage provides the most significant counterpoint to the author's description of Poe as "the saddest and the strangest figure in American literary history?"

    Ⓐ "He adopted the very effective means of absenting himself from roll calls and from classes, was court-martialed and formally expelled."

    Ⓑ "Before the end of his third year he was left an orphan, his mother dying in wretched poverty at Richmond, Virginia, 8 December, 1811, and his father a few weeks later, if we may believe the poet's own statement."

    Ⓒ "Before the end of 1824 he had somehow broken with his foster-father, and the breach between the two was never to be entirely healed."

    Ⓓ "He was promptly taken under the protection of a prosperous tobacco exporter of Richmond, John Allan, in whose family he lived, ostensibly as an adopted child, until 1827."

10. Which of the following phrases or words offer a negative connotation in the context of the passage?

   Ⓐ But there are few today who will not readily concede to him a place among the foremost writers of America.

   Ⓑ Here he made a creditable record.

   Ⓒ The boy possesses not a spark of affection for us.

   Ⓓ … though embarrassed by "an extravagant amount of pocket-money."

11. The description of Poe's life in paragraphs 2 and 3 is related to the entire passage because it

   Ⓐ shows how Poe's life quickly changed from "rags to riches."

   Ⓑ shows the wide range of private schools Poe attended.

   Ⓒ shows the reported demise of his parents soon after his birth.

   Ⓓ explains that he was born in Boston about thirty years after the revolutionary war.

12. In paragraph 5 the author quotes Poe's adoptive father.

"The boy possesses not a spark of affection for us," wrote John Allan in November, 1824, "not a particle of gratitude for all my care and kindness towards him. . . . I fear his associates have led him to adopt a line of thinking and acting very contrary to what he possessed when in England."

This excerpt reveals a relationship between Poe and his adoptive father primarily as

   Ⓐ an adoptive father who gave Poe a lot, which Poe did not appreciate.

   Ⓑ an adopted son who grew beyond the limited world of his adoptive father.

   Ⓒ an adopted son who fell into bad ways that his adoptive father did not approve of.

   Ⓓ an adoptive father who was just as happy to let his adoptive son go it alone.

13. Which excerpt below LEAST conveys what the author means in paragraph 1 when he writes, "But there are few today who will not readily concede him a place among the foremost writers in America?"

   Ⓐ "The year 1826 Poe spent as a student in the University of Virginia. Here he made a creditable record in his classes, winning honourable mention in Latin and French."

   Ⓑ "In May [1827] he [Poe] appeared in Boston and there, 26 May, was mustered into the army of the United States."

   Ⓒ "In the spring or summer of 1827 he brought out at Boston his first volume of poems, Tamerlane . . ."

   Ⓓ "In the preceding December he had published at Baltimore a second volume of poems."

14. In paragraph 9, the author best helps develop an understanding of Poe's character by

  Ⓐ noting that as a cadet at West Point Poe took "high rank in his classes."

  Ⓑ noting Poe was "determined to bring about his dismissal" because he would have no inheritance.

  Ⓒ describing the method Poe used to "a very effective means" "to be formally expelled."

  Ⓓ mentioning that in October 1830 "John Allen had married a second time."

15. The sentence below appears at the beginning of paragraph 7.

"Smarting under this disappointment and completely out of sympathy with the life marked out for him by his foster-father, Poe now determined to run away, and at some time in March, 1827, he left Richmond for parts unknown."

As it is used in this sentence, which of the following phrases come closet in meaning to the word "smarting?"

  Ⓐ Acting very intelligently

  Ⓑ Feeling mental distress

  Ⓒ Drawing on intelligence

  Ⓓ Drawing on courage

16. In paragraph 4, the author comments about how Poe earned the admiration of his fellows, which primarily serves what purpose in the passage?

  Ⓐ It provides a contrast to the reaction of the headmaster.

  Ⓑ It establishes his reputation among his peers.

  Ⓒ It explains why he wrote verses of his own.

  Ⓓ It shows his weakness because of his readiness to "cap" verses.

USE THIS PASSAGE TO ANSWER THE QUESTIONS THAT FOLLOW.

From *Dr. Heidegger's Experiment*, by Nathaniel Hawthorne

1 When the doctor's four guests heard him talk of his proposed experiment, they anticipated little. But without waiting for a reply, Dr. Heidegger hobbled across the chamber, and returned with the same ponderous folio, bound in black leather, which common report affirmed to be a book of magic. Undoing the silver clasps, he opened the volume, and took from among its black-letter pages a rose, or what was once a rose, though now the green leaves and crimson petals had assumed one brownish hue, and the ancient flower seemed ready to crumble to dust in the doctor's hands.

2 "This rose," said Dr. Heidegger, with a sigh, "this same withered and crumbling flower, blossomed five and fifty years ago. It was given me by Sylvia Ward, whose portrait hangs yonder; and I meant to wear it in my bosom at our wedding. Five and fifty years it has been treasured between the leaves of this old volume. Now, would you deem it possible that this rose of half a century could ever bloom again?"

3 "Nonsense!" said the Widow Wycherly, with a peevish toss of her head. "You might as well ask whether an old woman's wrinkled face could ever bloom again."

4   "See!" answered Dr. Heidegger.

5   He uncovered the vase, and threw the faded rose into the water which it contained. At first, it lay lightly on the surface of the fluid, appearing to imbibe none of its moisture. Soon, however, a singular change began to be visible. The crushed and dried petals stirred, and assumed a deepening tinge of crimson, as if the flower were reviving from a deathlike slumber; the slender stalk and twigs of foliage became green; and there was the rose of half a century, looking as fresh as when Sylvia Ward had first given it to her lover. It was scarcely full blown; for some of its delicate red leaves curled modestly around its moist bosom, within which two or three dewdrops were sparkling.

6   "That is certainly a very pretty deception," said the doctor's friends; carelessly, however, for they had witnessed greater miracles at a conjurer's show; "pray how was it effected?"

7   "Did you never hear of the 'Fountain of Youth?'" asked Dr. Heidegger, "which Ponce De Leon, the Spanish adventurer, went in search of two or three centuries ago?"

8   "But did Ponce De Leon ever find it?" said the Widow Wycherly.

9   "No," answered Dr. Heidegger, "for he never sought it in the right place. The famous Fountain of Youth, if I am rightly informed, is situated in the southern part of the Floridian peninsula, not far from Lake Macaco. Its source is overshadowed by several gigantic magnolias, which, though numberless centuries old, have been kept as fresh as violets by the virtues of this wonderful water. An acquaintance of mine, knowing my curiosity in such matters, has sent me what you see in the vase."

10   "Ahem!" said Colonel Killigrew, who believed not a word of the doctor's story; "and what may be the effect of this fluid on the human frame?"

11   "You shall judge for yourself, my dear colonel," replied Dr. Heidegger; "and all of you, my respected friends, are welcome to so much of this admirable fluid as may restore to you the bloom of youth. For my own part, having had much trouble in growing old, I am in no hurry to grow young again. With your permission, therefore, I will merely watch the progress of the experiment."

12   While he spoke, Dr. Heidegger had been filling the four champagne glasses with the water of the Fountain of Youth. It was apparently impregnated with an effervescent gas, for little bubbles were continually ascending from the depths of the glasses, and bursting in silvery spray at the surface. As the liquor diffused a pleasant perfume, the old people doubted not that it possessed cordial and comfortable properties; and though utter sceptics as to its rejuvenescent power, they were inclined to swallow it at once. But Dr. Heidegger besought them to stay a moment.

13   "Before you drink, my respectable old friends," said he, "it would be well that, with the experience of a lifetime to direct you, you should draw up a few general rules for your guidance, in passing a second time through the perils of youth. Think what a sin and shame it would be, if, with your peculiar advantages, you should not become patterns of virtue and wisdom to all the young people of the age!"

14   The doctor's four venerable friends made him no answer, except by a feeble and tremulous laugh; so very ridiculous was the idea that, knowing how closely repentance treads behind the steps of error, they should ever go astray again.

15 "Drink, then," said the doctor, bowing: "I rejoice that I have so well selected the subjects of my experiment."

16 With palsied hands, they raised the glasses to their lips. The liquor, if it really possessed such virtues as Dr. Heidegger imputed to it, could not have been bestowed on four human beings who needed it more woefully. They looked as if they had never known what youth or pleasure was, but had been the offspring of Nature's dotage, and always the gray, decrepit, sapless, miserable creatures, who now sat stooping round the doctor's table, without life enough in their souls or bodies to be animated even by the prospect of growing young again. They drank of the water, and replaced their glasses on the table.

17 Assuredly there was an almost immediate improvement in the aspect of the party, not unlike what might have been produced by a glass of generous wine, together with a sudden glow of cheerful sunshine brightening over all their visages at once. There was a healthful suffusion on their cheeks, instead of the ashen hue that made them look so corpse-like. They gazed at one another, and fancied some magic power had begun to smooth away the deep and sad inscriptions which Father Time had been so long engraving on their brows. The Widow Wycherly adjusted her cap, for she felt almost like a woman again.

Questions

17. This sentence appears in paragraph 1.

"But without waiting for a reply, Dr. Heidegger hobbled across the chamber, and returned with the same ponderous folio, bound in black leather, which common report affirmed to be a book of magic."

Which of the following words comes closest in meaning to "ponderous?"

Ⓐ Important
Ⓑ Wizardly
Ⓒ Large
Ⓓ Unwieldy

18. This excerpt is from paragraph 5.

"He uncovered the vase, and threw the faded rose into the water which it contained. At first, it lay lightly on the surface of the fluid, appearing to imbibe none of its moisture. Soon, however, a singular change began to be visible. The crushed and dried petals stirred, and assumed a deepening tinge of crimson, as if the flower were reviving from a deathlike slumber; the slender stalk and twigs of foliage became green; and there was the rose of half a century, looking as fresh as when Sylvia Ward had first given it to her lover. It was scarcely full blown; for some of its delicate red leaves curled modestly around its moist bosom, within which two or three dewdrops were sparkling."

In this excerpt, the author develops Dr. Heidegger's character by

Ⓐ describing him as a person who focuses on results.
Ⓑ showing that he has a flair for the dramatic.
Ⓒ demonstrating that he has mastered the art of illusion.
Ⓓ revealing that he has the ability to describe events in detail.

19. Which of the following excerpts from the passage does NOT reveal a skeptical tone?

Ⓐ "Nonsense!" said the Widow Wycherly, with a peevish toss of her head. "You might as well ask whether an old woman's wrinkled face could ever bloom again."

Ⓑ "They looked as if they had never known what youth or pleasure was, but had been the offspring of Nature's dotage, and always the gray, decrepit, sapless, miserable creatures, who now sat stooping round the doctor's table, without life enough in their souls or bodies to be animated even by the prospect of growing young again."

Ⓒ "That is certainly a very pretty deception," said the doctor's friends; carelessly, however, for they had witnessed greater miracles at a conjurer's show; "pray how was it effected?"

Ⓓ "Ahem!" said Colonel Killigrew, who believed not a word of the doctor's story; "and what may be the effect of this fluid on the human frame?"

20. The excerpt below appears in paragraph 13.

"Think what a sin and shame it would be, if, with your peculiar advantages, you should not become patterns of virtue and wisdom to all the young people of the age."

This excerpt best helps develop the characters of the four friends by

Ⓐ setting the stage for the next paragraph in which his friends laugh at the suggestion of returning to a misspent youth.

Ⓑ emphasizing that his friends are too old to contemplate the meaning of the words.

Ⓒ suggesting that his friends had led exemplary lives and were unlikely to repeat the few errors of their youth.

Ⓓ demonstrating that his friends are willing to consider the wise advice contained in the passage.

21. What is the best analysis of the reason why Dr. Heidegger did not himself drink the water from the vase?

Ⓐ He had obviously drunk the water before and already knew its effects.

Ⓑ He was a scientist conducting an experiment and did not want to also be a subject of the experiment.

Ⓒ He knew that the water did not confer a miraculous rejuvenation and intended this "experiment" as a lesson to his friends.

Ⓓ He wanted his friends to feel that he was doing something special for them and so did not include himself.

22. This sentence appears in paragraph 12.

While he spoke, Dr. Heidegger had been filling the four champagne glasses with the water of the Fountain of Youth.

The sentence is most closely connected to which part of paragraph 12?

Ⓐ Little bubbles were seen in the glass.

Ⓑ Dr. Heidegger asked them to wait a moment.

Ⓒ The water gave off a pleasant odor.

Ⓓ The guests did not believe in the water's special powers.

23. This is the last paragraph in the passage.

"Assuredly there was an almost immediate improvement in the aspect of the party, not unlike what might have been produced by a glass of generous wine, together with a sudden glow of cheerful sunshine brightening over all their visages at once. There was a healthful suffusion on their cheeks, instead of the ashen hue that made them look so corpse-like. They gazed at one another, and fancied some magic power had begun to smooth away the deep and sad inscriptions which Father Time had been so long engraving on their brows. The Widow Wycherly adjusted her cap, for she felt almost like a woman again."

The best analysis of this paragraph is that

Ⓐ the changes felt by the four friends are real in their own minds but not reflected in reality.

Ⓑ the youthful appearance is permanent and the friends are doomed to live their lives over again.

Ⓒ it demonstrates how a person can adjust to old age by finding some way to think positively about their youth.

Ⓓ it reveals that the effects of aging are only in the mind, and that these effects can be overcome with help developing a proper outlook.

24. In the paragraph below, the author describes Dr. Heidegger's explanation of how he came into possession of the water in the vase. This paragraph contains a warning about returning to youth.

"No," answered Dr. Heidegger, "for he never sought it in the right place. The famous Fountain of Youth, if I am rightly informed, is situated in the southern part of the Floridian peninsula, not far from Lake Macaco. Its source is overshadowed by several gigantic magnolias, which, though numberless centuries old, have been kept as fresh as violets by the virtues of this wonderful water. An acquaintance of mine, knowing my curiosity in such matters, has sent me what you see in the vase."

The best analysis of the paragraph is that it is likely

Ⓐ fiction because Ponce de Leon did discover the Fountain of Youth.

Ⓑ fact because of the apparent effects of the water.

Ⓒ fiction because the water would have been widely distributed.

Ⓓ fact because there is nothing in the passage to suggest that Dr. Heidegger is a liar.

USE THIS PASSAGE TO ANSWER THE QUESTIONS THAT FOLLOW.

Van Gogh's Letter

Vincent van Gogh was a post-Impressionist Dutch painter whose work had a significant influence on twentieth-century art. He lived from 1853 until 1890, and this letter to his younger brother Theo was written near the end of his life.

From: Vincent van Gogh
To: Theo van Gogh
Date: Saint-Rémy-de-Provence, Saturday, 5 October 1889

My dear Theo,

1   I was longing for your letter and so I was very happy to receive it, and to see from it that you're well, as are Jo and the friends you speak of.

2   I must ask you to send me the whites I asked for as soon as possible, and to add to them some canvas, 5 metres or 10, whichever suits. Then I must begin by telling you a piece of rather vexing news, as I see it. It's that during the stay here there have been a few expenses which I thought Mr. Peyron had notified you about as they occurred, which he told me the other day he hadn't done, with the result that it has mounted up to around 125 francs, deducting from it the 10 you sent by postal order.

3   It's for paint, canvas, frames and stretching frames, my trip the other day to Arles, a piece of linen clothing, and various repairs.

4   I'm using two colors here, lead white and ordinary blue, but in quite large quantities, and the canvas, that's for when I want to work on unprepared, stronger canvas.

5   This comes unfortunately just at this time when I would gladly have repeated my trip to Arles etc.

6   That said, I'll tell you that we're having some superb autumn days, and that I'm taking advantage of them. I have a few studies, among others a mulberry tree, all yellow on stony ground standing out against the blue of the sky, in which study I think that you'll see that I've found Monticelli's track. You'll have received the consignment of canvases I sent you last Saturday.

7   It surprises me a lot that Mr Isaäcson wants to do an article on studies of mine. I'd willingly urge him to wait a little longer, his article would lose absolutely nothing by it, and with another year of work I could hope to put more characteristic things in front of him with more willpower in the drawing, more knowledge of the Provençal south.

8   Mr. Peyron was very kind to talk of my case in those terms—I haven't dared ask him to go to Arles one of these days, which I'd very much like to do, believing that he would disapprove. Not, though, that I suspected that he believed there was a connection between my previous trip and the crisis that closely followed it. The thing is that there are a few people over there whom I felt and once again feel the need to see again.

9   While I don't have here in the south, like good Prévost, a mistress who holds me captive, I couldn't help becoming attached to people and things.

10 And now that I'm staying on here for the time being, and will most probably spend the winter here—in the spring –in the fine season, shall I not stay here too? That will depend on my health above all.

11 What you say of Auvers is nevertheless a very agreeable prospect to me, and sooner or later that ought to be fixed without seeking further. If I come to the north, even supposing that there's no room in this Doctor's home, it's probable that he would, on père Pissarro's recommendation and your own, find either board with a family or quite simply at the inn. The main thing is to know the doctor so that, in the event of a crisis, one doesn't fall into the hands of the police and isn't forcibly carried off into an asylum.

12 And I can assure you that the north will interest me like a brand-new country.

13 But anyway, for the moment there's therefore nothing that's absolutely hurrying us.

14 I reproach myself for being so behind with my correspondence, I'd like to write to Isaäcson, Gauguin and Bernard. But writing doesn't always come, and what's more, work is pressing. Yes, I'd like to say to Isaäcson that he would do well to wait longer, there isn't yet that in it that I hope to attain if my health continues. It's not worth mentioning anything about my work at the moment. When I'm back, at best it will form a kind of ensemble, 'Impressions of Provence'.

15 But what does he want to say now when the olive trees, the fig trees, the vineyards, the cypresses must be more accentuated, all characteristic things, the same as the Alpilles, which must get more character.

16 How I'd like to see what Gauguin and Bernard have brought back.

17 I have a study of two yellowed poplars on a background of mountains, and a view of the park here, autumnal effect, some of the draughtsmanship of which is more naive and more—at home.

18 Anyway, it's difficult to leave a land before having something to prove that one has felt and loved it.

19 If I come back to the north I plan to do a whole lot of Greek studies, you know, painted studies with white and blue and only a little orange, just like in the open air.

20 I must draw and seek style. Yesterday at the almoner's here I saw a painting that made an impression on me. A Provençal lady with an intelligent, pure-bred face, in a red dress. A figure like the ones Monticelli thought of.

21 It wasn't without great faults, but there was simplicity in it, and how sad it is to see how much they have degenerated from it here, as we have from ours in Holland.

22 I'm writing to you in haste so as not to wait to answer your kind letter, hoping that you'll write again without delaying long.

23 I've seen more very beautiful subjects for tomorrow—in the mountains.

24 Kind regards to Jo and to our friends, above all when you get the chance thank père Pissarro for his information, which will certainly be useful.

25 Shaking both your hands, believe me.

Ever yours,

Vincent

Questions

25. In which of the following excerpts from the passage does Van Gogh most clearly strike a tone of regret?

  Ⓐ "And I can assure you that the north will interest me like a brand-new country."
  Ⓑ "But anyway, for the moment there's therefore nothing that's absolutely hurrying us."
  Ⓒ "I reproach myself for being so behind with my correspondence. . . ."
  Ⓓ "I must draw and seek style."

26. Based on the passage as a whole, which of the following best characterizes Theo's relationship to Vincent?

  Ⓐ Friend
  Ⓑ Patron
  Ⓒ Confidant
  Ⓓ Critic

27. Which of the following excerpts from the passage most effectively demonstrates Van Gogh's dedication to art?

  Ⓐ "Yesterday at the almoner's here I saw a painting that made an impression on me. A Provençal lady with an intelligent, pure-bred face, in a red dress."
  Ⓑ "How I'd like to see what Gauguin and Bernard have brought back."
  Ⓒ "I'm using two colours here, lead white and ordinary blue, but in quite large quantities, and the canvas, that's for when I want to work on unprepared, stronger canvas."
  Ⓓ "Anyway, it's difficult to leave a land before having something to prove that one has felt and loved it."

28. The excerpt appears in paragraph 17 of the passage.

"I have a study of two yellowed poplars on a background of mountains, and a view of the park here, autumnal effect, some of the draughtsmanship of which is more naive and more—at home."

As it appears in the passage, this excerpt most clearly reveals

  Ⓐ the details of some of Van Gogh's recent art work.
  Ⓑ that Van Gogh had a sophisticated understanding of painting.
  Ⓒ that at that moment Van Gogh was interested in the outdoors as a setting for his art.
  Ⓓ that Van Gogh painted differently depending on the season.

29. Paragraph 10 reveals Van Gogh's awareness of his

  Ⓐ dependence on his brother for financial support as well as food and lodging.
  Ⓑ health issues.
  Ⓒ readiness to go north to Auvers.
  Ⓓ fear of arrest for his outspoken views.

30. This sentence appears in paragraph 2.

"Then I must begin by telling you a piece of rather vexing news, as I see it."

Which of the following words or phrases most captures the meaning of "vexing" in the context of the paragraph?

Ⓐ Bothersome
Ⓑ Delightful
Ⓒ Threatening
Ⓓ Something previously kept secret

31. In paragraph 14, Van Gogh describes his somewhat failed attempts at correspondence, which reveals that

Ⓐ he is more adept at expressing himself graphically than in words.
Ⓑ he is closely associated with the artistic establishment.
Ⓒ his impoverished state leaves him without the necessary means to carry on correspondence.
Ⓓ the early signs of the disease that killed him are starting to appear.

32. What is the best analysis of Van Gogh's discussion in paragraph 8 of Mr. Peyron and the crisis that followed Van Gogh's previous trip north?

Ⓐ Mr. Peyron was Van Gogh's patron, and that following a previous trip north, Van Gogh incurred a number of expenses that Mr. Peyron was not expecting.
Ⓑ Mr. Peyron was a friend of Theo who Van Gogh visited on a trip north.
Ⓒ The trip north was accompanied by a medical problem.
Ⓓ Mr. Peyron was a policeman, and Van Gogh got into legal trouble following a previous trip north.

USE THIS PASSAGE TO ANSWER THE QUESTIONS THAT FOLLOW.

Adapted from *The American Scholar* Ralph Waldo Emerson

1   I greet you on the re-commencement of our literary year. Our day of dependence, our long apprenticeship to the learning of other lands, draws to a close. The millions, that around us are rushing into life, cannot always be fed on the sere remains of foreign harvests. Events, actions arise, that must be sung, that will sing themselves. Who can doubt, that poetry will revive and lead in a new age, as the star in the constellation Harp, which now flames in our zenith, astronomers announce, shall one day be the pole-star for a thousand years?

2   In this hope, I accept the topic which not only usage, but the nature of our association, seem to prescribe to this day,—the AMERICAN SCHOLAR. Year by year, we come up hither to read one more chapter of his biography. Let us inquire what light new days and events have thrown on his character, and his hopes.

3   It is one of those fables, which, out of an unknown antiquity, convey an unlooked-for wisdom, that the gods, in the beginning, divided Man into men, that he might be more helpful to himself; just as the hand was divided into fingers, the better to answer its end.

4   The old fable covers a doctrine ever new and sublime; that there is One Man,—present to all particular men only partially, or through one faculty; and that you must take the whole society to find the whole man. Man is not a farmer, or a professor, or an engineer, but he is all. Man is priest, and scholar, and statesman, and producer, and soldier. In the divided or social state, these functions are parcelled out to individuals, each of whom aims to do his stint of the joint work, whilst each other performs his. The fable implies, that the individual, to possess himself, must sometimes return from his own labor to embrace all the other laborers.

5   Man is thus metamorphosed into a thing, into many things. The planter, who is Man sent out into the field to gather food, is seldom cheered by any idea of the true dignity of his ministry. He sees his bushel and his cart, and nothing beyond, and sinks into the farmer, instead of Man on the farm. The tradesman scarcely ever gives an ideal worth to his work, but is ridden by the routine of his craft, and the soul is subject to dollars. The priest becomes a form; the attorney, a statute-book; the mechanic, a machine; the sailor, a rope of a ship.

6   In this distribution of functions, the scholar is the delegated intellect. In the right state, he is, Man Thinking. In the degenerate state, when the victim of society, he tends to become a mere thinker, or, still worse, the parrot of other men's thinking.

7   And, finally, is not the true scholar the only true master? But the old oracle said, "All things have two handles: beware of the wrong one." In life, too often, the scholar errs with mankind and forfeits his privilege. Let us see him in his school, and consider him in reference to the main influences he receives.

8   The first in time and the first in importance of the influences upon the mind is that of nature. Every day, the sun; and, after sunset, night and her stars. Ever the winds blow; ever the grass grows. Every day, men and women, conversing, beholding and beholden.

9   To the young mind, every thing is individual, stands by itself. By and by, it finds how to join two things, and see in them one nature; then three, then three thousand; and so, tyrannized over by its own unifying instinct, it goes on tying things together, diminishing anomalies, discovering roots running under ground, whereby contrary and remote things cohere, and flower out from one stem. It presently learns, that, since the dawn of history, there has been a constant accumulation and classifying of facts.

10   Thus to him, to this school-boy under the bending dome of day, is suggested, that he and it proceed from one root; one is leaf and one is flower; relation, sympathy, stirring in every vein. And what is that Root? Is not that the soul of his soul?—A thought too bold,—a dream too wild. Yet when this spiritual light shall have revealed the law of more earthly natures,—when he has learned to worship the soul, and to see that the natural philosophy that now is, is only the first gropings of its gigantic hand, he shall look forward to an ever expanding knowledge as to a becoming creator. He shall see, that nature is the opposite of the soul, answering to it part for part. One is seal, and one is print. Its beauty is the beauty of his own mind. Its laws are the laws of his own mind. Nature then becomes to him the measure of his attainments. So much of nature as he is ignorant of, so much of his own mind does he not yet possess. And, in fine, the ancient precept, "Know thyself," and the modern precept, "Study nature," become at last one maxim.

Questions

33. The author's introduction in paragraph 1 serves mainly to

    (A) emphasize that poetry will be of paramount importance in a new age.
    (B) emphasize the independence from European thought.
    (C) mark the beginning of the new literary year.
    (D) describes the location of the new North or polar star.

34. The excerpt below is from paragraph 4.

    "The old fable covers a doctrine ever new and sublime; that there is One Man,— present to all particular men only partially, or through one faculty; and that you must take the whole society to find the whole man."

    Which of the following word or phrases is closest in meaning to "sublime"?

    (A) Futuristic
    (B) Substantial
    (C) Meaningful
    (D) Exalted

35. Which of the following excerpts from the passage supports the author's statement in paragraph 4 that, "Man is not a farmer, or a professor, or an engineer, but he is all?"

    (A) "Man is priest, and scholar, and statesman . . ."
    (B) "The planter who is Man sent out into the field to gather food . . ."
    (C) "Man is thus metamorphosed into a thing, many things . . ."
    (D) "The priest becomes a form, the attorney, a statute book . . ."

36. Paragraph 6 best relates to the entire passage in that it

    (A) provides an example of the theme developed in paragraph 5.
    (B) provides a counter example to the main idea of paragraph 1.
    (C) provides a new idea not found in paragraphs 1–5.
    (D) sets the stage for the discussion in paragraphs 9–10.

37. The reaction to European influence on American thought is best described in which of the following excerpts from the passage?

    (A) "Year by year we come hither to read one more chapter of his biography."
    (B) "Events, actions arise, that must be sung, that will sing themselves."
    (C) "Let us inquire what light new days and events have thrown on his character, and his hopes."
    (D) "Man is thus metamorphosed into a thing, into many things."

38. The excerpt from the passage, "The first in time and the first in importance of the influences upon the mind is that of nature" helps the author focus attention on a central theme of nature by emphasizing that

Ⓐ nature should be the main focus of mankind.
Ⓑ youth will lead the way in the development of thought in the New World.
Ⓒ just because it occurs first does not mean it is most important.
Ⓓ nature and achievement are two separate and distinct entities.

39. The excerpt below is from paragraph 9.

"To the young mind, everything is individual, stands by itself. By and by, it finds how to join two things . . ."

The excerpt serves to develop the main theme of the paragraph by

Ⓐ beginning a description of the evolution of thought as a person grows older.
Ⓑ showing that young people have a limited capacity to connect complex ideas.
Ⓒ emphasizing the egocentric nature of young people.
Ⓓ revealing the limited decision-making capability of young people.

40. Which of the following excerpts most clearly describes the author's view of the lesser role for "Man" as a scholar?

Ⓐ ". . . he tends to become a mere thinker."
Ⓑ ". . . the scholar errs with mankind and forfeits his privilege."
Ⓒ ". . . but is ridden by the routine of his craft"
Ⓓ "All things have two handles: beware of the wrong one."

Writing to Sources

You will see three exhibits. Two of the exhibits are original passages with differing views on a common topic. Note, passages are shown exactly as they appeared in the original.

The third exhibit is a graphic with information related to the topic.

Focused responses are 100 to 200 words each.

The extended response is 400 to 600 words and fully addresses a question or proposal related to the topic.

Use a word processor, with the spell check and grammar check disabled, to write your responses.

Plan before you write and do not rely on any outside sources.

Focused-Response Rating Scale

FOCUSED-RESPONSE CHARACTERISTICS

Focused responses are usually 100 to 200 words, but a minimum of 150 words should be your goal.

- The content of your response meets the requirements found in the prompt.
- Show evidence of engagement with the prompt's exhibits.
- Present a clear and coherent response.

4 Your focused response demonstrates a STRONG grasp of the writing skills and meets all the stated requirements of the focused-response prompt including a reference to the graphic.

3 Your focused response demonstrates a SATISFACTORY grasp of the writing skills and completely meets most of the stated requirements of the focused-response prompt.

2 Your focused response demonstrates a LIMITED grasp of the writing skills and completely meets few of the stated requirements of the focused-response prompt.

1 Your focused response demonstrates NO grasp of the writing skills and generally does not meet the stated requirements of the focused-response prompt.

U Your focused response cannot be scored because it is off topic, too short to score, or written in a language other than English. Even a well-written response that is off topic will be scored "U."

B You did not write a focused response

Extended-Response Rating Scale

EXTENDED-RESPONSE EXPECTATIONS

Extended responses must be 400 to 600 words; however, a minimum of 525 words should be your goal.

- Clearly communicate complex concepts and ideas in the context of the exhibits.
- Demonstrate that you have command of the evidence in the passages and the graphic.
- Organize complex ideas and write in a formal style with excellent word choice.
- Employ the standards of written English grammar, usage, and punctuation.

4 Your extended response demonstrates a STRONG grasp of the writing skills and meets all the stated requirements of the extended-response prompt including a reference to the graphic.

3 Your extended response demonstrates a SATISFACTORY grasp of the writing skills and completely meets most of the stated requirements of the extended-response prompt.

2 Your extended response demonstrates a LIMITED grasp of the writing skills and completely meets few of the stated requirements of the extended-response prompt.

1 Your extended response demonstrates NO grasp of the writing skills and generally does not meet the stated requirements of the extended-response prompt.

U Your extended response cannot be scored because it is off topic, too short to score, or written in a language other than English. Even a well-written response that is off topic will be scored "U."

B You did not write an extended response.

Topic: The Federal Debt Limit

PASSAGE A

Senator DeMint and other Senators
Adapted from a Letter to Mr. Timothy Geithner, Secretary of the Treasury

Dear Sir,

In light of your recent public comments conflating a decision not to raise the federal debt ceiling with outright default on the United States' debt obligations, we write seeking clarity about the administration's position.

In your February 3 letter to Sen. Toomey, you compare Sen. Toomey's proposal to an analogous decision by an average citizen: "A homeowner could decide to 'prioritize' and continue paying monthly mortgage payments, while opting to cease paying other obligations, such as car payments, insurance premiums, student loan and credit card payments, utilities, and so forth. Although the mortgage would be paid, the damage to that homeowner's creditworthiness would be severe."

But of course, making necessary payments on debts, like a home mortgage, a credit card, a car, or a student loan, is different from other personal spending. The consequences of missing those payments are truly dire—default, bankruptcy, repossession, and eviction. But they are not at all the same thing as belt-tightening and prioritizing when times are tight. In the same way, cutting spending programs, reducing the federal workforce, and prioritizing payments to vendors and contractors is not the same thing as sovereign default.

The Treasury Department suggests that efforts to prioritize debt payments would bring about "catastrophic economic consequences." Yet, this argument ignores the historical record. As you are well aware, the Treasury had to manage the nation's finances in the past when the debt ceiling was reached. In 1995–1996, for example, the Department prioritized certain payments—including debt service. During this period, hundreds of thousands of federal employees were furloughed and many programs were temporarily suspended as a result of the two government shutdowns that occurred. And yet, this prioritization did not result in default on our publicly held debt nor did it cause the "catastrophic economic consequences" the administration predicts.

Unfortunately, Washington has shown time and again that it is perfectly content to spend money on whatever suits its whims. That is why the debt limit exists in the first place—to restrict the government's profligate spending and borrowing impulses and so protect the citizens responsible for paying it all back.

In the event of reaching the debt limit in the course of that debate, the decision of whether to use available Treasury funds to honor the United States' debt obligations—and prevent the catastrophe of default—would ultimately fall to you. Recent comments conflating debt service with other spending notwithstanding, the markets, the courts, and the American people know differently.

And so we write today asking for your assurance that, as Treasury Secretary, you will not continue to encourage uncertainty as to whether or not the U.S. government will default on its publicly held debt by failing to use the Treasury's sufficient funds to make necessary payments on the United States' debt obligations. Such uncertainty could cause the markets to doubt the full faith and credit of the United States.

PASSAGE B

Mr. Timothy Geithner, Secretary of the Treasury

Adapted from Response to Senator DeMint (R-Utah) and other Senators

Dear Sir,

The debate over the debt limit can seem esoteric, but a failure to resolve it in the near term would have painful implications for people in every walk of American life.

In your letter, you suggest that the debt limit should not be raised, and instead the federal debt be "capped" at the current limit. You further propose that after the government's borrowing authority is exhausted in August, the United States should for some indefinite period pay only the interest on its debt, while stopping or delaying payment of a broad swath of other commitments the country has made under the law.

I have expressed my concerns about this idea before, but I will restate them to be clear: this "prioritization" proposal advocates a radical and deeply irresponsible departure from the commitments by Presidents of both parties, throughout American history, to honor all of the commitments our Nation has made.

"Prioritization" fails to account for how payments on *principal* would be made if investors were to lose confidence in U.S. creditworthiness. In August of this year, for example, more than $500 billion in U.S. Treasury debt will mature. Under normal circumstances, investors who hold Treasuries purchase new Treasury securities when the debt matures, permitting the United States to pay the principal on this maturing debt. Yet in the scenario you advocate, in which the United States would be defaulting on a broad range of its other obligations, there is no guarantee that investors would continue to re-invest in new Treasury securities.

If investors chose not to purchase a sufficient volume of new Treasury securities, the United States would be required to pay the principal on maturing debt, and not merely the interest, out of available cash. Yet the Treasury would be unable to make these principal payments without the continued confidence of market participants willing to buy new Treasury securities. Your proposal assumes markets would be unconcerned by our failure to pay other obligations. But if this assumption proved incorrect, then the United States would be forced to default on its debt.

I understand that you have a different view of what would happen if the United States were unable, for the first time in its history, to meet its legal obligations. Nevertheless, I hope we can all agree that we should not and must not gamble with the full faith and credit of the United States. The consequences of miscalculation are too grave. The full faith and credit of the United States is too precious an asset to risk. Ultimately, the notion of "prioritizing" payments is futile because the debt limit must be increased regardless of which spending path is adopted. There is no credible budget plan under which a debt limit increase can be avoided. In addition, a failure to enact a timely increase in the limit would have the perverse effect of *increasing* the government's borrowing costs and worsening our fiscal challenges.

For all of these reasons, the idea of "prioritization" has been rejected by every President and Secretary of the Treasury who have considered it. It is unwise, unworkable, unacceptably risky, and unfair to the American people. There is no alternative to enactment of a timely increase in the debt limit.

Graphic

At the end of 2008, federal debt held by the public stood at 39 percent of GDP, which was close to its average of the preceding several decades. Sinced then, large deficits have caused debt held by the public to grow sharply—to a projected 74 percent of GDP by the end of fiscal year 2014. Debt has exceeded 70 percent of GDP during only one other period in U.S. history: from 1944 through 1950, when it spiked because of a surge in federal spending during World War II to a peak of 106 percent of GDP (see the figure below).

Federal Debt Held by the Public

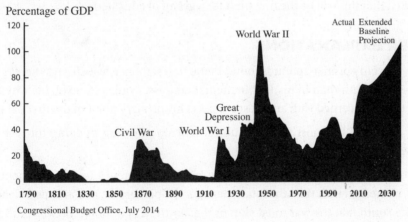

Congressional Budget Office, July 2014

ASSIGNMENT 1 FOCUSED RESPONSE

Use both Passage A and Passage B as you write your response to this assignment.

In about 100 to 200 words review each passage and compare and contrast the views each takes on raising the United States debt limit. To receive a high score your response should

- Review the claims found in each passage and how the contrasting views of raising the debt limit contributes to the presentation and the use of evidence found in the passages, and
- Include examples from each passage to support your response.

It is expected that this will be the first draft for a group of educated adults.

ASSIGNMENT 2 FOCUSED RESPONSE

Use both Passage A, Passage B and the graphic as you write your response to this topic.

In about 100 to 200 words explain how the information in the Federal Debt Graph can be combined with the arguments in each passage about raising the national debt limit. To receive a high score your response should

- Specifically detail how information in the National Debt Graph supports or refutes the claims found in each passage about the contrasting views of raising the debt limit.
- Include examples from the passages and the National Debt Graph to support your response.

It is expected that this will be the first draft for a group of educated adults.

ASSIGNMENT 3 EXTENDED RESPONSE

Use both passages and the Federal Debt Graph to respond to the following assignment. *Should action be taken to completely remove the National Debt Limit?*

This assignment is an essay of about 400 to 600 words that presents a fully developed persuasive argument about whether the National Debt Limit should be permanently removed.

To receive a high score your response should

- demonstrate that you understand the topic.
- use logical reasoning to expand and extend the points made in the passages.
- provide evidence from all three sources to support your claim, including the graphic.
- present and refute a counterclaim.

It is expected that this will be the first draft for a group of educated adults.

ANSWER EXPLANATIONS

1. **(A)** Lincoln's primary point is found in the first sentence, which says there is less to be concerned with than in his first inaugural address. Choice (A) explains why there was less to be concerned with and best supports his primary point of the first paragraph.

2. **(C)** In one of his most famous quotes, Lincoln offers an opening for reconciliation between the North and the South.

3. **(B)** The phrase "blood drawn with the lash" is a reference to the treatment of slaves and, combined with the other statements in the paragraph, constitutes a clear warning to the South that the war must stop or the North will continue the war until the South is defeated and the treatment of slaves is avenged. Choice (C) is incorrect because the excerpt does not discuss the higher price the South might pay.

4. **(D)** Lincoln is saying that the government initially did not try to abolish slavery, but rather halt its spread. This moderate position is notable among his other comments about slavery.

5. **(A)** The passage refers to the South as making war and the North as accepting war, and clearly places the blame for the war on the South.

6. **(B)** When Lincoln writes "progress of arms," he means progress on the battlefield, and his mention of "satisfactory and encouraging" indicates that the he believes that sup-

porters of the Union think the North is winning the war. Choice (C) is incorrect because it does not refer to the war itself and does not show progess.

7. **(A)** Lincoln used these words to refer to the North and South, putting both sides on a more or less equal footing.

8. **(A)** This is the best choice among those given. Tone is the author's attitude (position), and Lincoln made clear that the North was in the superior moral position. None of the remaining choices refers to Lincoln's tone; although, his speech did note a common thread between the two sides in the Civil War.

9. **(D)** A counterpoint creates a contrast, a dissonance. Choices (A), (B), and (C) align with the author's description. However, choice (D) creates a contrast between Poe as described by the author and Poe's good fortune at being taken in by a wealthy family.

10. **(C)** Choice (A) is a positive, even though the word "concede" is underlined. Choice (B) is similarly positive. The word "embarrassed" in choice (D) is not negative but positive similar to the idiom "embarrassment of riches," which signifies having a lot. That leaves choice (C), where the phrase "not a spark of" carries a negative connotation.

11. **(A)** The question asks about paragraphs 2 and 3, and we must consider both of these paragraphs when answering the question. Taken together they demonstrate that Poe's life changes quickly for the better, at least in a financial sense.

12. **(A)** One can read much into the excerpt; however, the question is about the quote, which reflects the adoptive father's view. That quote describes an adopted son who did not appreciate all that was done for him.

13. **(B)** Note that the question asks what *least* conveys the author's meaning of the quote. This choice meets that test because it is completely unrelated to writing or any other type of literary or academic activity.

14. **(B)** Poe's character was best revealed when he decided to arrange to be forced out of West Point after John Allen remarried and Poe realized that he would not receive an inheritance. Choice (C) is not the *best* choice because it describes what he did as a consequence of his character.

15. **(B)** In this context, the word "smarting" means acute mental distress, and it was this mental distress, combined with other factors, that caused Poe to leave home.

16. **(B)** This part of the passage establishes that Poe was held in academic regard by his peers. This regard among his peers helps explain why Poe was considered a literary talent.

17. **(D)** "Ponderous," in this context, means that the book is unwieldy, difficult to handle, because of its weight and size. Something can be (C) large without being ponderous.

18. **(B)** Above all, Dr. Heidegger shows he has a flair for the dramatic as he demonstrates the "experiment" for his friends.

19. **(B)** "Skeptical" means having doubts or reservations. All the other passages raise questions about the water and the "experiments," revealing their skepticism. The description in choice (B) reveals no skepticism. (Note the word "not" in the question.)

20. **(A)** Notice first, that (B), (C), and (D) are incorrect because they do not refer to the brief passage in the question. The character of the friends is best developed when in the next paragraph they laugh and dismiss any thought that they would return to the errors of their youth.

21. **(C)** The entire context of the story reveals that the water did not confer any special qualities, and, knowing this, Dr. Heidegger does not participate in the "experiment."

22. **(A)** The use of the term "champagne glasses" connects with the bubbles and leads us to believe that there may have been more in the glasses than water.

23. **(A)** Taken literally, the entire story is implausible, and so this paragraph cannot be referring to actual changes in a person's age. Choice (B) is incorrect because it presumes the changes in age are real. Choices (C) and (D) are incorrect because these adaptations to old age are not the best analysis.

24. **(C)** The explanation does not make sense because if the water was sent to Dr. Heidegger, it would have been sent to others as well and would be widely available.

25. **(C)** "Reproach" means disapproval. In this passage, Van Gogh reveals his reproach about not writing in a timelier manner. He clearly strikes a tone of regret about his failure to write sooner.

26. **(B)** A "patron" is a person who offers an artist support, whether by money or other efforts. Of all those listed, this choice most completely describes Theo's relationship with Vincent. Choice (A) "friend" and choice (C)"confidant," while true, do not best describe the relationship.

27. **(D)** The "something" Van Gogh refers to is paintings. In this passage, we sense the dedication of an artist who wants to paint the things he has felt and loved. The other choices refer to art in some fashion, but lack this dedication of Van Gogh as an artist.

28. **(B)** Von Gogh's analysis of his own work is quite sophisticated noting the various aspects of the painting that were of interest. Choice (A) is incorrect because we do not know that the paintings are recent. Similarly, we are unable to conclude that choices (C) and (D) are correct from the information in the passage.

29. **(B)** Van Gogh reveals his health concerns, which he understands could become a crisis, and perhaps cause him to lose his freedom. We see this issue in his desire to stay with a doctor, and in his need for a reliable doctor who could protect him from incarceration if he fell ill.

30. **(A)** The word "bothersome" is a synonym for the word "vexing." Van Gogh downplays somewhat the request for money by characterizing it as bothersome. None of the other words or phrases is a synonym for "vexing."

31. **(B)** The casual way he refers to Gauguin, a famous artist, demonstrates Von Gogh's close association with the art establishment. There is nothing in the passage to do with his failed attempts at correspondence that supports any of the other choices.

32. **(C)** The phrase "crisis that closely followed it" only makes sense if Van Gogh was referring to a medical crisis and not a monetary one.

33. **(B)** The author uses most of the paragraph to contrast the American scholar to the European scholar. He emphasizes independence from European thought, particularly in this excerpt: "our long apprenticeship to the learning of other lands, draws to a close. The millions, that around us are rushing into life, cannot always be fed on the sere [dry or withered] remains of foreign harvests."

34. **(D)** The word "sublime" describes something of such excellence, grandeur, or beauty as to inspire great admiration or awe. The word "exalted" comes closest to this definition.

35. **(A)** The statement from paragraph 4 refers to each "Man" as a complete person. That view is also found in choice (A), where "Man" is referred to as many things. The other choices show "Man" as just one thing, and not as many things.

36. **(A)** Paragraph 6 continues the theme developed in paragraph 5 of "Man" engaged in individual pursuits, as opposed to "Man" as a whole. In paragraph 6, it is the scholar who is engaged in the individual pursuit of "mere thinker" or "parrot of other men's thinking."

37. **(B)** The theme of the first part of this passage is independence from European thought, and this is what Emerson has in mind when he writes this sentence: that the songs "will be sung themselves," meaning free of European influence.

38. **(D)** Emerson makes this point to emphasize that the central theme of nature (things unchanged by Man) is the first concern of humans, and quite different from "work," by which most humans come to be defined. The other choices do not focus on the *central* theme of nature.

39. **(A)** The author uses this excerpt to start a series of parallel sentences describing how the complexity of thought advances with age.

40. **(A)** This excerpt comes from paragraph 6, in which the author uses the excerpt to describe the scholar in his "degenerate" or lesser state as a mere thinker. The word "mere," in choice (A), is similar in meaning to the word "lesser."

Constructed-Response Examples

There are many possible responses to a constructed-response item.

Assignment 1: Focused-Response Example

This 181-word response would likely earn a 3, or possibly a 4.

In the first passage, Senator DeMint raises questions about the necessity of raising the national debt limit. He has two main points. The first is that having a high national debt is just not a good idea. He thinks the government should just spend less and find a way to do it. He also makes the point of prioritizing debt payments. He draws on the common sense decisions that average Americans make every day as they decide which credit cards to pay in full and which to pay only partly.

In the second passage, Secretary Geithner argues that the national debt limit must be raised. He points out that the debt limit increase is needed for money that has already been authorized, and that not raising the debt to pay these bills would jeopardize the nation's credit rating. He supports his position by pointing out that Senator DeMint's proposal to prioritize debt payments is an unproven approach and that the federal government is not like an American consumer, and there is simply no way to responsibly avoid a debt limit increase.

Assignment 2: Focused Response Example

This 185-word response would likely earn a 4 or possibly a 3.

The Federal Debt Limit Graph shows the federal debt held by the public as a percent of GDP (Gross Domestic Product). This approach is useful because one could argue that a higher GDP means that the country can support a higher debt. The graph paints a troubling picture of a Debt to GDP ratio, which is already higher than any time since World War II. The graph predicts that the debt will surpass the GDP by 2030.

The graph itself is most supportive of the view in passage A, that raising the national debt does appear to present a significant issue. The essential view in passage A is that the federal government should spend less and so incur less debt. Interestingly, the author of passage B never addresses this issue. That writer's view is simple: we owe the money and we don't have enough to pay it so we have to borrow. He never addresses what got us there in the first place and so his position in passage B does not address the specific issue of the amount of national debt shown in the graph.

Assignment 3: Extended Response Example

This 473-word response would likely earn a 3.
The passages and the graph reveal to me that a national debt limit is important and should not be removed.

The initial support for this position is found in the graph itself. The graph predicts a national debt in excess of the country's GDP in fewer than 20 years from now. The impact of such an event would be profound. The predictions of a higher national debt would likely be higher if there was no debt limit. The limit compels lawmakers and the president to visit the issue of the national debt and make a decision about raising it, and not just pile on more and more debt without any checks and balances.

Support for my position that the national debt should not be removed is actually found in both passages. In passage A, the Senator argues that the national debt exists precisely because, Washington has shown time and again that it is perfectly willing to spend more money. That is why the debt limit exists in the first case. There is a certain amount of politics and jousting.

That is a fairly powerful reason for maintaining the debt limit. There is a certain amount of politics involved in both the passages, but this argument is nonetheless a good reason for maintaining a national debt limit.

Surprisingly, support for my position comes from passage B. In this passage the Secretary of the Treasury argues for raising the debt limit. He makes some compelling arguments, primarily to prevent the impending default of the United States. However, he never addresses the reason this debt limit increase is needed, and never suggests that the debt limit is a bad idea. It is true that his job is to make sure the country's bills are paid, and not the process of setting the debt limit. However, his unwillingness to address the existence of the debt limit adds more strength to my argument.

In summary, we have a graph that predicts what seems an unsustainable national debt that as interest rates increase as the Federal Reserve predicts will cost the American taxpayers two and three times the amount each year to just pay the debt interest. Just on those grounds alone, the debt needs to be monitored and controlled. Passage A comes out strongly against raising the national debt, while passage B just argues that the debt has to be raised out of necessity, but makes no recommendation for eliminating it.

The most effective argument against my position is that the removal of the debt limit would create less uncertainty about a potential default by the United States, and it is a good argument. As good as this argument is, the control of the debt through a fixed debt limit that can only be raised through affirmative congressional and presidential action outweighs any advantages of an unlimited debt.

40 Selected-Choice items

3 Constructed-Response Writing to Sources Items

Darken the lettered oval to show your choice for the multiple-choice items.

Use a word processor, without the spell or grammar checker, and type your constructed-response answers.

USE THIS PASSAGE TO ANSWER THE QUESTIONS THAT FOLLOW.

"Kew Gardens," by Virginia Woolf (1882–1941)

From *Monday or Tuesday*, by Virginia Woolf. New York: Harcourt, Brace and Company, Inc., 1921

1   FROM THE OVAL-SHAPED flower-bed there rose perhaps a hundred stalks spreading into heart-shaped or tongue-shaped leaves half way up and unfurling at the tip red or blue or yellow petals marked with spots of color raised upon the surface; and from the red, blue or yellow gloom of the throat emerged a straight bar, rough with gold dust and slightly clubbed at the end. The petals were voluminous enough to be stirred by the summer breeze, and when they moved, the red, blue and yellow lights passed one over the other. The light fell either upon the smooth, grey back of a pebble, or, the shell of a snail with its brown, circular veins, or falling into a raindrop, it expanded with such intensity of red, blue and yellow the thin walls of water that one expected them to burst and disappear.

2   Instead, the drop was left in a second silver grey once more, and the light now settled upon the flesh of a leaf, revealing the branching thread of fibre beneath the surface, and again it moved on and spread its illumination in the vast green spaces beneath the dome of the leaves. Then the breeze stirred rather more briskly overhead and the color was flashed into the air above, into the eyes of the men and women who walk in Kew Gardens in July.

3   The figures of these men and women straggled past the flower-bed with a curiously irregular movement not unlike that of the white and blue butterflies. The man was about six inches in front of the woman, strolling carelessly, while she bore on with greater purpose, only turning her head now and then to see that the children were not too far behind. The man kept this distance in front of the woman purposely, for he wished to go on with his thoughts.

4   "Fifteen years ago I came here with Lily," he thought. "We sat somewhere over there by a lake and I begged her to marry me all through the hot afternoon. All the time I spoke I knew without looking up what she was going to say. My love, my desire, were in the dragonfly; for some reason I thought that if it settled there, on that leaf, the broad one, if the dragonfly settled on the leaf she would say 'Yes' at once. But the dragonfly went round and round: it never settled anywhere—of course not, happily not, or I shouldn't be walking here with Eleanor and the children—"Tell me, Eleanor. Do you ever think of the past?"

5   "Why do you ask, Simon?"

6 "Because I've been thinking of the past. I've been thinking of Lily, the woman I might have married. . . . Well, why are you silent? Do you mind my thinking of the past?"

7 "Why should I mind, Simon? Doesn't one always think of the past, in a garden with men and women lying under the trees? Aren't they one's past, all that remains of it, those men and women, those ghosts lying under the trees, . . . one's happiness, one's reality?"

8 "For me, a square silver shoe buckle and a dragonfly—"

9 "For me, a kiss. Imagine six little girls sitting before their easels twenty years ago, down by the side of a lake, painting the water-lilies. And suddenly a kiss, there on the back of my neck. And my hand shook all the afternoon so that I couldn't paint. I took out my watch and marked the hour when I would allow myself to think of the kiss for five minutes only—it was so precious—the kiss of an old grey-haired woman with a wart on her nose, the mother of all my kisses all my life. "Come, Caroline, come, Hubert."

10 They walked on the past the flower-bed, now walking four abreast, and soon diminished in size among the trees and looked half transparent as the sunlight and shade swam over their backs in large trembling irregular patches.

11 In the oval flower-bed the snail, whose shell had been stained red, blue, and yellow for the space of two minutes or so, now appeared to be moving very slightly in its shell, and next began to labor over the crumbs of loose earth which broke away and rolled down as it passed over them. It appeared to have a definite goal in front of it, differing in this respect from the singular high stepping angular green insect who attempted to cross in front of it, and waited for a second with its antennae trembling as if in deliberation, and then stepped off as rapidly and strangely in the opposite direction.

12 Brown cliffs with deep green lakes in the hollows, flat, blade-like trees that waved from root to tip, round boulders of grey stone, vast crumpled surfaces of a thin crackling texture—all these objects lay across the snail's progress between one stalk and another to his goal. Before he had decided whether to circumvent the arched tent of a dead leaf or to breast it there came past the bed the feet of other human beings.

13 This time they were both men. The younger of the two wore an expression of perhaps unnatural calm; he raised his eyes and fixed them very steadily in front of him while his companion spoke, and directly his companion had done speaking he looked on the ground again and sometimes opened his lips only after a long pause and sometimes did not open them at all.

14 The elder man had a curiously uneven and shaky method of walking, jerking his hand forward and throwing up his head abruptly, rather in the manner of an impatient carriage horse tired of waiting outside a house; but in the man these gestures were irresolute and pointless. He talked almost incessantly; he smiled to himself and again began to talk, as if the smile had been an answer. He was talking about spirits—the spirits of the dead, who, according to him, were even now telling him all sorts of odd things about their experiences in Heaven.

Questions

1. In the first paragraph, the author's most likely reason for repeating the phrase "red or blue or yellow" is to

   Ⓐ evoke three of the colors of the rainbow.
   Ⓑ set the mood someone might experience as they strolled through the garden.
   Ⓒ describe the many representations of the petals' colors.
   Ⓓ to simply identify the petals' colors.

2. The author develops the idea in paragraph 3 that the man was contemplative by describing

   Ⓐ the distance he kept in front of the woman.
   Ⓑ the man and woman as straggling by.
   Ⓒ that the pace of the man and woman were like the movement of the butterflies.
   Ⓓ how the children were not too far behind.

3. This sentence appears in paragraph 9: "I took out my watch and marked the hour when I would allow myself to think of the kiss for five minutes only—it was so precious—the kiss of an old grey-haired woman with a wart on her nose, the mother of all my kisses all my life. 'Come, Caroline, come, Hubert.'"

   Which of the following words or phrases comes closest to the meaning of "marked" in the sentence?

   Ⓐ Clearly noticeable
   Ⓑ Noted
   Ⓒ Evident
   Ⓓ Detected

4. The author reveals that the man did not marry Lily. This is referred to in which of the following excerpts?

   Ⓐ "Why should I mind, Simon? Doesn't one always think of the past, in a garden with men and women lying under the trees?"
   Ⓑ "All the time I spoke I knew without looking up what she was going to say."
   Ⓒ "For me, a square silver shoe buckle and a dragonfly—"
   Ⓓ "Come, Caroline, come, Hubert."

5. Paragraph 4 contains the following sentence: "But the dragonfly went round and round: it never settled anywhere—of course not."

   This sentence most clearly connects to the paragraph in that it

   Ⓐ was a random event that reflected a larger idea of unpredictability.
   Ⓑ was considered predictive of an event.
   Ⓒ reflected a thought process of the man in the passage.
   Ⓓ was a metaphor for the thought process of the person making the decision.

6. You will find this sentence in paragraph 7: "Doesn't one always think of the past, in a garden with men and women lying under the trees? Aren't they one's past, all that remains of it, those men and women . . .?"

   In this sentence, the woman is

   (A) providing a context for the man's question.
   (B) offering a simile to help answer the man's question.
   (C) drawing a comparison between the current setting and the setting as it must have been years earlier.
   (D) explaining how the physical world around them is really an abstract expression of reality.

7. The discussion of the garden and its visitors in paragraphs 1 through 4 helps develop a central idea in the passage, which is

   (A) the unchanging nature of the garden compared to the humans who visit it.
   (B) the parallel but unrelated nature of the garden and its visitors.
   (C) a comparison of the colorful world of nature with the more mundane nature of humans.
   (D) the close relationship between the garden and the humans that visit it.

8. How does the discussion in paragraph 10 of four people walking abreast relate to the previous paragraphs 4 through 9?

   (A) It shows that the garden path has widened.
   (B) It shows that the man is less caught up in his own thoughts, and that the children have heeded their mother's request to catch up.
   (C) It indicates a symmetry that is in keeping with the symmetry we see in the garden.
   (D) It resolves the dissonance that was noted in the earlier paragraphs.

USE THIS PASSAGE TO ANSWER THE QUESTIONS THAT FOLLOW.

Committee on Commerce, Science, and Transportation

United States Senate, One Hundred Eighth Congress, First Session, November 17, 2004

Science and Transportation Subcommittee on Science, Technology and Space:

1 My name is Cheryl Sensenbrenner, a Board Member of the American Association of People with Disabilities (AAPD), a national non-profit, non-partisan membership organization promoting political and economic empowerment for the more than 56 million disabled children and adults in the U.S.

   I am here to testify about prenatal tests to detect genetic abnormalities. I am also here as a woman with a disability, and, probably most importantly, as the proud sister of a woman with Down syndrome, Tara Rae Warren. I am delighted that my sister, Tara, is able to be with us today for this important hearing. My comments today will be more personal.

2 Although we are certainly making progress in public attitudes, there is still a strong tendency in American society to underestimate the positive contributions that people with disabilities are capable of making if given a chance. I have seen people continually under-

estimate what my sister is capable of doing, and I have seen what can happen when people believe in her and give her an opportunity to shine.

3   Because Tara's mental disability is physically recognized, she is almost daily subjected to snide remarks, odd looks and put downs. Tara has faced many obstacles with no fear and total perseverance. Through her early education and with her family's support, Tara has been able to support herself with various jobs.

4   This financial independence has been a great source of pride for Tara. She has been able to pay for the car she drives and her car insurance. In the past few elections, Tara has been a non-partisan poll watcher in Wisconsin. Tara has completed her high school education and taken a couple of college courses. She has given speeches to students of special education on the challenges of her disability. Tara would be most happy to answer any questions you might have—once she stops blushing.

5   Although I don't often encounter the same degree of paternalism that my sister has faced, I can tell you from my personal experience living with a physical disability for all of my adult life that people frequently underestimate or overlook my capacities as well.

6   This has been a lifelong journey since I was twenty-two years old. I remember sitting in the lobby waiting for my father to conduct some personal business. I remember a bank executive looking at me and stating "people like that belong on the park benches out front and not in our lobby." I found it amazing that someone with a higher education would still think with such a closed mind. I can also remember back when the physically disabled were determined not qualified to serve on a jury. I am curious to know whether they truly believed that I would be mentally unfit due to my physical disability or if it was simply an issue of handicap accessibility. Being a disabled person can be difficult, but it is not impossible to deal with. On the positive side with the support of my dear family and friends, only certain sports and pretty shoes with heels remain unapproachable to me.

7   When I had my children, I didn't have to worry about prenatal genetic testing because the science hadn't evolved to a point where that kind of testing was widespread. I know that in recent years the science and practice of prenatal genetic testing has grown so that now it is very common for pregnant mothers to be offered screening tests to determine the likelihood that their baby will be born with conditions like Down syndrome and Spina Bifida.

8   I am concerned that expecting parents are being asked to consent to tests without really understanding the pros and cons of participating in this kind of testing. I am also even more concerned that expecting parents are being given the positive results of prenatal diagnostic tests for conditions like Down syndrome without getting good information about what it is like to raise a child with Down syndrome, or what supports and programs exist in the community for families with disabled children.

9   When you couple the uninformed fears and concerns many parents are likely to have when they receive this kind of prenatal diagnosis with the pressures they may perceive from their treating professionals, family, and friends to terminate the pregnancy, you have a recipe for uninformed decision making that can dramatically reduce the number of babies born with Down syndrome and other congenital disabilities. As someone who can testify to the great joy and love that my sister has brought to me and my family, I am

saddened and disheartened to think that the new genetic technologies would have this kind of impact.

10 As a parent, I am deeply troubled by any efforts to use prenatal genetic testing to identify genetically "normal" or "healthy" children and terminate pregnancies that fail to pass this test. Our responsibility as parents is to love and nurture our children, whatever challenges they may face. As a society, do we really want to live in a world where children must pass genetic tests in order to be born?

11 I believe we have a moral and ethical responsibility to maximize the likelihood that children with disabilities will be welcomed into the world like other children, and that their families will be supported in their efforts to help their children thrive. Science and medicine should be used to improve the quality of people's lives, not to encourage parents to try to engineer an advantage in the genetic lottery for their children.

12 If our experience with the prenatal screening and tests currently being used for Down syndrome and Spina Bifida is a harbinger of what is to come, I am very worried about how the new genetic technologies will be used moving forward. I believe that God created a beautifully diverse human population for a reason, and we should be humble and proceed with caution as we develop tools that can be manipulated to threaten that diversity.

Questions

9. Which of the following excerpts from the passage best expresses the author's central idea?

   Ⓐ "This has been a lifelong journey since I was twenty-two years old."
   Ⓑ "I am very worried about how the new genetic technologies will be used moving forward."
   Ⓒ "I believe we have a moral and ethical responsibility to maximize the likelihood that children with disabilities will be welcomed into the world like other children, and that their families will be supported in their efforts to help their children thrive."
   Ⓓ "Although we are certainly making progress in public attitudes, there is still a strong tendency in American society to underestimate the positive contributions that people with disabilities are capable of making if given a chance."

10. Which of the following best describes how the author develops the main idea of the passage?

   Ⓐ The author states her position on prenatal testing and then develops that main idea with a series of supporting details.
   Ⓑ The author develops her experience with disabilities and then moves on to state her position on prenatal research.
   Ⓒ The author discusses the impact of prenatal research on her disabled sister and then establishes that more in-depth testing would have caused more problems for her sister.
   Ⓓ The author discusses the problems with her disability and her sister's disability and uses this experience to discuss the unreliable nature of prenatal testing.

11. Which of the following sentences from the passage reveals part of the evolution of the author's thinking about the <u>perception</u> of disabilities?

Ⓐ "When I had my children, I didn't have to worry about prenatal genetic testing because the science had not evolved . . ."

Ⓑ "Because Tara's mental disability is physically recognized, she is almost daily subjected to snide comments, odd looks and put downs."

Ⓒ "I found it amazing that someone with a higher education could have such a closed mind."

Ⓓ "Being a disabled person can be difficult, but it is not impossible to deal with."

12. Use this portion of the passage from paragraphs 1 and 2 to answer the question that follows.

"I am also here as a woman with a disability, and, probably most importantly, as the proud sister of a woman with Down syndrome, Tara Rae Warren. I am delighted that my sister, Tara, is able to be with us today for this important hearing. My comments today will be more personal.

Although we are certainly making progress in public attitudes, there is still a strong tendency in American society to underestimate the positive contributions that people with disabilities are capable of making if given a chance."

Which of the following best describes how the author uses words to most effectively deliver the personal tone and a main point of the passage?

Ⓐ Phrases such as "delighted that my sister, Tara, is able to be with us," and "for this important hearing"

Ⓑ Phrases such as "comments today will be more personal," and "we are certainly making progress"

Ⓒ Phrases such as "strong tendency in American Society" and "underestimate the positive contribution"

Ⓓ Phrases such as "a woman with a disability" and the "proud sister of a woman with Down syndrome"

13. This excerpt is from paragraph 9:

"When you couple the uninformed fears and concerns many parents are likely to have when they receive this kind of prenatal diagnosis with the pressures they may perceive from their treating professionals, family, and friends to terminate the pregnancy, you have a recipe for uninformed decision making . . ."

This portion of the passage demonstrates the author's plan for developing the central idea by

Ⓐ emphasizing the concerns that many parents will have when they receive the results of prenatal testing.

Ⓑ showing how fears and pressure can be coupled.

Ⓒ laying a foundation for an argument against prenatal testing.

Ⓓ suggesting a relationship between prenatal testing and informed decision making.

14. This excerpt comes from paragraph 10:

"As a parent, I am deeply troubled by any efforts to use prenatal genetic testing to identify genetically "normal" or "healthy" children and terminate pregnancies that fail to pass this test. Our responsibility as parents is to love and nurture our children, whatever challenges they may face. As a society, do we really want to live in a world where children must pass genetic tests in order to be born?"

Which of the following statements best describes the way this excerpt relates to the rest of the passage?

Ⓐ It contrasts her situation as a parent with the situation of parents discussed in paragraphs 8 and 9.

Ⓑ It provides a contrast to her experience as a young woman, described in paragraph 6.

Ⓒ It shows how her life was different than her sister's life, which is described in paragraphs 3 and 4.

Ⓓ It provides further support for her experience as a disabled person described in paragraph 5.

15. This excerpt appears in paragraphs 3 and 4:

"Tara has been able to support herself with various jobs. This financial independence has been a great source of pride for Tara. She has been able to pay for her own car she drives and her car insurance."

In this excerpt, the author's words and the organization of the sentences most clearly conveys

Ⓐ her belief that gainful employment is the goal for most disabled people.

Ⓑ that pride comes from financial accomplishment.

Ⓒ that disabled people need not be financially dependent.

Ⓓ that her sister has achieved more than might have been expected of her.

16. In paragraph 6, the author uses a discussion of a physically disabled person serving on a jury to further develop the central idea by

Ⓐ musing on the reasons why physically disabled people were previously barred from jury duty.

Ⓑ showing the opportunities for further gains in how disabled people are treated.

Ⓒ presenting a fact with which many readers would be unaware.

Ⓓ raising the issue of how jury decisions might have been different if physically disabled people had been allowed to serve.

USE THIS PASSAGE TO ANSWER THE QUESTIONS THAT FOLLOW.

Adapted from *Narrative of the Life of Frederick Douglass, an American Slave,*
by Frederick Douglass

1   Colonel Lloyd kept from three to four hundred slaves on his home plantation, and owned a large number more on the neighboring farms belonging to him. It was the seat of government for the whole twenty farms. All disputes among the overseers were settled here. If a slave was convicted of any high misdemeanor, became unmanageable, or evinced a determination to run away, he was brought immediately here, severely whipped, carried to Baltimore, and sold to Austin Woolfolk, or some other slave-trader, as a warning to the slaves remaining.

2   Here, too, the slaves of all the other farms received their monthly allowance of food, and their yearly clothing. The allowance of the slave children was given to their mothers, or the old women having the care of them. The children unable to work in the field had neither shoes, stockings, jackets, nor trousers, given to them; their clothing consisted of two coarse linen shirts per year. When these failed them, they went naked until the next allowance-day. Children from seven to ten years old, of both sexes, almost naked, might be seen at all seasons of the year.

3   There were no beds given the slaves, unless one coarse blanket be considered such, and none but the men and women had these. This, however, is not considered a very great privation. They find less difficulty from the want of beds, than from the want of time to sleep; for when their day's work in the field is done, the most of them having their washing, mending, and cooking to do, and having few or none of the ordinary facilities for doing either of these, very many of their sleeping hours are consumed in preparing for the field the coming day; and when this is done, old and young, male and female, married and single, drop down side by side, on one common bed,—the cold, damp floor,—each covering himself or herself with their miserable blankets; and here they sleep till they are summoned to the field by the driver's horn.

4   At the sound of this, all must rise, and be off to the field. There must be no halting; every one must be at his or her post; and woe betides them who hear not this morning summons to the field. No age nor sex finds any favor. Mr. Severe, the overseer, used to stand by the door of the quarter, armed with a large hickory stick and heavy cowskin, ready to whip any one who was so unfortunate as not to hear, or, from any other cause, was prevented from being ready to start for the field at the sound of the horn.

5   Mr. Severe was rightly named: he was a cruel man. I have seen him whip a woman, causing the blood to run half an hour at the time; and this, too, in the midst of her crying children, pleading for their mother's release. He seemed to take pleasure in manifesting his fiendish barbarity. Added to his cruelty, he was a profane swearer. It was enough to chill the blood and stiffen the hair of an ordinary man to hear him talk. The field was the place to witness his cruelty and profanity. His presence made it both the field of blood and of blasphemy. From the rising till the going down of the sun, he was cursing, raving, cutting, and slashing among the slaves of the field, in the most frightful manner.

6   The home plantation of Colonel Lloyd wore the appearance of a country village. It was called by the slaves the Great House Farm. Few privileges were esteemed higher, by the slaves of the out-farms, than that of being selected to do errands at the Great House Farm. They regarded it as evidence of great confidence reposed in them by their overseers; and it was on this account, as well as a constant desire to be out of the field from under the driver's lash, that they esteemed it a high privilege, one worth careful living for. The competitors for this office sought as diligently to please their overseers, as the office-seekers in the political parties seek to please and deceive the people.

7   The slaves selected to go to the Great House Farm, for the monthly allowance for themselves and their fellow-slaves, were peculiarly enthusiastic. They would compose and sing as they went along, consulting neither time nor tune. The thought that came up, came out—if not in the word, in the sound;—and as frequently in the one as in the other. They would sometimes sing the most pathetic sentiment in the most rapturous tone, and the most rapturous sentiment in the most pathetic tone. Into all of their songs they would manage to weave something of the Great House Farm. They would then sing most exultingly the following words:—

8   "I am going away to the Great House Farm!

O, yea! O, yea! O!"

9   I did not, when a slave, understand the deep meaning of those rude and apparently incoherent songs. I was myself within the circle; so that I neither saw nor heard as those without might see and hear. They told a tale of woe which was then altogether beyond my feeble comprehension; they were tones loud, long, and deep; they breathed the prayer and complaint of souls boiling over with the bitterest anguish. Every tone was a testimony against slavery, and a prayer to God for deliverance from chains. The hearing of those wild notes always depressed my spirit, and filled me with ineffable sadness.

10   If any one wishes to be impressed with the soul-killing effects of slavery, let him go to Colonel Lloyd's plantation, and, on allowance-day, place himself in the deep pine woods, and there let him, in silence, analyze the sounds that shall pass through the chambers of his soul. If he is not thus impressed, it will only be because "there is no flesh in his obdurate heart."

Questions

17. The word "obdurate," underlined in paragraph 10, most likely means

    Ⓐ elusive.

    Ⓑ empty.

    Ⓒ unyielding.

    Ⓓ lifeless.

18. Which of the following sentences from the passage most nearly conveys the author's central theme?

    Ⓐ "If any one wishes to be impressed with the soul-killing effects of slavery, let him go to Colonel Lloyd's plantation, and, on allowance-day, place himself in the deep pine woods, and there let him, in silence, analyze the sounds that shall pass through the chambers of his soul."

    Ⓑ "If a slave was convicted of any high misdemeanor, became unmanageable, or evinced a determination to run away, he was brought immediately here, severely whipped, carried to Baltimore, and sold to Austin Woolfolk, or some other slave-trader, as a warning to the slaves remaining."

    Ⓒ "Children from seven to ten years old, of both sexes, almost naked, might be seen at all seasons of the year."

    Ⓓ "I have seen him whip a woman, causing the blood to run half an hour at the time; and this, too, in the midst of her crying children, pleading for their mother's release."

19. Which of the following best summarizes how the author develops the central theme of the passage?

    Ⓐ The author is describing only the worst practices among slave owners, and omits those slave owners who regularly freed slaves.

    Ⓑ The author emphasizes inappropriate treatment of women and children to make his point about cruelty.

    Ⓒ The author gives many details of slavery to establish the central theme of the passage.

    Ⓓ The author described impromptu slave music to contrast the reality of slavery with the techniques used by slaves to endure their hardship.

20. Which of the following parts of the passage have the most positive connotation in the context of the passage?

    Ⓐ "At the sound of this, all must rise, and be off to the fields."

    Ⓑ "Children . . . of both sexes, almost naked, might be seen at all seasons of the year."

    Ⓒ ". . . and sold to Austin Woolfolk, or some other slave-trader, as a warning to the slaves remaining."

    Ⓓ "There were no beds given the slaves . . ."

21. The author's comments about slaves chosen to go to the Great House Farm in paragraph 7 relates to the rest of the passage by

   (A) describing how the relative advantages of this selection are seen as a positive compared to the other choices available to them.

   (B) showing how slaves who were good workers were given the advantages that good workers might normally expect to receive.

   (C) describing circumstances under which the positive feelings of the slaves were released, as evidenced by their spontaneous singing.

   (D) revealing that there was a deep-seated desire among the slaves to advance and better themselves, the first step of which was this acknowledgement of their accomplishments.

22. The excerpt below appears in paragraph 2:

   "The children unable to work in the field had neither shoes, stockings, jackets, nor trousers, given to them; their clothing consisted of two coarse linen shirts per year. When these failed them, they went naked until the next allowance-day. Children from seven to ten years old, of both sexes, almost naked, might be seen at all seasons of the year."

   The author contrasts the adult slaves and the slave children who could not work as adult slaves by indicating that adult slaves

   (A) were regularly given the same shoes, stockings, jackets, and trousers, as slave children.

   (B) shared clothing with slave children even though the slave children often preferred to be naked.

   (C) and slave children had to go naked if the clothing they were given failed before allowance day.

   (D) were given more than slave children.

23. In which of the following excerpts from the passage does the author describe the reason why "Few privileges were esteemed higher, by the slaves of the out-farms, than that of being selected to do errands at the Great House Farm"?

   (A) "The competitors for this office sought as diligently to please their overseers, as the office-seekers in the political parties seek to please and deceive the people."

   (B) "They regarded it as evidence of great confidence reposed in them by their overseers."

   (C) "The slaves selected to go to the Great House Farm, for the monthly allowance for themselves and their fellow-slaves, were peculiarly enthusiastic."

   (D) "Every tone was a testimony against slavery, and a prayer to God for deliverance from chains."

24. In the first paragraph, the author gives us some insight into Colonel Lloyd's practices, which help us understand Colonel Lloyd as someone who

   (A) had no respect for African Americans and was determined to punish them.

   (B) took slave children from their mothers and fathers.

   (C) managed his "business" through fear and intimidation.

   (D) punished slaves by whipping and selling their relatives.

USE THIS PASSAGE TO ANSWER THE QUESTIONS THAT FOLLOW.

From *My Antonia*, by Willa Cather

1   WE KNEW THAT THINGS were hard for our immigrant neighbors, but the two girls were lighthearted and never complained. They were always ready to forget their troubles at home, and to run away with me over the prairie, scaring rabbits or starting up flocks of quail.

2   I remember Antonia's excitement when she came into our kitchen one afternoon and announced: "My papa find friends up north, with Russian mans. Last night he take me for see, and I can understand very much talk. Nice mans. Everybody laugh. The first time I see my papa laugh in this country. 'Oh, very nice!'"

3   I asked her if she meant the two immigrants who lived up by the big dog-town. I had often been tempted to go to see them when I was riding in that direction, but one of them was a wild-looking fellow and I was a little afraid of him. Russia seemed to me more remote than any other country—farther away than China, almost as far as the North Pole.

4   Of all the strange, uprooted people among the first settlers, those two men were the strangest and the most aloof. Their last names were unpronounceable, so they were called Pavel and Peter. They went about making signs to people, and until the Shimerdas came they had no friends. Pavel, the tall one, was said to be an anarchist; since he had no means of imparting his opinions, his generally excited and rebellious manner gave rise to this supposition. He must once have been very strong, but now his great frame had a wasted look, and the skin was drawn tight over his high cheekbones.

5   Peter, his companion, was a very different sort of fellow; short, bow-legged, and as fat as butter. He always seemed pleased when he met people on the road, smiled and took off his cap to everyone, men as well as women. At a distance, on his wagon, he looked like an old man; his hair and beard were of such a pale flaxen color. His rosy face, with its snub nose, set in this fleece, was like a melon among its leaves. He was usually called "Curly Peter," or "Rooshian Peter."

6   The two Russians made good farm-hands. I had heard our neighbors laughing when they told how Peter always had to go home at night to milk his cow. Other bachelor homesteaders used canned milk. Sometimes Peter came to church at the sod schoolhouse. It was there I first saw him, sitting on a low bench by the door, his plush cap in his hands, his bare feet tucked apologetically under the seat.

7   After Mr. Shimerda discovered the Russians, he went to see them almost every evening, and sometimes took Antonia with him. She said they came from a part of Russia where the language was not very different from their own, and if I wanted to go to their place, she could talk to them for me.

8   One afternoon, before the heavy frosts began, we rode up there together on my pony. The Russians had a neat log house built on a grassy slope. As we rode up the draw, we skirted a big melon patch, and a garden with squashes and yellow cucumbers. We found Peter out behind his kitchen, bending over a washtub. He was working so hard that he did not hear us coming. When he straightened himself up to greet us, drops of perspiration were rolling from his thick nose down onto his curly beard. Peter took us down to see his chickens and his cow. He told Antonia that in his country only rich people had cows, but here any man could have one. The milk was good for Pavel, who was often sick, and he could make butter by beating sour cream with a wooden spoon. Peter was very fond of his cow.

9   After he had shown us his garden, Peter trundled a load of watermelons up the hill in his wheelbarrow. Pavel was not at home. The house I thought very comfortable for two men who were "batching." Besides the kitchen, there was a living-room, with a wide double bed built against the wall, properly made up with blue gingham sheets and pillows. There was a little storeroom, too, with a window. That day the floor was covered with garden things, drying for winter; corn and beans and fat yellow cucumbers. There were no screens or window-blinds in the house, and all the doors and windows stood wide open, letting in flies and sunshine alike.

10   Peter put the melons in a row on the oilcloth-covered table and stood over them, brandishing a butcher knife. Before the blade got fairly into them, they split of their own ripeness, with a delicious sound. I had never seen anyone eat so many melons as Peter ate. He assured us that they were good for one—better than medicine; in his country people lived on them at this time of year. He was very hospitable and jolly. Once, while he was looking at Antonia, he sighed and told us that if he had stayed at home in Russia perhaps by this time he would have had a pretty daughter of his own. He said he had left his country because of a "great trouble."

11   When we got up to go, Peter looked about in perplexity for something that would entertain us. He ran into the storeroom and brought out a gaudily painted harmonica, sat down on a bench, and he began to play like a whole band. The tunes were either very lively or very doleful, and he sang words to some of them.

12   Before we left, Peter put ripe cucumbers into a sack for Mrs. Shimerda and gave us a lard-pail full of milk to cook them in. I had never heard of cooking cucumbers, but Antonia assured me they were very good. We had to walk the pony all the way home to keep from spilling the milk.

Questions

25. In the first paragraph, the author notes, "we knew that things were hard for our immigrant neighbors." Which of the following information from the paragraph supports that statement?

   Ⓐ They had only one parent.
   Ⓑ They were from Russia.
   Ⓒ They were always able to forget their troubles at home.
   Ⓓ The family was uprooted.

26. In which excerpt from the passage is the underlined phrase most consistent with being wistful?

   Ⓐ "Of all the strange, <u>uprooted people</u> among the first settlers, those two men were the strangest and the most aloof."
   Ⓑ "He said he had left his country because of a '<u>great trouble.</u>'"
   Ⓒ "He ran into the storeroom and brought out a <u>gaudily painted</u> harmonica, sat down on a bench, and he began to play like a whole band."
   Ⓓ "Once, while he was looking at Antonia, <u>he sighed</u> and told us that if he had stayed at home in Russia perhaps by this time he would have had a pretty daughter of his own."

27. The discussion of the Russians in paragraphs 4 and 5 is related to the rest of the passage because it

   Ⓐ develops the characters and sets the stage for further discussion.
   Ⓑ shows the limited resources that these other immigrants had.
   Ⓒ raises questions about how much they can be trusted to fit into the area's society.
   Ⓓ describes the characteristics of Russian immigrants to give insight into Antonia's family.

28. This excerpt is from paragraph 2.

"I remember Antonia's excitement when she came into our kitchen one afternoon and announced: "My papa find friends up north, with Russian mans. Last night he take me for see, and I can understand very much talk. Nice mans. Everybody laugh. The first time I see my papa laugh in this country. 'Oh, very nice!'"

In this portion of the passage, the author characterizes the relationship between Antonia and her father primarily by describing

   Ⓐ her father as someone who sought out other immigrants "up north" for her to associate with.
   Ⓑ "Antonia's excitement" when her father met other immigrants.
   Ⓒ Antonia's pleasure that it was the first time she had seen her papa "laugh in this country."
   Ⓓ Antonia's reaction that the other immigrants were "nice mans."

29. This is a portion of paragraph 3: "but one of them was a wild-looking fellow"

   In context, which of the following excerpts most directly refers to that portion of paragraph 3?

   Ⓐ "... further away than China almost as far as the North Pole."
   Ⓑ "He said he had left his country because of a 'great trouble' ..."
   Ⓒ "... he had no means of imparting his opinions, his generally excited and rebellious manner ..."
   Ⓓ "... the two immigrants who lived up by the big dog-town ..."

30. This sentence appears in paragraph 11: "When we got up to go, Peter looked about in perplexity for something that would entertain us."

   Which phrase below is the closest in meaning to the word "perplexity?"

   Ⓐ Wanting to please
   Ⓑ Unable to locate something
   Ⓒ A state of confusion
   Ⓓ A sense of disbelief

31. The author's report in paragraph 6 that "I had heard our neighbors laughing when they told how Peter always had to go home at night to milk his cow," serves what primary purpose in the passage?

   Ⓐ It emphasizes an important fact about Peter's life.
   Ⓑ It establishes Peter's work ethic.
   Ⓒ It provides a contrast with his ability to own a cow in his native country.
   Ⓓ It shows that Peter was the subject of scorn in the community.

32. This sentence appears in paragraph 10: "He assured us that they were good for one—better than medicine; in his country people lived on them at this time of year."

   In the sentence, Peter's comparison of melons and medicine presents the reader with

   Ⓐ a more natural "green view" of effective medicine.
   Ⓑ insight into effective approaches to healthy living followed in other countries.
   Ⓒ an example of the folklore in other countries.
   Ⓓ affirmation of the well-known effectiveness of melons as an anti-carcinogen.

USE THIS PASSAGE TO ANSWER THE QUESTIONS THAT FOLLOW.

From *Hiawatha and the Iroquois Confederation,* by Horatio Hale

1   The formation of the Iroquois confederacy likely dates from about the middle of the fifteenth century. There is reason to believe that prior to that time the five tribes, who are dignified with the title of nations, had held the region south of Lake Ontario, extending from the Hudson to the Genesee river. They were then isolated tribes, at war occasionally with one another, and almost constantly with the fierce Algonquins who surrounded them.

2   At this time two great dangers, the one from without, the other from within, pressed upon these tribes. The Mohegans, or Mohicans, a powerful Algonquin people waged a desperate war against them. In this war the most easterly of the Iroquois, the Mohawks and Oneidas, bore the brunt and were the greatest sufferers. The two westerly nations, the Senecas and Cayugas, had a peril of their own to encounter. The central nation, the Onondagas, were then under the control of a dreaded chief. The chiefs who ventured to oppose him were taken off one after another by secret means, or were compelled to flee.

3   The name Atotarho signifies "entangled." The usual process by which mythology, after a few generations, makes fables out of names, has not been wanting here. In the legends which the Indian story-tellers recount in winter about their cabin fires, Atotarho figures as a being of preterhuman nature, whose head, in lieu of hair, is adorned with living snakes. A rude pictorial representation shows him seated and giving audience, in horrible state, with the upper part of his person enveloped by these writhing and entangled reptiles. But the grave Counsillors Canadian Reservation, who recite his history as they have heard it from their fathers at every installation of a high chief, do not repeat these inventions of marvel-loving gossips, and only smile with good-humored derision when they are referred to.

4   Among the Onondagas a chief of high rank whose name, variously written—Hiawatha, Hayonwatha, Ayongwhata, Taoungwatha—is rendered, "he who seeks the wampum belt." He had made himself greatly esteemed by his wisdom and his benevolence. He was now past middle age. Though many of his friends and relatives had perished by the machinations of Atotarho, he himself had been spared.

5   Hiawatha had long beheld with grief the evils which afflicted all tribes through the continual wars in which they were engaged, and the misgovernment and miseries at home. With much meditation he had elaborated in his mind the scheme of a vast confederation which would ensure universal peace. But the plan which Hiawatha had evolved differed from all others because it was to be a permanent government. While each nation was to retain its own council, general control was to be lodged in a federal senate, composed of representatives elected by each nation. Still further, and more remarkably, the confederation was to be indefinitely expansible. The avowed design of its proposer was to abolish war altogether. He wished the federation to extend until all the tribes of men should be included in it, and peace should everywhere reign.

6   Hiawatha's first endeavor was to enlist his own nation in the cause. He summoned a meeting of the chiefs and people of the Onondaga towns. The summons, proceeding from a chief of his rank and reputation, attracted a large concourse. "They came together, along the creeks, from all parts, to the general council-fire." However there appeared among them a well-known figure, grim, silent and forbidding, whose terrible aspect overawed the assemblage. The unspoken displeasure of Atotarho was sufficient to stifle all debate, and the meeting dispersed. Atotarho had organized among the more reckless warriors of his tribe a band of unscrupulous partisans, who did his bidding without question, and took off by secret murder all persons against whom he bore a grudge.

7   Hiawatha alone was undaunted. He summoned a second meeting, which was attended by a smaller number, and broke up as before, in confusion, on Atotarho's appearance. The unwearied reformer sent forth his runners a third time; but the people were disheartened. When the day of the council arrived, no one attended.

8   Hiawatha seated himself on the ground in sorrow. He enveloped his head in his mantle of skins, and remained for a long time bowed down in grief and thought. At length he arose and left the town and plunged into the forest; he climbed mountains; he crossed a lake; he floated down the Mohawk river in a canoe. Indeed, the flight of Hiawatha from Onondaga to the country of the Mohawks is to the Five Nations what the flight of Mohammed from Mecca to Medina is to the votaries of Islam. It is the turning point of their history.

9   Eventually he arrived at village of the residence of the noted chief Dekanawidah, whose name, in point of celebrity, ranks in Iroquois tradition with those of Hiawatha and Atotarho. One of Dekanawidah's brothers came out and approached Hiawatha, who sat silent and motionless. Something in his aspect awed the warrior. He returned to the house, and said to Dekanawidah, "a man, or a figure like a man, is seated nearby." "It is a guest," replied the chief; "go and bring him in. We will make him welcome." Thus Hiawatha and Dekanawidah first met.

10 The sagacity of the Mohawk chief grasped at once the advantages of the proposed plan, and, after much discussion, the agreement of the Mohawk nation was secured. Dekanawidah sent ambassadors to the nearest tribe, the Oneidas. Dekanawidah had good reason to expect that it would not prove difficult to win the consent of the Oneidas.

11 The Seneca's leading chief, Odatshehte, received their message in a friendly way, but "Come back in another day," he said. In the political speech of the Indians, a day is understood to mean a year. Dekanawidah and Hiawatha knew that they had to wait. After a year, they repaired to the place of meeting. The treaty which initiated the great league was then and there ratified between the Mohawk and Oneida nations.

Questions

33. The discussion in paragraph 2 primarily relates to the passage as a whole by establishing

    Ⓐ the Iroquois were in a constant state of warfare.
    Ⓑ the Onondagas represented the most significant internal threat to the Iroquois.
    Ⓒ there was a duality of threats facing the Iroquois.
    Ⓓ the formation of the Iroquois nation occurred about the time of the arrival of Columbus.

34. Which of the following excerpts from the passage best supports a central theme of the passage?

    Ⓐ "Among the Onondagas a chief of high rank whose name, variously written—Hiawatha, Hayonwatha, Ayongwhata, Taoungwatha—is rendered, "he who seeks the wampum belt." He had made himself greatly esteemed by his wisdom and his benevolence. He was now past middle age. Though many of his friends and relatives had perished by the machinations of Atotarho, he himself had been spared."
    Ⓑ "The name Atotarho signifies "entangled." The usual process by which mythology, after a few generations, makes fables out of names, has not been wanting here. In the legends which the Indian story-tellers recount in winter about their cabin fires, Atotarho figures as a being of preterhuman nature, whose head, in lieu of hair, is adorned with living snakes."
    Ⓒ "Hiawatha had long beheld with grief the evils which afflicted all tribes through the continual wars in which they were engaged, and the misgovernment and miseries at home. With much meditation he had elaborated in his mind the scheme of a vast confederation which would ensure universal peace."
    Ⓓ "The formation of the Iroquois confederacy likely dates from about the middle of the fifteenth century. There is reason to believe that prior to that time the five tribes, who are dignified with the title of nations, had held the region south of Lake Ontario, extending from the Hudson to the Genesee river."

35. The excerpt below is from paragraph 3:

    "The usual process by which mythology, after a few generations, makes fables out of names, has not been wanting here. In the legends which the Indian story-tellers recount in winter about their cabin fires, Atotarho figures as a being of preterhuman nature, whose head, in lieu of hair, is adorned with living snakes. A rude pictorial representation shows him seated and giving audience, in horrible state, with the upper part of his person enveloped by these writhing and entangled reptiles. But the grave Counsillors Canadian Reservation, who recite his history as they have heard it from their fathers at every installation of a high chief, do not repeat these inventions of marvel-loving gossips . . ."

    In the development of the character of Atotarho in this excerpt, the author

    Ⓐ demonstrates how Atotarho's nature was exaggerated in mythology.
    Ⓑ describes Atotarho as a fierce chief who used clandestine methods.
    Ⓒ contrasts the mythological depiction with a more realistic assessment.
    Ⓓ relies on old images of Atotarho.

36. This excerpt comes from paragraph 8:

"Hiawatha seated himself on the ground in sorrow. He enveloped his head in his mantle of skins, and remained for a long time bowed down in grief and thought. At length he arose and left the town and plunged into the forest; he climbed mountains; he crossed a lake; he floated down the Mohawk river in a canoe."

The tone of the passage is best developed in this selection through using details in the passage

Ⓐ to show the lengths Hiawatha went to get away from his tribe.
Ⓑ to suggest Hiawatha's determination.
Ⓒ to show the diversity of the area surrounding Hiawatha's village.
Ⓓ to show the fear Hiawatha felt from the retribution of the chief Atotarho.

37. Which of the following words or phrases come closest in meaning to the word "sagacity" in this excerpt from paragraph 10? "The sagacity of the Mohawk chief grasped at once the advantages of the proposed plan, and, after much discussion, the agreement of the Mohawk nation was secured."

Ⓐ Pursue personal advantages
Ⓑ Pursue political gains
Ⓒ Self-interest
Ⓓ Soundness of judgment

38. In which of the excerpts below does the author most obviously employ a euphemism?

Ⓐ "The unwearied reformer sent forth his runners a third time; but the people were disheartened."
Ⓑ "Indeed, the flight of Hiawatha from Onondaga to the country of the Mohawks is to the Five Nations what the flight of Mohammed from Mecca to Medina is to the votaries of Islam."
Ⓒ "The chiefs who ventured to oppose him were taken off one after another by secret means, or were compelled to flee."
Ⓓ "He wished the federation to extend until all the tribes of men should be included in it, and peace should everywhere reign."

39. Which of the following excerpts from the passage best reflects the author's point of view?

Ⓐ "The formation of the Iroquois federation likely dates from about the middle of the fifteenth century."
Ⓑ "Hiawatha had long beheld with grief the evils which afflicted all tribes through the continual wars in which they were engaged, and the misgovernment and miseries at home."
Ⓒ "Eventually he arrived at the village of the residence of the noted chief Dekanawidah, whose name, in point of celebrity, ranks in Iroquois tradition with those of Hiawatha and Atotarho."
Ⓓ "Indeed, the flight of Hiawatha from Onondaga to the country of the Mohawks is to the Five Nations what the flight of Mohammed from Mecca to Medina is to the votaries of Islam."

40. The excerpt below is from paragraph 4:

"Among the Onondagas a chief of high rank whose name, variously written—Hiawatha, Hayonwatha, Ayongwhata, Taoungwatha—is rendered, "he who seeks the wampum belt." He had made himself greatly esteemed by his wisdom and his benevolence. He was now past middle age. Though many of his friends and relatives had perished by the machinations of Atotarho, he himself had been spared."

Which of the following best characterizes how the author develops Atotarho's character?

Ⓐ Atotarho was ruthless, but careful not to lose popularity or face by "removing" a highly regarded chief whom others may have held in respect.

Ⓑ Atotarho kept his potential enemies and political adversaries in check by dealing harshly with their relatives and friends through clandestine methods.

Ⓒ Atotarho was a crafty chief who posed no threat to anyone who stood up to him.

Ⓓ Atotarho portrayed himself as ruthless, but he actually used threats to keep other members of the tribe in check.

Writing to Sources

You will see three exhibits. Two of the exhibits are original passages with differing views on a common topic. Note, passages are shown exactly as they appeared in the original.

The third exhibit is a graphic with information related to the topic.

Focused responses are 100 to 200 words each.

The extended response is 400 to 600 words and fully addresses a question or proposal related to the topic.

Use a word processor, with the spell check and grammar check disabled, to write your responses.

Plan before you write and do not rely on any outside sources.

Focused-Response Rating Scale

FOCUSED-RESPONSE CHARACTERISTICS

Focused responses are usually 100 to 200 words, but a minimum of 150 words should be your goal.

- The content of your response meets the requirements found in the prompt.
- Show evidence of engagement with the prompt's exhibits.
- Present a clear and coherent response.

4 Your focused response demonstrates a STRONG grasp of the writing skills and meets all the stated requirements of the focused-response prompt including the graphic.

3 Your focused response demonstrates a SATISFACTORY grasp of the writing skills and completely meets most of the stated requirements of the focused-response prompt.

2 Your focused response demonstrates a LIMITED grasp of the writing skills and completely meets few of the stated requirements of the focused-response prompt.

1 Your focused response demonstrates NO grasp of the writing skills and generally does not meet the stated requirements of the focused-response prompt.

U Your focused response cannot be scored because it is off topic, too short to score, or written in a language other than English. Even a well-written response that is off topic will be scored "U."

B You did not write a focused response

Extended-Response Rating Scale

EXTENDED-RESPONSE EXPECTATIONS

Extended responses must be 400 to 600 words; however, a minimum of 525 words should be your goal.

- Clearly communicate complex concepts and ideas in the context of the exhibits.
- Demonstrate that you have command of the evidence in the passages and the graphic.
- Organize complex ideas and write in a formal style with excellent word choice.
- Employ the standards of written English grammar, usage, and punctuation.

4 Your extended response demonstrates a STRONG grasp of the writing skills and meets all the stated requirements of the extended-response prompt including the graphic.

3 Your extended response demonstrates a SATISFACTORY grasp of the writing skills and completely meets most of the stated requirements of the extended-response prompt.

2 Your extended response demonstrates a LIMITED grasp of the writing skills and completely meets few of the stated requirements of the extended-response prompt.

1 Your extended response demonstrates NO grasp of the writing skills and generally does not meet the stated requirements of the extended-response prompt.

U Your extended response cannot be scored because it is off topic, too short to score, or written in a language other than English. Even a well-written response that is off topic will be scored "U."

B You did not write an extended response.

Topic: Slavery Just Before the Civil War

PASSAGE A

Stephen Douglas, from the Lincoln-Douglas Debates

[The 1858 Lincoln-Douglas debates were between Abraham Lincoln, Republican candidate for the Illinois Senate, and Stephen Douglas, the Democratic candidate. The main topic of the debates was slavery.]

Uniformity in the local laws and institutions of the different States is neither possible or desirable. If uniformity had been adopted when the Government was established, it must inevitably have been the uniformity of slavery everywhere, or else the uniformity of negro citizenship and negro equality everywhere . . . .

I ask you, are you in favor of conferring upon the negro the rights and privileges of citizenship? Do you desire to strike out of our State Constitution that clause which keeps slaves and free negroes out of the State, and allow the free negroes to flow in, and cover your prairies with black settlements? Do you desire to turn this beautiful State into a free negro colony, in order that when Missouri abolishes slavery she can send one hundred thousand emancipated slaves into Illinois, to become citizens and voters, on an equality with yourselves?

If you desire negro citizenship, if you desire to allow them to come into the State and settle with the white man, if you desire them to vote on an equality with yourselves, and to make them eligible to office, to serve on juries, and to adjudge your rights, then support Mr. Lincoln and the Black Republican party, who are in favor of the citizenship of the negro.

For one, I am opposed to negro citizenship in any and every form. I believe this Government was made on the white basis. I believe it was made by white men for the benefit of white men and their posterity forever, and I am in favor of confining citizenship to white men, men of European birth and descent, instead of conferring it upon negroes, Indians, and other inferior races.

Mr. Lincoln, following the example and lead of all the little Abolition orators, who go around and lecture in the basements of schools and churches, reads from the Declaration of Independence, that all men were created equal, and then asks, how can you deprive a negro of that equality which God and the Declaration of Independence awards to him?

Now, I hold that Illinois had a right to abolish and prohibit slavery as she did, and I hold that Kentucky has the same right to continue and protect slavery that Illinois had to abolish it. I hold that New York had as much right to abolish slavery as Virginia has to continue it, and that each and every State of this Union is a sovereign power, with the right to do as it pleases upon this question of slavery, and upon all its domestic institutions.

And why can we not adhere to the great principle of self-government, upon which our institutions were originally based? I believe that this new doctrine preached by Mr. Lincoln and his party will dissolve the Union if it succeeds. They are trying to array all the Northern States in one body against the South, to excite a sectional war between the free States and the slave States, in order that the one or the other may be driven to the wall.

PASSAGE B

Abraham Lincoln, from the Lincoln-Douglas Debates

[The 1858 Lincoln-Douglas debates were between Abraham Lincoln and Senator Stephen Douglas, who were candidates for the Illinois State Senate. The main topic of the debates was slavery.]

I agree with Judge Douglas that he is not my equal in many respects—certainly not in color, perhaps not in moral or intellectual endowment. But in the right to eat the bread, without the leave of anybody else, which his own hand earns, he is my equal and the equal of Judge Douglas, and the equal of every living man.

This declared indifference, but, as I must think, covert real zeal for the spread of slavery, I cannot but hate. I hate it because of the monstrous injustice of slavery itself. I hate it because it deprives our republican example of its just influence in the world—enables the enemies of free institutions, with plausibility, to taunt us as hypocrites—causes the real friends of freedom to doubt our sincerity, and especially because it forces so many really good men amongst ourselves into an open war with the very fundamental principles of civil liberty—criticizing the Declaration of Independence, and insisting that there is no right principle of action but self-interest.

I am not, nor ever have been, in favor of bringing about in any way the social and political equality of the white and black races, that I am not nor ever have been in favor of making voters or jurors of negroes, nor of qualifying them to hold office, nor to intermarry with white people; and I will say in addition to this that there is a physical difference between the white and black races which I believe will forever forbid the two races living together on terms of social and political equality.

And in as much as they cannot so live, while they do remain together there must be the position of superior and inferior, and I as much as any other man am in favor of having the superior position assigned to the white race. I say upon this occasion I do not perceive that because the white man is to have the superior position the negro should be denied everything. I do not understand that because I do not want a negro woman for a slave I must necessarily want her for a wife. My understanding is that I can just let her alone.

The authors of the Declaration of Independence intended to include all men, but they did not mean to declare all men equal in all respects. They did not mean to say all men were equal in color, size, intellect, moral development or social capacity. They defined with tolerable distinctness in what they did consider all men created equal—equal in certain inalienable rights, among which are life, liberty, and the pursuit of happiness . . . They meant to set up a standard maxim for free society which should be familiar to all: constantly looked to, constantly labored for, and even, though never perfectly attained, constantly approximated, and thereby constantly spreading and deepening its influence and augmenting the happiness and value of life to all people, of all colors, everywhere.

GRAPHIC

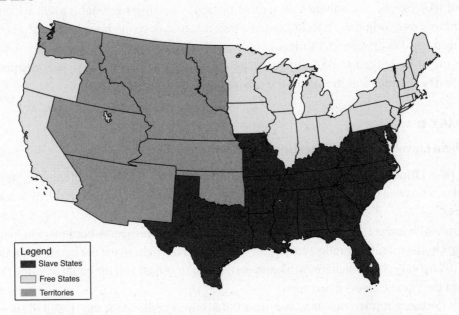

1860 Map of Slave States, Free States, and Territories (National Park Service)

Type the assignments on a word processor with spell checking and grammar checking turned off.

ASSIGNMENT 1

Use passages A and B as you write your response to this assignment.

In about 100 to 200 words, review each passage and compare and contrast the views each takes on slavery and abolition in the United States. To receive a high score, your response should

- review the claims found in each passage about how the contrasting views of slavery and abolition contribute to the presentation and make use of evidence found in the passages; and
- include examples from each passage to support your response.

It is expected that this will be the first draft for a group of educated adults.

ASSIGNMENT 2

Use passages A and B and the state map as you write your response to this topic.

In about 100 to 200 words, explain how the information in the state map can be combined with the arguments in each passage about slavery and abolition. To receive a high score your response should

- specifically detail how information in the state map explains claims found in each passage about the authors' views on slavery and abolition; and
- include examples from the passages and the state map to support your response.

It is expected that this will be the first draft for a group of educated adults.

ASSIGNMENT 3

Use both passages and the state map to respond to the following assignment.

Is the view of Lincoln as anti-slavery at the time of these debates supported by these exhibits?

This assignment is a response of about 400 to 600 words that presents a fully developed persuasive essay about whether Lincoln is correctly viewed as anti-slavery at the time of these debates.

To receive a high score your response should

- demonstrate that you understand the topic;
- use logical reasoning to expand and extend the points made in the passages;
- provide evidence from all three sources to support your claim; and
- present and refute a counterclaim.

It is expected that this will be the first draft for a group of educated adults.

ANSWER EXPLANATIONS

1. **(C)** The author repeats the phrase to describe the petals' colors of red, blue, or yellow in many ways, including the colors themselves.

2. **(A)** The author describes how the man maintained his position ahead of the woman so that the man could go on with his thoughts. Choice (C) is incorrect because it does not focus on the man's actions.

3. **(B)** The word "marked" has many meanings. In this context, "marked" means that the person noted or identified the hour.

4. **(A)** It helps to remember that we are limited to the choices given. Paragraph 6 makes direct reference to the man not marrying Lily. However, that paragraph is not one of the choices. Choice (B) is incorrect because it gives no information about the man's relation to Lily.

5. **(B)** The man described in the paragraph considered the dragonfly's actions a prediction of Lily's acceptance of his marriage proposal.

6. **(C)** The woman is drawing a relationship between the men and women present and what the man remembers of his past. (B) is incorrect because a simile uses words such as "like" or "as," and these words are not found here.

7. **(B)** The garden has its own existence, and the human visitors have theirs. Each exists side by side without affecting the other.

8. **(D)** The four people were physically separated as the man struggled with his past. They are now joined together indicating that the dissonance created by those thoughts has been resolved.

9. **(B)** In the first paragraph, the author indicates she is here to comment on prenatal testing. It follows that her central idea would be related to that topic, and choice (B) best expresses the central idea about that issue.

10. **(B)** The author spends most of the first part of what is testimony before congress describing her personal experiences with disabilities and waits until the last part of the passage to discuss her views on prenatal testing.

11. **(C)** This encounter was part of her evolution about the perception of disabilities. She was amazed that an educated person could act in such an inappropriate way. None of the other choices reveals this indication of evolution of thought about the perception of disabilities.

12. **(B)** The author notes that her comments are personal as reflected in the first phrase, while the second phrase describes a main point of the passage—"we are making progress." None of the other phrase pairs reveals this duality.

13. **(C)** The author wants to limit prenatal testing and presents living examples of what she sees as the flawed decision making this type of testing can generate. This excerpt reveals her plan by linking the uninformed fears of parents and the pressure from those around them as a basis for limiting testing.

14. **(A)** The author was unaware of prenatal testing as an expectant mother, and she contrasts that view with the situation of expectant parents, who are not only aware of prenatal testing but also receive the results of that testing.

15. **(C)** The author is obviously proud of her sister, but this passage goes beyond that and presents her sister as a living example that disabled people can be self-supporting.

16. **(B)** The author presents two equally unacceptable reasons for barring physically disabled people from jury service to demonstrate the faulty and illogical reasoning for this type of discrimination.

17. **(C)** Dictionary definitions of the difficult word "obdurate" include: stubbornly resistant to moral influence, not easily moved by feelings, and hardened in wrongdoing or wickedness. You may notice from the context that Mr. Douglass is saying that anyone unmoved by the privations of slavery would have to be hardened to the reality of a slave's life. Choice (C) alone comes closest to any of these definitions. Choice (D), "lifeless," is a common error among students.

18. **(A)** The main theme of the passage is not conveyed by the horrific details of slavery—the beatings, the naked children, the treatment of people as property to be bought and sold. Rather, these details serve as the evidence for the main theme: that slavery kills the soul.

19. **(C)** The author describes the many details of his personal experiences as a slave and then uses those experiences to lead to the main theme of this passage. Choices (A), (B), and (D) are true, but these choices do not describe how the author develops the central theme.

20. **(D)** The author states that the absence of beds was not considered a great privation, and so among the choices given has the most positive connotation in the context of the passage.

21. **(A)** The author describes how going to the Great House Farm is considered by slaves to be better than working in the fields and gives the slaves a sense of privilege. In these ways, going to the Great House Farm is presented as better than the other choices available to the slaves.

22. **(D)** Many of the words in other choices are from the passage, but the unmistakable contrast is that adult slaves were given more than slave children who could not work. Nothing in the passage suggests the adult slaves gave any of their clothing to the slave children.

23. **(B)** Choice (B) alone describes the main reason why going to the Great House Farm was considered a privilege. The privilege made the slaves feel important. Choice (A) describes competing to be chosen for the privilege, and choice (C) describes a slave's reaction to being selected. Choice (D) is not related to the question; however, this choice conveys a powerful message that might attract some test takers.

24. **(C)** This choice alone directly answers the question. The author states that the reason for the punishment and sale of slaves was "as a warning to the slaves remaining." This tells us that Colonel Lloyd used fear and intimidation to manage his "business." The other choices may or may not be true; however, none of this is mentioned in the passage.

25. **(C)** The only support for this excerpt from the first paragraph is the author's statement in the first paragraph that, "They were always ready to forget their troubles at home."

26. **(D)** "Wistful" means to feel sad or melancholy, and at the moment of that sigh, Peter was sad because he did not have a daughter like Antonia.

27. **(A)** These paragraphs provide background information about the two Russians and lay the foundation for understanding them throughout the passage.

28. **(C)** This portion of the passage shows a close relationship because of Antonia's reaction to her father's good feelings. Choice (B) is incorrect because it does not address the relationship between Antonia and her father, as found in choice (C).

29. **(C)** This portion of the passage refers to "one of them," one person. This choice, which is from paragraph 4, and the portion of the passage in the question each refers to Pavel. Choice (A) is incorrect because it does not refer to a person. Choice (B), from paragraph 10, is incorrect because it refers to Peter. Choice (D) is incorrect because it refers to two immigrants, not one.

30. **(C)** "Perplexity" means confusion. Peter is confused as he looks around for something that would entertain his guests.

31. **(B)** The report establishes that Peter was hard working. Choice (D) is incorrect because the laughter the author reports does not carry with it a negative connotation.

32. **(C)** Peter "tells" the reader that this is a practice followed in his country, and thus folklore, or popular beliefs and customs included in the traditions of his country.

33. **(C)** As the passage states, the Iroquois faced threats from without and from within. These two threats can be referred to as a duality of threats. It is worth noting that the date of the formation of the tribes is not mentioned in the second paragraph, and that Columbus never set foot on the mainland of North America.

34. **(C)** A major theme in the passage is how the five tribes joined together to become a nation. This excerpt, which describes Hiawatha's vision of that passage, best supports a central theme.

35. **(C)** In this passage, the author describes the mythological descriptions of Atotarho that developed over the years, and then brings us to earth noting that those with direct knowledge of Atotarho, don't pay attention to these "inventions of marvel-living gossips." Choice (A) is incorrect because the passage does not describe how Atotarho's nature was exaggerated.

36. **(B)** The tone of the passage is built around Hiawatha's determination, and the author mentions the extreme steps that Hiawatha took to achieve his goal to highlight that determination, without expressly mentioning that term.

37. **(D)** The context of the excerpt reveals that "sagacity" must refer to some positive attribute. That effectively eliminates choices (B) and (C). The goal was to benefit the entire federation, not only the tribe. Choice (D), which indicates that the chief was capable of sound judgment, must be correct.

38. **(C)** A "euphemism" is the substitution of a mild, indirect, or vague expression for one thought to be offensive, harsh, or blunt. In this excerpt, the words "taken off one after another" refers to the more accurate and harsh words of kidnappings and killing.

39. **(D)** The author's point of view is unique to the author and independent from the other facts and opinions found in a passage. Choice (D) is the best example of the unique view of the author found among the four listed excerpts from the passage. The remaining passages are directly related to the passage, but unrelated to the author's view or opinion.

40. **(A)** The author portrays Atotarho as a ruthless chief, but someone who spared a highly regarded chief like Hiawatha, most likely because he did not want the consequences of dealing harshly with someone held in high regard.

Constructed-Response Examples

There are many possible responses to a constructed-response item.

Assignment 1: Constructed-Response Example

This 228-word response would likely earn a 3, or possibly a 4.

Douglas begins by noting it is not possible to have uniformity of local laws. This is a reference to states' rights, and that some states have abolished slavery, while others have not. Then Douglas condemns citizenship for the group of people he refers to as "negroes." Douglas appeals to the predominately white citizens in the audience, asking them if they want to have "negro" citizens with the same rights as theirs. Douglas does object to some states abolishing slavery, while others have not. Douglas draws a clear line between the abolishment of slavery, about which he seems ambivalent, and citizenship for blacks, to which he is opposed.

Lincoln comes out against slavery, saying that it is a "monstrous injustice." He then goes on later to say that the authors of the Declaration of Independence did not mean that all men are created equal in every way, but they did mean that all men were indeed created equal in the certain inalienable rights of "life, liberty, and the pursuit of happiness" as spelled out in the constitution. It is in the muddles of his speech that we find Lincoln sounding more like Douglas. He says that he has not been and is not now in favor of "equality of the white and black races." He alludes to the superiority of whites, and implies that blacks should be just left alone.

Assignment 2: Constructed-Response Example

This 201-word response would likely earn a 3, or possibly a 4.

The state map shows states in which slavery is legal and the states in which it is not. Vast areas are classified as territories. It was inevitable that states would be formed from these territories, and with a small number more free states than slave states. There was great concern about which of the new states would be admitted as slave states, and which as free states. The arrangement of the free and slave states seems to offer equal opportunity for either type of state becoming a majority. So it is clear the maps depiction of free and slave states provides the backdrop for these debates.

We have two men, Douglas and Lincoln, debating in the state of Illinois, but each had aspirations for political office. Each was a politician, and so they crafted their words in the quest for national office at this time when the issue of free states was at its height. Both are careful to avoid being abolitionists, those in favor of the national abolition of slavery. Each in his own way is careful to distance himself from "negroes" becoming citizens, Douglas more directly and Lincoln with a somewhat more egalitarian view of the rights of black Americans.

Assignment 3: Extended-Response Sample

This 467-word response would likely earn a 3, but unlikely a 4.

Reading Lincoln's actual words during the debate leads me to the inescapable conclusion that Lincoln did not declare himself as anti-slavery at the time of these debates. So my response to the statement is that Lincoln did not deserve to be viewed as anti-slavery at the time of these debates. What we have is political debate with two candidates trying to present themselves to an electorate in a way that was designed to garner the most votes with the backdrop of the reality in the state map that the country could swing either predominately anti-slavery or pro-slavery. One has to assume though that they would not compromise their principles during this debate.

We can analyze Lincoln from two perspectives, the national abolition of slavery and citizenship for "Negroes." In fact, Douglas and Lincoln are closer on this issue than one might seem. Neither is in favor of the national abolition of slavery. Lincoln is more direct and speaks out against the <u>spread</u> of slavery and he mentions civil liberty, but this falls far short of saying he is entirely against it. It is very clear from his words that he is not in favor of the national abolition of slavery. Douglas is actually a little more direct saying that it is up to the states to decide whether or not slavery is legal. But when it comes to citizenship for black Americans, Lincoln and Douglas sound quite alike. The passage contains a quote from Lincoln that I was actually shocked to read. He says he is now and always has been against "the social and political equality of black and white races."

He goes on to oppose blacks holding office, being jurors, and intermarriage. He goes further still when he says that the physical difference between whites and blacks will prevent them from living in "social and political equality." And then still further when he "as much as anyone" is in favor of having the superior position assigned to the white race. While Lincoln was opposed to the spread of slavery, he held a low opinion of the black race and never presented himself as anti-slavery, and we must take him at his word.

Some might argue that these were merely political statements by Lincoln who knew he could never win an election if he campaigned on a strict anti-slavery platform, or was not in favor of a pseudo-slavery in which slaves could not be owned, but were actually inferior and not entitled to much. That's a very convenient but unconvincing argument, because it means that Lincoln would not have been a man of his convictions and would have kept those convictions to himself just to win an election. I have never had the opinion that Lincoln was the kind of person to hide his true convictions.

SECTION IV
edTPA

Overview of the edTPA

7

ELEMENTARY EDUCATION edTPA
(FOUR TASKS AND 18 RUBRICS)

Task 1: Planning for Literacy Instruction and Assessment

1: Planning for Literacy Learning

2: Planning to Support Varied Student Learning Needs

3: Using Knowledge of Students to Inform Teaching and Learning

4: Identifying and Supporting Language Demands

5: Planning Assessments to Monitor and Support Student Learning

Task 2: Instructing and Engaging Students in Literacy Learning

6: Learning Environment

7: Engaging Students in Learning

8: Deepening Student Learning

9: Subject-Specific Pedagogy: Elementary Literacy

10: Analyzing Teaching Effectiveness

Task 3: Assessing Students' Literacy Learning

11: Analysis of Student Learning

12: Providing Feedback to Guide Further Learning

13: Student Use of Feedback

14. Analyzing Students' Language Use and Literacy Learning

15: Using Assessment to Inform Instruction

Task 4: Assessing Students' Mathematics Learning

16: Analyzing Whole Class Understandings

17: Analyzing Individual Student Work Samples

18: Using Evidence to Reflect on Teaching

THE EARLY CHILDHOOD edTPA
(THREE TASKS AND 15 ASSESSMENT RUBRICS)

Task 1: Planning for Instruction and Assessment

1: Planning for the Whole Child

2: Planning to Support Varied Learning Needs

3: Using Knowledge of Children to Inform Teaching and Learning

4: Identifying and Supporting Language Development

5: Planning Assessments to Monitor and Support Children's Learning

Task 2: Instructing and Engaging Children in Learning

6: Learning Environment Rubric

7: Engaging Children in Learning Rubric

8: Deepening Children's Learning Rubric

9: Subject-Specific Pedagogy Rubric

10: Analyzing Teaching Effectiveness

Task 3: Assessing Children's Learning

USING THIS CHAPTER

Most of the useful information about the edTPA is copyrighted, and we cannot publish it here. Rely on the booklets mentioned in the Test Info Box. Review the preparation information you find below, and then visit the websites, which contain the most up-to-date information and sample videos.

As of press time for this book, the full implementation of the edTPA has been delayed until June 2015. Prospective teachers who complete but do not pass the edTPA may substitute the ATS-W. Read a description of the policy and check for recent updates here:

www.highered.nysed.gov/updateedtpa.html.

There is continued pressure for a further delay of implementation. It is not possible yet to predict the final outcome. State wide, during 2013–2014 school year, edTPA passing rates were about 80 percent but from a very small sample. Those passing students have worked closely with faculty and teachers to develop the written and video materials.

PASSING THE edTPA

The edTPA is not a traditional test. You don't sit at a computer or go to a testing center. The edTPA is a developmental process that stretches across your teaching preparation program. The edTPA is a portfolio or authentic assessment of your ability to (a) plan, (b) teach, and (c) assess learning. The idea is that you will actually demonstrate that you can do these things, not just write about doing them or talk about doing them, and that does make sense.

The planning and assessment part consist of written documents. The teaching part consists of unedited videos of you working in a school with students at an appropriate grade level.

The edTPA is a highly individualized process that will usually be different for each person. You go through the process with college faculty members and teachers in the schools. The videos are usually made in conjunction with student teaching. Pearson Education has a series of rubrics, or guidelines, for evaluating your written work and lesson videos. The completed edTPA materials are submitted to Pearson electronically.

WHAT SHOULD I DO?

You must complete the edTPA. Under the current rules, you can take and pass the ATS-W only after you fail the edTPA. Check the link above for the most up-to-date information.

Do your best on the edTPA, and use the steps below to increase the likelihood of passing. If you do not pass, evaluate the results with your faculty mentor and decide whether to resubmit or to take the ATS-W. The decision will be influenced by the current regulations and the timing of any resubmission.

If you passed the ATS-W before April 30, 2014, and subsequently did not pass the edTPA, your earlier passing score will be accepted in lieu of the edTPA passing score.

PREPARATION STRATEGIES AND REVIEW

This section gives you the important preparation steps and links to online resources.

Get a Good Faculty Mentor

Your goal is to find a college faculty member who is willing to guide you through this process. You want a faculty member who is "on your side," but still willing to point out the areas of needed growth and improvement. Growth and improvement are the real goals of the edTPA, and it is what leads to passing scores.

A good faculty mentor will be able to demystify the whole process and put you on the path to success. A faculty member who is a good match for someone else, may not be a good match for you.

Don't Be Afraid of the Video

When the time comes, just make the required videos and see how they go. DO NOT evaluate the videos yourself. Show them to your mentor and other faculty and get feedback about how the videos stack up against other successful videos. Let your mentor and other faculty members guide your choice about whether these are good videos to submit.

It is fine if you have to do more videos. Use the feedback and give it another try. The evaluators will not know if this is the first video or the sixth. So just relax.

Discuss questions about the links below with your mentor.

Review the New York State edTPA Guidelines and Information

The comprehensive information and many valuable links found on the NYSTCE website will be most up to date and your best source of edTPA information. The comprehensive resources include an extensive list of edTPA guides and newsletters:

www.nystce.nesinc.com/NY_annTPA.asp.

Review the steps to prepare for the edTPA:

www.edtpa.com/PageView.aspx?f=GEN_Candidates.html.

Review videos of teacher candidates who have taken the edTPA. The videos include advice for preparing for the edTPA:

http://edtpa.aacte.org/resources/candidate-to-candidate-reflections-on-taking-edtpa.

Browse the edTPA resource library with particular attention to the recent entries:

https://secure.aacte.org/apps/rl/resource.php?resid=268&ref=edtpa.

Review this posting of the most recent New York passing edTPA scores:

www.highered.nysed.gov/edtpapassscores2.PNG.

GUIDELINES AND SAMPLES FOR SUCCESSFUL edTPA SUBMISSIONS

Review this college developed module about preparing successful videos. Other edTPA modules may be available in the right margin of the page:

www.slideshare.net/lhbaecher/edtpa-online-session-7video-analysis-of-teaching

Review this description of high-scoring edTPA lessons:

www.passedtpa.com/.

Not Successful?

Visit this site for guidance about retaking the edTPA.

www.edtpa.com/Content/Docs/edTPARetakeGuidelines.pdf

SECTION V
Multi-Subject CST

Preparing for the Multi-Subject Elementary and Early Childhood CSTs

8

Each CST is actually three separate tests. You must achieve a passing score on each one.

The test items are distributed as shown below. Refer to the NYSTCE Test Frameworks (*www.nystce.nesinc.com/NY_viewobjs_opener.asp*) to view the extensive list of topics covered on each test. This webpage is your best source of information about test changes.

There are many topics covered on each test. Each topic may lead to any number of different items. The model CST in this chapter will provide insight about the type and difficulty of items you will encounter. However, the test you take may cover topics not found on this test.

Part One: Literacy and English Language Arts (2 hours)
40 selected-response items; 1 constructed-response item

Area	Approximate Number of Selected-Response Items	Percent of Score
Knowledge of Literacy and English Language Arts	17	30%
Instruction in Foundational Literacy Skills	17	20%
Instruction in English Language Skills	6	10%
Student-based Constructed-response Item	—	30%

Part Two: Mathematics (2 hours 15 minutes)
40 selected-response items; 1 constructed-response item

Area	Approximate Number of Selected-Response Items	Percent of Score
Number and Operations	3	5%
Ratio, Proportion, Percent, Number Systems	15	30%
Algebra, Geometry, Measurement, and Data	17	25%
Instruction in Mathematics	5	10%
Student-based Constructed-response Item	—	20%

Part Three: Arts and Sciences (1 hour)
This part is the same for every multi-subject test.
40 selected-response items; no constructed-response items

Area	Approximate Number of Selected-Response Items	Percent of Score
Science and Technology	16	40%
Social Studies	16	40%
Fine Arts, Family/Consumer Science, and Health/Fitness Careers	8	20%

SCORES

The new Multi-Subject CSTs were administered for the first time in September 2014, and full scoring information is not available. Overall, CST passing rates will likely be lower than in previous years.

Passing the Multi-Subject CSTs

The new Multi-Subject CSTs administrations began shortly before this book went to press. We developed our practice tests around overall student feedback about the tests, the test frameworks, and the truly enormous number of topics specified for each CST. It is possible to develop many thousands of different CSTs based on those topics.

Students report a wide variation in the specific topics and difficulty level found on administered tests. State testing officials can adjust the scale scores to account for these variations.

This indicates that the tests you take may cover different topics and be at a different difficulty level than the practice tests in this book. These practice CSTs will be very helpful as you prepare for the real tests; however, because of this variation, you will not be able to predict the scale score you would receive on a practice test.

PREPARATION STRATEGIES

Use the Reviews in this Chapter

Complete the summary Mathematics, Literacy and English Language Arts, and Arts and Sciences reviews that follow. These reviews are designed to be helpful, but they cannot cover every area on the multi-subject CST.

Mathematics is usually the most challenging, so that review is the most detailed.

Take a Related Practice Test

Pearson Education creates the Multi-Subject CST for New York State. Pearson also creates a multi-subject test for California called the California Subject Matter Examination for Teachers (CSET): Multiple Subjects. The CST is a different test; however, there are some strong subject matter similarities between the two. The multi-subject CSET has selected-response items in Reading, Language and Literature, History and Social Science, Mathematics, Science, Physical Education, and Visual and Performing Arts.

Here is the link to practice test questions and a complete multi-subject CSET, showing the correct letter answer for each item:

www.ctcexams.nesinc.com/PM_CSET.asp?t=101

The question types will not be identical; however, this is an excellent way to prepare for the types of questions you may find on the Multi-Subject CST. Skip the CSET constructed-response items. They are not similar to the CST constructed-response items.

Use the CSET practice test results to identify possible opportunities for further study in areas covered on the CST. Immediately following the subject reviews are additional review recommendations.

Read the review to familiarize yourself with the topics that may be covered on the test. Work through the examples.

NUMBERS

Understanding and Ordering Whole Numbers

Whole numbers are the numbers you use to tell how many. They include 0, 1, 2, 3, 4, 5, 6 . . . . The dots tell us that these numbers keep going on forever. There are an infinite number of whole numbers, which means you will never reach the last one.

Cardinal numbers such as 1, 9, and 18 tell how many. There are 9 players on the field in a baseball game. Ordinal numbers such as 1st, 2nd, 9th, and 18th tell about order. For example, Lynne batted 1st this inning.

You can visualize whole numbers evenly spaced on a number line.

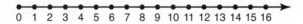

You can use the number line to compare numbers. Numbers get smaller as you go to the left and larger as you go to the right. The terms *equal to* (=), *less than* (<), *greater than* (>), and *between* are used to compare numbers.

12 equals 10 + 2	2 is less than 5	9 is greater than 4	6 is between 5 and 7
$12 = 10 + 2$	$2 < 5$	$9 > 4$	$5 < 6 < 7$

Place Value

We use ten digits, 0–9, to write out numerals. We also use a place value system of numeration. The value of a digit depends on the place it occupies. Look at the following place value chart.

millions	hundred thousands	ten thousands	thousands	hundreds	tens	ones
3	5	7	9	4	1	0

The value of the 9 is 9,000. The 9 is in the thousands place. The value of the 5 is 500,000. The 5 is in the hundred thousands place. Read the number three million, five hundred seventy-nine thousand, four hundred ten.

Some whole numbers are very large. The distance from Earth to the planet Pluto is about six trillion (6,000,000,000,000) yards. The distance from Earth to the nearest star is about 40 quadrillion (40,000,000,000,000,000) yards.

A. What is the value of 8 in the numeral 47,829?

The value of the 8 is 800; this is because the 8 is in the hundreds place.

B. Use $<$, $>$, or $=$ to compare 2 and 7.

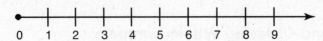

Use the number line to see that $2 < 7$ (2 is less than 7).

Positive Exponents

You can show repeated multiplication as an exponent. The exponent shows how many times the factor appears.

$$\text{Base—}3^{\overset{\text{[Exponent]}}{5}} = 3 \times 3 \times 3 \times 3 \times 3 = 243$$
[Factors]

RULES FOR EXPONENTS

Use these rules to multiply and divide exponents with the *same base*.

$$7^8 \times 7^5 = 7^{13} \qquad\qquad a^n \times a^m = a^{m+n}$$
$$7^8 \div 7^5 = 7^3 \qquad\qquad a^n \div a^m = a^{n-m}$$

EXAMPLES

A. $4^3 + 6^2 \qquad = 4 \times 4 \times 4 + 6 \times 6 \qquad = 64 + 36 \quad = 100$

B. $(2^3)(4^2) \qquad = (2 \times 2 \times 2) \times (4 \times 4) \quad = 8 \times 16 \quad = 128$

C. $(3^2)^2 \qquad = 3^4 \qquad = 3 \times 3 \times 3 \times 3 \quad = 81$

D. $(10 - 9)^2 \qquad = 1^2 \qquad = 1$

Scientific Notation

Scientific notation uses powers of 10. The power shows how many zeros to use.

$$10^0 = 1 \qquad 10^1 = 10 \qquad 10^2 = 100 \qquad 10^3 = 1,000 \qquad 10^4 = 10,000$$
$$10^{-1} = 0.1 \qquad 10^{-2} = 0.01 \qquad 10^{-3} = 0.001 \qquad 10^{-4} = 0.0001$$
$$10^5 = 100,000$$
$$10^{-5} = 0.00001$$

Write whole numbers and decimals in scientific notation. Use a decimal with one numeral to the left of the decimal point.

2,345	=	2.345×10^3	The decimal point moved three places to the left. Use 10^3.
176.8	=	1.768×10^2	The decimal point moved two places to the left. Use 10^2.
0.0034	=	3.4×10^{-3}	The decimal point moved three places to the right. Use 10^{-3}.
2.0735	=	2.0735×10^0	The decimal is in the correct form. Use 10^0 to stand for 1.

EXAMPLES

A. Write 7,952 in scientific notation.

Move the decimal point three places to the left and write $7,952 = 7.952 \times 10^3$.

B. Write 0.03254 in scientific notation.

Move the decimal point two places to the right and write 3.254×10^{-2}.

Understanding and Ordering Decimals

Decimals are used to represent numbers between 0 and 1. Decimals can also be written on a number line.

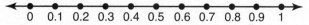

We also use ten digits 0–9 and a place value system of numeration to write decimals. The value of a digit depends on the place it occupies. Look at the following place value chart.

ones	tenths	hundredths	thousandths	ten thousandths	hundred thousandths	millionths	ten millionths	hundred millionths	billionths
0	3	6	8	7					

The value of 3 is three tenths. The 3 is in the tenths place. The value of 8 is eight thousandths. The 8 is in the thousandths place.

Comparing Whole Numbers and Decimals

To compare two numbers line up the place values. Start at the left and keep going until the digits in the same place are different.

Compare	9,879 and 16,459	23,**8**01 and 23,798	58.1289 and 58.132
Line up the place values	9,879	23,**8**01	58.1289
	16,459	23,798	58.132
	9,879 < 16,459	23,801 > 23,798	58.1289 < 58.132
	Less than	Greater than	Less than

A. What is the value of the digit 2 in the decimal 35.6829?

The 2 is in the thousandths place. $2 \times 0.001 = 0.002$.

The value of the 2 is 0.002 or 2 thousandths.

B. Use <, >, or = to compare 1248.9234 and 1248.9229.

1248.9234 ◯ 1248.9229. The digits in the numerals are the same until you reach the thousandths place where $3 > 2$. Since $3 > 2$, then $1248.9234 > 1248.9229$.

Rounding Whole Numbers and Decimals

Follow these steps to round a number to a place.

- Look at the digit to the right of the number.
- If the digit to the right is 5 or more, round up. If the digit is less than 5, leave the numeral to be rounded as written.

A. *Round 859,465 to the thousands place.*
Underline the thousands place.
Look to the right. The digit 4 is less than 5 so leave as written.
859,465 rounded to the thousands place is 859,000.
859,465 rounded to the ten-thousands place 860,000.

B. *Round 8.647 to the hundredths place.*
Underline the hundredths place.
Look to the right. The digit 7 is 5 or more so you round up.
8.647 rounded to the *hundredths* place is 8.65.
8.647 rounded to the *tenths* place is 8.6.

Rational and Irrational Numbers and Fractions

Most numbers can be written as a fraction or a ratio, with an integer in the numerator and in the denominator. These are called rational numbers.

Some numbers cannot be written as fractions with an integer in the numerator and denominator. These are called irrational numbers.

Never write 0 in the denominator. These numbers are undefined.

Look at these examples.

9 is rational because it can be written as the ratio 9/1 (or 18/2 and so on).

0.25 is rational because it can be written as the ratio 1/4.

0.4 is rational because it can be written as the ratio 4/10 (2/5 in simplest form).

0.666 . . . (6 continues to repeat) is rational because it can be written as the ratio 2/3.

Rational numbers can be written as decimals that terminate or repeat.

0.25 and 0.4 are examples of decimals that terminate.

$\frac{1}{3} = 0.333\ldots$ and $\frac{1}{7} = 0.14285714285\ldots$ (the "142857" repeats) are examples of decimals that repeat.

Every fraction can be represented by a decimal that terminates or repeats.

IRRATIONAL NUMBERS

Irrational numbers cannot be written as a fraction.

The most famous irrational number is π.

You could try forever and never find a fraction or a terminating or repeating decimal that equals π.

$\pi = 3.141592653\ldots$

The calculator for this test does not have a π key, so you will have to use rational numbers to approximate π. Use 3.14, 3.1416 or 22/7 (= 3.14285). The test item will indicate which approximation to use or the answer will be so obvious that you will not need that specific information.

Square Root of 2

Another famous irrational number is the square root of $2 (\sqrt{2})$. If you draw a diagonal in a square with sides equal to 1, the Pythagorean theorem tells you that the length of that diagonal is $\sqrt{2}$.

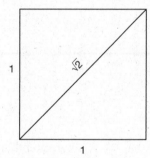

$$a^2 + b^2 = c^2 = 1^2 + 1^2 \qquad c^2 = 1 + 1 = 2 : c = \sqrt{2}$$

$\sqrt{2} = 1.41421356\ldots$

You can use 99/70 (≈ 1.41429) to approximate $\sqrt{2}$. You can see that this approximation is very close to the decimal value of the number.

The test calculator has a square root key so you could approximate the square root of 2. Most often just leave it as is and write the answer in radical form, such as $3\sqrt{2}$.

Understanding and Ordering Fractions

A fraction names a part of a whole or of a group. A fraction has two parts, a numerator and a denominator. The denominator tells how many parts in all. The numerator tells how many parts are identified.

EQUIVALENT FRACTIONS

Two fractions that stand for the same number are called equivalent fractions. Multiply or divide the numerator and denominator by the same number to find an equivalent fraction.

$$\frac{2\times3}{5\times3}=\frac{6}{15} \qquad \frac{6\div3}{9\div3}=\frac{2}{3} \qquad \frac{6\times4}{8\times4}=\frac{24}{32} \qquad \frac{8\div2}{10\div2}=\frac{4}{5}$$

Fractions can also be written and ordered on a number line. You can use the number line to compare fractions. Fractions get smaller as you go to the left and larger as you go to the right. Use the terms equivalent to (=), less than (<), greater than (>), and between to compare fractions.

$\frac{1}{2}$ is equivalent to $\frac{2}{4}$ $\qquad$ $\frac{2}{3}$ is less than $\frac{3}{4}$ $\qquad$ $\frac{5}{8}$ is greater than $\frac{1}{2}$ $\qquad$ $\frac{1}{3}$ is between $\frac{1}{4}$ and $\frac{3}{8}$

$$\frac{1}{2}=\frac{2}{4} \qquad\qquad \frac{2}{3}<\frac{3}{4} \qquad\qquad \frac{5}{8}>\frac{1}{2} \qquad\qquad \frac{1}{4}<\frac{1}{3}<\frac{3}{8}$$

COMPARE TWO FRACTIONS

Use this method to compare two fractions. For example, compare $\frac{13}{18}$ and $\frac{5}{7}$. First write the two fractions and cross multiply as shown. The larger cross product appears next to the larger fraction. If cross products are equal, then the fractions are equivalent.

$$91 = \qquad = 90$$

$$91 > 90 \text{ so } \frac{13}{18} > \frac{5}{7}$$

MIXED NUMBERS AND IMPROPER FRACTIONS

Change an improper fraction to a mixed number:

$$\frac{23}{8} = 8\overline{)23}\ \ 2\frac{7}{8}$$

Change a mixed number to an improper fraction:

$$3\frac{2}{5} = \frac{17}{5}$$

Multiply denominator and whole number. Then add the numerator.

$$\frac{(3\times5)+2}{5} = \frac{15+2}{5} = \frac{17}{5}$$

EXAMPLES

A. Compare $\frac{5}{7}$ and $\frac{18}{19}$,

Use cross multiplication.

$\frac{5}{7} \times \frac{18}{19}$, $5 \times 19 = 95$ and $7 \times 18 = 126$, therefore $\frac{5}{7} < \frac{18}{19}$.

B. Write $\frac{27}{7}$ as a mixed number.

$$7\overline{)27}\ \ 3\,R6$$

$$\frac{21}{6}$$

$$\frac{27}{7} = 3\frac{6}{7}$$

C. Write $6\frac{5}{8}$ as a fraction.

$6 \times 8 = 48$. Multiply the denominator and the whole number.

$48 + 5 = 53$. Add the numerator to the product.

$$6\frac{5}{8} = \frac{53}{8}$$

Integers

The number line can also show negative numbers. There is a negative whole number for every positive whole number. Zero is neither positive nor negative. The negative whole numbers, the positive whole numbers, and zero, together, are called integers. Integers are smaller as you go left on the number line and larger as you go to the right.

$$^-10 < {}^-1 \qquad {}^-8 < {}^-3 \qquad {}^+1 > {}^-9 \qquad {}^+6 > {}^+4$$

When to Add, Subtract, Multiply, and Divide

ORDER OF OPERATIONS

Use this phrase to remember the order to do operations:

Please Excuse My Dear Aunt Sally

(1) **P**arentheses (2) **E**xponents (3) **M**ultiplication or **D**ivision (4) **A**ddition or **S**ubtraction

For example,

$$4 + 3 \times 7^2 \quad = \quad 4 + 3 \times 49 \quad = \quad 4 + 147 \quad = \quad 151$$
$$(4 + 3) \times 7^2 \quad = \quad 7 \times 7^2 \quad \quad = \quad 7 \times 49 \quad = \quad 343$$
$$(6 - 10 \div 5) + 6 \times 3 = (6 - 2) + 6 \times 3 = 4 + 6 \times 3 = 4 + 18 = 22$$

EXAMPLES

$$7 + 3 \times 6 + 4^2 - (8 + 4) \quad = \quad 7 + 3 \times 6 + 4^2 - \underline{12} \quad =$$
$$7 + 3 \times 6 + \underline{16} - 12 \quad \quad = \quad 7 + \underline{18} + 16 - 12 \quad \quad = 29$$

DECIDE WHETHER TO ADD, SUBTRACT, MULTIPLY, OR DIVIDE

Before you can solve a problem, you should know which operation to use. You can use key words to decide which operation to use or you can use a problem-solving strategy called choosing the operation.

Key Words

Addition	sum, and, more, increased by
Subtraction	less, difference, decreased by
Multiplication	of, product, times
Division	per, quotient, shared, ratio
Equals	is, equals

You cannot just use these key words without thinking. You must check to be sure that the operation makes sense when it replaces the key word. See the examples below.

EXAMPLES

19 and 23 is 42	16 is 4 more than 12	What percent of 19 is 5.7
$19 + 23 = 42$	$16 = 4 + 12$	$\underline{\quad\quad}\% \times 19 = 5.7$

CHOOSING THE OPERATION

To use the choosing-the-operation strategy, you think of each situation in this way. What do I know? What am I trying to find? The answers to these questions lead you directly to the correct operation.

You Know	You Want to Find
Add	
1. How many in two or more groups	How many in all
2. How many in one group How many join it	The total amount
3. How many in one group How many more in the second group	How many in the second group
Subtract	
4. How many in one group Number taken away	How many are left
5. How many in each of two groups	How much larger one group is than the other
6. How many in one group How many in part of that group	How many in the rest of the group

Common Factors and Multiples

FACTORS

The factors of a number evenly divide the number with no remainder. For example, 2 is a factor of 6, but 2 is not a factor of 5.

Here are the factors for the numbers 1–10.

The number 1 is a factor of every number. Each number is a factor of itself.

1	The only factor is 1	6	1, 2, 3, 6
2	1, 2	7	1, 7
3	1, 3	8	1, 2, 4, 8
4	1, 2, 4	9	1, 3, 9
5	1, 5	10	1, 2, 5, 10

LEAST COMMON MULTIPLE (LCM), GREATEST COMMON FACTOR (GCF)

Multiples

The multiples of a number are all the numbers you get when you count by that number. Here are some examples.

Multiples of 1: 1, 2, 3, 4, 5, . . .
Multiples of 2: 2, 4, 6, 8, 10, . . .
Multiples of 3: 3, 6, 9, 12, 15, . . .
Multiples of 4: 4, 8, 12, 16, 20, . . .
Multiples of 5: 5, 10, 15, 20, 25, . . .

Least Common Multiple

The least common multiple is the smallest multiple shared by two numbers.

The least common multiple of 6 and 8 is 24.

List the multiples of 6 and 8. Notice that 24 is the smallest multiple common to both numbers.

Multiples of 6: 6, 12, 18, **24**, 30, 36
Multiples of 8: 8, 16, **24**, 32, 40

Greatest Common Factor

The greatest common factor is the largest factor shared by two numbers.

The greatest common factor of 28 and 36 is 4.

List the factors of 28 and 36.

Factors of 28: 1, 2, **4**, 7, 28
Factors of 36: 1, 2, 3, **4**, 9, 12, 18, 36

EXAMPLES

A. Find the factors of 24.

The factors are 1, 2, 3, 4, 6, 8, 12, and 24.
These are the only numbers that divide 24 with no remainder.

B. Find the GCF of 14 and 22.

Write out the factors of each number.
14: 1, 2, 7, 14
22: 1, 2, 11, 22

The greatest common factor is 2.

C. Find the LCM of 6 and 9.

List some of the multiples of each number.
6: 6, 12, 18, 24, . . .
9: 9, 18, 27, . . .

The least common multiple is 18.

PROPERTIES OF OPERATIONS

Subtraction and division are not commutative or associative.

| **Commutative** | $a + b = b + a$ | $a \times b = b \times a$ |
| | $3 + 5 = 5 + 3$ | $3 \times 5 = 5 \times 3$ |

| **Associative** | $(a + b) + c = a + (b + c)$ | $(a \times b) \times c = a \times (b \times c)$ |
| | $(3 + 4) + 5 = 3 + (4 + 5)$ | $(3 \times 4) \times 5 = 3 \times (4 \times 5)$ |

| **Identity** | $a + 0 = a$ | $a \times 1 = a$ |
| | $5 + 0 = 5$ | $5 \times 1 = 5$ |

| **Inverse** | $a + (-a) = 0$ | $a \times \dfrac{1}{a} = 1$ |
| | $5 + (-5) = 0$ | $5 \times \dfrac{1}{5} = 1 \ (a \neq 0)$ |

Distributive property of multiplication over addition $a(b + c) = (a \times b) + (a \times c)$
$3(4 + 5) = (3 \times 4) + (3 \times 5)$

EXAMPLES

A. Use a property of operations to write an expression equivalent to $8y - 4x$.
These items ask you to identify equivalent statements produced by the properties.
The distributive property creates the equivalent expressions
$4(2y - x)$ or $2(4y - 2x)$.

B. What property is illustrated by $7^2 + 8^3 = 8^3 + 7^2$?
This statement demonstrates the commutative property.

Add, Subtract, Multiply, and Divide Decimals

ADD AND SUBTRACT DECIMALS

Line up the decimal points and add or subtract.

Add: $14.9 + 3.108 + 0.16$ Subtract $14.234 - 7.14$

$$
\begin{array}{r}
14.9 \\
3.108 \\
+\,0.16 \\
\hline
18.168
\end{array}
\qquad
\begin{array}{r}
14.234 \\
-\,7.14 \\
\hline
7.094
\end{array}
$$

MULTIPLY DECIMALS

Multiply as with whole numbers. Count the total number of decimal places in the factors. Put that many decimal places in the product. You may have to write leading zeros.

Multiply: 17.4×1.3

$$
\begin{array}{r}
17.4 \\
\times\ 1.3 \\
\hline
522 \\
174 \\
\hline
22\,6\,2
\end{array}
$$

Multiply: 0.016×1.7

$$
\begin{array}{r}
0.016 \\
\times\ 1.7 \\
\hline
112 \\
16 \\
\hline
02\,7\,2
\end{array}
$$

DIVIDE DECIMALS

Make the divisor a whole number. Match the movement in the dividend and then divide.

$$0.16)\overline{1.328}$$

$$0.16)\overline{1.32.8}$$

$$
\begin{array}{r}
8.3 \\
16)\overline{132.8} \\
\underline{128} \\
48 \\
\underline{48} \\
0
\end{array}
$$

Multiply, Divide, Add, and Subtract Fractions and Mixed Numbers

MULTIPLY FRACTIONS AND MIXED NUMBERS

Write any mixed number as an improper fraction. Multiply numerator and denominator. Write the product in simplest form. For example, multiply $\frac{3}{4}$ and $\frac{1}{6}$.

$$\frac{3}{4} \times \frac{1}{6} = \frac{3}{24} = \frac{1}{8}$$

Now, multiply $3\frac{1}{3}$ times $\frac{3}{5}$.

$$3\frac{1}{3} \times \frac{3}{5} = \frac{10}{3} \times \frac{3}{5} = \frac{30}{15} = 2$$

DIVIDE FRACTIONS AND MIXED NUMBERS

To divide $1\frac{4}{5}$ by $\frac{3}{8}$:

$$1\frac{4}{5} \div \frac{3}{8} = \frac{9}{5} \div \frac{3}{8} = \frac{9}{5} \times \frac{8}{3} = \frac{72}{15} = 4\frac{12}{15} = 4\frac{4}{5}$$

Write any mixed numbers as improper fractions   Invert the divisor and multiply   Write the product   Write in simplest form

ADD FRACTIONS AND MIXED NUMBERS

Write fractions with common denominators. Add and then write in simplest form.

Add: $\dfrac{3}{8} + \dfrac{1}{4}$

$\dfrac{3}{8} = \dfrac{3}{8}$

$+\dfrac{1}{4} = \dfrac{2}{8}$

$\dfrac{5}{8}$

Add: $\dfrac{7}{8} + \dfrac{5}{12}$

$\dfrac{7}{8} = \dfrac{21}{24}$

$+\dfrac{5}{12} = \dfrac{10}{24}$

$\dfrac{31}{24} = 1\dfrac{7}{24}$

Add: $2\dfrac{1}{3} + \dfrac{5}{7}$

$2\dfrac{1}{3} = 2\dfrac{7}{21}$

$+\dfrac{5}{7} = \dfrac{15}{21}$

$2\dfrac{22}{21} = 3\dfrac{1}{21}$

SUBTRACT FRACTIONS AND MIXED NUMBERS

Write fractions with common denominators. Subtract and then write in simplest form.

Subtract: $\dfrac{5}{6} - \dfrac{1}{3}$

$\dfrac{5}{6} = \dfrac{5}{6}$

$-\dfrac{1}{3} = \dfrac{2}{6}$

$\dfrac{3}{6} = \dfrac{1}{2}$

Subtract: $\dfrac{3}{8} - \dfrac{1}{5}$

$\dfrac{3}{8} = \dfrac{15}{40}$

$-\dfrac{1}{5} = \dfrac{8}{40}$

$\dfrac{7}{40}$

Subtract: $3\dfrac{1}{6} - 1\dfrac{1}{3}$

$3\dfrac{1}{6} = 3\dfrac{1}{6} = 2\dfrac{7}{6}$

$-1\dfrac{1}{3} = 1\dfrac{2}{6} = 1\dfrac{2}{6}$

$1\dfrac{5}{6}$

Square Roots

The square root of a given number, when multiplied by itself, equals the given number. This symbol means the square root of 25: $\sqrt{25}$. The square root of 25 is 5. $5 \times 5 = 25$.

SOME SQUARE ROOTS ARE WHOLE NUMBERS

The numbers with whole-number square roots are called perfect squares.

$$\sqrt{1} = 1 \quad \sqrt{4} = 2 \quad \sqrt{9} = 3 \quad \sqrt{16} = 4 \quad \sqrt{25} = 5 \quad \sqrt{36} = 6$$

$$\sqrt{49} = 7 \quad \sqrt{64} = 8 \quad \sqrt{81} = 9 \quad \sqrt{100} = 10 \quad \sqrt{121} = 11 \quad \sqrt{144} = 12$$

The fractional exponent $a^{\frac{1}{2}}$ is another way to write square root.

$$16^{\frac{1}{2}} = \sqrt{16} = 4 \qquad 324^{\frac{1}{2}} = \sqrt{324} = 18$$

USE THIS RULE TO WRITE A SQUARE ROOT IN ITS SIMPLEST FORM

$$\sqrt{a \times b} = \sqrt{a} \times \sqrt{b} \qquad \sqrt{5 \times 3} = \sqrt{5} \times \sqrt{3}$$

$$\sqrt{72} = \sqrt{36 \times 2} = \sqrt{36} \times \sqrt{2} = 6 \times \sqrt{2}$$

EXAMPLES

A. Write the square root of 162 in simplest form.

$$\sqrt{162} = \sqrt{81 \times 2} = \sqrt{81} \times \sqrt{2} = 9\sqrt{2}$$

B. Write the square root of 112 in simplest form.

$$\sqrt{112} = \sqrt{16 \times 7} = \sqrt{16} \times \sqrt{7} = 4\sqrt{7}$$

Ratio and Proportion

RATIO

A ratio is a way of comparing two numbers with division. It conveys the same meaning as a fraction. There are three ways to write a ratio.

Using words   3 to 4   As a fraction $\dfrac{3}{4}$ Using a colon   3 : 4

PROPORTION

A proportion shows two ratios that have the same value; that is, the fractions representing the ratios are equivalent. Use cross multiplication. If the cross products are equal, then the two ratios form a proportion.

$\dfrac{3}{8}$ and $\dfrac{27}{72}$ form a proportion. The cross products are equal. ($3 \times 72 = 8 \times 27$)

$\dfrac{3}{8}$ and $\dfrac{24}{56}$ do not form a proportion. The cross products are not equal.

SOLVING A PROPORTION

You may have to write a proportion to solve a problem. For example, the mason mixes cement and sand using a ratio of 2 : 5. Twelve bags of cement will be used. How much sand is needed?

To solve, use the numerator to stand for cement. The denominator will stand for sand.

$$\frac{2}{5} = \frac{12}{S} \qquad\qquad \frac{2}{5} = \frac{12}{S}$$

$$2 \times S = 5 \times 12$$
$$2S = 60$$
$$S = 30$$

Write the proportion   Cross multiply to solve

Thirty bags of sand are needed.

The problem compares loaves of whole wheat bread with loaves of rye bread. Let the numerators stand for loaves of whole wheat bread. The denominators stand for loaves of rye bread.

Ratio of whole wheat to rye. $\dfrac{3}{7}$ Ratio of whole wheat to rye for $\dfrac{51}{R}$
51 loaves of whole wheat.

Write a proportion. $\dfrac{3}{7} = \dfrac{51}{R}$

Solution: $3R = 357$ $R = 119$

There are 119 loaves of bread.

Percent

Percent comes from per centum, which means per hundred. Whenever you see a number followed by a percent sign it means that number out of 100.

DECIMALS AND PERCENTS

To write a decimal as a percent, move the decimal point two places to the right and write the percent sign.

$$0.34 = 34\% \qquad 0.297 = 29.7\% \qquad 0.6 = 60\% \qquad 0.001 = 0.1\%$$

To write a percent as a decimal, move the decimal point two places to the left and delete the percent sign.

$$51\% = 0.51 \qquad 34.18\% = 0.3418 \qquad 0.9\% = 0.009$$

FRACTIONS AND PERCENTS

Writing Fractions as Percents

- Divide the numerator by the denominator. Write the answer as a percent.

  Write $\dfrac{3}{5}$ as a percent.   Write $\dfrac{5}{8}$ as a percent.

  $\begin{array}{r} 0.6 \\ 5\overline{)3.0} \end{array}$ $0.6 = 60\%$ $\begin{array}{r} 0.625 \\ 8\overline{)5.000} \end{array}$ $0.625 = 62.5\%$

- Write an equivalent fraction with 100 in the denominator. Write the numerator followed by a percent sign.

  Write $\dfrac{13}{25}$ as a percent.

  $$\dfrac{13}{25} = \dfrac{52}{100} = 52\%$$

Writing Percents as Fractions

Write a fraction with 100 in the denominator and the percent in the numerator. Simplify.

$$18\% = \frac{18}{100} = \frac{9}{50} \qquad 7.5\% = \frac{7.5}{100} = \frac{75}{1000} = \frac{3}{40}$$

EXAMPLES

A. Write 0.567 as a percent.

Move the decimal two places to the right and write a percent sign, therefore, $0.567 = 56.7\%$.

B. Write $\frac{1}{4}$ as a percent.

Write $\frac{1}{4}$ as a decimal $(1 \div 4) = 0.25$

Write 0.25 as a decimal $0.25 = 25\%$

C. Write 26% as a fraction.

Place the percent number in the numerator and 100 in the denominator.

$26\% = \frac{26}{100} = \frac{13}{50}$. Simplify: $\frac{26}{100} = \frac{13}{50}$

Three Types of Percent Problems

FINDING A PERCENT OF A NUMBER

To find a percent of a number, write a number sentence with a decimal for the percent and solve.

$$\text{Find } 40\% \text{ of } 90.$$
$$0.4 \times 90 = 36$$

It may be easier to write a fraction for the percent.

$$\text{Find } 62\frac{1}{2}\% \text{ of } 64.$$
$$\frac{5}{8} \times 64 = 5 \times 8 = 40$$

FINDING WHAT PERCENT ONE NUMBER IS OF ANOTHER

To find what percent one number is of another, write a number sentence and solve to find the percent.

$$\text{What percent of 5 is 3?}$$
$$n \times 5 = 3$$
$$n = \frac{3}{5} = 0.6 = 60\%$$

FINDING A NUMBER WHEN A PERCENT OF IT IS KNOWN

To find a number when a percent of it is known, write a number sentence with a decimal or a fraction for the percent and solve to find the number.

$$5\% \text{ of what number is } 2?$$

$$0.05 \times n = 2$$
$$n = 2 \div 0.05$$
$$n = 40$$

EXAMPLES

A. What percent of 70 is 28?

$\square \times 70 = 28$

$\square = \dfrac{28}{70} = \dfrac{4}{10}$

$\square = 40\%$

B. 30% of 60 is what number?

$30\% \times 60 = \square$

$0.3 \times 60 = \square$

$\square = 18$

C. 40% of what number is 16?

$0.40 \times \square = 16$

$\square = \dfrac{16}{0.4}$

$\square = 40$

Percent of Increase and Decrease

PERCENT OF INCREASE

A price increases from $50 to $65. What is the percent of increase?

Subtract to find the amount of increase.	$65 − $50 = $15 $15 is the amount of increase
Write a fraction. The amount of increase is the numerator. The original amount is the denominator.	$15 Amount of increase —————————————— $50 Original amount
Write the fraction as a percent. The percent of increase is 30%.	$\overset{0.3}{50 \overline{)15.00}}$ $0.3 = 30\%$

PERCENT OF DECREASE

A price decreases from $35 to $28. What is the percent of decrease?

Subtract to find the amount of decrease.	$35 − $28 = $7 $7 is the amount of decrease
Write a fraction. The amount of decrease is the numerator. The original amount is the denominator.	$7 Amount of decrease —————————————— $35 Original amount
Write the fraction as a percent. The percent of decrease is 20%.	$\dfrac{7}{35} = \dfrac{1}{5} = 20\%$

A. The price increased from $30 to $36. What is the percent of increase?

$36 − $30 = $6

$$\frac{6}{30} = \frac{1}{5} = 20\%$$

B. An $80 item goes on sale for 25% off. What is the sale price?

$80 × 25% = $80 × 0.25 = $20

$80 − $20 = $60. $60 is the sale price.

PROBABILITY AND STATISTICS

Probability

The probability of an occurrence is the likelihood that it will happen. Most often, you write probability as a fraction.

Flip a fair coin and the probability that it will come up heads is $\frac{1}{2}$. The same is true for tails. Write the probability this way.

$$P(H) = \frac{1}{2} \qquad P(T) = \frac{1}{2}$$

If something will never occur the probability is 0. If something will always occur, the probability is 1. Therefore, if you flip a fair coin,

$$P(7) = 0 \qquad P(H \text{ or } T) = 1$$

Write the letters A, B, C, D, and E on pieces of paper. Pick them randomly without looking. The probability of picking any letter is $\frac{1}{5}$.

$$P(\text{vowel}) = \frac{2}{5} \qquad P(\text{consonant}) = \frac{3}{5}$$

RULES FOR COMPUTING PROBABILITY

$$P(A \text{ or } B) = P(A) + P(B) = \frac{1}{5} + \frac{1}{5} = \frac{2}{5}$$

when A and B have no common elements

$$P(A \text{ and } B) = P(A) \times P(B) = \frac{1}{5} \times \frac{1}{5} = \frac{1}{25}$$

$$P(\text{not } C) = 1 - P(C) = 1 - \frac{1}{5} = \frac{4}{5}$$

In one high school, 40% of the students go on to college. Two graduates of the high school are chosen at random. What is the probability that they both went to college?

Write the probabilities you know.

$$P(\text{college}) = \frac{40}{100} = \frac{2}{5}$$

Solve the problem.

$P(A \text{ and } B)$ probability the two students went to college.

$$P(A \text{ and } B) = P(A) \times P(B) = \frac{2}{5} \times \frac{2}{5} = \frac{4}{25}$$

The probability that they both went to college is $\frac{4}{25}$.

Independent and Dependent Events

Events are *independent* when the outcome of one event does not affect the probability of the other event. Each coin flip is an independent event. No matter the outcome of one flip, the probability of the next flip remains the same.

Flip heads 10 times in a row with a fair coin. On the next flip, the $P(H)$ is still $1/2$. Coin flips are independent events.

Events are *dependent* where the outcome of one event does affect the probability of the other event. For example, you have a full deck of cards. The probability of picking the Queen of Hearts is $1/52$.

You pick one card and it is not the Queen of Hearts. You do not put the card back. The probability of picking the Queen of Hearts is now $1/51$. Cards picked without replacement are dependent events.

Permutations, Combinations, and the Fundamental Counting Principle

PERMUTATIONS

A permutation is the way a set of things can be arranged in order. There are 6 permutations of the letters A, B, and C.

| ABC | ACB | BAC | BCA | CAB | CBA |

Permutation Formula

The formula for the number of permutations of n things is **n! (n factorial)**.

$$6! = 6 \times 5 \times 4 \times 3 \times 2 \times 1 \qquad 4! = 4 \times 3 \times 2 \times 1 \qquad 2! = 2 \times 1$$

There are 120 permutations of 5 things.

$$n! = 5! = 5 \times 4 \times 3 \times 2 \times 1 = 120$$

COMBINATIONS

A combination is the number of ways of choosing a given number of elements from a set. The order of the elements does not matter. There are 3 ways of choosing 2 letters from the letters A, B, and C.

AB AC BC

FUNDAMENTAL COUNTING PRINCIPLE

The fundamental counting principle is used to find the total number of possibilities. Multiply the number of possibilities from each category.

EXAMPLE

An ice cream stand has a sundae with choices of 28 flavors of ice cream, 8 types of syrups, and 5 types of toppings. How many different sundae combinations are available?

28	×	8	×	5	=	1,120
flavors		syrups		toppings		sundaes

There are 1,120 possible sundaes.

Statistics and Scatter Plots

Descriptive statistics are used to explain or describe a set of numbers. Most often you use the mean, median, or mode to describe these numbers.

MEAN (AVERAGE)

The mean is a position midway between two extremes. To find the mean:

1. Add the items or scores.
2. Divide by the number of items.

For example, find the mean of 24, 17, 42, 51, 36.

$$24 + 17 + 42 + 51 + 36 = 170 \qquad 170 \div 5 = 34$$

The mean or average is 34.

MEDIAN

The median is the middle number. To find the median:

1. Arrange the numbers from least to greatest.
2. If there are an odd number of scores, then find the middle score.
3. If there is an even number of scores, average the two middle scores.

For example, find the median of these numbers.

6, 9, 11, <u>17</u>, <u>21</u>, 33, 45, 71

There are an even number of scores.

$$17 + 21 = 38 \qquad 38 \div 2 = 19$$

The median is 19.

Do not forget to arrange the scores in order before finding the middle score!

MODE

The mode is the number that occurs most often.

For example, find the mode of these numbers.

6, 3, 7, 6, 9, 3, 6, 1, 2, 6, 7, 3

The number 6 occurs most often so 6 is the mode.

Not all sets of numbers have a mode. Some sets of numbers may have more than one mode.

EXAMPLE

What is the mean, median, and mode of 7, 13, 18, 4, 14, 22?

Mean Add the scores and divide by the number of scores.

$$7 + 13 + 18 + 4 + 14 + 22 = 78 \div 6 = 13 \qquad \text{The mean is 13.}$$

Median Arrange the scores in order. Find the middle score.

$$4, 7, 13, 14, 18, 22 \quad 13 + 14 = 27 \div 2 = 13.5 \qquad \text{The median is 13.5.}$$

Mode Find the score that occurs most often.

Each score occurs only once. There is no mode.

Scatter Plots

Scatter plots are an indication about the trend of a set of data. They indicate how the data are correlated. Correlation can be complicated, but test questions will not ask for a sophisticated understanding of scatter plots or correlation.

Look at these examples.

Example A shows a positive correlation. The dots in the plot move generally from lower left to upper right. Example B shows a negative correlation. The dots move generally from upper left to lower right. Example C shows little or no correlation. The dots do not show any organized pattern.

Negative and positive linear correlations are also called negative and positive linear relationships. You may come across this term on the test.

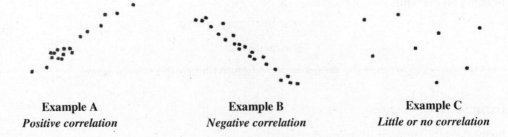

Example A
Positive correlation

Example B
Negative correlation

Example C
Little or no correlation

Scatter plots are usually based on sets of data.

GEOMETRY AND MEASUREMENT
Symmetry

Symmetric objects, figures, and designs have a pleasing, balanced appearance.

There are three primary types of symmetry—line (reflection), rotational, and translational.

LINE OR REFLECTIVE SYMMETRY

A figure with line symmetry can be folded in half so that one half exactly matches the other half.

This letter M has line symmetry.

Fold the M in half at the line and one half exactly matches the other half.

Flip the M over the line and it looks the same.

Place a mirror on that line and half the M and the reflection will form the entire M.

The line is called the line of symmetry.

ROTATIONAL SYMMETRY

A figure has rotational symmetry if it can be turned less than a full turn and look exactly as it did before it was turned.

This letter N has rotational symmetry.

N ↧ Z ↧ N

Turn the Z half a turn and it looks exactly as it did before the turn.

TRANSLATIONAL SYMMETRY

A design has translational symmetry if it repeats a pattern.

Many wallpaper patterns have translational symmetry.

This simple pattern has translational symmetry because it shows a repeating pattern.

A B C A B C

A. Which of these letters has line symmetry?

B. Which of these letters has rotational symmetry?

A   B   C   D   E   F   G   H   I

These letters have both line and rotational symmetry: H, I

These letters have only line symmetry: A, B, C, D, E

None of the letters has only rotational symmetry.

These letters have neither type of symmetry: F, G

Two-Dimensional Geometry

Geometry has two or three dimensions. A two-dimensional model is this page. A three-dimensional model is the room where you will take the test.

DEFINITION	MODEL	SYMBOL
Point—a location	. A	A
Plane—a flat surface that extends infinitely in all directions		plane ABC
Line—a set of points in a straight path that extends infinitely in two directions		$\overleftrightarrow{AB}$
Line segment—part of a line with two endpoints		$\overline{AB}$
Ray—part of a line with one endpoint		$\overrightarrow{AB}$
Parallel lines—lines that stay the same distance apart and never touch		$\overleftrightarrow{AB} \parallel \overleftrightarrow{DF}$
Perpendicular lines—lines that meet at right angles		$AB \perp CD$

DEFINITION	MODEL	SYMBOL

Angle—two rays with a common endpoint, which is called the vertex

$\angle ABC$

Acute angle—angle that measures between 0° and 90°

Right angle—angle that measures 90°

Obtuse angle—angle that measures between 90° and 180°

Complementary angles—angles that have a total measure of 90°

Supplementary angles—angles that have a total measure of 180°

Congruent angles have the same angle measure.
$\angle p$ and $\angle q$ measure 90°.
$\angle p$ and $\angle q$ are congruent.
$m\angle p = m\angle q$

$\angle p \cong \angle q$

CIRCLES

A circle is a shape with all points the same distance from its center. A circle is named by its center. The distance around the circle is called the circumference.

The region inside a circle is not part of the circle. It is called the area of a circle.

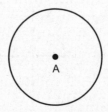

The diameter of a circle is a line segment across a circle through the center.

The radius of a circle is a line segment from the center of the circle to any point on the circle. Two radii lined up end-to-end form a diameter. The diameter and radius each has a length, and the length of the diameter is twice the length of the radius.

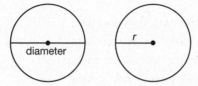

A chord is a line segment with endpoints on a circle. A diameter is the longest chord of a circle. Every diameter is a chord but not every chord is a diameter.

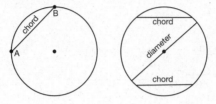

Polygon

A closed figure made up of line segments; if all sides are the same length, the figure is a regular polygon.

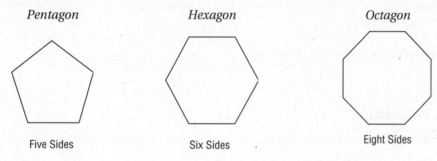

Pentagon   *Hexagon*   *Octagon*

Five Sides   Six Sides   Eight Sides

TRIANGLE

A polygon with three sides and three angles; the sum of the angles is always 180°.

Equilateral triangle—all the sides are the
same length; all the angles are the
same size, 60°.

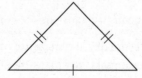

Isosceles triangle—two sides the
same length; two angles the same size.

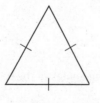

Scalene triangle—all sides different lengths; all angles different sizes.

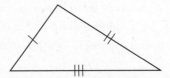

Congruent triangle—Two triangles are congruent if the lengths of each corresponding pair of sides are equal and the measures of each corresponding pair of angles are equal. That means one triangle fits exactly on top of the other triangle.

QUADRILATERAL

A polygon with four sides

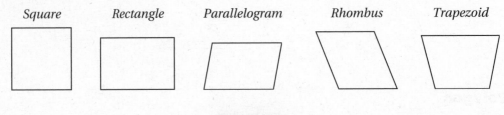

Square   Rectangle   Parallelogram   Rhombus   Trapezoid

EXAMPLE

Which types of quadrilaterals can be constructed using four congruent line segments *AB*, *BC*, *CD*, and *DA*?

You can create a square and a rhombus.

SIMILAR TRIANGLES

In similar triangles, corresponding angles are congruent. The ratio of the lengths of corresponding sides are equal.

These triangles are similar.

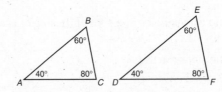

Corresponding angles of the two triangles are congruent.

  $\angle A$ and $\angle D$ $\angle B$ and $\angle E$ $\angle C$ and $\angle F$

That means the measures of congruent angles are equal.

  measure of $\angle A$ = measure of $\angle D$ = 40°
  measure of $\angle B$ = measure of $\angle E$ = 60°
  measure of $\angle C$ = measure of $\angle F$ = 80°

Corresponding sides (Corresponding sides are opposite corresponding angles)

  $\overline{BC}$ and $\overline{EF}$ $\overline{AC}$ and $\overline{DF}$ $\overline{AB}$ and $\overline{DE}$

The ratios of the lengths of corresponding sides are equal.

$$\frac{BC}{EF} = \frac{AC}{DF} = \frac{AB}{DE}$$

Are these triangles similar?

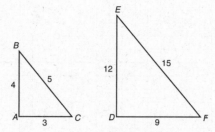

Corresponding sides: $\overline{AB}$ and $\overline{DE}$, $\overline{BC}$ and $\overline{EF}$, $\overline{AC}$ and $\overline{DF}$

Does $\dfrac{AB}{DE} = \dfrac{BC}{EF}$? $\quad \dfrac{AB}{DE} = \dfrac{4}{12}$; $\dfrac{BC}{EF} = \dfrac{5}{15}$; $\dfrac{4}{12} = \dfrac{1}{3}$; $\dfrac{5}{15} = \dfrac{1}{3}$

These triangles are similar. Ratios of corresponding sides of the two triangles are equal.

EXAMPLE

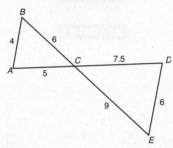

Are triangle *ABC* and triangle *CDE* similar triangles?

The ratios of the lengths of corresponding sides are equal.

$\overline{AB}$ and $\overline{DE}$ are corresponding sides.

Does $\dfrac{AC}{CD} = \dfrac{AB}{DE}$? Yes. $\dfrac{5}{7.5} = \dfrac{4}{6} \left(\dfrac{20}{30} = \dfrac{20}{30} \right)$

Coordinate Grid and Translations

You can plot ordered pairs of numbers on a coordinate grid.

The *x* axis goes horizontally from left to right. The first number in the pair tells how far to move left or right from the origin. A minus sign means move left. A plus sign means move right.

The *y* axis goes vertically up and down. The second number in the pair tells how far to move up or down from the origin. A minus sign means move down. A plus sign means move up.

Pairs of numbers show the *x* coordinate first and the *y* coordinate second (*x*, *y*). The origin is point (0, 0) where the *x* axis and the *y* axis meet.

Plot these pairs of numbers on the grid.

A (+3, −7)   **B** (+5, +3)   **C** (−6, +2)   **D** (−3, −6)

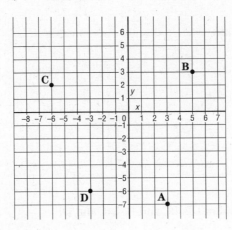

TRANSLATIONS ON A COORDINATE GRID

You can slide or translate points and geometric shapes on the coordinate grid. You can describe the translations by what happens to the positions of the vertices. Look at these simple examples:

EXAMPLE 1

This triangle slid right 4 units horizontally on the coordinate plane. The y values remain the same. The x values increase by 4. The coordinates of point A (−4, 3) on the triangle became (0, 3) after the slide.

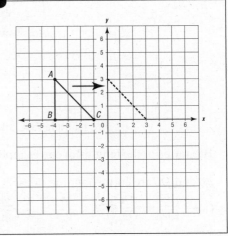

EXAMPLE 2

This triangle slid down five units vertically. The x values remain the same. The y values decrease by 3. The coordinate of point Q (4, 3) became (4, −2) after the slide.

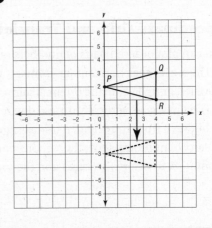

EXAMPLE 3

This triangle slid right 6 units and up 3 units. The *x* values increased by 6 and the *y* values increased by 5. The coordinate of point *M* (–2, –2) became (4, 1) after the slide.

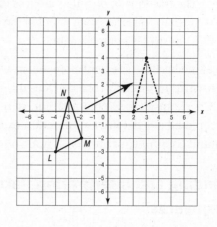

PROBLEM SOLVING

The problem-solving strategies of choosing a reasonable answer, estimating, choosing the operation, writing a number sentence, and identifying extra or needed information were discussed earlier in the review. This section shows you how to use more problem-solving strategies.

Estimate to Be Sure Your Answer Is Reasonable

You can use estimation and common sense to be sure that the answer is reasonable. You may make a multiplication error or misalign decimal points. You may be so engrossed in a problem that you miss the big picture because of the details. These difficulties can be headed off by making sure your answer is reasonable.

   A few examples follow.

   A question involves dividing or multiplying. Multiply: 28×72.

   Estimate first: $30 \times 70 = 2{,}100$. Your answer should be close to 2,100. If not, then your answer is not reasonable. A mistake was probably made in multiplication.

   A question involves subtracting or adding. Add: $12.9 + 0.63 + 10.29 + 4.3$.

   Estimate first: $13 + 1 + 10 + 4 = 28$. Your answer should be close to 28. If not, then your answer is not reasonable. The decimal points may not have been aligned.

   A question asks you to compare fractions to $\frac{11}{10}$.

   Think: $\frac{11}{10}$ is more than 1. Any number 1 or less will be less than $\frac{11}{10}$. Any

   number larger than $1\frac{1}{10}$ will be more than $\frac{11}{10}$. You have to look

   closely only at numbers from 1 to $1\frac{1}{10}$.

A question asks you to multiply two fractions or decimals.

The fractions or decimals are less than 1. The product of two fractions or decimals less than one is less than either of the two fractions or decimals. If not, you know that your answer is not reasonable.

Stand back for a second after you answer each question and ask, "Is this reasonable? Is this at least approximately correct? Does this make sense?"

Check answers to computation, particularly division and subtraction. When you have completed a division or subtraction example, do a quick, approximate check. Your check should confirm your answer. If not, your answer is probably not reasonable.

Finding and Interpreting Patterns

SEQUENCES

Arithmetic Sequence

A sequence of numbers formed by adding the same nonzero number.

3, 11, 19, 27, 35, 43, 51	Add 8 to get each successive term.
52, 48, 44, 40, 36, 32	Add (−4) to get each successive term.

Geometric Sequence

A sequence of numbers formed by multiplying the same nonzero number.

3, 15, 75, 375	Multiply by 5 to get each successive term.
160, 40, 10, $2\frac{1}{2}$	Multiply by $\frac{1}{4}$ to get each successive term.

Harmonic Sequence

A sequence of fractions with a numerator of 1 in which the denominators form an arithmetic sequence.

$$\frac{1}{2} \quad \frac{1}{9} \quad \frac{1}{16} \quad \frac{1}{23} \quad \frac{1}{30}$$

Each numerator is 1. The denominators form an arithmetic sequence.

Relationships

Linear Relationships

Linear relationships are pairs of numbers formed by adding or multiplying the same number to the first term in a pair. Here are some examples.

(3, 12), (5, 14), (11, 20), (15, 24)	Add 9 to the first term to get the second.
(1, 6), (2, 12), (3, 18), (4, 24), (5, 30)	Multiply the first term by 6 to get the second.
(96, 12), (72, 9), (56, 7), (24, 3), (16, 2)	Multiply the first term by $\frac{1}{4}$ to get the second.

A. What term is missing in this number pattern?

2   5   10   17   ___

  +3 +5 +7 +9

26 is the missing term.

B. These points are all on the same line.
Find the missing term.

$(-7, -15)\left(\dfrac{2}{3}, \dfrac{1}{3}\right)$ (2, 3) (4, 7) (8, ___)

Multiply the first term by 2 and subtract 1.
The missing term is (8, 15).

Formula Problems

Concentrate on substituting values for variables. If you see a problem to be solved with a proportion, set up the proportion and solve.

EXAMPLES

A. A mechanic uses this formula to estimate the displacement (P) of an engine. $P = 0.8 (d^2)(s)(n)$ where d is the diameter, s is the stroke length of each cylinder, and n is the number of cylinders. Estimate the displacement of a 6-cylinder car whose cylinders have a diameter of 2 inches and a stroke length of 4 inches.

1. Write the formula. $P = 0.8(d^2)(s)(n)$
2. Write the values of the variables. $d = 2,\ s = 4,\ n = 6$
3. Substitute the values for the variables. $P = 0.8(2^2)(4)(6)$
4. Solve. $P = 0.8(4)(24) = (3.2)(24)$

                                         $P = 76.8$

The displacement of the engine is about 76.8 cubic inches.

B. The accountant calculates that it takes $3 in sales to generate $0.42 in profit. How much cost does it take to generate a profit of $5.46?

1. Write a proportion
Use s for sales. $\dfrac{3}{0.42} = \dfrac{s}{5.46}$

2. Cross multiply. $0.42s = 16.38$

3. Solve. $s = \dfrac{16.38}{0.42}$

                                     $s = 39$

It will take $39 in sales to generate $5.46 in profits.

Pythagorean Theorem Problems

Follow these steps to solve this type of problem.

1. Sketch and label the right triangle.
2. Use the Pythagorean formula.
3. Solve the problem.

EXAMPLE

A radio tower sticks 40 feet straight up into the air. Engineers attached a wire with no slack from the top of the tower to the ground 30 feet away from the tower. If it costs $95 a foot to attach the wire, how much did the wire cost?

1. Sketch and label the right triangle.

2. Use the Pythagorean formula.

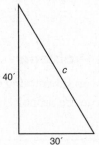

$$a^2 + b^2 = c^2$$
$$(40)^2 + (30)^2 = c^2$$
$$1{,}600 + 900 = c^2$$
$$2{,}500 = c^2$$
$$50 = c$$

The wire is 50 feet long.

3. Solve the problem.

50 feet at $95 a foot.

$50 \times 95 = 4{,}750$. The wire costs $4,750 to install.

Geometric Figure Problems

Follow these steps to solve this type of problem.

1. Identify the figure or figures involved.
2. Use the formulas for these figures.
3. Use the results of the formulas to solve the problem.

A circular pool with a radius of 10 feet is inscribed inside a square wall. What is the area of the region outside the pool but inside the fence?

1. There is a square with $s = 20$ and a circle with $r = 10$. The side of the square is twice the radius of the circle.

2. Find the areas.
   Square: $(A = s^2)$ $(20) \times (20) = 400$
   Circle: $(A = \pi r^2)$ $3.14 \times 10^2 = 3.14 \times 100 = 314$

3. Subtract to find the area inside the square but outside the circle.
   $400 - 314 = 86$

Interpreting Remainder Problems

When you divide to solve a problem there may be both a quotient and a remainder. You may need to (1) use only the quotient, (2) round the quotient to the next greater whole number, or (3) use only the remainder.

Stereo speakers are packed 4 to a box. There are 315 stereo speakers to be packed.

Questions:
1. How many boxes can be filled?
2. How many boxes would be needed to hold all the stereo speakers?
3. How many stereo speakers will be in the box that is not completely full?

   Divide 315 by 4.

$$\begin{array}{r} 78 \text{ R}3 \\ 4\overline{)315} \\ \underline{28} \\ 35 \\ \underline{32} \\ 3 \end{array}$$

Answers:
1. Use only the quotient—78 of the boxes can be filled.
2. Round the quotient to the next higher number. It would take 79 boxes to hold all the stereo speakers.
3. Use only the remainder. Three stereo speakers would be in the partially filled box.

LEARNING TO READ

Reading is the most important subject addressed in school. Students who cannot read effectively are denied access to most other learning. There are dire practical consequences for those who cannot read. Teaching reading is a sophisticated, technical process that requires careful study.

This section reviews five areas of reading instruction: phonemic awareness, phonics, fluency, vocabulary, and text comprehension. You will find a description of each topic, some specific examples, and a summary of the most current research about reading instruction.

PHONEMIC AWARENESS

Here are some essential definitions related to phonemic awareness.

Phoneme

A phoneme is the smallest part of *spoken* language that makes a difference in the meaning of words. Phonemes are represented by letters between slash marks. English has about forty-one phonemes. A few words have one phoneme, but most words have more than one phoneme: The word "at" has two phonemes, one for each letter; "check" has three phonemes (/ch/ /e/ /k/).

Grapheme

A grapheme is the smallest part of *written* language that represents a phoneme in the spelling of a word. A grapheme may be just one letter, such as "b" or "s" or several letters, such as "sh" or "ea."

Phonics

Phonics is the fairly predictable relationship between phonemes and graphemes.

Phonemic Awareness

Phonemic awareness is the ability to hear, identify, and manipulate the individual sounds—phonemes—in spoken words.

Phonological Awareness

Phonological awareness is a broad term that includes phonemic awareness. In addition to phonemes, phonological awareness activities can involve work with rhymes, words, syllables, and onsets and rimes.

Onset and Rime

Onsets and rimes are parts of spoken language that are smaller than syllables but larger than phonemes. An onset is the initial consonant(s) sound of a syllable (the onset of bag is b-; of swim, sw-). A rime is the part of a syllable that contains the vowel and all that follows it (the rime of bag is -ag; of swim, -im).

Children learn phonemes—the sounds of a language—before they learn to read. Phonemic awareness is the ability to notice, think about, and work with those individual sounds in spoken words. Children who have well-established phonemic awareness skills generally find it easier to read and spell than children who do not.

Phonemic awareness is not phonics, as we can see from the definitions above. Phonemic awareness is not the same as phonological awareness, although phonemic awareness is a subcategory of phonological awareness. The focus of phonemic awareness is narrow—identifying and manipulating the individual sounds in words. The focus of phonological awareness is much broader. It includes identifying and manipulating larger parts of spoken language, such as words, syllables, and onsets and rimes—as well as phonemes. It also encompasses awareness of other aspects of sound, such as rhyming, alliteration, and intonation.

Here are some activities to build phonemic awareness.

PHONEME ISOLATION—recognize individual sounds in a word.

PHONEME IDENTITY—recognize the same sounds in different words.

PHONEME CATEGORIZATION—recognize a word with a sound that does not match the sounds in other words.

PHONEME BLENDING—combine the phonemes to form a word. Then they write and read the word.

PHONEME SEGMENTATION—break a word into its separate sounds, saying each sound.

PHONEME DELETION—recognize the word that remains when a phoneme is removed from another word.

PHONEME ADDITION—make a new word by adding a phoneme to an existing word.

PHONEME SUBSTITUTION—substitute one phoneme for another to make a new word.

Phonemic Awareness Instruction Helps Children Learn to Read.

Phonemic awareness instruction aids reading comprehension primarily through its influence on word reading. For children to understand what they read, they must be able to read words rapidly and accurately. Rapid and accurate word reading frees children to focus their attention on the meaning of what they read. Of course, many other things, including the size of children's vocabulary and their world experiences, contribute to reading comprehension.

Phonemic Awareness Instruction Helps Children Learn to Spell.

Teaching phonemic awareness, particularly how to segment words into phonemes, helps children learn to spell. The explanation for this may be that children who have phonemic awareness understand that sounds and letters are related in a predictable way. Thus, they are able to relate the sounds to letters as they spell words.

Phonemic Awareness Instruction Is Most Effective When Children Are Taught to Manipulate Phonemes by Using the Letters of the Alphabet.

Phonemic awareness instruction makes a stronger contribution to the improvement of reading and spelling when children are taught to use letters as they manipulate phonemes than when instruction is limited to phonemes alone. Teaching sounds along with the letters of the alphabet is important because it helps children to see how phonemic awareness relates to their reading and writing.

If children do not know letter names and shapes, they need to be taught them along with phonemic awareness. Relating sounds to letters is, of course, the heart of phonics instruction, which is discussed later in this section.

Phonemic Awareness Instruction Is Most Effective When It Focuses on Only One or Two Types of Phoneme Manipulation.

Children who receive instruction that focuses on one or two types of phoneme manipulation make greater gains in reading and spelling than children who are taught three or more types of manipulation.

Phonics

Phonics is the relationships between the letters (graphemes) of written language and the individual sounds (phonemes) of spoken language. It teaches children to use these relationships to read and write words. Phonics instruction teaches children a system for remembering how to read words. The alphabetic system is a mnemonic device that supports our memory for specific words.

Systematic Phonics Instruction Is More Effective than Non-Systematic or No Phonics Instruction.

Systematic phonics instruction is the direct teaching of a set of letter–sound relationships in a clearly defined sequence. The set includes the major sound/spelling relationships of both consonants and vowels.

Systematic and Explicit Phonics Instruction Significantly Improves Kindergarten and First-Grade Children's Word Recognition and Spelling.

Systematic phonics instruction produces the greatest impact on children's reading achievement when it begins in kindergarten or first grade.

Both kindergarten and first-grade children who receive systematic phonics instruction are better at reading and spelling words than kindergarten and first-grade children who do not receive systematic instruction.

Systematic and Explicit Phonics Instruction Significantly Improves Children's Reading Comprehension.

Systematic phonics instruction results in better growth in children's ability to comprehend what they read than non-systematic or no phonics instruction. This is not surprising because the ability to read the words in a text accurately and quickly is highly related to successful reading comprehension.

Systematic and Explicit Phonics Instruction Is Effective for Children from Various Social and Economic Levels.

Systematic phonics instruction is beneficial to children regardless of their socioeconomic status. It helps children from various backgrounds make greater gains in reading than non-systematic instruction or no phonics instruction.

Systematic and explicit phonics instruction is particularly beneficial for children who are having difficulty learning to read and who are at risk for developing future reading problems.

Systematic phonics instruction is significantly more effective than non-systematic or no phonics instruction in helping to prevent reading difficulties among at risk students and in helping children overcome reading difficulties.

Systematic and Explicit Phonics Instruction Is Most Effective When Introduced Early.

Phonics instruction is most effective when it begins in kindergarten or first grade. To be effective with young learners, systematic instruction must be designed appropriately and taught carefully. It should include teaching letter shapes and names, phonemic awareness, and all major letter–sound relationships. It should ensure that all children learn these skills. As instruction proceeds, children should be taught to use this knowledge to read and write words.

Phonics Instruction Is Not an Entire Reading Program for Beginning Readers.

Along with phonics instruction, young children should be solidifying their knowledge of the alphabet, engaging in phonemic awareness activities, and listening to stories and informational texts read aloud to them. They also should be reading texts (both out loud and silently) and writing letters, words, messages, and stories.

Examples of Non-Systematic Programs

Here are examples of non-systematic programs that may be important in other ways but that do not achieve the essential outcomes of systematic phonics instruction.

Literature-Based Programs That Emphasize Reading and Writing Activities

Phonics instruction is embedded in these activities, but letter–sound relationships are taught incidentally, usually based on key letters that appear in student reading materials.

Basal Reading Programs That Focus on Whole-Word or Meaning-Based Activities

These programs pay only limited attention to letter–sound relationships and provide little or no instruction in how to blend letters to pronounce words.

Sight-Word Programs That Begin by Teaching a Sight-Word Reading Vocabulary of from 50 to 100 Words

Only after they learn to read these words do children receive instruction in the alphabetic principle.

Adding Phonics Workbooks or Phonics Activities

Just adding phonics workbooks or phonics activities to these programs has not been effective. Such "add-ons" tend to confuse rather than help children to read.

Fluency

Fluency means to read a text accurately and quickly. Fluent readers recognize words automatically and they group words quickly to help them gain meaning. Fluent readers read aloud effortlessly and with expression. Readers who have not yet developed fluency read slowly, word by word. Their oral reading is choppy and plodding.

Fluency is the bridge between word recognition and comprehension. Fluent readers can concentrate on meaning because they do not have to concentrate on decoding words. Less fluent readers, however, must focus their attention on the words and not on meaning.

Fluency develops gradually through substantial practice. At the earliest stage of reading development, students' oral reading is slow and labored and even when students recognize many words automatically, their oral reading may still not be fluent. To read with expression, readers must be able to divide the text into meaningful chunks and know when to pause appropriately.

Fluency varies, depending on what readers are reading. Even very skilled readers may read in a slow, labored manner when reading texts with many unfamiliar words or topics. For example, readers who are usually fluent may not be able to fluently read unfamiliar technical material.

Repeated and Monitored Oral Reading Improves Reading Fluency and Overall Reading Achievement.

Students who read and reread passages orally as they receive guidance and/or feedback become better readers. Repeated oral reading substantially improves word recognition, speed, and accuracy as well as fluency. To a lesser but still considerable extent, repeated oral reading also improves reading comprehension. Repeated oral reading improves the reading ability of all students throughout the elementary school years. It also helps struggling readers at higher grade levels.

Round-robin reading means students take turns reading parts of a text aloud (though usually not repeatedly). But round-robin reading in itself does not increase fluency. This may be because students only read small amounts of text, and they usually read this small portion only once.

Students should read and reread a text a certain number of times or until a certain level of fluency is reached. Four rereadings are sufficient for most students. Oral reading practice is increased through the use of audiotapes, tutors, and peer guidance.

No Research Evidence Currently Confirms That Silent, Independent Reading with Minimal Guidance Improves Reading Fluency and Overall Reading Achievement.

One of the major differences between good and poor readers is the amount of time they spend reading. But research has not yet confirmed whether independent silent reading with minimal guidance or feedback improves reading achievement and fluency. Neither has it proven that more silent reading in the classroom cannot work. But the research does suggest that there are more beneficial ways to spend reading instructional time than to have students read independently in the classroom without reading instruction.

Students Should Hear Models of Fluent Reading.

Primary teachers should read aloud daily to their students. By reading effortlessly and with expression, the teacher is modeling how a fluent reader sounds during reading. After a teacher models how to read students should reread the selection.

A teacher should encourage parents or other family members to read aloud to their children at home. The more models of fluent reading the children hear, the better. Of course, hearing a model of fluent reading is not the only benefit of reading aloud to children. Reading to children also increases their knowledge of the world, their vocabulary, their familiarity with written language, and their interest in reading.

Students Should Read Orally from Text They Can Easily Master.

Fluency develops as a result of many opportunities to practice reading with a high degree of success. Therefore, students should practice orally rereading text that contains mostly words that they know or can decode easily. In other words, the texts should be at the students' independent reading level, which means the student can read it with about 95 percent accuracy. If the text is more difficult, students will focus so much on word recognition that they will not have an opportunity to develop fluency.

The text your students practice rereading orally should also be relatively short—probably 50–200 words, depending on the age of the students. You should also use a variety of reading materials, including stories, nonfiction, and poetry. Poetry is especially well suited to fluency practice because poems for children are often short and they contain rhythm, rhyme, and meaning, making practice easy, fun, and rewarding.

Vocabulary

Vocabulary refers to the words people must know to communicate effectively. In general, vocabulary can be described as oral vocabulary or reading vocabulary. Oral vocabulary refers to words used in speaking or recognized in listening. Reading vocabulary refers to words we recognized or used in print.

Vocabulary plays an important part in learning to read. As beginning readers, children use the words they have heard to make sense of the words they see in print. Beginning readers have a much more difficult time reading words that are not already part of their oral vocabulary.

Vocabulary also is very important to reading comprehension. Readers cannot understand what they are reading without knowing what most of the words mean. As children learn to read more advanced texts, they must learn the meaning of new words that are not part of their oral vocabulary.

Children Learn the Meanings of Most Words Indirectly, Through Everyday Experiences with Oral and Written Language.

Children learn word meanings indirectly in three ways:

Children Engage in Oral Language Daily.

Young children learn word meanings through conversations with other people, especially adults. As they engage in these conversations, children often hear adults repeat words several times. They also may hear adults use new and interesting words. The more oral language experiences children have, the more word meanings they learn.

Children Listen to Adults Read to Them.

Children learn word meanings from listening to adults read to them. Reading aloud is particularly helpful when the reader pauses during reading to define an unfamiliar word and, after reading, engages the child in a conversation about the book. Conversations about books help children to learn new words and concepts and to relate them to their prior knowledge and experience.

Children Read Extensively on Their Own.

Children learn many new words by reading extensively on their own. The more children read on their own, the more words they encounter and the more word meanings they learn.

Teaching Specific Words Before Reading Helps Both Vocabulary and Reading Comprehension.

Before students read a text, it is helpful to teach them specific words they will see in the text. Teaching important vocabulary before reading can help students learn new words and comprehend the text.

Extended Instruction That Promotes Active Engagement with Vocabulary Improves Word Learning.

Children learn words best when they work actively with the words over an extended period of time. The more students use new words and the more they use them in different contexts, the more likely they are to learn the words.

Repeated Exposure to Vocabulary in Many Contexts Aids Word Learning.

Students learn new words better when they encounter them often and in various contexts. When the students read those same words in their texts, they increase their exposure to the new words.

Word-Learning Strategies

Of course, it is not possible for teachers to provide specific instruction for all the words their students do not know. Therefore, students also need to be able to determine the meaning of words that are new to them but not taught directly to them. They need to develop effective word-learning strategies. Word-learning strategies include:

1. how to use dictionaries and other reference aids to learn word meanings and to deepen knowledge of word meanings;
2. how to use information about word parts to figure out the meanings of words in text; and
3. how to use context clues to determine word meanings.

Using Dictionaries and Other Reference Aids

Students must learn how to use dictionaries, glossaries, and thesauruses to help broaden and deepen their knowledge of words, even though these resources can be difficult to use. The most helpful dictionaries include sentences providing clear examples of word meanings in context.

PARTS OF WORDS

Word parts include *affixes* (prefixes and suffixes), *base words*, and *word roots*.

AFFIXES are word parts that are "fixed to" either the beginnings of words (prefixes) or the ending of words (suffixes). The word "unremarkable" has two affixes, a prefix "un" and a suffix "able."

BASE WORDS are words from which many other words are formed. For example, many words can be formed from the base word migrate: migration, migrant, immigration, immigrant, migrating, migratory.

WORD ROOTS are the words from other languages that are the origin of many English words. About 60 percent of all English words have Latin or Greek origins.

Using Context Clues

Context clues are hints about the meaning of an unknown word that are provided in the words, phrases, and sentences that surround the word. Context clues include definitions, restatements, examples, or descriptions. Because students learn most word meanings indirectly, or from context, it is important that they learn to use context clues effectively.

Text Comprehension

Comprehension is the reason for reading. Without comprehension, reading is a largely meaningless activity. Good readers are both purposeful and active as they read.

Good Readers Are Purposeful.

Good readers have a purpose for reading. They may read to find out how to use a food processor, read a guidebook to gather information about national parks, read a textbook to satisfy the requirements of a course, read a magazine for entertainment, or read a classic novel to experience the pleasures of great literature.

Good Readers Are Active.

Good readers think actively as they read. To make sense of what they read, good readers engage in a complicated process. Using their experiences and knowledge of the world, their knowledge of vocabulary and language structure, and their knowledge of reading strategies (or plans), good readers make sense of the text and know how to get the most out of it. They know when they have problems with understanding and how to resolve these problems as they occur.

Over 30 years of research has shown that instruction in comprehension can help students understand what they read, remember what they read, and communicate with others about what they read.

Specific Comprehension Strategies Help Improve Text Comprehension.

Comprehension strategies are conscious sets of steps that good readers use to make sense of text. Comprehension strategy instruction helps students become purposeful, active readers who are in control of their own reading comprehension.

The following six strategies appear to have a firm scientific basis for improving text comprehension.

METACOGNITION. Metacognition can be defined as "thinking about thinking." Good readers use metacognitive strategies to think about and have control over their reading. Before reading, they might clarify their purpose for reading and preview the text. During reading, they might monitor their understanding, adjusting their reading speed to fit the difficulty of the text and "fixing up" any comprehension problems they have. After reading, they check their understanding of what they read.

COMPREHENSION MONITORING. Comprehension monitoring is a critical part of metacognition. Students who are good at monitoring their comprehension know when they understand what they read and when they do not. They have strategies to "fix up" problems in their understanding as the problems arise. Research shows that instruction, even in the early grades, can help students become better at monitoring their comprehension.

USING GRAPHIC AND SEMANTIC ORGANIZERS. Graphic organizers illustrate concepts and interrelationships among concepts in a text, using diagrams or other pictorial devices. Graphic organizers may be maps, webs, graphs, charts, frames, or clusters. Semantic organizers (also called semantic maps or semantic webs) are graphic organizers that look somewhat like a spider web. In a semantic organizer, lines connect a central concept to a variety of related ideas and events.

Regardless of the label, graphic organizers can help readers focus on concepts and how they are related to other concepts. Graphic organizers help students read to learn from informational text in the content areas, such as science and social studies textbooks and trade books. Used with informational text, graphic organizers can help students see how concepts fit common text structures. Graphic organizers are also used with narrative text, or stories, as story maps.

RECOGNIZING STORY STRUCTURE. Story structure refers to the way the content and events of a story are organized into a plot. Students who can recognize story structure have greater appreciation, understanding, and memory for stories. In story structure instruction, students learn to identify the categories of content (setting, initiating events, internal reactions, goals, attempts, and outcomes) and how this content is organized into a plot. Often, students learn to recognize story structure through the use of story maps. Story maps, a type of graphic organizer, show the sequence of events in simple stories. Instruction in the content and organization of stories improves students' comprehension and memory of stories.

SUMMARIZING. A summary is a synthesis of the important ideas in a text. Summarizing requires students to determine what is important in what they are reading, to condense this information, and to put it into their own words. Instruction in summarizing helps students identify or generate main ideas; connect the main or central ideas; eliminate redundant and unnecessary information; and remember what they read.

Students Can Be Taught to Use Comprehension Strategies.

In addition to identifying which comprehension strategies are effective, scientific research provides guidelines for how to teach comprehension strategies.

Effective Comprehension Strategy Instruction Is Explicit, or Direct.

Research shows that explicit teaching techniques are particularly effective for comprehension strategy instruction. In explicit instruction, teachers tell readers why and when they should use strategies, what strategies to use, and how to apply them. The steps of explicit instruction typically include direct explanation, teacher modeling ("thinking aloud"), guided practice, and application.

DIRECT EXPLANATION. The teacher explains to students why the strategy helps comprehension and when to apply the strategy.

MODELING. The teacher models, or demonstrates, how to apply the strategy, usually by "thinking aloud" while reading the text that the students are using.

GUIDED PRACTICE. The teacher guides and assists students as they learn how and when to apply the strategy.

APPLICATION. The teacher helps students practice the strategy until they can apply it independently.

Effective Comprehension Strategy Instruction Can Be Accomplished Through Cooperative Learning.

Cooperative learning (and the closely related concept, collaborative learning) involves students working together as partners or in small groups on clearly defined tasks. Cooperative learning instruction has been used successfully to teach comprehension strategies in content-area subjects. Students work together to understand content-area texts, helping each other learn and apply comprehension strategies. Teachers help students learn to work in groups, demonstrate comprehension strategies, and monitor student progress.

Effective Instruction Helps Readers Use Comprehension Strategies Flexibly and in Combination.

Good readers must be able to coordinate and adjust several strategies to assist comprehension. Multiple-strategy instruction teaches students how to use strategies flexibly as they are needed to assist their comprehension. In a well-known example of multiple-strategy instruction called "reciprocal teaching," the teacher and students work together so that the students learn these four comprehension strategies.

1. Ask questions about the text they are reading;
2. Summarize parts of the text;
3. Clarify words and sentences students don't understand;
4. Predict what might occur next in the text.

Teachers and students use these four strategies flexibly as they are needed in reading literature and informational texts.

TEXTS

Literary Forms

CHILDREN'S LITERATURE

Children's literature, as we know it, did not exist until the late 1700s. Jean Rousseau, in his influential *Emile*, was among the first writers to popularize the view that children were not just small adults. A collection of age-old fairy tales, *The Tales of Mother Goose*, was published in France about 1700. The first illustrated book was probably *The Visible World in Pictures*, which was written in Latin about 1760 by John Comenius.

Before this time, most children's literature conveyed a religious or moral message or was designed for instruction. A few adult books appealed to children including *Robinson Crusoe* and the satirical *Gulliver's Travels*.

In the United States during the 1800s, James Fenimore Cooper wrote *The Last of the Mohicans*, Washington Irving wrote *The Legend of Sleepy Hollow*, and Nathaniel Hawthorne wrote *A Wonder Book for Boys and Girls*. Louisa May Alcott wrote *Little Women* and Samuel Clemens, writing as Mark Twain, wrote *The Adventures of Huckleberry Finn*. Horatio Alger wrote a series of "rags to riches" books at the end of the century.

On the European continent, the Brothers Grimm published *Grimm's Fairy Tales*, which included "Snow White and the Seven Dwarfs." Hans Christian Anderson published a number of stories including "The Ugly Duckling." Heidi and the *Adventures of Pinocchio* were also published about this time.

In England, Charles Dodgson, writing as Lewis Carroll, penned *Alice's Adventures in Wonderland*. John Tenniel provided the illustrations for this famous work. Robert Louis Stevenson wrote *Treasure Island*, Rudyard Kipling wrote *The Jungle Book*, and Edward Lear wrote the *Nonsense Book*.

At the beginning of this century, Frank Baum wrote the first *Wizard of Oz* book and Lucy Maud Montgomery wrote *Anne of Green Gables*. Also in this century, Hugh Loftig penned the famous Dr. Doolittle books, A. A. Milne published a series of Winnie-the-Pooh books and P. L. Travers wrote the Mary Poppins books. Albert Payson Terhune wrote a series of dog stories, most notably *Lad a Dog*.

The Little Prince and *Charlotte's Web* were published in the mid-1900s. About this time, Theodore Geisel, writing as Dr. Seuss, began to write a popular series of books, including *Green Eggs and Ham*. Notable books of the past twenty years include *The Snowy Day*, and *Where the Wild Things Are*.

The Newbery Medal and Caldecott Medal are given annually to the most notable American children's books. The Newbery Medal is named after publisher John Newbery and is awarded to the best American children's book. The Caldecott Medal is named after illustrator Randolph Caldecott and is given to the best picture book.

POETRY

Poetry usually communicates through linguistic imagery, sounds of words, and a rhythmic quality. Poetry and poems are among the oldest forms of literature and date to ancient Greece. Ancient poems were originally sung, and poetry has been slowly emancipated from this reliance on music, replacing it with a linguistic cadence.

Poetry is often associated with rhyming. However, many poems do not rhyme. Some poems rely on their rhythmic patterns alone, others are composed of open verses, while still others, such as Japanese haiku, rely on special features such as the number of syllables in a line.

The epic, the lyric, and some romances are examples of early poetry.

EPIC

The epic is a very long narrative poem, usually about a single heroic person. Epics have a monumental sweep, embrace the essence of an entire nation, and frequently include mythical forces that influence the inevitable battles and conflicts. Epics include the *Odyssey* and the *Iliad*, which were written by Homer and embrace Greek national themes, as well as *Beowulf*, set in Scandinavia.

LYRIC

The lyric is related to the epic, but it is shorter and presents profound feelings or ideas. The terms elegy and ode both refer to lyric poems. Lyric poems were called rondeaus when sung by French troubadours and madrigals when sung by English balladeers. During the 1800s both Robert Browning and Tennyson wrote lyrics. Modern lyrics are still written but no longer occupy a central place in culture.

FABLE A short literary piece designed to present a moral or truth. Fables frequently involve animals. The most famous fables are attributed to a reputed Greek slave, Aesop, who lived in the sixth century.

ROMANCE

The romance and the epic are similar. However, the romance is concerned with love and chivalry and, originally, was written in one of the romance languages. This genre of literature dates from the 1100s and was most popular during the 1200s. Stories of *King Arthur and the Knights of the Round Table* are romances.

LEGEND A heroic story or collection of stories about a specific person or persons. Legends are presented as fact but are actually a combination of fact and fiction. Legends with differing degrees of factual content have been built around Davy Crockett, who "kilt him a bar when he was only three," and the gigantic logger Paul Bunyan and his blue ox Babe. Paul Bunyan reputedly cleared out entire Maine forests with one swing of the ax.

SATIRE

Satire exposes the frailty of the human condition through wit, irony, mockery, sarcasm, or ridicule. For example, the sentence, "The doctor looked down at the man sneaking away from the impending flu shot and said, 'At least he knows to avoid sharp objects,'" is an example of satire. Occasionally, entire works such as Jonathan Swift's *Gulliver's Travels* are satirical.

DOGGEREL A work that features awkward or rough verbiage. Most often, this clumsy verse is the result of an inept writer, although it may occasionally be intended as humor.

SHORT STORY

The short story is a short fictional piece, usually with a single theme. The first short stories date from ancient Egypt. O. Henry and Mark Twain were famous writers who penned short stories in the late 1800s and early 1900s. Hemingway and Faulkner wrote short stories before mid-century with John Cheever and Eudora Welty noted as prominent short story writers in the latter half of the century.

NOVEL

The novel is a fictional story that depicts characters in a plot. The novel builds on the epic and the romance. The first novels were written during the Renaissance (1300–1600) and were developed more fully during the 1700s and 1800s in England.

The modern novel developed in the 1800s. Novels with strong historical and social themes, including dialogue, were written by the English authors Dickens, Thackeray, and Eliot. American novels written during this time tended to be allegorical.

American novels in the early 1900s focused on social ills. These novels include *The Jungle* by Upton Sinclair, *Studs Lonigan* by James Farrell, and *The Grapes of Wrath* by John Steinbeck. In the late 1900s American novels of great strength appeared including *The Naked and the Dead* by Norman Mailer and *Catch-22* by Joseph Heller.

BIOGRAPHY A full account of a person's life. An autobiography is a biography written by the person.

SCIENCE GLOSSARY

Here is a list of about 100 science terms to support and augment your science review.

Science Terms

ALTIMETER An instrument that uses air pressure to record height, such as the height of a plane.

ANEMOMETER An instrument to measure wind speed.

ANGIOSPERM A group of plants that produce seeds enclosed within an ovary, which may mature into a fruit.

ANNUALS Plants that die after one growing season.

ASEXUAL REPRODUCTION Reproduction involving only one parent.

ATMOSPHERE The Earth's atmosphere is primarily nitrogen and oxygen. The atroposphere extends from the surface to about 10 km; the stratosphere from 10 km to 50 km; the mesosphere from 50 km to 80 km; and the thermosphere is the atmosphere beyond 80 km.

AURORA BOREALIS (NORTHERN LIGHTS) Light emission from the upper atmosphere that appear in many shapes and colors.

BACILLUS A rod-shaped bacteria.

BLOOD Fluid that circulates throughout the body of an animal, distributing nutrients, and usually oxygen.

CANOPY A layer of tree branches and other vegetation elevated above the ground.

CARBON DIOXIDE (CO$_2$) A colorless, odorless gas that is important in the Earth's atmospheric greenhouse effect. Frozen CO$_2$ is dry ice.

CARCINOGEN A substance that can lead to cancer.

CARCINOMA A malignant tumor, which forms in the skin and outside of internal organs.

CARNIVORE An organism that eats meat, which includes animals, fungi, and plants.

CEILOMETER An instrument that measures cloud height.

CELL The fundamental unit of all life. The cell consists of an outer plasma membrane, the cytoplasm, and genetic material (DNA).

CELSIUS A temperature scale in which water freezes at 0 degrees and boils at 100 degrees.

CHEMOTHERAPY A cancer treatment that includes chemicals toxic to malignant cells.

CHINOOK WIND A warm, dry wind on the eastern side of the Rocky Mountains.

CHLOROPHYLL The green substance that absorbs light during photosynthesis.

CHROMOSOME A single DNA molecule, a tightly coiled strand of DNA, condensed into a compact structure.

CLONE An identical copy of an organism.

CLOUD A visible group of water or ice particles in the atmosphere.

COMMENSALISM A relationship between dissimilar organisms that is advantageous to one and doesn't affect the other.

CONTINENTAL DIVIDE In the United States, the part of the western mountains that separates water flowing toward opposite sides of the country.

CONVECTION The movement up in the atmosphere of heated moisture. Thunderstorms are often caused by convection.

CORE The portion of Earth from beneath the mantle to the Earth's center.

CROSS-POLLINATION Fertilization of one plant by pollen from a different plant species.

DIABETES A disease related to lowered levels of insulin.

DIPLOID CELL A cell with two copies of each chromosome.

DNA (DEOXYRIBONUCLEIC ACID) This primary component of chromosomes carries an organism's genetic code.

DOUBLE HELIX A term used to describe the coiling strands of DNA molecule that resembles a spiral staircase.

ECOLOGY The study of the interactions of organisms with their environment and with each other.

ECOSYSTEM All the organisms in an area and the environment in which they live.

EL NINO Warming of Pacific Ocean seawater along the coast of South America that leads to significant weather changes in the United States.

EMBRYO The stage of cellular divisions that develops from a zygote.

ENZYME A protein that aids biochemical reactions.

EPICENTER The place on the surface of the Earth immediately above the *focus* of an earthquake.

ESOPHAGUS The part of the gut that connects the pharynx and stomach.

ESTUARY A place where fresh water and seawater mix.

FLOWER The reproductive parts of flowering plants.

FOSSIL Evidence of past life.

FRUIT The part of flowering plants that contains seeds.

GAMETE Reproductive haploid cells that combine to create a zygote.

GENUS The level of plant and animal between the species and the family.

GERMINATION The process by which seeds develop into seedlings.

GILL The tissues aquatic animals use to breathe in water.

GLUCOSE A simple sugar and a product of photosynthesis.

GUT That part of the body cavity between the mouth and anus including in most animals the mouth, pharynx, esophagus, stomach, intestine, and the anus.

HAPLOID CELL A cell with one set of chromosomes, which is half the regular (diploid) number.

HEART A muscle that pumps to circulate the blood.

HERBIVORE An organism that relies primarily on plants for food.

HYPOTHESIS A preliminary proposition that can be tested through scientific study.

INSULIN A hormone needed to transport glucose to cells.

INTERFERON Small proteins that stimulate viral resistance in cells.

INTESTINE The digestive tract between the stomach and anus where most nutrients are absorbed.

ISOTOPE Atoms of the same chemical element with a different number of neutrons but the same number of protons. Isotopes of an element have the same atomic number but may not have the same mass.

JET STREAM Strong upper wind currents in a narrow stream that flow west to east in the United States. Weather patterns are related to the position of the jet stream, which changes often.

KELVIN A temperature scale in which 1° Kelvin equals 1° C. 0° Kelvin is about –273° C. 0° Kelvin is called absolute zero because there is no movement of molecules.

KNOT One nautical mile per hour or about 1.15 miles per hour.

LARVA In the metamorphosis of insects, the larva becomes a pupa before it becomes an adult.

LENTICULAR CLOUD An almond-shaped cloud usually seen on windy days.

LIPIDS Compounds that are fats and oils.

MAGMA Molten rock formed in the Earth that may appear on the surface.

MANTLE The part of Earth located between the crust and the core.

MARSUPIAL A mammal whose young crawl into its mother's pouch to complete development.

MEIOSIS The process in which a diploid cell divides to form haploid cells.

METAMORPHOSIS In most amphibians, a process in which larva goes through significant changes, perhaps including a pupa stage, before becoming an adult.

MIRAGE The phenomenon when refraction of light makes objects appear where they are not.

MITOSIS Cell division consisting of prophase, metaphase, anaphase, and telophase, that usually creates in two new nuclei, each with a full set of chromosomes.

MORAINE Material deposited by a glacier and often marking a glacier's furthest advance.

NEBULA An interstellar cloud of dust and gas.

NERVE A bundle of neurons, or nerve cells.

NEURON A cell that reacts to stimuli and transmits impulses consisting of a body with a nucleus and dendrites to receive and axons to transmit impulses.

NICHE An organism's unique place in the environment.

NIMBOSTRATUS A dark cloud, but not a thundercloud, that frequently produces rain.

NUCLEUS An organelle in a cell that contains chromosomes.

NYMPH The larval stage of an aquatic insect.

PALEONTOLOGY Study and interpretation of fossils.

PARASITISM A relationship between organisms in which one organism benefits and the other does not die, even though the second organism may be harmed.

PERENNIALS Plants that live through more than one growing season.

PERMAFROST Soil beneath the earth's surface that stays frozen throughout the year.

PHLOEM The tissue in plants that conducts nutrients.

PHYLUM A level of plant and animal classification between class and kingdom.

PLACENTA A tissue in the uterus through which nutrients pass from the mother to the fetus.

PLANKTON Floating aquatic plants (phytoplankton) and animals (zooplankton).

PLATE TECTONICS The movement of plates and the interaction across the Earth's surface to form land masses.

POLLINATION Movement of pollen to a plant egg cell, often by wind, bees, or other animals.

PUPA In metamorphosis, the stage between the larva and adult.

RADIOCARBON DATING A way to date organic substances based on the carbon-14 remaining.

RAINBOW Light refracted through raindrops to form colors of a spectrum from red to blue.

REEF A ridge built in water by organisms such as coral.

SEED In plants, a seed includes the embryo.

SONIC BOOM A loud noise caused by a shock wave when an object exceeds the speed of sound.

SUMMER SOLSTICE When the sun is highest in the sky and directly above the Tropic of Cancer 23½° North Latitude. This date usually falls on June 22.

TREE RINGS Rings that show how many years a tree has been growing. The thickness of the rings may reveal other information about climatic conditions.

VERNAL EQUINOX When the sun is directly over the equator. This date usually occurs on March 20.

VIRGA Precipitation that evaporates before it reaches the Earth's surface.

WEATHERING The physical, chemical, and biological processes by which rock is broken down into smaller pieces.

WIND CHILL The combined cooling effect of wind and temperature. Higher wind chills indicate that a body will cool more quickly to the air temperature.

FINE ARTS OVERVIEW

Here is brief section about analyzing art with a glossary of art terms.

Analyzing Art

Art appears in many incarnations, including paintings, photographs, prints, carvings, sculpture, and architecture. When asked to analyze any work of art, you can comment on the content, the form, the style, and the method used by the artist.

The *content* is what actually appears in a work of art. It is the subject matter of the art. Don't take the obvious subject matter for granted when considering your analysis. Choose descriptive words as you search for ways to capture the content of the image in front of you. For example, a landscape may contain peaceful blue skies, a raging river, cows and horses grazing, or seemingly endless grassy fields. A portrait may show a happy person or someone filled with concern or worry. A sculpture may show a smoothly muscled athlete. A building may have cascading stairs or a series of columns that thrust upward to the ceiling.

The *form* of a work of art is the order imposed by the artist. Form is the design of the work regardless of the content. A painting or photograph may show strong horizontal or vertical orientation. Perhaps the work is symmetrical, with one part a mirror image of the other. Some works may be tilted or asymmetrical.

The *style* refers to the artist's way of expressing ideas including formal styles such as gothic, high renaissance, baroque, or impressionist. In a painting or picture you can notice how the artist uses color. The colors may blend or clash. There may be an overall dark tone to the picture, or it may be light and airy. Perhaps the artist used dots of paint to produce the image.

The *method* is the medium used by the artist to create the work. It may be an oil painting or a watercolor. Perhaps the artist created prints or an etching. A three-dimensional work of art may have been sculpted, cast, carved, molded, or turned on a potter's wheel.

Keep these elements of content, form, style, and method in mind as you respond to the questions on the CST.

Glossary of Art Terms

ALLEGORY Art that represents or symbolizes some idea or quality.

AMPHORA An egg-shaped Grecian urn.

ANKH An Egyptian hieroglyph that represents life. See illustration.

ANNEALING Softening by heating glass or metal that has become hardened.

ARCH A curved span. See illustration.

Ankh

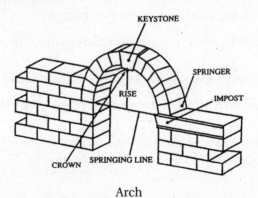

Arch

AREBESQUE Very intricate designs based on plant forms.

ATRIUM An open rectangular-shaped court, often in front of a church.

AVANT-GARDE Art considered ahead of its time.

BALUSTER A small curved post or pillar.

BALUSTRADE A railing usually supported by balusters.

BATTEN Strips of wood used as a base for plastering or for attaching tile.

BEVEL To round off a sharp edge.

BISCUIT Unglazed porcelain.

BUST A sculpture showing the head and shoulders.

CALLIGRAPHY Decorative writing.

CANOPY A fabric covering.

CASEMENT A vertically hinged window frame.

CERAMICS All porcelain and pottery.

CHALICE An ornamental cup often used in religious services.

CHANCEL The part of a church reserved for clergy.

COLLAGE Art created by pasting together many media including newspaper, fabric, and wood. A collage may also include paintings or drawings.

COLORS Many colors can be created by combining the primary colors. See illustration.

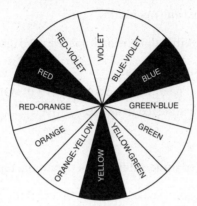

Color Wheel

COLUMN A free-standing, circular pillar. Several different styles exist. See illustration.

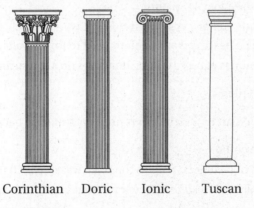

Corinthian   Doric   Ionic   Tuscan

COURSE A row of bricks or stones.

CUNEIFORM Wedge-shaped writing associated with Babylonians and Sumerians.

DECOUPAGE Cutting out designs to be used in a collage.

ECLECTIC Drawing on many styles.

ENAMEL Powdered glass bonded to a metal surface by firing.

ENGRAVING Inscribing a design on glass, metal, or some other hard surface.

ETCHING Designs created on metal plates by applying acid to initial scratchings and the prints made from these plates.

FILIGREE Gold or silver soldered to create elaborate, delicate patterns.

FOCAL POINt The place on a work of art to which the eye is drawn.

FORESHORTENED Objects painted or drawn as though they were seen from an angle projecting into space.

FRESCO A painting applied to wet plaster.

GENRE The type of painting—portrait, landscape, etc.

GOLDEN RATIO The proportion of approximately 1.6 to 1, which is said to represent the most pleasing artistic proportion. For example, a window 3 feet wide would meet this proportion by being 4.8 feet high.

HIEROGLYPHICS Egyptian symbols representing letters or words.

ILLUSTRATION An idea or scene represented in art.

KIOSK A small booth with a roof and open sides.

LINEAR A way of representing three-dimensional space in two dimensions.

MACRAME Artwork made of knotted fabrics.

MONOLITH A figure sculpted or carved from a single block of stone.

MURAL A painting made on or attached to a wall.

NICHE A wall recess.

OBELISK A rectangular block of stone, often with a pyramidal top.

PAPIER MACHÉ Paper (newspaper) soaked with water and flour and shaped into figures.

PARQUET A floor made of wooden tile.

PERSPECTIVE Representing three dimensions on a flat surface.

PIGMENT The material used to color paint.

PLASTER Limestone and sand or gypsum mixed with water, which can be shaped and then hardened. Plaster can also be carved and is often used to finish walls and ceilings.

PROJECTION The techniques of representing buildings on a flat surface.

QUARRY TILE Unglazed tile.

RELIEF Carved or molded art in which the art projects from the background.

SARCOPHAGUS A stone coffin.

SCALE The relative size of an object, such as the scale was one inch to one foot.

SIZING Gluelike material used to stiffen paper or to seal a wall or canvas.

STIPPLE Dab on paint.

TAPESTRY Fabric woven from silk by hand.

TEMPERA A type of painting that binds the pigment with a mixture of egg and water or egg and oil.

UPPERCASE Capital letters.

VIHARA A Buddhist monastery.

WARP In weaving, the thick, fixed threads.

WEFT In weaving, the thin threads that are actually woven.

Additional resources are available online to review subjects appropriate for the multi-subject tests. Here are some suggestions.

Reading Instruction

For a summary of the most up-to-date information about reading instruction, go to

www.nichd.nih.gov/publications/pubs/nrp/pages/smallbook.aspx

Mathematics

IXL Mathematics

www.ixl.com/math/

This math website created for elementary students has proven useful for elementary teachers as well. The site is organized by grade level. Fourth, fifth, or sixth grade would be a good choice for you.

The Khan Academy

The Khan Academy has an extensive set of instructional videos. Visit the website and set up a free account to access them:

www.khanacademy.org/

United States History

The Wikipedia U.S. History Site (*http://en.wikipedia.org/wiki/History_of_the_United_States*) covers all aspects of U.S. history. Links in the article access opportunities for further study.

World History

The Wikipedia History of the World site (*http://en.wikipedia.org/wiki/History_of_the_world*) gives a quick overview of world history. Links in the article offer opportunities for further study.

Science and Technology

The Smith County School Board's Dictionary of Technology Terms (*www.scsb.org/glossary.html*) is a good list of nontechnical technology terms that might help on the test.

The Pennsylvania State Education Association's Technology Terms and Definitions (*www.psea.org/general.aspx?id=830*) provides a nice list of more than 100 science terms to support and augment your review.

One Last Reminder

The Multi-Subject CST is a content-based test. You are going to see questions about topics that may be unfamiliar. Don't let that bother you. Make your best guess at the answer and move on. Everyone else will have the same issues.

Final Step

Take the Model CSTs in Chapter 9. Review the answer explanations.

Three Model Multi-Subject CSTs with Answer Explanations

9

LITERACY AND ENGLISH LANGUAGE ARTS CST

2 hours

40 selected-choice items

1 extended constructed-response item based on a classroom situation

Darken the lettered oval to show your choice for the selected-response items.

Use a word processor, without the spell or grammar checker, and type your constructed-response answers.

1. Many English words follow common spelling patterns. Which of the following words has a pronunciation that does not follow the spelling pattern usually associated with that word?

   Ⓐ Save
   Ⓑ Axe
   Ⓒ Sleigh
   Ⓓ Neat

2. Phonemic awareness instruction is most effective with children when

   Ⓐ it focuses on many different types of phoneme manipulation.
   Ⓑ it is taught as phonological awareness.
   Ⓒ they learn the sounds along with the phonemes.
   Ⓓ the children understand that phoneme awareness is the same as phonics.

3. Which of the following sentences is grammatically incorrect, but would be grammatically correct except for the irregular nature of English verb construction?

Ⓐ Blaire bringed the car to the mechanic.
Ⓑ Blaire hopped happily down the street.
Ⓒ Blaire were practicing a play.
Ⓓ Blaire speak to her friend yesterday.

4. Which of the following most accurately describes how the English language is linked to other world languages?

Ⓐ The English language was first developed about 2,500 years ago from the Spanish language.
Ⓑ Languages such as German and French contain many English words.
Ⓒ English uses the 26-letter Latin alphabet.
Ⓓ English developed first from languages in East Africa.

5. Based on recent findings, which of the following is the best approach to teach reading to young children?

Ⓐ Sight word programs
Ⓑ Literature-based programs
Ⓒ Phonics instruction integrated with literature-based approaches
Ⓓ Phonics programs

6. Based on recent findings, silent independent reading

Ⓐ has not been shown to improve reading achievement.
Ⓑ has been shown to improve reading achievement but not fluency.
Ⓒ has not been shown to improve reading achievement, but it has been proven to improve reading fluency.
Ⓓ has been shown to improve both reading achievement and fluency.

7. Which of the following is the best example of the phonemic awareness skill of phonemic identity?

Ⓐ A child recognizes the sound of "w" in the word "was."
Ⓑ A child recognizes the sound of the word "was."
Ⓒ A child recognizes the sound of "w" is the same for "was" and "want."
Ⓓ A child substitutes the sound of "w" in "was" with the sound of "h" to form the new word "has."

8. Which of the following is NOT an effective text comprehension strategy?

Ⓐ Using graphic organizers
Ⓑ Careful detailed reading
Ⓒ Employing metacognition
Ⓓ Writing summaries

9. When we talk about teaching onsets and rimes to young children, we are talking about

    Ⓐ written language that matches each syllable.
    Ⓑ the initial consonant sound of a word followed by the vowel and all that follows.
    Ⓒ written language found at the very beginning or the very end of a poem.
    Ⓓ spoken language units smaller than a phoneme that combine to make up individual phonemes.

10. Which of the following sentences contains a possessive pronoun?

    Ⓐ They were happy to have the day off.
    Ⓑ John likes to ride his bike.
    Ⓒ We don't know what to do with them.
    Ⓓ They don't know whom to ask first.

USE THE PASSAGE BELOW TO ANSWER QUESTION 11.

(1) Choosing educational practices sometimes seems like choosing fashions. (2) Fashion is driven by whims, tastes, and the zeitgeist of the current day. (3) The education system should not be driven by these same forces. (4) Three decades ago, teachers were told to use manipulative materials to teach mathematics. (5) But consider the way mathematics is taught. (6) In the intervening years, the emphasis was on drill and practice. (7) Now teachers are told again to use manipulative materials. (8) Even so, every teacher has the ultimate capacity to determine his or her teaching practices.

11. Which of the following revisions to a sentence in this passage would be most likely to improve the style of the passage?

    Ⓐ Sentence 1: The choice of educational practices sometimes seems like choosing fashions.
    Ⓑ Sentence 3: The education system should not have to react to these forces.
    Ⓒ Sentence 5: But consider mathematics and the way it is taught.
    Ⓓ Sentence 8: Even so, every teacher can determine his or her teaching practices.

12. Linguists' assertion that each phoneme is associated with a grapheme is NOT well represented by which of the following.

    Ⓐ o
    Ⓑ ay
    Ⓒ ch
    Ⓓ hg

13. Which of the following would indicate that a student is using a metacognitive approach to reading comprehension?

    Ⓐ A student grasps the overall structure of a story.
    Ⓑ A student summarizes the essence of a story.
    Ⓒ A student adjusts his or her reading speed.
    Ⓓ A student works cooperatively with others to comprehend a story.

14. Phonics is the predictable relationship between graphemes and phonemes. In general, experts say

    Ⓐ systematic and explicit phonics instruction is the essential element of early grade reading programs.
    Ⓑ literature-based instruction that emphasizes reading and writing is the essential element of early grade reading programs.
    Ⓒ sight word programs are the essential element in early grade reading programs.
    Ⓓ basal programs that focus on whole-word or meaning-based activities are the essential element of early grade reading programs.

15. Some oral presentation experts suggest that a speaker should use rhetorical questions to capture the attention of an audience, meaning the speaker should ask questions

    Ⓐ that engage audience members in a rhetorical response.
    Ⓑ to determine audience members' knowledge of rhetorical techniques.
    Ⓒ to which no response is expected.
    Ⓓ when audience members already know the answer.

16. It is most likely that a child has learned the meaning of a word

    Ⓐ indirectly, through context clues.
    Ⓑ directly, through phonics learning experiences.
    Ⓒ indirectly, through everyday experiences.
    Ⓓ directly, through phonemic learning experiences.

17. As a rule, using a script instead of note cards to make an oral presentation can make the presentation

    Ⓐ more accurate.
    Ⓑ more organized.
    Ⓒ more detailed.
    Ⓓ more monotonous.

18. Which of the following is the most effective way for children to develop phonemic awareness?

    Ⓐ Become familiar with an appropriate number of symbolic phonemic spellings such as /b/ /eI/.
    Ⓑ Focus on the unique sounds of each phoneme.
    Ⓒ Learn how the building blocks of individual phonemes combine to form sounds that are more complex.
    Ⓓ Learn phonemic awareness along with the letters of the alphabet.

19. Fifth-grade students are starting to read a book about American colonists. Students are most likely to use context to learn the meaning of new social studies terms when the teacher

    Ⓐ shows students how to examine surrounding words and phrases.

    Ⓑ shows students how to use a dictionary and to distinguish among the various meanings of a word.

    Ⓒ asks students to try to activate their prior knowledge about the word's meaning.

    Ⓓ provides content material about American colonists and events occurring during Colonial times.

20. Which of the following would be most appropriate for an upper elementary teacher to use to evaluate students' writing techniques and plan for further writing experiences?

    Ⓐ Administer a standardized grammar test and use the scores as a planning device.

    Ⓑ Use a writing checklist to assess a variety of creative writing samples that include writing summaries and samples.

    Ⓒ Have the student prepare a composition on a subject of his or her choice and holistically evaluate the composition.

    Ⓓ Have the student answer a series of higher-level, short-answer questions about a specific writing sample.

21. Lisa writes well and understands verbal directions, but often has trouble understanding written directions. Her difficulty might be related to all of the following EXCEPT

    Ⓐ auditory discrimination.

    Ⓑ visual discrimination.

    Ⓒ sight vocabulary.

    Ⓓ context clues.

22. A student has trouble reading the problems in the mathematics textbook. This difficulty is most likely to be the result of

    Ⓐ faulty word identification and recognition.

    Ⓑ inability to locate and retain specific facts.

    Ⓒ deficiencies in basic comprehension abilities.

    Ⓓ inability to adapt to reading needs in this content field.

23. A child has difficulty pronouncing a printed word. The problem may reflect all of the following EXCEPT

    Ⓐ phonetic analysis.

    Ⓑ sight vocabulary.

    Ⓒ language comprehension.

    Ⓓ context analysis.

24. During a unit on animal stories, sixth-grade students read *Lad a Dog*, by Albert Payson Terhune. The teacher uses transactional strategy instruction to help students develop a deeper understanding of the cognitive process involved in understanding Lad's "motivations," as described in the book. Which of the following indicates the teacher is using this approach?

Ⓐ The teacher explicitly explains the processes involved in successful reading comprehension.

Ⓑ The teacher encourages students to explore the processes involved in successful reading comprehension.

Ⓒ The teacher and students cooperate to jointly explore the processes involved in successful reading instruction.

Ⓓ The teacher asks students to explore the processes involved in successful reading comprehension.

25. A third-grade teacher, who emphasizes the relationship between reading and mathematics, posts this problem for his students to read critically and solve:

Charles is traveling on a bus. Charles leaves work at 6:15 PM. The bus travels 15 minutes on Forest Street, then 20 minutes on Quincy Avenue, then 25 minutes on Chestnut Street. At what time does Charles get home?

The teacher most likely asked the students to read the problem critically in order to

Ⓐ experience a reading passage that includes both words and numerals.

Ⓑ detect if there is too much or too little information in a passage.

Ⓒ notice that a story about a boy's life could include numerical information.

Ⓓ develop a visual image of the trip described in the passage.

26. Your class reads a science fiction story about space travel. Which of the following actions on your part is most likely to help students differentiate between science fact and science fiction?

Ⓐ Guide students to understand that science fiction stories are creative writing and not based on science fact.

Ⓑ Guide students as they identify examples of science fact and science fiction based on the story they just completed.

Ⓒ Ask students to work independently to make their own list of science fact and science fiction.

Ⓓ Ask students to work independently as they identify examples of science fact and science fiction in the story they just completed.

27. Which of the following reading activities would engage a student at the highest level of the *Revised Taxonomy of Educational Objectives: Cognitive Domain*?

Ⓐ Evaluate a reading passage.

Ⓑ Create a written work.

Ⓒ Analyze a reading passage.

Ⓓ Apply the contents of a reading passage to a real world situation.

28. You have a number of long newspaper articles about whales. Which of the following is an approach most likely to inform students about the main idea(s) of each article?

Ⓐ Students work independently and summarize for themselves the main point(s) of each article.

Ⓑ Students work in cooperative learning groups to summarize and present the main point(s) of each article.

Ⓒ You present a brief summary of the main point(s) of each article.

Ⓓ You prepare a brief summary of the main point(s) of each article and distribute them to your students.

29. A teacher finishes a three-day unit on nouns. He or she wants to be sure students learned the material in the unit. Which of the following assessment techniques would be best for the teacher to use?

Ⓐ Obtain and have the students complete a standardized assessment.

Ⓑ Prepare and have the students complete a teacher-made assessment.

Ⓒ Observe students' writing over the next week.

Ⓓ Review writing that students have previously completed.

30. A teacher wants to use the Orton-Gillingham approach with a student who is having difficulty reading. The following actions on the part of the teacher are consistent with that approach EXCEPT

Ⓐ teaching synthetic phonics.

Ⓑ generally discouraging independent reading.

Ⓒ emphasize reading for meaning.

Ⓓ use a dictionary to learn word pronunciation.

31. A fourth-grade teacher wants to conduct on ongoing assessment of his or her language arts program. Which one of the following actions on the part of the teacher would NOT indicate that the assessment was underway?

Ⓐ The teacher walks around the room regularly observing students' writing.

Ⓑ The teacher asks students to hand in their written work at the end of the day.

Ⓒ The teacher gives students an in-class composition assignment about the environment.

Ⓓ The teacher regularly collects performance samples of students' work.

32. Which of the following would be the best opportunity for a formative evaluation of student's writing?

Ⓐ A discussion with the student

Ⓑ A portfolio of students' writing samples

Ⓒ Iowa test of basic skills

Ⓓ End-of-unit test

33. A teacher is using an ESL approach to teach reading to a group of LEP students. Which of the following is most consistent with that approach?

(A) Use context clues to help students identify English words.
(B) Help students learn to read in their native language.
(C) Translate English reading passages into the students' native language.
(D) Ask students to bring in original literature in their native language.

34. A fourth-grade teacher keeps a portfolio of written work for a student. In her opinion, the writing samples are well above average for fourth graders overall. A standardized language arts test administered last month shows a writing grade equivalent of 3.2. Which of the following is the best description of the child's language arts achievement?

(A) The child is above average in writing for his grade level.
(B) The child is below average in writing for his grade level.
(C) The child needs intensive help in writing at his grade level.
(D) The child seems to do better when evaluated in real world settings.

35. A fifth-grade student hands in this writing sample.

> I sat in the audience while my
> sister play the clarinet. I
> saw her play while sit there.
> I guess I will never be a
> profesional musician.

The teacher is most likely to help improve this student's writing by providing instruction in which of the following areas?

(A) Nouns
(B) Pronouns
(C) Spelling
(D) Verbs

36. A primary teacher wants to produce the most significant reading benefits for his or her students. Which of the following actions on the part of the teacher is most likely to create that benefit?

(A) Providing a literature rich environment
(B) Providing effective phonics instruction
(C) Providing opportunities for oral expression and listening
(D) Using real literature sources instead of basal texts

37. In a class, students will have the opportunity to produce and direct a brief dramatic work. Which of the following would best help distinguish the student's role as producer and the student's role as director?

   Ⓐ The producer is responsible for planning and writing a performance, while the director is actually responsible for implementing the producer's overall scheme.
   Ⓑ The producer follows the director's lead and makes arrangements for stage sets and props.
   Ⓒ The producer is responsible once the performance begins, while the director is responsible for everything leading up to the actual performance.
   Ⓓ The producer has overall administrative responsibility for the dramatic work, while the director has creative responsibility for the work.

38. A teacher using phoneme deletion activities promotes phonemic awareness by

   Ⓐ breaking a word into separate sounds and saying each sound.
   Ⓑ recognizing the sounds in a word that do not match the sounds in another words.
   Ⓒ recognizing the word remaining when a phoneme is removed from a longer word.
   Ⓓ substituting one phoneme for another to make a new word.

39. A teacher incorporating recent research findings will most likely use which of the following approaches to improve a student's reading fluency?

   Ⓐ Round-robin reading in which students take turns reading a passage
   Ⓑ Monitored oral reading
   Ⓒ Silent independent reading
   Ⓓ Hearing models of fluent reading

40. A teacher uses semantic organizers because this approach is most likely to help students

   Ⓐ understand the meaning of words, expressions, and sentences in relation to reference and truth.
   Ⓑ identify the underlying structure of a story.
   Ⓒ relate pictures and diagrams in the text to the text itself.
   Ⓓ identify related ideas and concepts in a text.

Constructed Response

Use the information in the exhibits that follow to complete the task.

Use a word processor, without the spell check or the grammar check, to type your response, which should be about 400 to 600 words.

Identify one significant strength the student demonstrates.

Identify one significant need the student demonstrates.

Identify a learning activity or strategy that would advance the student's strength or remediate the student's need.

Explain why the learning activity or strategy would be effective.

Teacher's Notes

Jeannie is just a delight. She loves to come to school every day, and she likes to read; although, it takes an extra effort to motivate her to read. More than anything, Jeannie is interested in history. She seems to have a good grasp of the history of New York State, and she has brought in articles about the Iroquois and the Revolutionary War in New York. I must say, it is quite something to see, and I seldom encounter, a fourth grader with this much interest in these topics.

I met both her parents during our regular early start parent conferences. I did not inquire, but it may be that English is not their first language; however, there were no communication issues. They reiterated what I had noticed about Jeannie—she loves history. The parents say they download books for her to the tablet she owns, and the books she requests are always about history. They are concerned that she may use the tablet's speech recognition capability to listen to the books rather than read them herself. The parents noted that her interest in using her tablet is second only to her interest in history.

Her overall reading scores are below average for the class. I am always careful about test scores because some students do not test well, but I feel more confident in my personal observations. Just talking to her I notice that her vocabulary seems quite good, but that she makes noticeable errors in grammar and usage.

Informal Assessment of Spoken English

Quinn—What are you going to do this weekend?

Jeanie—I are going shopping.

Quinn—What store?

Jeanie—It's the store down by the school.

Quinn—I guess your brother is going?

Jeanie—That is what he say.

Quinn—What do you think you'll buy?

Jeanie—I ain't sure.

Quinn—Take a guess.

Jeanie—I are not sure.

Quinn—It was crowded the last time I went there.

Jeanie—I hope it is not when I went there this weekend.

Quinn—See you later.

Jeanie-Just keep it among us.

I conducted an informal language assessment as I recorded and transcribed this brief interaction of and Jeannie with her friend Quinn, about what Jeannie was doing this weekend. The transcript is above.

Reading Informational Text

In order to learn more about Jeannie's reading ability, I gave Jeannie this brief passage to read about the Iroquois, a topic that should interest her, followed by a few comprehension questions that called for a constructed response.

> The Iroquois were present in upstate New York about 500 years before Europeans arrived. Iroquois oral history says that this Indian nation was once a single tribe. The Iroquois nation eventually had five main tribes. They were called the five nations or the League of Five Nations. The tribes were arranged from east to west. That region was called the Long House of the Iroquois.
>
> The Iroquois economy was based mainly on agriculture. The main crop was corn, or maize. The Iroquois also grew pumpkins, beans, and fruit. Hollow beads called wampum were used for money.
>
> The Iroquois had a democratic form of government. All the tribes spoke an Algonquin language. At the end of the American Revolutionary War, the tribes scattered. Only some members of two tribes remained in their original tribal lands.

1. How would you describe the overall structure of the story?

2. What is the topic of each paragraph?

3. What do you think it would have been like to be an Iroquois?

Jeannie's Response

1. The structure was a story about the history of the Iroquois.

2. Who the Iroquois is
   The Iroquois Agriculture
   Iroquois government and what happened to them

3. It has been amazing to be an Iroquois. You is part of a nice culture. You live happily with all the other tribes. The nation had a long history and you will be a part of that history when other tribe members make the nation even bigger or better. There is a lot of healthy food to eat and you gets to have your own garden where you will grow pumpkins. You can even have your own Halloween.

ANSWER EXPLANATIONS

1. **(B)** Words with <u>a</u> pronounced as in "<u>a</u>xe" usually do not end in "e." The word axe does not follow a regular spelling pattern. (A), (C), and (D) are all incorrect because each choice follows the regular spelling pattern for word pronunciation.

2. **(C)** Phonemic awareness is the ability to hear, identify, and manipulate phonemes in spoken words. (A) is incorrect because phonemic manipulation is just one part of phonemic awareness. (B) is incorrect because phonological awareness includes phonemic awareness, but it also includes words and syllables. It is not effective to include words and syllables with phonemic awareness. (D) is incorrect because phonemic awareness is not the same as phonics.

3. **(A)** Substitute "brought" for "bringed." The word "bringed" would be appropriate, except for the irregular nature of English verb construction. (B), (C) are incorrect because the verbs "hopped" and "practicing" are used correctly in the sentence. (D) is incorrect because, while a writer should substitute "spoke" for "speak," the problem is not caused by the irregular nature of English verb construction.

4. **(C)** English uses the 26-letter Latin alphabet and this is the clearest link among those presented to world languages. (A) is incorrect because English did not develop from Spanish. (B) is incorrect because most English words have foreign origins, including many German and French words. (D) is incorrect because English did not develop from languages in East Africa.

5. **(D)** According to experts, the research overwhelmingly supports phonics programs alone as the best approach to teach reading to young children. (A), (B), and (C) are all incorrect because research shows the programs listed, including the blended phonics approaches, are not as effective as phonics alone.

6. **(A)** Studies have consistently failed to confirm that silent reading helps students become better readers. (B), (C), and (D) are all incorrect because research does not show that silent reading improves either reading achievement or reading fluency.

7. **(C)** Phonemic identity means to recognize the same sound in different words. (A) is incorrect because it is an example of phoneme isolation. (B) is incorrect because it is an example of phoneme blending. (D) is incorrect because it is an example of phoneme substitution.

8. **(B)** Careful reading is not an effective text comprehension strategy. Good readers use strategies that are more flexible. (A), (C), and (D) are all incorrect because each of these choices presents an effective text comprehension strategy.

9. **(B)** This choice gives the definition of onsets and rimes. For the word jump, "j" is the onset and "ump" is the rime. (A) is incorrect because onsets and rimes are smaller than syllables. (C) is incorrect because onsets and rimes are not directly related to poetry. Notice the different spellings of "rime" and "rhyme." (D) is incorrect because onsets and rimes show an order of sounds in words.

10. **(B)** The pronoun "his" shows possession. The bike belongs to John. (A) is incorrect because the pronoun "they" does not show possession. (C) is incorrect because neither

the pronoun "we" nor the pronoun "them" show possession. (D) is incorrect because neither the pronoun "they" nor the pronoun "whom" show possession.

11. **(D)** This sentence is too wordy. Replacing the wordy "has the ultimate capacity to" with "can" materially improves the style of the passage. (A) is incorrect because this change removes the parallel structure of the original sentence. (B) is incorrect because changing the words "driven by" to "react to" changes the meaning of the sentence and does not improve the style. (C) is incorrect because it alters the meaning from "consider the way mathematics is taught" to "consider mathematics" and it does not improve the style of the passage.

12. **(D)** The letter combination "hg" is not a grapheme because it does not represent a phoneme. (A) is incorrect because the grapheme "o" can represent the phoneme in sow. (B) is incorrect because the grapheme "ay" represents the phoneme in s<u>ay</u>. (C) is incorrect because the grapheme "ch" represents the phoneme in <u>ch</u>eck.

13. **(C)** Metacognition means thinking about thinking, and in this case, thinking about reading. A student who adjusts his or her reading speed is thinking about the reading process and reacting appropriately. (A) is incorrect because understanding story structure is an effective comprehension technique, but it is not metacognition. (B) is incorrect because summarizing a story is another effective comprehension strategy that is not metacognition. (D) is incorrect because cooperative learning can be an effective way to learn comprehension strategies, but cooperative learning is neither an approach to reading comprehension nor a metacognitive strategy.

14. **(A)** Early grade students need systematic and explicit phonics instruction to become good readers. This approach is not the only approach that could be included; however, it is the only approach that must be included. Choices (B), (C), and (D) are all incorrect because they are examples of nonsystematic phonics approaches. The evidence is clear that these nonsystematic approaches are not as effective in early grades as systematic phonics approaches.

15. **(C)** This is the definition of a rhetorical question, a question to which no response is expected. (A) and (B) are incorrect because a rhetorical question has nothing to do with rhetoric or rhetorical techniques. (D) is incorrect because audience members may or may not know the answer to a rhetorical question.

16. **(C)** Children are surrounded by words, and they learn most words by talking with others, overhearing conversations, and reading by themselves. (A) is incorrect because context clues are an important way for children to learn word meanings, but context clues are just a part of the indirect experiences that lead to understanding a word's meaning. (B) and (D) are incorrect because explicit phonics instruction and phonemic awareness instruction are essential, but this is not the way children learn the meaning of most words.

17. **(D)** Reading from a script can make the presentation more monotonous than when note cards are used. (A), (B), and (C) are all incorrect because using note cards can create just as accurate, organized, and detailed a presentation as using a script.

18. **(D)** This approach is most effective because it helps children see how phonemes relate directly to their reading and writing. (A) is incorrect because there is never a reason

to introduce children to phonemic symbols. (B) and (C) are incorrect because, while they can be effective phonemic awareness approaches, they are not the most effective approaches.

19. **(A)** It describes how to use context clues to find the meaning of a word. Choice (B) is incorrect because using a dictionary is not using context to find meaning. Choice (C) is incorrect because prior knowledge is something students already know, not something students have to learn. Choice (D) is incorrect because content material will not help students understand word meaning.

20. **(B)** A writing checklist is an excellent way to determine a student's writing ability to prepare for further writing experiences. Choice (A) is incorrect. Standardized grammar tests do not reveal a student's writing ability. Choice (C) is incorrect. Holistic evaluations reflect the evaluator's overall view of the quality of the writing. A holistic evaluation does not yield a specific analysis that can lead to instructional plans. Choice (D) is incorrect. This assessment evaluates reading, not writing.

21. **(A)** Note the word EXCEPT in the item. This choice has to do with listening and NOT reading. Difficulty with auditory discrimination does not itself interfere with reading. Early hearing problems can inhibit reading and writing development. However, Lisa writes well and understands verbal directions. Choices (B), (C), and (D) could be the cause of Lisa's trouble with understanding written directions. Of course, there are other factors that could cause her difficulty.

22. **(D)** The phrase "most likely" is key to answering this question. It is most likely that this student is having difficulty reading in the content area of mathematics. We do not have more information, so choices (A), (B), and (C) might be correct, but they are not the most likely cause.

23. **(C)** Note the word EXCEPT in the item. You don't have to understand the meaning of a word to pronounce it. This item points out the important distinction between recognizing a word and knowing what the word means. Word recognition and comprehension are both important parts of reading instruction. Choices (A), (B), and (D) are incorrect. Difficulty with any of these might make it harder for a child to pronounce a word. It is clear how difficulty with phonics or with sight vocabulary might lead to the problem. Difficulty with content analysis could also lead to this problem. A young child reads the sentence, "Jamie went to the store," but the child does not remember if the "e" in "went" is pronounced "eh" or "ah." That is, the child is not sure if the word "went" is pronounced "went" or "want," but, the context of the word shows clearly the correct pronunciation is "went."

24. **(C)** The word "transactional" in the term "transactional strategy instruction" means a give and take between students and teachers as they explore the processes involved in successful reading comprehension. Choice (A) is incorrect. This choice describes the direct explanation of cognitive processes. Both direct explanation and the transactional strategy hold tremendous promise for reading instruction. Choices (B) and (D) explain neither of these approaches.

25. **(B)** The problem does not provide enough information to determine what time Charles arrived home. The relationship between reading and mathematics is very important, and this is more a reading problem than a mathematics problem. A child might consider

the following points when solving the problem. The problem never says that Charles arrived home. Charles left work a 6:15 P.M., but we don't know what time he got on the bus. We also don't know that the bus is traveling toward his house.

26. **(B)** Guiding students as they work is a very effective strategy for teaching reading. Picking out science fact and science fiction in a space exploration science fiction story is certainly the best kind of guidance among the choices given. Choice (A) is incorrect. Many science fiction stories contain science facts. Choices (C) and (D) are incorrect. Working independently is one of the least effective ways to learn about reading because it lacks interaction with the teacher and other students.

27. **(B)** "Create" is the highest level in Bloom's Revised Cognitive Taxonomy. Choice (A), evaluation, was the highest level of the original taxonomy. Choices (C), analyze, and (D), apply, are the fourth and third levels of this six-level revised taxonomy.

28. **(B)** This is exactly the situation in which cooperative learning groups excel. Students learn from interaction in the group, from the presentation made by other groups, and from the teacher's reaction to the presentations. Choice (A) is incorrect. Working independently is one of the least effective ways to learn about reading because it lacks interaction with teachers and other students. Choices (C) and (D) are incorrect because the approach involves direct instruction, which is not the best approach for this situation.

29. **(B)** For a brief unit such as this, a teacher-made assessment is almost always the best choice. Choice (A) is incorrect. Standardized tests are used to establish an achievement level or to compare results between students or groups of students. Standardized tests are not particularly useful for finding out whether or not a student has learned a particular skill or concept. Choices (C) and (D) are incorrect because neither approach gives the teacher current achievement information.

30. **(C)** Note the word EXCEPT in the item. The Orton-Gillingham method does not emphasize reading for meaning. That is not to say that meaning is not important, it's just not an Orton-Gillingham emphasis. Choices (A), (B), and (D) are incorrect. The actions described in these choices are consistent with the Orton-Gillingham approach.

31. **(C)** Note the word "NOT" in the item. Note also the word "indicate," which means the incorrect choices show an ongoing assessment is underway. This choice is correct because an in-class composition does not indicate that an ongoing assessment is underway. Choice (A) is incorrect. Observing students' work while they are writing indicates that ongoing assessment is underway. Choice (B) is incorrect. The teacher's review of students' daily work indicates an ongoing assessment is underway. Choice (D) is incorrect. The regular collection of performance samples indicates an ongoing assessment is underway.

32. **(B)** A formative evaluation helps a teacher plan lessons. Samples of a student's writing best further that goal. Choice (A) is incorrect. A discussion with a student may help a teacher, particularly if the discussion follows a review of the student's writing. But a discussion is not the best opportunity for a formative evaluation. Choice (C) is incorrect. The Iowa Test of Basic Skills does not evaluate writing, and it is more useful as a summative evaluation than a formative evaluation. Choice (D) is incorrect. An end-of-unit test is also more useful as a summative evaluation.

33. **(A)** ESL means English as a second language. This approach encourages the teaching and use of English. The approaches in Choices (B), (C), and (D) rely on the student's native language.

34. **(D)** The only conclusive information is that the student appears to do better in real world situations. This just underscores the importance of portfolio assessment. Even though portfolio assessment is often not a reliable indicator, portfolio assessment gives students the opportunity to demonstrate their "real world" proficiency.

35. **(D)** The student's writing contains several verb tense shifts. In the first sentence, "sat" is past tense while "play" is present tense. In the second sentence, "saw" is past tense while "sit" is present tense. Choices (A) and (B) are incorrect. The nouns and pronouns are used correctly. Choice (C) is incorrect. The spelling error in the last sentence requires less of the teacher's attention than the tense shift errors.

36. **(B)** Reading is a unique skill, and different from language. Studies show that students benefit most from early, effective phonics instruction. This should not be taken to mean that every phonics program is effective. Choice (A) is incorrect. This is a good idea, of course, and it would likely improve language development, but it is not a significant factor in reading development, particularly when compared to phonics instruction. Choice (C) is incorrect. Oral expression and effective listening are altogether different from reading. Choice (D) is incorrect. Replacing basal texts with real literature sources can help increase a student's interest in reading. However, this practice does not significantly contribute to reading development.

37. **(D)** The student's role as director is to create the performance, as opposed to the producer's overall responsibility. (A), (B), and (C) are all incorrect because these choices do not show the correct comparison between director and producer.

38. **(C)** Phonemic deletion means to remove a phoneme from one word and to leave another word for students to identify. In an easy example, remove the /s/ from stack to form tack. (A) is incorrect because phoneme segmentation involves recognizing or counting each phoneme in a word. (B) is incorrect because phoneme categorization involves recognizing a sound not found in another word or words. (D) "Phonemic substitution" is the term for the technique of substituting one phoneme for another to make a new word.

39. **(B)** Fluency is the ability to read accurately and quickly. Monitored oral reading that includes feedback from the teacher is the most effective way to help a student achieve fluency. (A) is incorrect because round robin reading does not increase fluency, probably because each student reads a relatively small part of the passage. (C) is incorrect because there is no current evidence that silent independent reading improves fluency or reading comprehension. There is no final proof that it does not help; although, it is certainly clear that a teacher can't be sure a student is actually reading. (D) is incorrect because, while students need to hear models of fluent reading, this approach is less likely to improve fluency than choice (B).

40. **(D)** Semantic organizers are a special type of graphic organizer that may look like a spider web and help students identify related events and concepts in a text. (A) is incorrect because semantic organizers are not related to the linguistic study of semantics described in this choice. (B) and (C) are incorrect because they describe some types of graphic organizers, but not semantic organizers.

SAMPLE CONSTRUCTED RESPONSE

Constructed-Response Scoring

SCORING EXPECTATIONS

The response should meet the stated specific requirements.

- The response should demonstrate an understanding of the applicable exhibits.
- The response should draw on information from the assignment and give examples to support the main themes.

SCORING

4 The response demonstrates a STRONG grasp of the applicable content and skills and always includes all required response elements.

3 The response demonstrates an ACCEPABLE grasp of the applicable content and skills and always includes all required response elements.

2 The response demonstrates a LESS THAN ACCEPTABLE grasp of the applicable content and skills and may not include all required response elements.

1 The response is INCOMPLETE AND/OR OFF TRACK and usually does not include required response elements.

U The response can't be scored because it is off topic, written in a language other than English, or contains too little information to score. Note, a well-written but off-topic response will be scored U.

B You did not write anything.

Sample Response

This 635-word response would likely receive a 4.

This student has a number of strengths. As the teacher notes, Jeannie loves to come to school every day. The teacher also notes that she loves to read, at the same time noting it can be difficult to motivate her to do just that. It is a confusing picture, as is often the case in real classrooms.

Jeannie's most significant strength is her love of history. The teacher notes that she brings information about history to school. During the interview, Jeannie's parents note that she loves history, and the electronic books that she requests for download to her tablet are about history. Even her response to the history passage about the Iroquois shows that passion as she describes her wonder at the thought of being an Iroquois. Her reading strength shows up in the other responses to the history passage in which she does a credible job writing responses to the question.

Jeannie's needs are primarily in subject verb agreement (SVA) and tense (T) errors. These issues appear several places in the description, but are most evident in the transcribed dialog with Quinn. I have noted some of her specific errors below.

In Line 1, Jeannie says, "I are going shopping." This is a subject-verb error in which the plural verb "are" should be changed to the singular "am."

In Line 6, Jeannie says, "That is what he say." This is a tense error in which the present tense "say" should be changed to the past tense "said."

In Line 8, Jeannie uses the word "ain't," which can variously be a slang contraction for am not, is not, are not, has not, and have not. It is inappropriate slang, but does not itself reveal a specific grammatical error. In this case, "ain't" should be changed to "am not."

In my view, SVA errors are the dominant error pattern and the issue that should be addressed. In Jeannie's case, the first step is agreement in number between subject and verb. English is a complex language and identification of singular or plural verbs can be a particular problem. I would institute a four-step approach to help Jeannie with this issue.

1. Plural Verbs and Nouns: As a first step, I would discuss plural verbs with Jeannie and show her a list of simple plural verbs. Then I would give her index cards with plural and singular nouns and plural and singular verbs. We would work on the cards together and match nouns and verbs until Jeannie was successful about 80 percent of the time.

2. Identification: We would review some of Jeannie's writing and identify instances in which she had made verb agreement errors. Jeannie would correct the errors.

3. Practice: I would give Jeannie worksheets with samples of mismatched subjects and verbs. I would ask Jeannie to identify and correct the mismatching until she could complete these tasks accurately about 80 percent of the time.

4. Application: I would ask Jeannie to write brief passages. We would review the passages for examples of SVA errors and make needed corrections. After successfully writing five passages that were free of SVA errors, I would consider the remediation complete, although still expecting these errors to continue to occur, but with decreasing frequency.

This approach would be successful because SVA is not a natural act. It must be learned. The approach takes Jeanie through the essential learning steps. She is taught to identify singular and plural verbs and then to associate the verbs with the appropriate subjects. She receives mediated practice with the teacher, matching subjects and verbs. Next she works independently to identify and correct SVA errors. Finally, Jeannie is asked to show what she has learned by writing brief passages with additional interaction with the teacher to produce passages free of errors.

2 hours 15 minutes

40 selected-choice items

1 extended constructed-response item based on a classroom situation.

Darken the lettered oval to show your choice for the selected-response items.

Use a word processor, without the spell or grammar checker, and type your constructed-response answers.

---

1. An even number has two different prime factors. Which of the following could be the product of those factors?

    Ⓐ 6

    Ⓑ 12

    Ⓒ 36

    Ⓓ 48

2. Two types of elevators travel up and down inside a very tall building. One elevator starts at the first floor and stops every x floors. Another elevator starts at the first floor and stops every y floors. Which of the following is the best way to find at which floors both elevators stop?

    Ⓐ Find the common multiples of x and y.

    Ⓑ Find the common factors of x and y.

    Ⓒ Find the prime factors of x and y.

    Ⓓ Find the divisors of x and y.

3 The school received $5,300 to use for eight different activities. A total of 91 percent of the money was allocated for seven of the activities, with the remainder used for the school trip. How much money was used for the school trip?

    Ⓐ $477

    Ⓑ $663

    Ⓒ $757

    Ⓓ $4,293

4. The landscaper recommended a mix of $3\frac{1}{2}$ pounds of rye grass seed with $\frac{3}{4}$ pound of blue grass seed. If the lawn needs $5\frac{1}{4}$ pounds of rye grass seed, how many pounds of blue grass seed would that be?

    Ⓐ $\frac{3}{8}$ pounds

    Ⓑ $1\frac{1}{8}$ pounds

    Ⓒ $1\frac{1}{2}$ pounds

    Ⓓ $4\frac{1}{3}$ pounds

5. A car is set on cruise control to travel at a steady rate of 45 miles per hour. The scale on the map for the area is 1 inch = 10 miles. What is the most likely length of the line on the map for the distance the car will travel in 90 minutes?

  Ⓐ 3 inches
  Ⓑ 4.5 inches
  Ⓒ 6.75 inches
  Ⓓ 27 inches

6. A fair penny is flipped three times, and each time the penny lands heads up. What is the probability that this same penny will land heads up on the next flip?

  Ⓐ $\dfrac{1}{16}$

  Ⓑ $\dfrac{1}{8}$

  Ⓒ $\dfrac{1}{4}$

  Ⓓ $\dfrac{1}{2}$

7. Three of the same item is for sale in a store. The original price of each item is $83.00. What would the sale price of each item be after a 35 percent discount?

  Ⓐ $161.85
  Ⓑ $53.25
  Ⓒ $53.95
  Ⓓ $41.50

8. An oil truck pumps oil at the rate of 100 gallons per hour. The truck filled an empty oil tank in three hours. How long will it take another oil truck pumping at the rate of 80 gallons per hour to fill the same empty oil tank?

  Ⓐ $2\dfrac{2}{5}$ hours

  Ⓑ $3\dfrac{2}{5}$ hours

  Ⓒ $3\dfrac{3}{8}$ hours

  Ⓓ $3\dfrac{3}{4}$ hours

9. The bakers make brownies and cookies in a ratio of 2:9. Today, the bakers made 1,350 cookies. How many brownies did the bakers make?

  Ⓐ 150
  Ⓑ 300
  Ⓒ 675
  Ⓓ 2,750

Tax money spent on town services

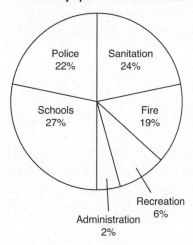

10. A town collects $2,600,000 in taxes. The town needs $624,000 for police. Any needed money will come from sanitation. The percents in the circle graph are recalculated. What percent is left for sanitation?

   Ⓐ 22%
   Ⓑ 20%
   Ⓒ 19%
   Ⓓ 18%

11. The disaster relief specialist found that 289, or 85 percent, of the houses on the beach had been damaged by Hurricane Sandy. How many houses were on the beach?

   Ⓐ 294
   Ⓑ 332
   Ⓒ 340
   Ⓓ 400

12. After a discount of 25 percent, the savings for a pair of inline skates is $12.00. What is the sale price?

   Ⓐ $48.00
   Ⓑ $36.00
   Ⓒ $25.00
   Ⓓ $24.00

13. The class kept track of rainy and sunny days. During the 54 days, classified rainy or sunny, the ratio of rainy days to sunny days is 7 to 14. How many sunny days were there?

   Ⓐ 4
   Ⓑ 8
   Ⓒ 18
   Ⓓ 36

14. Serena is an account executive. She receives a base pay of $18 an hour plus a 15 percent bonus for all the sales she generates. Last week she generated $1,200 worth of sales. What is the minimum number of hours she could have worked to make $500?

    (A) 17
    (B) 18
    (C) 25
    (D) 26

15. At sea level, sound travels about 34,000 centimeters per second, while light travels almost instantaneously. You see a lightning bolt, and five seconds later you hear the thunder clap associated with that lightning bolt. Which of the following is the best estimate of how far away the lightning bolt was using scientific notation?

    (A) 17.0×10^4 cm
    (B) 1.7×10^5 cm
    (C) 1.7×10^6 cm
    (D) 0.017×10^7 cm

16. A student draws a square with an area of one square meter. Then, the student draws a diagonal from one corner of the square to the other. Which of the following is the best approximation of the length of the diagonal?

    (A) 0.92
    (B) 1.00
    (C) 1.41
    (D) 1.66

17. As a part of a manufacturing process, two spheres, each with a radius of 3 centimeters, are dipped into water. Engineers use the product of the water displaced as a part of their calculations. What is the formula for the product of the water displaced by two identical spheres? [Volume of a sphere $= \frac{4}{3}\pi r^3$]

    (A) $9\pi^2 r^6$
    (B) $\frac{16}{9}\pi^2 r^5$
    (C) $\frac{16}{9}\pi^2 r^6$
    (D) $48\pi^2 r^5$

18. A mathematical relationship is represented by this expression: $3 \cdot \sqrt{7a}$. How is this expression best represented using fractional exponents?

    (A) $3^{1/2} \cdot 7a^{1/2}$
    (B) $3\,(7^{1/2} \cdot a^{1/2})$
    (C) $(21\,a)^{1/2}$
    (D) $(3 \cdot 7\,a^{1/2})^{1/2}$

19. Cubes one centimeter on a side are used to form a square pyramidal shape. The bottom square on the pyramid measures six cubes on a side. The top of the pyramid shape has a single centimeter cube. How many centimeter cubes are used to make the pyramid?

  Ⓐ 81
  Ⓑ 91
  Ⓒ 100
  Ⓓ 216

20. Use this coordinate grid to answer the question that follows.

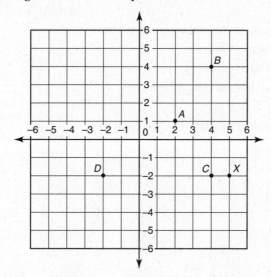

Point X is on a line with a slope of −1, meaning that which of the other points is also on that line?

  Ⓐ A
  Ⓑ B
  Ⓒ C
  Ⓓ D

21. A phone company has a rate plan of $0.29 a call and $0.04 a minute. Which of the following expressions could be used to find the cost of a call?

  Ⓐ $(0.29 + 0.04)$
  Ⓑ $0.04m + 0.29$
  Ⓒ $0.29m + 0.04$
  Ⓓ $m(0.29 + 0.04)$

22. Triangle *ABC* is an equilateral triangle. The length of side *AB* is 40 centimeters. What is the measure of angle *B*?

  Ⓐ 30°
  Ⓑ 40°
  Ⓒ 60°
  Ⓓ 90°

23. A sphere with a volume of 36π is cut in half. One of the circles formed by the cut is shown above. Which of the following is an accurate statement about this sphere if the formula for the volume of a sphere is $V = \frac{4}{3}\pi r^3$ and the formula for the area of a circle is πr^2?

   Ⓐ The surface area of the entire sphere is 18π.
   Ⓑ The area of each circle is 9π.
   Ⓒ The radius of each circle is 6.
   Ⓓ The surface area of half the sphere is 6π.

24. Use this diagram to answer the item that follows.

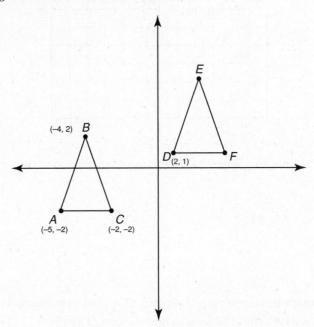

$\triangle ABC$ and $\triangle DEF$ are congruent. Translate $\triangle ABC$ to $\triangle DEF$. What are the coordinates at point E?

   Ⓐ (3, 4)
   Ⓑ (3, 5)
   Ⓒ (4, 4)
   Ⓓ (5, 5)

25. Cutting through a cylinder could produce all of the figures below, except

   Ⓐ

   Ⓑ

   ©

   Ⓓ

26. The area of a garden is 12 square yards. How many square feet is that?

   Ⓐ 4
   Ⓑ 36
   © 72
   Ⓓ 108

27. There are 9 toll booths at a toll plaza. In 1 hour, the mode of the number of cars passing through a toll booth is 86, the median is 97, and the range is 108. From this information we can tell that (carefully consider the meaning of median, mode, and range)

   Ⓐ at least 6 toll booths have fewer than 97 cars passing through.
   Ⓑ the toll booth with the most cars had at least 108 cars pass through.
   © most toll booths had more than 86 cars pass through.
   Ⓓ most toll booths had 86 cars pass through.

28. Use these statements to answer the question:

   1. Some of the triangles are isosceles triangles.
   2. Some of the triangles are equilateral triangles.

   Which of the following conclusions is true?

   Ⓐ Some of the triangles have three sides of equal length.
   Ⓑ None of the triangles contains a right angle.
   © All of the triangles have three sides of equal length.
   Ⓓ None of the triangles has two sides of equal length.

29. The points (−4, +3) and (+4, −3) are plotted on a coordinate grid. At what point would a line connecting these two points cross the y-axis?

   Ⓐ (+1, 0)
   Ⓑ (0, 0)
   © (0, −1)
   Ⓓ (−1, 0)

30. Light travels about 186,000 miles in a second. Which of the following choices shows how to find about how far light travels in an hour?

    Ⓐ Multiply 186,000 by 24
    Ⓑ Multiply 186,000 by 60
    Ⓒ Multiply 186,000 by 360
    Ⓓ Multiply 186,000 by 3600

31. In a standard deck of 52 cards, what is the probability of being dealt a king, a queen, or a jack?

    Ⓐ $\dfrac{1}{3}$

    Ⓑ $\dfrac{2}{13}$

    Ⓒ $\dfrac{3}{13}$

    Ⓓ $\dfrac{4}{13}$

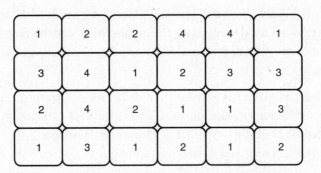

32. A ball is dropped randomly into the container shown above. What is the probability that the ball will land in a section labeled with a composite number?

    Ⓐ $\dfrac{8}{12}$

    Ⓑ $\dfrac{1}{2}$

    Ⓒ $\dfrac{1}{3}$

    Ⓓ $\dfrac{1}{6}$

33. The third person (T) in line is taller than the first person. The first person (F) in a line is the same height or smaller than the second person (S). Using the letters F, S, and T, which of the following choices best represents the height order of these three people?

    Ⓐ $F > S > T$
    Ⓑ $F \geq S > T$
    Ⓒ $S > T \geq F$
    Ⓓ $T > F \leq S$

34. The triangle *ABC* below is shifted 3 units down and shifted 2 units left. What are the coordinates of point *C* after the shifts?

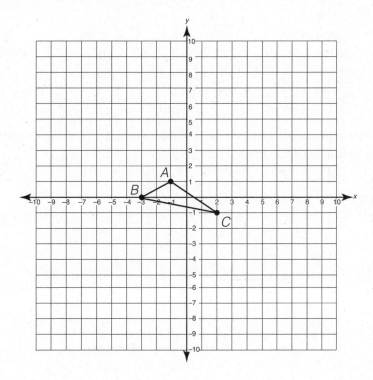

Ⓐ   (–1, 1)

Ⓑ   (0, –4)

Ⓒ   (0, 3)

Ⓓ   (5, –3)

35. All the letters of the alphabet are written on plastic discs and placed in a bag. The vowels in the bag are A. E, I, O, U. Two letters are randomly chosen and not replaced. Both letters are consonants. What is the probability that the next letter chosen is a vowel?

Ⓐ $\dfrac{1}{5}$

Ⓑ $\dfrac{1}{3}$

Ⓒ $\dfrac{5}{26}$

Ⓓ $\dfrac{5}{24}$

36. These are examples of a student's work.

$$\begin{array}{r} 0.036 \\ \times\ \ 1.23 \\ \hline 0108 \\ 0072 \\ 0036 \\ \hline 0.4428 \end{array}$$
$$\begin{array}{r} 1.24 \\ \times\ \ 1.04 \\ \hline 496 \\ 000 \\ 124 \\ \hline 12.896 \end{array}$$
$$\begin{array}{r} 5.79 \\ \times\ \ 2.4 \\ \hline 2316 \\ 1158 \\ \hline 13.896 \end{array}$$

The student continues to make the same type of error. Which of the following is the student's answer to 0.08×1.04?

Ⓐ 0.0832

Ⓑ 0.832

Ⓒ 8.32

Ⓓ 83.2

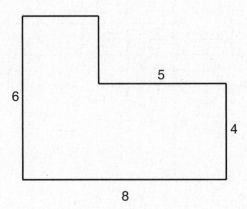

37. After examining the diagram of the polygon above, the student states the perimeter is 23 units. Which of the following statements by the teacher is most likely to help the student?

Ⓐ Check your addition.

Ⓑ Trace each side of the shape with your finger.

Ⓒ Count the number of sides of the polygon.

Ⓓ Use the rule for finding perimeter.

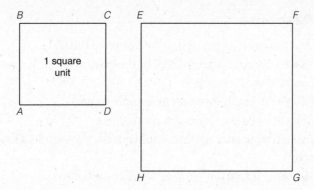

38. After examining the illustration above, a student gave an answer of 2 for the area of the larger polygon. How can the teacher best help the student understand the error?

    Ⓐ Suggest the student trace the small square and compare that to the tracing of the larger square.
    Ⓑ Suggest the student get a ruler and measure.
    Ⓒ Suggest the student cut out the small square and find out how many small squares fit inside the large square.
    Ⓓ Suggest the student estimate the increase in distance between $\overline{BC}$ and $\overline{EF}$.

39. Which of the following is the LEAST appropriate mathematics objective to teach using manipulative materials?

    Ⓐ Adding single-digit numbers
    Ⓑ Solving problems using the strategy "make an organized list"
    Ⓒ Adding double-digit numbers
    Ⓓ Dividing decimals

40. A teacher is helping young students learn about counting. The teacher uses shapes as counters and makes sure students point to a shape each time the student says the next numeral. Why is the teacher using this approach?

    Ⓐ The teacher wants to be sure the students are paying attention to what they are doing.
    Ⓑ The teacher wants to be sure students are developing eye-hand coordination.
    Ⓒ The teacher is going to ask the students questions about the shapes once they have finished counting.
    Ⓓ The teacher wants to be sure the students are not just saying counting words.

Constructed Response

Use the information in the exhibits that follow to complete the task.

Use a word processor, without the spell check or the grammar check, to type your response, which should be about 400 to 600 words.

Identify one significant strength the student demonstrates.

Identify one significant need the student demonstrates.

Identify a learning activity or strategy that would advance the student's strength or remediate the student's need.

Explain why the learning activity or strategy would be effective.

Teacher's Notes

Derek is a student in a fourth-grade mathematics class. Ms. Stendel, Derek's teacher, notices that Derek has trouble with some relatively simple computation problems. Derek is frequently distracted during class. Derek's ability test scores and his insights and comments during class reveal that he is unusually intelligent. When asked do something he can complete quickly or to solve a problem mentally, he is amazing and is great at solving logical thinking problems.

Ms. Stendel's Classroom Observation of Derek in a Mathematics Group

The class was given a project to work on for thirty minutes that involves solving two mathematics problems. The first problem requires logical thinking, while the second problem involves complicated addition, subtraction, multiplication, and division. The students do not have their calculators. Derek is working in a group with four other students.

The five students are seated around a table and each student has a copy of the problem to be solved. Derek seems disinterested. He suggests that the group talk about other things besides the problem in front of them.

Some of the students seem interested in his distraction, but the group decides to focus on the first problem. Derek is not happy, and he sulks and withdraws from the group and stares at his copy of the problem. The other students are talking about the first problem when Derek interrupts them saying, "I've got it." After fifteen minutes the group has not solved the first problem, and Derek will not share the solution he says he has. The group turns their attention to the second problem.

Students have sheets of plain paper and Derek begins to work on his calculations for the second problem. I can see that his numerals are hard to read and are not aligned well.

Sample of Derek's Calculations

$$
\begin{array}{r}
1 \\
174 \\
+\ 286 \\
\hline
4510
\end{array}
$$

$$
\begin{array}{r}
31 \\
\times\ 42 \\
\hline
62 \\
124 \\
\hline
186
\end{array}
$$

$$\begin{array}{r} 121 \text{ R } 15 \\ 58\overline{)7053} \\ \underline{58} \\ 125 \\ \underline{116} \\ 93 \\ \underline{58} \\ 15 \end{array}$$

Derek's Discussion with the Teacher

After class I had a conversation with Derek about his work. A copy of this conversation follows.

Ms. Stendel: Derek, can you stay just a minute?

Derek: OK.

Ms. Stendel: You seemed to know the answer to that first problem. But you would not tell them what your answer was.

Derek: Let them get it.

Ms. Stendel: But it could help them to know what your answer is. And what if your answer was not correct?

Derek: It was.

Ms. Stendel: Will you tell me what it was?

Derek: It's 26.

Ms. Stendel: Oh Derek, that's correct!

ANSWER EXPLANATIONS

1. **(A)** The number 6 has two different prime factors, 2 and 3.

    The product of 2 and 3 is 6: $2 \times 3 = 6$

    (B), (C), and (D) are incorrect.

    (B) The number 12 has two prime factors, 2 and 3.

    The product of 2 and 3 is not 12.

    (C) The number 36 two prime factors, 2 and 3.

    The product of 2 and 3 is not 36.

    (D) The number 48 two prime factors, 2 and 3

    The product of 2 and 3 is not 48.

2. **(A)** The multiples of x and y will reveal at which floors each elevator stops. Find the common multiples to find at which floors both elevators stop.

    For example, the multiples of 2 are 2, 4, 6, 8, 10, . . .

    The multiples of 3 are 3, 6, 9, . . .

    The common multiples we can see show that both elevators stop at the sixth floor. (B), (C), and (D) are all incorrect because the factors of a number are the same as the divisors of that number. Prime factors are factors that are also prime numbers. Divisors do not show at which floors elevators stop. The largest divisor of a number is the number itself.

3. **(A)** 91 percent is spent on other things, and 9 percent is left for the class trip.

Find 9 percent of $5,300.

9 percent of $5,300 = $0.09 \times \$5300 = \$477$

Choice (A) shows the correct answer.

4. **(B)** This is a proportion problem, and there are a few ways to approach it. Here's the more classic approach. It is a little easier to use decimals.

Write a fraction for what you know about the grass seed mix: $\dfrac{3.5 \text{ rye grass}}{0.75 \text{ blue grass}}$

Write a fraction with an unknown for the total amount of seed: $\dfrac{5.25 \text{ rye grass}}{b \text{ blue grass}}$

Write a proportion $\quad \dfrac{3.5}{0.75} = \dfrac{5.25}{b}$

Cross multiply $\quad 3.5b = 3.9375 \quad b = \dfrac{3.9375}{3.5} \quad b = 1.125 \quad$ That's $1\frac{1}{8}$.

(B) is the only correct answer.

5. **(C)** To find the distance, write 90 minutes is 1.5 hours. Then multiply 1.5 and 45 to find how far the car travels in 90 minutes: $1.5 \times 45 = 67.5$ miles.

Divide 67.5 by 10 to find the number of inches $\quad 67.5 \div 10 = 6.75$ inches

(A), (B), and (D) are all incorrect because these choices do not show this answer.

6. **(D)** The probability that a fair coin will land heads up is $\dfrac{1}{2}$, regardless of what has happened before the flip. (A), (B), and (C) are all incorrect because these choices do not show this answer.

7. **(C)** The discount is 35 percent of $83 =

Find the discount: $0.35 \times \$83 = \$29.05$

Subtract to find the new price: $\$83 - \$29.05 = \$53.95$

Note, choice (A) is incorrect because the question asks for the discounted price of one item, not all three items.

8. **(D)** Use these steps to solve this problem.

Find the capacity of the oil tank: 3 hours $\times$ 100 gallons per hour = 300 gallons.

Divide 300 by 80 to find the filling time at 80 gallons per hour to get 3.75 hours.

3.75 hours $= 3\frac{3}{4}$ hours.

9. **(B)** Write a proportion and solve.

$\dfrac{2}{9} = \dfrac{b}{1,350}$

$9b = 2,700$

$b = 300$

The bakers made 300 brownies.

10. **(A)** Divide to find what percent $624,000 is of $2,600.000. (An estimate shows it is going to be <u>about</u> $\frac{1}{4}$, or 0.25.)

Divide: $624,000 ÷ $2,600,000 = 0.24. (To get the answer, "cancel out" zeros and divide 624 by 2600.) The town needs 24 percent for police, 2 percent more than in the pie chart. Take the 2 percent from sanitation, leaving 22 percent for sanitation.

11. **(C)** Think of the percent equation 85% = 0.85, $0.85x = 289$

So, $x = 289 ÷ 0.85$.

Divide 289 by 0.85 to find how many houses were on the beach.

$289 ÷ 0.85 = 340$. (You could also multiply each answer by 0.85. Only choice (C), $340 × 0.85 = 289$.)

12. **(B)** Find the original price: 25 percent of the original price is $12.

$\frac{1}{4}$ of original price is $12

original price = $12 × 4 = $48

Find the sale price: original price – $12 = sale price.

$48 – $12 = $36.

The sale price is $36.

13. **(D)** The ratio 7 to 14 (7:14) can be expressed as 1:2. Use the equation $x + 2x = 54$, where x represents the number of rainy days and $2x$ the number of sunny days. The total number of classified days equals 54. So $x + 2x = 54$ and $3x = 54$, $x = 18$.

$x = 18$, the number of rainy days

$2x = 36$, the number of sunny days

$18 + 36 = 54$. That checks.

14. **(B)** Multiply to find her bonus: $1,200 × 15% = $180

She needs to work enough hours to make $500 – $180 = $320.

Divide to find the number of hours $320 ÷ 18 = 17 R 14.

Seventeen hours would be too few, so she would have to work a minimum of 18 hours.

Notice that choices (C) and (D) are incorrect because they are <u>more</u> than the minimum number of hours she needed to work.

15. **(B)** Start by multiplying $5 × 34,000$ cm = 170,000 cm.

Then, write the answer using scientific notation, which has a digit in the ones place multiplied by a power of 10.

That's $1.7 × 10^5$

Note, choices (A) and (D) are mathematically correct but do not correctly represent the number using scientific notation.

16. **(C)** If you draw a diagonal in a square with sides equal to 1, the Pythagorean theorem tells you that the length of that diagonal is $\sqrt{2}$.

$a^2 + b^2 = c^2 = 1 + 1 = c^2 = 2$ $c = \sqrt{2}$

The best decimal approximation is $\sqrt{2} = 1.41421356\ldots$

That is closest to choice (C).

17. **(C)** The answers are formulas, so the first step is to notice that the spheres are the same size. Square the volume formula to find the product of the volume of two identical spheres.

$$[\frac{4}{3}\pi r^3]^2 =$$

Square each term.

$$(\frac{4}{3})^2 = \frac{16}{9}$$

$(\pi)^2$ becomes π^2

$r^{3(2)} = r^6$ (Multiply exponents to find the square of r^3)

$$[\frac{4}{3}\pi r^3]^2 = \frac{16}{9}\pi^2 r^6$$

(C) is the only correct answer choice.

18. **(B)** Begin by writing $\sqrt{7a}$ in this form: $\sqrt{7} \cdot \sqrt{a} = 7^{1/2} \cdot a^{1/2}$

(remember $\sqrt{x} = x^{1/2}$)

Multiply by 3:3 $(7^{1/2} \cdot a^{1/2})$

We are done. (That is choice (B).)

(B) is the only correct answer.

19. **(B)** There are 36 cubes in the bottom square and then 25, 16, 9, 4 cubes on the fifth to second squares, with 1 cube on top.

Add $36 + 25 + 16 + 9 + 4 + 1 = 91$

That is 91 cubes all together.

(A), (C), and (D) are all incorrect because these choices do not show this answer.

20. **(A)** The slope of –1 means the line goes generally from upper left to lower right on the grid. That immediately eliminates points B, C, and D.

A slope of –1 means move right one square for every square down. A line through point A and point X follows that pattern and shows the slope of that line is –1.

21. **(B)** This expression correctly shows multiplying $0.04 times the number of minutes plus the general charge of $0.29. (A), (C), and (D) are all incorrect because these choices do not show this answer.

22. **(C)** Equilateral triangles, triangles with all sides the same length, have three 60° angles, regardless of how long a side is. (A), (B), and (D) are all incorrect because these choices do not show this answer.

23. **(B)** Eliminate choices (A) and (D). The question gives no information about the surface area.

Write the volume formula equal to 36π to find the length of the radius:

$$\frac{4}{3}\pi r^3 = 36\pi$$

$$\frac{4}{3}r^3 = 36$$

$$r^3 = 27$$

$$r = 3$$

That eliminates choice (C), so the answer is probably (B). Let's check.

The formula for the area of a circle is πr^2.

$\pi 3^2 = 9\pi$. That is choice (B).

24. **(B)** Add (+1, +4) to get from point A to point B.

Now add (+1, +4) to point D (2, 1) to find point E (3, 5).

The coordinates for point E are (3, 5). Other approaches yield the correct answer.

(A), (C), and (D) are all incorrect because these choices do not show this answer.

25. **(C)** There is no way to cut through a cylinder to produce rounded ends and straight sides. (A) Cut straight through the height to create this shape. (B) Cut through the diameter when the diameter and height are equal to create this shape. (D) Cut diagonally through the cylinder to create this shape.

26. **(D)** One square yard measures 3 feet by 3 feet = 9 square feet.

12 square yards is $12 \times 9 = 108$ square feet.

27. **(B)** Start by eliminating incorrect answers. (A) is incorrect because a median of 97 means no more than 4, not 6, tollbooths have fewer than 97 cars pass through. (C) is incorrect because the mode tells which number occurs most often. We do not know how many numbers are above or below the mode. (D) is incorrect because we cannot tell how many booths had 86 cars pass through. It could be just two toll booths. (B) must be correct. The range is the greatest number of cars to pass through a toll booth, minus the smallest number of cars that pass through a toll booth. Even if no cars passed through one tollbooth, AT LEAST 108 cars will pass through one toll booth.

28. **(A)** This conclusion is supported by BOTH of the statements. (B) is incorrect because neither statement gives any information about right angles or right triangles. (C) is incorrect because of statement 2. (D) is incorrect because both statements describe at least one triangle with two sides of equal length.

29. **(B)** The points are symmetrical, and so the line passes through the origin, where the x-axis and y-axis cross. The coordinates for the origin are (0, 0). Choice (B) is the only correct answer.

30. **(D)** There are 60 seconds in a minute and 60 minutes in an hour. So there are $60 \times 60 = 3,600$ seconds in an hour. The product $186,000 \times 3,600$ is a reasonable approximation of how far light travels in an hour. (A), (B), and (C) are all incorrect because these choices do not show the number of seconds in an hour.

31. **(C)** In a standard deck of cards, there are 12 "face cards"—4 kings, 4 queens, and 4 jacks—out of 52 possible cards.

P (face card) $= \dfrac{12}{52} = \dfrac{3}{13}$.

Choice (C) is the only correct answer.

32. **(D)** A composite number has factors other than itself and 1. That means 4 is the only composite number in the container.

Write a fraction to represent the number of fours: $\dfrac{4}{24}$

Write the fraction in lowest terms: $\dfrac{4}{24} = \dfrac{1}{6}$.

33. **(D)** Use the letters F, S, and T for the first, second, and third person. The third person is taller than the first person. Write T > F to show this relationship. The first person's height is less than or equal to the second person's height, so write F ≤ S to show this relationship. Put T > F together with F ≤ S and we get this result: T > F ≤ S.

Choice (D) is the only correct choice.

34. **(B)** Remember that "up" (add) and "down" (subtract) describe the movement of the y-coordinate, while "left" (subtract) and "right" (add) describe the movement of the x-coordinate.

The original coordinates of point C are (2, –1)

Subtract 2 to find the x-coordinate $2 - 2 = 0$.

Subtract 3 to find the y-coordinate $-1 - 3 = -4$

The coordinates of point C after the shifts are (0, –4).

35. **(D)** There are 26 letters in the alphabet. Removing two consonants leaves 24 letters, 5 of which were vowels. The probability of randomly picking a vowel is $\frac{5}{24}$.

36. **(C)** This choice shows the student's incorrect answer. To multiply decimals, multiply the numbers, count the number of digits to the right of the decimal point in both factors, and put that many decimal places in the answer. This student does not count "0" when it appears to the right of the decimal point. Choice (A) shows the correct answer to $0.08 \times 1.04 = 0.0832$. The student should move the decimal point four places to the left to get 0.0832. Choices (B) and (D) do not show the student's incorrect answer.

37. **(B)** The student failed to include the sides that do not show the lengths. Tracing each side will most likely lead the student to realize this omission. (The length of the missing horizontal side is $8 - 5 = 3$. The length of the missing vertical side is $6 - 4 = 2$.) Choice (A) is incorrect because the student added correctly but omitted the lengths of some of the sides. Choice (C) is incorrect because counting sides might help; however, choice (B) with physical involvement of the student is much more likely to help. Choice (D) is incorrect because the student did use the rule "add the sides to find the perimeter." The student just did not include all sides.

38. **(C)** A student is most likely to be helped if he or she actually sees four small squares fit inside the large square. Choice (A) is incorrect. Tracing and comparing might help the student, but choice (C) is the best way. Choice (B) is incorrect. A ruler might help the student calculate the area, but the task here is to help the student see the relationship visually. Choice (D) is incorrect. Estimating the increase in distance might help the student calculate the area; however, this is less effective than choice (C).

39. **(D)** Note the word LEAST in the item. Dividing decimals is too complex to represent with manipulatives. Choice (A) is incorrect. Counters can help student learn single-digit addition. Choice (B) is incorrect. Students might use this strategy to find how many ways to arrange three different shapes in order. Shapes or other objects can be used to represent elements in the list. Choice (C) is incorrect. Tens blocks or bean sticks can help students learn addition of double-digit numbers.

40. **(D)** Just because a student can say counting words in order does not mean the student can count. You may have seen a child correctly count to 5 as the child counts 7 objects. It is the correspondence between the counting words and the objects being counted that is important.

SAMPLE CONSTRUCTED RESPONSE

Constructed-Response Scoring

SCORING EXPECTATIONS

The response should meet the stated specific requirements.

- The response should demonstrate an understanding of the applicable exhibits.
- The response should draw on information from the assignment and give examples to support the main themes.

SCORING

4 The response demonstrates a STRONG grasp of the applicable content and skills and always includes all required response elements.

3 The response demonstrates an ACCEPABLE grasp of the applicable content and skills and always includes all required response elements.

2 The response demonstrates a LESS THAN ACCEPTABLE grasp of the applicable content and skills and may not include all required response elements.

1 The response is INCOMPLETE AND/OR OFF TRACK and usually does not include required response elements.

U The response can't be scored because it is off topic, written in a language other than English, or contains too little information to score. Note, a well-written but off-topic response will be scored U.

B You did not write anything

Sample Response

This 564-word response might earn 4 or a 3.

As is quite common, Derek's needs in mathematics go beyond mathematics ability and extends to his lack of care and awareness when calculating. As the written calculations demonstrate, he also has issues with the correct methods for writing addition, multiplication, and division algorithms. There may be additional issues with an awareness of place value. In his addition example, he does not carry the "1" to the tens place but writes it in the answer. The rest of the problem is correctly done. In the multiplication example, he does not start the second partial product in the correct location, resulting in an incorrect answer. His division problem has a careless subtraction error which may be due to his lack of concentration due to the fact that the rest of his facts were correct. His difficulty with group work interferes with his ability to learn from others.

His strength lies mainly in his ability to think logically and to quickly solve problems. That strength can be seen in the difficult pattern problem he solved during my observation. He would not reveal the answer to others in the group. He only shared the answer with me when I implied he may not have the correct answer. Even so, he never shared the method he used, and he may have used a specific approach, or it may just have been a quick intuitive grasp of the problem that led to the correct answer.

My efforts to help Derek will focus on his difficulty with computation. I will give Derek Place Value Mats or Calculation paper with Place Value columns to record his answers. I will carefully point out where his errors are and model the correct regrouping techniques he needs to use in his addition. I will be alert for the careless placement of the "1" in his regrouping of the ones column.

The Place Value Mats or Place Value Calculation paper can also help in his multiplication error. I will remind him that the "4" in the second factor of "42" really means 4 tens, so the partial product of 4 "tens" × 1 "ones" is "40" not 4. I will model the use of the written problem for Derek using the Place Value Calculation paper, and then allow him to do a few on his own with supervision and guided practice, before giving him some independent practice.

When Derek looks at his division steps again, he probably may find the error on his own. If he does not, I will guide him through the problem until his error is evident to him. I will give Derek just a few problems at a time to help hold his attention.

I expect this lesson to be successful because it will help Derek focus on one thing at a time. The Place Value Mats and Place Value Calculation paper also help to remind him to take the time to align his calculations properly. Once he sees how simple it will be for him to get correct answers, it will help his confidence and hopefully interest him in taking care when doing other work in and out of school. He is a good problem solver, and I will treat this as a problem he can solve with a little more effort and time.

---

1 hour

40 selected-response items

Darken the lettered oval to show your choice for the selected response items.

---

1. Which of the following stages of skiing represents potential energy?

   Ⓐ The skier is going to the top of the hill on a ski lift.
   Ⓑ The skier is waiting at the top of the hill.
   Ⓒ The skier pushes off from the top of the hill
   Ⓓ The skier is skiing down the hill.

2. Which of the following involves the most work?

   Ⓐ Using all your might to try to lift a 50-story building.
   Ⓑ Holding 100 pounds of weight perfectly still over your head.
   Ⓒ Lifting 10 pounds over your head.
   Ⓓ Dropping 100 pounds of weight to the floor.

3. Which of the following best describes what happens to light when it strikes a flat mirror?

   Ⓐ Light is reflected straight back from the flat mirror.
   Ⓑ The light ray reflects back from the mirror at the same angle it strikes.
   Ⓒ The light ray is refracted at many different angles back from the mirror.
   Ⓓ The light is absorbed leaving only an image of the light waves to be viewed.

4. Written as a formula, Newton's second law of motion is

$$(F)orce = (M)ass \times (A)cceleration.$$

   Which of the following is the best everyday explanation of this law?

   Ⓐ Something heavier will move slower than something lighter.
   Ⓑ It is easier to move something if it has less mass.
   Ⓒ The more the acceleration you apply the less mass there is.
   Ⓓ The more mass there is means there is more force applied to it.

5. Which of the following best illustrates heat transfer through conduction?

   Ⓐ A person feels heat when he stands near an electric stove.
   Ⓑ A person feels heat when he stands in the sunlight.
   Ⓒ A person feels heat when he stands in front of a hot air blower.
   Ⓓ A person feels heat when he touches a steam radiator.

6. A green plant is placed in a terrarium and subjected to continuous light and watering. Which of the following is certain to happen as a result of photosynthesis?

    Ⓐ The plant will produce oxygen.
    Ⓑ The plant will produce carbon dioxide.
    Ⓒ The plant will produce water.
    Ⓓ The plant will produce carbon monoxide.

7. Which one of the body systems listed below includes a mechanical process?

    Ⓐ Nervous system
    Ⓑ Digestive system
    Ⓒ Endocrine system
    Ⓓ Immune system

8. Some cells respire aerobically while others respire anaerobically. Fermentation is most like anaerobic respiration in that

    Ⓐ the process occurs only during cell division.
    Ⓑ the process does not require oxygen.
    Ⓒ the process only occurs in aquatic animals.
    Ⓓ the process produces oxygen.

9. Which of the following examples of cell reproduction results in a doubling of the number of chromosomes?

    Ⓐ A human egg cell is formed.
    Ⓑ A human sperm cell is formed.
    Ⓒ A human cell enters the metaphase stage of mitosis.
    Ⓓ Human sperm and egg cells combine.

10. The best way to characterize Earth's location in the Milky Way, our galaxy, is

    Ⓐ at the center.
    Ⓑ near the outer edge.
    Ⓒ near the top.
    Ⓓ that we don't know.

11. A weather observer would use a hygrometer to measure which of the following?

    Ⓐ Rainfall
    Ⓑ Humidity
    Ⓒ Wind speed
    Ⓓ Air pressure

12. The hottest temperature on record in the Western Hemisphere—134 degrees F—was recorded in Death Valley. Which of the following is the best explanation of why Death Valley can be hotter than surrounding areas?

Ⓐ Death Valley is a desert area.
Ⓑ Death Valley is lower in elevation.
Ⓒ Death Valley is a high desert.
Ⓓ Death Valley is more isolated.

13. A teacher wants to add salt to 100 ml of freshwater to match the salinity of sea water. About how much salt should be added?

Ⓐ 3.5 ml
Ⓑ 5 ml
Ⓒ 7.5 ml
Ⓓ 10 ml

14. A geologist is reviewing topographic maps for northern New York, knowing that the maps will show

Ⓐ the land features as viewed from the perspective of a hiker.
Ⓑ the rainfall and snowfall characteristics of a region.
Ⓒ the land features as viewed from above.
Ⓓ the location of cultural groups in the region.

15. Meiosis is a very important cell reproduction process. This process always involves

Ⓐ cells making carbon copies of themselves.
Ⓑ reducing the number of chromosomes by half.
Ⓒ the creation of cells equal to all others in terms of DNA.
Ⓓ the production of identical daughter cells.

16. The half-life of plutonium is about 82 years. Approximately how much of the mass of plutonium would remain after about 330 years?

Ⓐ $\frac{1}{2}$

Ⓑ $\frac{1}{4}$

Ⓒ $\frac{1}{8}$

Ⓓ $\frac{1}{16}$

17. Which of the following describes the similarity between feudalism in Japan and feudalism in Europe?

    Ⓐ Shoguns were like lords.
    Ⓑ Christians were persecuted.
    Ⓒ Leaders were overthrown by the people.
    Ⓓ Shoguns were like popes.

18. The Reformation in Europe led to which of the following developments?

    Ⓐ The establishment of protestant religions in Spain
    Ⓑ The rediscovery of literature and art
    Ⓒ The painting of the Sistine Chapel
    Ⓓ The establishment of the Protestant Church of England

19. Which of the following statements best summarizes aspects of the Mayan culture in Mexico?

    Ⓐ The Mayans had no human sacrificial ceremonies.
    Ⓑ The Mayans had the most accurate calendar in the world at the time.
    Ⓒ The Mayans extended their culture to the western coast of South America.
    Ⓓ The Mayan culture was predominant in South America before the arrival of Columbus.

20. When Christopher Columbus sailed, he

    Ⓐ never returned to Europe from his explorations.
    Ⓑ first established a settlement in what is now the state of North Carolina.
    Ⓒ never reached the mainland of North America.
    Ⓓ first established a settlement in what is now the state of Virginia.

21. Which of the following is the most accurate account of the battle leading up to the surrender of the British general Cornwallis at Yorktown in Virginia on October 17, 1781?

    Ⓐ American troops trapped Cornwallis in and around Yorktown and forced him to surrender.
    Ⓑ American troops surrounded Cornwallis at Yorktown and forced him to surrender.
    Ⓒ French troops and American troops surrounded Cornwallis at Yorktown and forced him to surrender.
    Ⓓ The French Navy and American troops surrounded Cornwallis at Yorktown and forced him to surrender.

22. During the state ratification process following the Constitutional Convention, the Federalist Papers were authored to support the ratification. In response, anti-Federalists expressed their concerns, which were that

Ⓐ there should be no federal or national government.
Ⓑ the Constitution replaced the Articles of Confederation, which formed a nation just from southern states.
Ⓒ the Constitution did not adequately protect individual rights.
Ⓓ the states could not properly ratify a document that established a federal government.

23. Use this excerpt from Article II, Section 1 of the U.S. Constitution to answer the item below.

> The executive Power shall be vested in a President of the United States of America. He shall hold his Office during the Term of four Years, and, together with the Vice President, chosen for the same Term, be elected, as follows:
> Each State shall appoint, in such Manner as the Legislature thereof may direct, a Number of Electors, equal to the whole Number of Senators and Representatives to which the State may be entitled in the Congress: but no Senator or Representative or Person holding an Office of Trust or Profit under the United States, shall be appointed an Elector.

What is the impact of Article II, Section 1 on the election of the President of the United States of America?

Ⓐ The President of the United States is elected directly by the people of the United States.
Ⓑ The President of the United States is elected by a majority of the states.
Ⓒ The President of the United States can be elected by less than a majority of the voters.
Ⓓ The number of presidential electors is equal to the number of representatives.

24. The Declaration of Independence featured six self-evident truths including which of the following?

Ⓐ The right of the people to alter or abolish a destructive government.
Ⓑ Equality of all who were not slaves.
Ⓒ Freedom of religion, speech, press, assembly, and petition.
Ⓓ Right to bear arms.

Use this map to answer item 25.

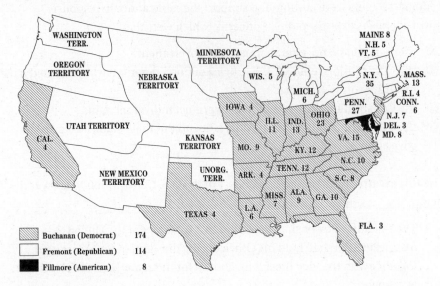

25. Which of the following conclusions can reasonably be drawn from the map above?

Ⓐ Were it not for Texas and California, Fremont would have won the election.
Ⓑ Buchanan was a strong supporter of the rebel cause.
Ⓒ Fremont was favored by those living in the northernmost states.
Ⓓ Fremont was favored by the states that fought for the Union in the Civil War.

26. The Jim Crow South emerged following Reconstruction in part because of

Ⓐ the Supreme Court's decision in the Amistad case, which freed the slaves held on the ship.
Ⓑ the Supreme Court's decision in *Plessy v. Ferguson* that ruled separate but equal accommodations were legal.
Ⓒ the Supreme Court's decision in *Marbury v. Madison* that established the court's right to rule that federal actions were unconstitutional.
Ⓓ the Supreme Court's decision in *Brown v. Board of Education* that essentially overturned the *Plessy v. Ferguson* ruling.

27. The dance form ballet is based on

Ⓐ positions of the arms.
Ⓑ positions of the legs.
Ⓒ positions of the feet.
Ⓓ relative position of torso and legs.

28. Which of the activities listed below would be most likely to help elementary school students develop an aesthetic perception, an appreciation, of dance?

Ⓐ Ask students to view a dance performance and identify the time and space elements in the performance.

Ⓑ Ask students to view a dance performance and identify the cultural style of the performance.

Ⓒ Ask students to view a dance performance and interpret the meaning found in the performance.

Ⓓ Ask students to view a dance performance and interpret the history of the dance form.

29. Floods along the Nile River about 4000 years ago were most responsible for which of the following?

Ⓐ The destruction of agricultural land

Ⓑ The establishment of cataracts

Ⓒ The birth of geometry

Ⓓ The construction of boats that could withstand the floods

30. The first democracy in the Americas was formed in New York State when

Ⓐ George Washington became the first President of the United States and New York City became the first U.S. capital.

Ⓑ the Iroquois formed a nation of five tribes in northern New York.

Ⓒ the Dutch founded the capital of New Netherland, called New Amsterdam, located at the southern tip of the island of Manhattan.

Ⓓ the Dutch founded what became Albany, New York, as the trading post of Fort Nassau in 1614.

31. The state's name New York most likely originated as which of the following?

Ⓐ The Duke of York purchased Manhattan and named the city New York, and the name eventually came to refer to the entire state.

Ⓑ In 1664, an English fleet arrived at New Amsterdam; England took control of the colony and renamed both the city and the colony New York, after the Duke of York.

Ⓒ The French named the upstate region of current New York near the Canadian border "Yorke," and the name spread throughout the state where it was eventually applied to the state and the city.

Ⓓ York was a name that applied to what is present-day New England and New York. As the New England colonies formed states, the name York was changed to New York.

32. New York became a state in the United States when

    (A) its representatives were the first to sign the Declaration of Independence.

    (B) England surrendered the entire colony of New York to the American Continental Army.

    (C) on July 26, 1788, New York became the eleventh state to ratify the new U.S. Constitution.

    (D) Albany became the state capital in 1797.

33. Which of the following is the most appropriate way to monitor the impact of exercise on a child?

    (A) Monitor the child's pulse rate.

    (B) Observe how "hard" a child is breathing.

    (C) Take note of how much the child's eyes are dilated.

    (D) Feel the child's forehead to detect elevated body temperature.

34. An elementary school student knows about the pitch of a musical note. Which of the following will the child also need to know to fully understand the "note"?

    (A) Chord

    (B) Harmony

    (C) Duration

    (D) Timbre

35. A person viewing the visual art technique called a fresco is most likely viewing it

    (A) on a canvas.

    (B) on a wall.

    (C) in a church.

    (D) on a board or piece of wood.

36. What color results from mixing two complementary colors?

    (A) A supplementary color

    (B) Reddish brown

    (C) Black

    (D) A primary color

37. Jazz music, developed by African American musicians about 100 years ago, is best characterized by

    (A) chaotic sounds interspersed with individual solos.

    (B) a "battle" between two musicians to create the most pleasing sound.

    (C) popular songs interspersed with individual solos and improvisation.

    (D) solos accompanied by repetition of chords from popular music.

38. Which scale uses all the white and black keys on a piano?

    Ⓐ Chromatic

    Ⓑ Diatonic

    Ⓒ Harmonic

    Ⓓ Piano

39. Which of the following descriptions of a child is LEAST likely to require an intervention to help them with a transition to adult life?

    Ⓐ A first-grade student is very careful about trying out new ideas.

    Ⓑ A sixth-grade student exhibits a well-defined gender identity.

    Ⓒ A third-grade student who feels he or she is accepted by their peer group, when he or she is not.

    Ⓓ A kindergarten student who feels somewhat inhibited in school.

40. Students lives are most influenced by their families. Today's family is LEAST accurately characterized by which of the following?

    Ⓐ A majority of families have mothers who work.

    Ⓑ An increasing number of children are "latchkey" children.

    Ⓒ Less than 10 percent of American families have a mother (as a homemaker), a father (as the breadwinner), and children.

    Ⓓ Families are groups of people living together who are related to one another.

ANSWER EXPLANATIONS

1. **(B)** Energy is the ability to do work, and the skier at the top of the hill represents the most potential to create kinetic energy by skiing down the hill. (A) is incorrect because this choice does not represent any energy potential because there is no way to activate it. (C) is incorrect because a skier pushing off the top of the hill represents activation energy, not potential energy. (D) is incorrect because the skier skiing down the hill represents kinetic motion and energy.

2. **(C)** In science, "work" means movement of a body by force. This choice is the only one that involves movement. (A) and (B) are incorrect because these choices involve no movement, so there is no work. (D) is incorrect because no force is involved when an object is dropped, which means there is no work.

3. **(B)** The phrase most often used is "angle of incidence equals angle of reflection." Light rays reflect back at the same angle they strike the mirror. (A) In general, light is not reflected straight back. (C) Light refracts through a prism, but it reflects back from a mirror. (D) The majority of the light that strikes a mirror reflects back.

4. **(B)** This formula means: the more mass there is, the more force you need to accelerate it. Less mass means you need less force. (A) A common sense example of a heavy airplane moving faster than a lighter bicycle explains why this choice is incorrect. (C) is incorrect because making something go faster does not reduce its mass. (D) is incorrect because more mass does not mean more force will be applied to it.

5. **(D)** "Conduction" means heat transfer by direct contact, as described in this choice. (A) and (B) are incorrect because these choices give examples of heat transfer by radiation (no physical contact). (C) is incorrect because this choice gives an example of heat transfer by convection (moving air).

6. **(A)** Photosynthesis in a green plant produces oxygen, along with carbohydrates (sugar and starch). (B) is incorrect because photosynthesis uses, but does not produce, carbon dioxide. (C) is incorrect because photosynthesis uses, but does not produce, water. (D) is incorrect because photosynthesis as described here neither uses nor produces carbon monoxide.

7. **(B)** The teeth help digestion through a mechanical process. Stomach muscle contractions during digestion are also a mechanical process. (A), (C), and (D) are all incorrect because none of these systems include a mechanical process.

8. **(B)** Anaerobic respiration means respiration without oxygen. (A) is incorrect because anaerobic respiration is not related to cell division. (C) is incorrect because fermentation occurs most frequently in yeast and bacteria. (D) is incorrect because anaerobic respiration does not produce oxygen.

9. **(D)** A human sperm cell and a human egg cell each have half the number of chromosomes normally found in a human. When they combine, they form a zygote that has double the number of cells found in the sperm cell or the egg cell. (C) is incorrect because cell reproduction through mitosis maintains the number of chromosomes found in the parent cell.

10. **(B)** Earth is located at the outer edge of the Milky Way. (A) is incorrect because Earth is not located at the center of our galaxy. (C) is incorrect because Earth is not located at the top of the Milky Way. (D) is incorrect because we do know where Earth is located in the Milky Way.

11. **(B)** A hygrometer measures humidity. (A) is incorrect because a rain gauge measures rainfall. (C) is incorrect because an anemometer measures wind speed. (D) is incorrect because a barometer measures air pressure.

12. **(B)** Death Valley's very low elevation explains why the temperature is higher there than in the nearby desert. (A) and (C) are incorrect because there are many desert and high desert regions that do not experience the extreme temperatures found in Death Valley. (D) is incorrect because there are many more isolated areas that do not experience Death Valley's extreme temperatures.

13. **(A)** Seawater is about 3.5 percent salt. Adding 3.5 ml of salt to 100 ml of water would make the freshwater about 3.5 percent salt. Grams (g) are also used to measure salt, but milliliters make the comparison easier. (B), (C) and (D) are all incorrect because adding these amounts of salt would not approximate the salinity of seawater.

14. **(C)** Topographic maps show an aerial view of land features. (A) is incorrect because a topographic map shows elevations, so it would be useful to a hiker. However, it would not show things from a hiker's perspective. (B) and (D) are incorrect because topographic maps do not show rainfall or snowfall information, nor do they show information about cultural groups.

15. **(B)** Meiosis is a type of cell division common to sexually reproducing organisms. Meiosis reduces the chromosome number by half, enabling sexual recombination to occur.

(A), (C), and (D) are all incorrect because these steps are all common to mitosis, but not meiosis.

16. **(D)** Divide 330 years by 82. That's about 4. Plutonium will lose half its mass about four times during those 330 years.

Multiply $\frac{1}{2}$ four times to find the answer.

$$\frac{1}{2} \times \frac{1}{2} \times \frac{1}{2} \times \frac{1}{2} = \frac{1}{16}$$

Choice (D) shows the correct answer.

17. **(A)** Feudalism refers to a European system in which lords protected vassals (knights), and then serfs, in return for their service. The role of lords in this system very closely resembles the role of shoguns in Japan. (B) is incorrect because persecution is not an element of feudalism. (C) is incorrect because the overthrow of leaders by "the people" may have occurred during feudalism, but it is not a part of feudalism. (D) is incorrect because a pope is a religious leader, and shoguns did not have a primary religious role in Japan.

18. **(D)** The reform movement in Europe created Protestant religions, protesting Catholicism. Protestant religions spread to England and led to the creation of the protestant Church of England. (A) is incorrect because the Reformation did not have a significant impact on religion in Spain, which remained a largely Catholic nation. (B) is incorrect because the rediscovery of literature and art occurred in the Renaissance, not the Reformation. (C) is incorrect because the Sistine Chapel was painted at about the same time the Reformation started, and it did not result from the Reformation.

19. **(B)** The very accurate calendar created by the Mayans, which features a circular design, is still in use today. (A) is incorrect because the Mayans did have human sacrificial ceremonies. These sacrifices were also found among the Aztecs. (C) and (D) are incorrect because the Mayans were located in Central America and Mexico, which is in North America.

20. **(C)** Columbus sailed the Caribbean and landed in what is now the Dominican Republic and the island of Hispaniola. He never reached the mainland. (A) is incorrect because Columbus did return to Europe during his explorations. (B) is incorrect because Sir Walter Raleigh helped establish a settlement in North Carolina. (D) is incorrect because John Smith established the Jamestown Colony in Virginia.

21. **(D)** American troops trapped Cornwallis and his forces against the coast in Yorktown, Virginia, but it was the French fleet that made it impossible for British forces to escape. (A), (B), and (C) are all incorrect because it was the combination of American troops and French naval forces that forced the British to surrender.

22. **(C)** The anti-Federalists were not opposed to a federal government, but they were concerned that the Constitution did not protect individual rights. (A) is incorrect because the anti-Federalists were not opposed to a federal government. (B) is incorrect because the Articles of Confederation were the first U.S. constitution and had nothing to do with the Confederacy of the Civil War. (D) is incorrect because many of those who preferred the Articles of Confederation and did not favor a central government were concerned whether individual states could act to form a central government. However, this was not a view held by the anti-Federalists.

23. **(C)** This Article of the Constitution establishes the Electoral College. The popular vote chooses electors, not the president. The electors then vote for the president. In three recent presidential elections, a candidate received a majority of the electoral votes but did not receive a majority of the popular vote. (A) is incorrect because this article says that the people of the United States do not directly elect the president. (B) is incorrect because a plurality in a majority of the states is not enough to elect a president, even though most elected presidents do win in a majority of states. (D) is incorrect because as the article says, the number of electors is equal to the number of senators and representatives combined.

24. **(A)** This basic right was essential in order to formulate a document that abolished the British government. Look at the underlined portion of this excerpt from the Declaration of Independence.

> We hold these truths to be self-evident, that all men are created equal, that they are endowed by their Creator with certain inalienable rights, which among these are Life, Liberty and the Pursuit of Happiness. That, to secure these rights, Governments are instituted among Men, deriving their just powers from the consent of the governed. <u>That is, when any form of government becomes destructive of these ends, it is the Right of the People to alter or abolish it.</u>

(B) is incorrect because the Declaration of Independence says that all men are created equal, with no exception for slaves; although, delegates removed from a draft a section condemning the slave trade. (C) is incorrect because the First Amendment outlines these rights. (D) is incorrect because the Second Amendment mentions the right to bear arms.

25. **(C)** The map shading clearly shows that Freemont won in the northernmost states. (A) is incorrect because Texas and California did not have enough electoral votes to change the outcome of the election. (B) is incorrect because Buchanan did win in states that did not join the Confederacy and this is not the best choice from among the answers given. (D) is incorrect because not all of the states that fought for the Union in the Civil War favored Fremont.

26. **(B)** Jim Crow laws imposed racial segregation. The Supreme Court ruled shortly after the Civil War in *Plessy v. Ferguson* that it was legal to have "separate but equal" accommodations, opening the door for segregationist legislation. (A) is incorrect because the Court's ruling in the Amistad case was about twenty-five years before the Civil War began. (C) is incorrect because the Court's ruling in *Marbury v. Madison* was about sixty years before the Civil War. (D) is incorrect because the Court's ruling in *Brown v. Board of Education* was in 1954.

27. **(C)** Just observing ballet reveals that the dance form is based primarily on the position of the feet. (A), (B), and (D) are all incorrect because these choices do not most accurately describe the basis of ballet.

28. **(A)** Only this choice is related to an appreciation of dance and dance elements. (B) is incorrect because this choice is related to the cultural style of a dance. (C) is incorrect because this choice is related to interpretation of dance and not appreciation. (D) is incorrect because this choice is related to the history of dance.

29. **(C)** Floods along the Nile destroyed land boundaries, and mathematicians say that geometry and surveying were developed to reestablish these boundaries. (A) is incor-

rect because the floods actually added rich soil to agricultural lands. (B) is incorrect because the cataracts lengths of shallow water along the Nile were long in existence and not established by the flooding. (D) is incorrect, because while this may have happened, the floods were much more responsible for the establishment of geometry.

30. **(B)** The five original tribes that formed the Iroquois Nation were founded in the 1400s or earlier, and this nation of tribes was the first democracy in the Americas. The other answer choices are accurate, but they are not the correct answer to this question.

31. **(B)** The name originated when New Amsterdam was surrendered to an English naval squadron under Colonel Richard Nicolls, and the English renamed the city and the entire colony New York. The other answer choices contain incorrect information about New York State.

32. **(C)** The ratification of the U.S. Constitution was the act that established New York as a state. Choice (D) is an accurate statement, but the establishment of Albany as the capital came after New York became a state. (A) Several members of the New York delegation signed the Declaration. However, other members of the delegation refused to sign. (B) England's surrender in the Revolutionary War occurred in Yorktown, Virginia.

33. **(A)** Pulse rate is the best way to determine if an exercise has become too demanding. (B) is incorrect because hard breathing is not as effective as pulse rate. (C) and (D) are incorrect because these choices do not include an effective way to determine if an exercise has become too demanding.

34. **(C)** The real meaning of a musical note is found in the pitch, sound, and the duration of that sound. This elementary school student knows about the pitch, and "sound" is not listed as an answer choice. That leaves choice (C), duration, as the correct answer.

35. **(B)** A fresco is created in wet plaster on a wall. (A), (C), and (D) are all incorrect because these choices do not indicate where a fresco would appear.

36. **(C)** Complementary colors are opposing colors on the color wheel. Mixing complementary colors produces black. (A), (B), and (D) are all incorrect because mixing complimentary colors does not produce the colors listed for these choices.

37. **(C)** Jazz consists of popular songs interspersed with individual solos and improvisation. (A), (B), and (D) are incorrect because they do not contain the most accurate description of jazz music.

38. **(A)** The chromatic scale uses all of the piano's black keys and white keys. (B) is incorrect because the diatonic scale refers to only the piano's white keys. (C) is incorrect because the harmonic scale refers to only a portion of the white and black keys on the piano. (D) is incorrect because there is no specific scale called the piano scale.

39. **(B)** This choice, alone, represents an appropriate developmental trait and is least likely among the choices given to require an intervention. (A), (C), and (D) are all incorrect because these choices all represent deviations from appropriate development that are most likely, among the choices given, to require intervention.

40. **(D)** This choice LEAST accurately characterizes the American family from among the choices given. This does not mean this choice is never accurate, just that it is not as accurate as the other choices. (A), (B), and (C) are all incorrect because these choices are the three most accurate characterizations of the American family among the choices given.

Index

Independent clause, 136

Independent event, 261

Individualized education plan, 44

Inductive reasoning, 26

Inference, 150

Inquiry learning, 25

Instruction

   adapting of, 45

   resources for, 25

Instruction planning

   Common Core State Standards

      Initiative, 28

   objectives. *See* Objectives

Instructional environment, 31–34

Integers, 249

Internet, 27–28

Interpersonal thinkers, 21

Intrapersonal thinkers, 21

Intrinsic motivation, 19

Introductory phrases, 139

Invention, 26

Inverse property, 253

IQ, 42

Irrational numbers, 246–247

Irregular verbs, 130–131

Isosceles triangle, 267

K

Kahn Academy, The, 295

Kinesthetic learning, 22–23

Kounin, 33

L

LCM. *See* Least common multiple

Leadership, classroom, 33

Learning

   cooperative, 24

   inquiry, 25

   student-centered approaches,

      24–25

   successful, 20

   teacher-centered approaches,

      23–24

   teaching for, 31

Learning disabilities, 41

Learning styles, 22–25

Learning-disabled students, 45

Least common multiple, 252

Least restrictive environment, 44

Lecture, 23

Legends, 287

Lesson

   attention on, 34

   teaching of, 30–31

Limited English proficiency students,
   29

Line, 265

Line segment, 265

Line symmetry, 264

Linear relationships, 272–273

Linguistic diversity, of ELL students, 37

Linguistic thinkers, 21

Linking verbs, 130

Literacy and English Language Arts CST,
   5, 297–347

Literary forms, 286–288

Logical-mathematical thinkers, 21

Logs, 46

Love, 22

Lyric, 287

M

Main idea, 149

Mainstreaming, 44

Maslow's hierarchy of needs, 22

Mathematics

   geometry, 264–271

   model test of, 315–325

   numbers. *See* Numbers

   problem solving, 271–275

   scatter plots, 263–264

   statistics, 262–263

Mathematics CST, 5

Mean, 262–263

Median, 262–263

Memorization, 26

Mentor, 236

Metacognition, 23, 284

Mildly handicapped students, 45

Misplaced modifiers, 135–136

Mistakes, 11

Mixed numbers, 249, 254–255

Mobile devices, 3

Mode, 263

Modeling, 38

Modifiers

   dangling, 135–136

   misplaced, 135–136

Motivation, 19–20, 22

Multiple intelligences, 21

Multiple-choice questions, 12

Multiplication

   of decimals, 254

   description of, 250

   of fractions, 254

Multi-subject CST

   English language arts, 276

   info box for, 241

   literacy, 276

   mathematics review, 243–275

   model tests, 297–348

   passing of, 242

   scores on, 242

   test-preparation strategy for, 10–11, 242

Multi-Subject Elementary Education
   and Early Childhood CSTs, 5, 7

Musical learners, 21

N

Naturalistic thinkers, 21

Negative reinforcement, 46

Nonverbal communication, 31

Norm-referenced tests, 35–36

Nouns, 129–130

Novel, 288

Number(s)

   addition of, 250–251

   cardinal, 243

   division of, 250

   fractions, 248–249

   integers, 250

   irrational, 246–247

   mixed, 249, 254–255

   multiples of, 252

   multiplication of, 250

   order of operations, 250

   ordering of, 243

   percent. *See* Percent

   place value, 243–244

   positive exponents, 244

   rational, 246–247

   scientific notation, 244–245

   subtraction of, 250–251

   whole, 243, 245–246

Number line, 249

Numerator, 246, 248

NYSTCE

   alternative arrangements for, 7

   description of, 5–6

   passing of, 4, 14

   passing rates for, 7

   scores, 7, 14